THE ANCHOR YALE BIBLE REFERENCE LIBRARY

The Origins of Judaism

An Archaeological-Historical Reappraisal

T0244541

YONATAN ADLER

YALE
AYBRL
Yale
UNIVERSITY
PRESS
NEW HAVEN
AND
LONDON

Yale University Press books may be purchased in quantity for educational, business, or promotional use. For information, please email sales.press@yale.edu (U.S. office) or sales@yaleup.co.uk (U.K. office).

Set in Adobe Caslon and Bauer Bodoni type by Newgen North America.
Printed in the United States of America.

Library of Congress Control Number: 2022931886
ISBN 978-0-300-25490-7 (hardcover : alk. paper)
ISBN 978-0-300-27665-7 (paperback)

A catalogue record for this book is available from the British Library.

10 9 8 7 6 5 4 3 2 1

The Origins of Judaism

THE ANCHOR YALE BIBLE REFERENCE LIBRARY is a project of international and interfaith scope in which Protestant, Catholic, and Jewish scholars from many countries contribute individual volumes. The project is not sponsored by any ecclesiastical organization and is not intended to reflect any particular theological doctrine.

The series is committed to producing volumes in the tradition established half a century ago by the founders of the Anchor Bible, William Foxwell Albright and David Noel Freedman. It aims to present the best contemporary scholarship in a way that is accessible not only to scholars but also to the educated nonspecialist. It is committed to work of sound philological and historical scholarship, supplemented by insight from modern methods, such as sociological and literary criticism.

John J. Collins
General Editor

Dedicated with love to Netanel, Emuna, Avital, Techiya, Elyada, and Aviya

Contents

Preface

The biblical tradition provides a sweeping narrative, spanning the course of a millennium, about the reception of the Torah among the people of Israel. The account begins when the God of Israel first gives his set of laws to Moses at Mt. Sinai and continues until the time when Ezra and Nehemiah bring about a restoration of this Torah in Persian-era Jerusalem. This is a chronicle of discontinuities, characterized by long periods when the Torah was entirely neglected, but punctuated by intermittent episodes of rediscovery and restoration at the hands of virtuous leaders. Already before Moses descends from the mountain, the people transgress by setting up a golden calf. Subsequent prophets through the centuries repeatedly scold Israel for its various iniquities, and time after time the nation is punished for its sins. This dim narrative of disobedience is punctuated now and again when a righteous leader returns the people to observance of the Torah's laws. Jehoshaphat, for example, sends teachers throughout the land to teach Torah to the people (2 Chr 17:7–9). Hezekiah restores observance of the Passover, as it had not been celebrated "since the days of Solomon son of David, king of Israel" (2 Chr 30:26). Josiah similarly restores observance of the Passover, as it had not been offered "since the days of the judges who judged Israel nor in all the days of the kings of Israel and the kings of Judah" (2 Kgs 23:22; see also 2 Chr 35:18). On the authority of a Persian king, Ezra arrives in Jerusalem and publicly expounds from a long-forgotten Torah, restoring observance of Sukkot rites that had been neglected "from the days of Jeshua son of Nun to that day" (Neh 8:17). And finally, Nehemiah discovers the populace of Persian-era Jerusalem negligent of the Sabbath and immediately sets about to restore proper observance of the day (Neh 13:15–22).

This biblical tradition is certainly not "history" in the modern sense of the word. "History," from the ancient Greek "*historía*," refers to the open-ended, methodical investigation into questions that people in the present choose to pose about the past. That the biblical tradition was never "history" becomes abundantly evident when we consider the fact that the tradition provides no citations, includes no footnotes, and affords no bibliographic lists of sources. Rather than a methodical inquiry into the past, the biblical tradition about Israel's reception of the Torah is very much a *living declaration in the present*, a call to action in the here and now. It proclaims that the Torah is divine, and as such its commandments are sacred and to be kept assiduously. It warns against complacency, as the Torah is liable to be ignored and even forgotten if sufficient care is not taken to maintain its continual observance. It comforts that even if transgression occurs, full repentance through restoration of Torah observance is always possible. Its message is acutely relevant to the lives of those who inherited the tradition, and it adjures those who have thus received it to pass it onward as a legacy to subsequent generations.

As a call to action in the present, the biblical tradition about how the Torah came to be observed by Israel is undeniably *true* in the deepest, most fundamental sense of the word. It is this tradition that has fostered not only the survival but also the astonishing development and flourishing of Jewish communities throughout the many centuries of frequently recurring persecutions and hardships. To paraphrase the Hebrew thinker Ahad Ha'am (1856–1927), more than the Jewish people have kept the Torah, the Torah has kept the Jewish people. Undoubtedly, the biblical tradition about the early reception of the Torah has served as the bedrock of Jewish identity, and hence existence, through the generations.

Despite its crucial place in forging the Jewish past and present, the biblical tradition about the origins of the Torah and how it came to be observed is decidedly *not* the point of departure of the book that is before you. The biblical account has been studied in the past from countless angles, both traditional and critical, and doubtless will continue to be a subject of intense interest well into the future. As crucial as the biblical tradition has been as a call to action throughout the millennia, it will not be subject to investigation within the framework of the present study.

Instead of the biblical tradition about Israel's reception of the Torah, this book takes as its starting point the lived experiences of the Jewish people as they have actually *practiced* their Judaism over the centuries through the observance of the laws of the Torah in their everyday lives. It is this *practical* Judaism, rather than the biblical tradition *about* it, that stands at the center of the present book. The aim of this study is to apply systematic historical and archaeological methods to seek the earliest evidence for the emergence of precisely this practical Judaism within the routine lives of ordinary people in antiquity.

The title of this book announces that it will conduct a "reappraisal" of Judaism's origins. What is to be reappraised here is not the biblical tradition, however, which as I have just explained will not be subject to investigation. Rather, my aim is to reevaluate a certain scholarly hypothesis, dating back to the nineteenth century but still current today, that locates the emergence of Judaism in the so-called postexilic period.

The Origins of Judaism is actually a play on the title of a volume published by Eduard Meyer in 1896, *Die Entstehung des Judentums: Eine historische Untersuchung* (The origin of Judaism: A historical investigation). Meyer's work represents the culmination of a century of Protestant biblical scholarship which posited that the Babylonian exile marked a complete rupture in the history of Israel, dividing between a preexilic "ancient Israel" and a postexilic "Judaism." The postulate was that the Pentateuch was promulgated as the law of the Jews among the returnees to Judea from Babylonia during the Persian period, and that with this an entirely new creation called "Judaism" was born. The evidence adduced for this idea derived primarily from literary-critical analyses of the biblical texts themselves, and therefore scholars' attention focused more on *intellectual* history—the history of ideas communicated by biblical authors—rather than on *social* history surrounding the actual behaviors and practices of the general populace of Judea.

Since the late nineteenth century, we have experienced an explosion of archaeological and epigraphic discoveries that have consequentially led to the exponential expansion of our knowledge about the practical observance of Torah among ordinary Judeans in antiquity. This new body of material evidence allows us today to turn our attention to social history, and specifically to the question of when rank-and-file Judeans first began to observe the rules and regulations of the Torah on a wide-scale basis. The present study seeks to do just that; it aims to mine this treasure trove of new data, and concurrently to reexamine the long-available historical resources in order to assess the origins of what we might call "Judaism."

A Note on Translations and Transliterations

Translations of ancient texts mostly follow standard editions, but I have emended these in some cases as I deemed necessary. For the Hebrew Bible, Apocrypha, and the New Testament, I have usually followed the New Revised Standard Version. For Jewish Pseudepigrapha, I have usually followed *OTP*. For Philo, I have generally followed Colson and Whitaker, *Philo*. For Josephus, I have mostly followed Thackeray, Marcus, and Feldman, *Josephus*. For other Greek and Latin sources, unless otherwise indicated, I have followed M. Stern, *GLAJJ*. All other translations of ancient and modern texts are my own, unless otherwise noted.

Transliterations from Hebrew, Aramaic, and Syriac mostly follow the Society of Biblical Literture's "academic style" as described in B. J. Collins et al., *The SBL Handbook of Style*, 56–58, 63. Exceptions are the fricative *bêt*, which I transliterate as "*v*," the fricative *kāp*, which I transliterate as "*kh*," and the fricative *pê*, which I transliterate as "*f*." Transliterations from Greek follow the online transliteration software at https://www.lexilogos.com/keyboard/greek_conversion.htm. Names of people, places, and written works are provided according to their standard spellings in English, without diacritical marks.

Abbreviations

Standard abbreviations are followed for names of ancient sources (e.g., Bible, Apocrypha, Pseudepigrapha, Dead Sea Scrolls, Philo, Josephus, rabbinic literature, and classical and ancient Christian writings).

b.	Bavli (Babylonian Talmud)
CBQ	*Catholic Biblical Quarterly*
CIIP	*Corpus Inscriptionum Iudaeae/Palaestinae* (Cotton et al., 2010–2018)
CIJ	*Corpus Inscriptionvm Ivdaicarvm* (Frey, 1936–1952)
CPJ	*Corpus Papyrorum Judaicarum* (vols. 1–3: Tcherikover, 1957–1964; vol. 4: Hacham and Ilan, 2020)
DJD	Discoveries in the Judaean Desert
DSD	*Dead Sea Discoveries*
GLAJJ	*Greek and Latin Authors on Jews and Judaism* (Stern, 1974–1984)
HUCA	*Hebrew Union College Annual*
IAA	Israel Antiquities Authority
IAHUJ	Institute of Archaeology, the Hebrew University of Jerusalem
IEJ	*Israel Exploration Journal*
IES	Israel Exploration Society
JAJ	*Journal of Ancient Judaism*
JBL	*Journal of Biblical Literature*
JIGRE	*Jewish Inscriptions of Graeco-Roman Egypt* (Horbury and Noy, 1992)

JJS	*Journal of Jewish Studies*
JSJ	*Journal for the Study of Judaism*
LXX	Septuagint
m.	Mishnah
NEAEHL	*New Encyclopedia of Archaeological Excavations in the Holy Land* (Stern, 1993–2008)
OTP	*The Old Testament Pseudepigrapha* (Charlesworth, 1983–1985).
SBL	Society of Biblical Literature
SOA	Staff Officer of Archaeology—Civil Administration of Judea and Samaria
t.	Tosefta
TAD	*Textbook of Aramaic Documents from Ancient Egypt* (Porten and Yardeni, 1986–1999)
TJC	*Treasury of Jewish Coins* (Meshorer, 2001)
VT	*Vetus Testamentum*
y.	Yerushalmi (Jerusalem Talmud, or Palestinian Talmud)
ZAR	*Zeitschrift für Altorientalische und Biblische Rechtsgeschichte*
ZAW	*Zeitschrift für die Alttestamentliche Wissenschaft*

Introduction

In this introductory chapter, I will lay out the aims of the present book, situate this study within the history of scholarship, and describe the methods to be followed in pursuing the stated aims. Because the aims of this book are predicated on precise definitions of key concepts such as Judaism, Torah, and Jews (or Judeans), we begin by defining these terms as they will be used throughout the book. This will be followed by a brief survey of scholarly treatments of the problem of Judaism's origins, beginning with early nineteenth-century scholarship and ending with a review of recent work on the question. After this, I will present the methodological procedure to be followed in investigating the central question posed in this study, along with an overview of the kinds of data to be consulted. The chapter will close with an explanation of how the subsequent chapters of the book are arranged.

The Aims of This Book

Throughout most of the past two millennia, the Jewish way of life has been characterized by adherence to the manifold laws of the Torah. The myriad prohibitions and positive commandments that comprise the Torah came to regulate all aspects of Jewish life, from morning until night and from cradle to grave. The ambit of Torah law is so broad as to give the impression that no sphere of human experience has been left unregulated: daily prayers and rituals, weekly Sabbaths and annual festivals, dietary laws, life-cycle events, conjugal life and family law, criminal and civil laws, regulations pertaining to agriculture, rules relating to ritual purity (fig. 1), and (in antiquity) rites pertaining to the temple cult.[1]

1

Figure 1. *Jewish women preparing for immersion in a ritual bath, eighteenth-century Germany. (From Kirchner,* Jüdisches Ceremoniel, *205.)*

In speaking of a "Jewish way of life," I am referring to a manner of living shared by most rank-and-file Jews, with the emphasis on the masses of ordinary people as opposed to any special pietists. Since it is the masses that we are speaking about, when I say that their way of life was characterized by adherence to the laws of the Torah, I do not for a moment imagine that the common folk were necessarily well versed in the intricacies of the law, or that they were universally punctilious in its observance. Rather, what is implied is that most people were at least rudimentarily aware of the existence of something like the Torah and were at least nominally committed to obeying its rules.

Rabbinic interpretations of Torah, especially as these were collected in the Babylonian Talmud, eventually came to exert a tremendous amount of influence on the Jewish way of life. But while certainly very influential, rabbinic *hălākhāh* (as the rabbis' system of Torah law is commonly called) was never the *only* way that all Jews chose to put the rules of the Torah into practice.² Even before the rabbis entered upon the stage of history, groups such as Pharisees, Sadducees, and Essenes were all characterized by adherence to the laws of the Torah as each group interpreted them.³ Also after the rise of the rabbinic movement, following the destruction of Jerusalem and its temple in 70 CE, large segments of the Jewish population continued to adhere to the laws of the Torah in ways that did not necessarily correspond with rabbinic interpretations. Famously, in the early Middle Ages some such Jews organized themselves into a group whose members called themselves "Karaites," but also less organized examples of Jews following the Torah in non-rabbinic ways may be found throughout Jewish history.⁴ The point is that all throughout this time, the Jewish masses were following a distinctive way of life guided by the rules and regulations of the Torah—however these may have been interpreted.

The aim of the present book is to investigate when and how the ancestors of today's Jews first came to know about the regulations of the Torah, to regard these rules as authoritative law, and to put these laws into actual practice in their daily lives. My interest here is to investigate when and why adherence to the Torah became the way of life of the Jewish population at large: the farmers and the craftsmen, the men, the women, and the children. The questions of when and why the laws of the Torah were themselves first conceptualized and written down, while certainly important, will *not* be explored in this book. My interest here is decidedly not in the history of *ideas* or *intellectual* history, but rather in *social* history, focused on the behavior of a society at large.

Key Definitions

Judaism

Having described the subject of this study, I now turn to the question of what term might best be used when referring to this "thing." I have decided here on the term "Judaism," in line with both modern uses of this term in twenty-first-century English and the etymological origins of this term in ancient Greek.

Among the definitions of "Judaism" in *Webster's Third New International Dictionary*, one finds: "conformity to Jewish rites, ceremonies and practices ... the total complex of cultural, social and religious beliefs and practices of the Jews."⁵ It seems to me that something very much akin to these definitions is what many if not most English speakers today have in mind when

Figure 2. *The avowedly irreligious prime minister of Israel David Ben-Gurion participating in a Passover seder at Kibbutz Sde Boker, April 16, 1973. (Photo courtesy of the Sde Boker Archive.)*

they use the term "Judaism." I should add that no matter what contemporary Jewish denomination (if any) is involved, modern-day observance of "Jewish rites, ceremonies and practices" remains deeply indebted to the Torah as its source of inspiration, if not formal authority. A modern-day Jew who on the first night of Passover sits down to a seder, eats matzah and bitter herbs, and drinks four cups of wine is by our definition engaged in "Judaism" whether he or she identifies as Haredi, Modern Orthodox, Conservative, Reform, Reconstructionist—or none of the above (fig. 2).[6]

The etymological root of the English "Judaism" is undoubtedly the ancient Greek "*Ioudaïsmós*," although there is some question as to precisely what the term would have meant in antiquity. The word first appears in a handful of texts penned by ancient Judeans (2 Maccabees, Paul's epistle to the Galatians, 4 Maccabees, and two third-century-CE inscriptions), and then more frequently in the writings of late antique Christian authors.[7] "*Ioudaïsmós*" represents in nominal form the ongoing action of the verb "*Ioudaïzō*," probably as it was used in the intransitive sense of "to act like the Judeans."[8] "*Ioudaïsmós*," then, would mean something like "acting in the manner of the Judeans." From the contexts in which it is used, the term

"*Ioudaïsmós*" likely denotes not just any Judaic behavior but specifically conduct that is in accordance with the laws of the Torah.[9]

Throughout the present study, I will be using the term "Judaism" in line with the modern English usage cited above, and in close agreement with my understanding of the ancient Greek "*Ioudaïsmós*." For the purposes of this book, "Judaism" will serve as the technical term for what I have described here: the Jewish way of life characterized by conformity to the rules and regulations of the Torah. In regarding Judaism as the ways *of the Jews* as governed by Torah, the implication is that the term refers to a manner of living characterizing the Jews *as a people*. In speaking of Judaism, then, it is not individual practitioners of Torah that will interest us here, but rather Jewish society at large.[10]

It should be stressed that our focus here is on the Jewish way of life centered on *practices* rather than beliefs. The reason for this focus is quite simple: practices are far more visible than beliefs, especially when studying a sizable group of people. When it comes to such a mercurial category of experience as "belief," any generalizations we moderns might choose to make about what a large segment of the population in the ancient past might have *believed* about a certain matter begins to border on the meaningless.[11] From the etic perspective, from the outside looking in, we can view and describe patterns of *behaviors* practiced by a large group of individuals far more readily than we can discern the abstract *beliefs* shared by such a collective.[12]

Torah

Until this point, I have allowed myself the liberty of using the term "Torah" rather unreflectively. As this term has been used in at least three ways in the literature (both ancient and modern), it is crucial to devote some space here to clarify precisely how I will be using the word "Torah" throughout this book.

The first way that the Hebrew term "*tôrāh*" has been used may be found in the Hebrew Bible, where the word appears more than two hundred times. The noun likely derives from the verbal stem "*y-r-h*," meaning "to instruct" or "to teach" ("*hôrāh*" in *hif'îl* form), and as such carries a meaning approximating "instruction" or "teaching."[13] As the word often appears in the Hebrew Bible with unambiguously legal terms such as "*ḥōq*" (statute) and "*mišpāṭ*" (ordinance), the word "*tôrāh*" is best understood in many instances as denoting some sort of *legal* "instruction."[14] This idea finds expression in the Septuagint, where "*tôrāh*" is invariably rendered as "*nómos*," the standard Greek term for "law." Throughout the Hebrew Bible, "*tôrāh*" as legal instruction is frequently associated with the figure of Moses. Several times in the Pentateuch, YHWH is said to give Moses several discrete sets of instructions, each called a "*tôrāh*," and each relating to a limited body of regulations.[15] In Deuteronomy, the term "*tôrāh*" is used numerous times to refer to a seemingly larger body of instruction relayed by Moses to Israel in the land of Moab in Transjordan, immediately prior to the death of Moses and the planned incursion into Canaan.[16] It is this entire body of instruction, it seems, that Moses is said to have written down in the form of a book.[17] Moses further instructs that a "copy of this instruction [*mišnēh hatôrāh hazō't*]" is to be written in a book by the future king, and that "all these words of instruction [*kol dīvrê hatôrāh hazō't*]" are to be written upon large, plastered stones, to be set up upon Mt. Ebal on the day Israel crosses the river Jordan.[18] References to some sort of "*tôrāh*" associated with Moses appear several times outside the Pentateuch as well; often it is not made explicit that this Mosaic instruction was written down, while in other instances it is said to be found in a "book" or else simply "written."[19]

The second way that "*tôrāh*" is used first emerges in literature written toward the end of the Second Temple period. By this time, the term "*tôrāh*"—together with its Greek translation "*nómos*"—began to take on an entirely new meaning as the standard name for the Pentateuch.[20] This novel usage of the term is almost certainly reflected in first-century texts that tell of public readings from the "*nómos*" in synagogue settings and in later rabbinic texts that discuss communal readings from the "*tôrāh*."[21] This is also the apparent meaning of first-century and rabbinic texts that use the term "*nómos*"/"*tôrāh*" when referring to a physical scroll.[22]

A third and far most expansive way the term "*tôrāh*" came to be used is especially common in rabbinic literature, although it may have its roots already in the late Second Temple period.[23] While continuing to be used as the commonly accepted term for the Pentateuch itself, the word "*tôrāh*" took on the additional sense of *the entire system of law* that had developed surrounding the Pentateuch. The legal material in the Pentateuch is written in language so opaque and oftentimes so self-contradictory that it could hardly have been implementable in real life without its readers deploying considerable interpretive efforts. Exegetical activity of this sort is in evidence in the late Second Temple period, especially in legal material from

Qumran, and is ubiquitous throughout rabbinic literature.[24] Certain individuals living in the late Second Temple period were said to have been experts in interpreting the laws of the Pentateuch, as were the later rabbis.[25] The major sects of the late Second Temple period (Pharisees, Sadducees, and Essenes) are known to have quarreled over the details of numerous Pentateuchal interpretations, as well as over whether ancillary traditions not recorded in the Pentateuch are to be treated as authoritative.[26] It is this entire living system of law, centered on the dynamic interpretation of the Pentateuch, which itself eventually came to be known as "*tôrāh*."[27]

In the present study, I will be using the term "Torah"—capitalized and without italics—to refer exclusively to this third, most expansive sense of the term. In order to avoid confusion, I will use the term "Pentateuch" when referring strictly to the text comprising the first five books of the Hebrew Bible. And when citing ancient sources that use the Hebrew "*tôrāh*" or the Greek "*nómos*," I will provide a transliteration of these words utilizing italics and diacritical marks, together with my translation of these terms into English as "instruction" and "law," respectively.

To reiterate a crucial point from above, the present study does *not* seek to explore the origins of the notion of a Mosaic "instruction" (*tôrāh*), the origins of the Pentateuch, or the origins of the Torah as a legal system. All of these are certainly vital questions, but their focus is on the history of ideas whereas my interest here is in the entirely distinct realm of social history. A Mosaic "*tôrāh*," the Pentateuch, and the Torah may all have manifested as ideas in the minds of a small cadre of individuals, who might even have decided to put these notions into practice in their personal lives. What concerns us here is when and by what historical processes the rules and regulations of the Torah—once these mental constructs had come into existence—came to be widely known and put into practice as a way of life by an entire society.

Jews and Judeans

In texts dating to the first half of the first millennium BCE, we begin to encounter a group that both self-identified and was identified by others using a name formed from the consonantal root "*y-h-d*."[28] Hebrew texts refer to this group as "*yəhûdîm*," and Aramaic texts render the name as "*yəhûdāyē*·." In the latter half of the first millennium BCE, alongside these Semitic-language names we begin to encounter renderings of the name into Greek as "*Ioudaîoi*" and into Latin as "*Iudaei.*" In some European languages used in the medieval period, the sound *d* in the name was altogether dropped through elision (the common linguistic process whereby a sound or syllable is omitted), thus in English taking on forms such as "*Giwis,*" "*Giws,*" "*Gywes,*" "*Iuwes,*" and eventually "Jews."[29]

In recent years, a rather curious debate has developed within English language scholarship about which name is most suitable when referring to this group in the ancient past.[30] There seems to be a common assumption among those engaged in this dispute that the modern English word "Jew" signifies some *religious* character, as it is commonly located within the same semantic category as "Christian" and "Muslim." As such, so the argument goes, it is appropriate to use the term "Jews" only when considering a time after this group had developed a specifically *religious* identity, while prior to this time it is preferable to refer to these people as "Judeans." The key question that divides these scholars is exactly when in historical time this supposed seminal movement from "Judeans" to "Jews" might have taken place.

I do not intend to stake out a position on this problem in the present study. Because my interest is in exploring when *Judaism* first emerged among this group of people, I will require a neutral term to discuss this group and its members diachronically without predetermining my own conclusions. Considering the current debate, it seems that "Judeans" is the most unobjectionable term available for our purposes of considering the *longue durée* from the middle of the first millennium BCE through the first century CE. Using this term will especially facilitate our discussion of such early epochs as the Iron Age, regarding which current scholarship is in rather broad agreement that the term "Jews" should be altogether avoided.

It bears stressing here that the present study will not investigate the origins of the Judeans (or of "Israel" for that matter) as a *people*. When and how the Judeans first coalesced into a distinct identity group is undoubtedly a fascinating question, but it will not detain us here.[31] Instead, we will begin our investigation once the Judeans have already appeared upon the stage of history within the framework of a clearly named group. The focus will be on when and how these Judeans, as a well-established collective, first began to adopt the Torah as the central regulating principle of their shared way of life.

The History of Scholarship

In order to properly situate the present study within the history of research, it would be necessary to present a detailed account of scholarly investigations into early Judaism, beginning with the dawn of the modern era until today. Considering the vast volume of scholarship on this subject, however, this is clearly an impossible task. Instead, I will focus here on what appear to me to be the most salient studies relevant to the precise topic at hand—the question of when the Torah first came to regulate the way of life of the Judean masses. I will demonstrate that, for the most part, modern scholarship on early Judaism has focused on intellectual history—as reflected in the writings of biblical authors—rather than on social history. Although several key scholars from the nineteenth century onward have posited that the Pentateuch was promulgated and accepted by the people at large as normatively binding Torah following a return to Zion after the Babylonian exile, the hypothesis remains one that has never been subject to any kind of sustained examination. Our survey will conclude with an overview of some recent scholarship that has investigated problems bordering closely on the question that stands at the center of the present study.

Nineteenth Century

Wilhelm Martin Leberecht de Wette (1780–1849) has been described as the founder of modern biblical criticism for his pivotal role in developing methods and ideas that served as the groundwork for practically all future work within the discipline of historical criticism of the Hebrew Bible.[32] In his dissertation submitted in 1804, de Wette argued that Deuteronomy was written later than the other four books of the Pentateuch.[33] In an extensive footnote, he famously identified Deuteronomy as the "book of instruction" (*sēfer hatôrāh*) or "book of the covenant" (*sēfer habərît*) purportedly "discovered" in the days of Josiah.[34] In his later works, beginning in 1813 with the publication of his first volume of *Lehrbuch der christlichen Dogmatik*, de Wette posited that the Babylonian exile marked a clear watershed in the religion and culture of the Judeans: "We must view the nation [*Nation*] after the exile as a different one, with a different worldview and religion."[35] He argued that the preexilic people should be called "Hebrews" (*Hebräer*) and their culture "Hebraism" (*Hebraismus*), while the postexilic people should be called "Jews" (*Juden*) and their culture "Judaism" (*Judenthum*).[36] His case rested entirely upon his own interpretation of the history of the literary composition of the Hebrew Bible rather than on any actual evidence of ritual and cultic practices among the Judean populace either before or after the exile.[37]

De Wette's ideas about the dating of Deuteronomy and his model of a radical rupture between preexilic "Hebraism" and postexilic "Judaism" proved extremely influential upon subsequent scholarship. Expanding on de Wette's work, Karl Heinrich Graf (1815–1869) argued in a study published in 1866 that since the ritual legislation found in Exodus, Leviticus, and Numbers was ignored in the works of the preexilic prophets, but is quite close to postexilic works such as Ezekiel, these parts of the Pentateuch must therefore date to the postexilic period—and consequentially must be later than Deuteronomy.[38] Working independently, the Dutch scholar Abraham Kuenen (1828–1891) published a similar argument four years later and named this hypothesized late source the "Priestercodex" (in Dutch; "Priest code" in English), which he abbreviated with the letter "P."[39] Kuenen believed that it was Ezra and Nehemiah who introduced these laws as part of a complete Pentateuch, and that with this "Judaism" itself first emerged: "A new period in the history of Israel's religion begins with Ezra and Nehemiah. That which had long been in preparation comes into existence under their influence: *Judaism* is founded."[40] Like de Wette, both Graf and Kuenen focused their interests on the *literary history* of the Hebrew Bible; neither sought to investigate evidence outside this literature for the actual practices of the Judean masses.

Building on the work of these scholars, Julius Wellhausen (1844–1918) began in the mid-1870s to argue for his fourfold "documentary hypothesis," in which he dated the so-called Jehovistic (J) and Elohistic (E) sources (redacted together as JE) to the centuries before the Deuteronomic (D) source, while the Priestly Code (RQ) he dated to the postexilic period.[41] The classical formulation for his ideas appears in his 1883 *Prolegomena zur Geschichte Israels*, a foundational work that was to have an extraordinary impact upon subsequent scholarship.[42] Picking up from de Wette, Wellhausen established as the aim of his *Prolegomena* to show that the promulgation of the Mosaic law marks the endpoint of "ancient Israel" (*altes Israel*) (equivalent to de Wette's "Hebraism") and the starting point of "Judaism" (*Judentum*).[43] In so doing, he went so far as to provide the exact dates for when the Pentateuch was "published and introduced" as "the constitution of Judaism": in the year 444 BCE, between the first and the twenty-fourth of the seventh month.[44] This surprisingly precise claim was based entirely upon the narrative of Ezra's public reading of the Mosaic "*tôrāh*" in Neh 8, a story that Wellhausen paraphrased at length. This purported event served as the watershed that distinguished Wellhausen's "ancient Israel" from his "Judaism," the latter of which could now claim both a father (in the guise of Ezra) and a precise birthday. But why did Wellhausen think that this story should be accepted as *historical*? This he explained in a footnote: "The credibility of the narrative appears on the face of it."[45] Like his predecessors', Wellhausen's research concentrated on textual evidence relating to the *literary development of the Hebrew Bible*. Aside from his naïve acceptance of the veracity of Neh 8, however, he never sought historical data that might point to the Torah being well known and its laws being put into widespread practice by the general populace of Persian-era Judea.

Twenty years after Wellhausen began to publish his views on the Pentateuch, Eduard Meyer (1855–1930) published his 1896 *Die Entstehung des Judentums*, in which he contended that the origins of Judaism lie in the Persian Empire's mandate of the Torah as the official law of the Judeans living in the province of Yehud. Meyer went to great lengths to argue for the authenticity of the Aramaic document presented in Ezra 7:12–26 as an official letter given to Ezra by Artaxerxes, king of Persia, and commanding him to enforce the laws of the Judean god upon all denizens of the province.[46] Whereas Wellhausen had emphasized Neh 8, which presents the promulgation of the Torah as an internal *Judean* matter, Meyer stressed Ezra 7, which presents Ezra's project as an *imperial Persian* initiative. Wellhausen himself published a contemptuous review of Meyer's book the year after it came out, to which Meyer immediately responded with a no-less-scathing reply.[47] Putting aside the detail of Persian imperial sanction, however, both Wellhausen and Meyer remained in essential agreement in positing that the Judeans at large first adopted the Pentateuch as the legal foundation for their distinct way of life during the time of Ezra. And beyond accepting the claims of the authors of Ezra-Nehemiah as essentially historical, neither sought actual evidence demonstrating that ordinary Judeans in Persian-era Yehud knew anything about the existence of a Torah and that they were in fact keeping its laws.

Twentieth Century

BIBLICAL SCHOLARSHIP

The groundwork laid by the biblical scholars of the nineteenth century served as the foundational support for the vast output of biblical scholarship that came to be produced throughout the twentieth century. While building on these underpinnings, scholars forged manifold new lines of inquiry into the literary history of the Hebrew Bible, including the Pentateuch. The discovery of law collections and vassal treaty documents in Mesopotamia proved especially profitable in providing for comparative studies with legal material in the Pentateuch.[48] Discoveries of biblical manuscript remains in the Judean Desert around the middle of the century provided vital data for conducting textual criticism of the Pentateuch and the rest of the Hebrew Bible.[49] And later in the century, the long-standing consensus surrounding the Graf-Wellhausen documentary hypothesis began to open up to competing models such as the "supplementary hypothesis" and the "fragmentary hypothesis."[50]

Despite all these important developments, biblical scholars in the twentieth century primarily continued down the path trodden by their nineteenth-century forebears in focusing their efforts almost exclusively on the ideas and writings produced by the intellectual circles who authored the biblical texts. To the best of my knowledge, no studies were ever dedicated to a detailed investigation of the evidence pertaining to when and how the legal portions of the Pentateuch eventually came to be known and widely regarded as authoritative *outside* these intellectual circles. De Wette's notion of a rupture between a preexilic "Hebraism" and a postexilic "Judaism" persisted as the standard hypothesis among twentieth-century biblical scholars, even as the proposition itself remained untested.[51]

In the 1990s, biblical scholars revisited Meyer's century-old hypothesis which had posited that the Persian imperial authorities authorized the Pentateuch as the official law of the Judeans. This hypothesis, which became known as the "theory of Persian imperial authorization," was hotly debated for several years throughout the 1990s but went out of favor by the first decade of the new millennium. At the time, the conversation focused on whether the available evidence suggests a unified Achaemenid policy of granting imperial authorization to local legal norms and, even if so, whether we should necessarily presume that it would have been *the Pentateuch* specifically that the Persians would have ratified. We will survey the specifics of this debate in greater detail in chapter 7. For our purposes here, however, I will simply note that neither side in the discussion pursued any serious examination of the (albeit limited) available evidence to determine whether the general populace of Persian Yehud were in fact aware of the existence of the Pentateuch and whether they put its rules and regulations into actual practice.

EPIGRAPHY AND ARCHAEOLOGY

The late nineteenth and twentieth centuries witnessed an explosion in the volume of epigraphic discoveries holding the potential to shed light on the ritual and cultic practices of ancient Judeans. These included remains of writing with ink on papyrus, skin, and pottery shards (ostraca); inscriptions etched into materials such as stone and metal; texts inscribed into clay tablets; and inscriptions engraved on stone seals, pressed into seal impressions, and stamped on coins.[52] As a rule, epigraphic remains associated with Persian- and Hellenistic-era Judeans were interpreted in light of the standard assumption among biblical scholars that the Torah had already become authoritative law for rank-and-file Judeans by this time. Finds that appeared to undermine this assumption were either dismissed as aberrations or apologetically interpreted in such a way as to make them align with Torah law. The assemblage of fifth-century-BCE Judean writings unearthed at Elephantine in southern Egypt is an excellent case in point. Represented in these texts is a Judean community that seemed to know nothing of the rules and regulations found in the Pentateuch, and on certain matters the community's practices clearly *contravened* Pentateuchal law (for more on this, see chapter 7). Some scholars, beginning with Wellhausen himself, dismissed this community as a vestigial fossil of "ancient Israel," a group living on the periphery of Judean society who had not yet come to adopt Judaism.[53] Other scholars, like Bezalel Porten, forcibly interpreted these texts so as to make the Judeans of Elephantine not only knowledgeable of Torah laws but generally also quite observant.[54] Either way, the result was that no serious efforts were made to test the hypothesis that the Judean masses of the Persian period knew of the Torah and regarded its laws as authoritative.[55]

Aside from these important epigraphic discoveries, archaeological finds associated with Judeans in the Persian and Hellenistic periods were spotty throughout the twentieth century—and indeed have remained patchy until today. Considering the dearth of relevant finds, it is hardly surprising that there have been no archaeological studies focused on investigating possible Judean observance of the Torah during these periods. The closest we get are studies published by Ephraim Stern which have argued that a lack of figurines in Judea (and Samaria) during the Persian period suggests that at this time a "religious revolution" took place wherein "Jewish monotheism was at last consolidated."[56]

Recent Scholarship

SANDERS'S "COMMON JUDAISM"

In his *Judaism: Practice and Belief*, published in 1992, Ed P. Sanders first introduced the term "common Judaism" to describe a system of practices and beliefs that was shared by practically all Judeans living during the first century CE.[57] Sanders broke fundamentally new ground here in his focus on the "ordinary" or "common" people. His method involved a critical examination of both first-century texts and (to a more limited extent) contemporary archaeological remains, from which he sought to uncover the behaviors and beliefs of rank-and-file Judeans. His analysis of the data suggested to him that, during the first century, Judeans throughout the Roman world shared a common set of practices and beliefs centered on the Mosaic Torah and the remainder of what were jointly regarded by this time as hallowed scriptures.

As far as I can tell, Sanders's was the first rigorous investigation into the observance of the Torah among *the Judean masses* in antiquity, and furthermore the first to examine both texts and archaeological finds toward this end.[58] Although not all aspects of Sanders's arguments were subsequently taken up as scholarly consensus, his proposition that a common set of practices and beliefs was shared among ordinary Judeans has proven very influential.[59] It is important to note here that Sanders's interest focused exclusively on the first century CE; he made no attempt to investigate when and by what historical means his "common Judaism" might have first emerged.

COHEN'S *THE BEGINNINGS OF JEWISHNESS*

We again encounter an investigation into "origins" with Shaye Cohen's *The Beginnings of Jewishness*, published in 1999. Here, Cohen investigated the questions of when and how a distinct category of identity he called "Jewishness" first emerged out of an earlier "Judean" one. According to Cohen, the Hebrew "*yəhûdîm*" and the Aramaic "*yəhûdāyē*" were at first purely ethnic terms, taken from the geographic name of the homeland with which these people were associated. Like other groups bearing ethnic-geographic names, at this early stage the *yəhûdîm/yəhûdāyē* "have their own language, customs, institutions, dress, cuisine, religion and so on, but no one of these characteristics is necessarily more important than any other" in defining what it meant to be a member of this group.[60] Cohen maintained that this was the state of affairs throughout the Persian and Early Hellenistic periods, up until the late second century BCE when a seismic shift occurred. It was precisely at this time, argued Cohen, that, under the influence of Hellenistic culture and politics, the Hasmoneans refashioned the Judean state into a league that would allow the incorporation of non-Judeans. For the first time in history, non-Judeans could be enfranchised either politically or religiously but without taking on the ethnic-geographic identity of the Judeans. From this point onward—once one could *convert* to *become* a "Judean" in the purely religious conception of the term—we can rightly begin to speak of the beginning of what Cohen called "Jewishness."

Cohen's book broke radically new ground in identifying the Hasmonean era—rather than the Babylonian exile—as the crucial watershed in Judeans' "religious" history.[61] Importantly, the book concentrated entirely on identity categories and the possibility of movement between them, or as Cohen framed the questions at the heart of his study: "What is it that makes us *us* and them *them*?" and, consequentially, "Can one of 'them' become one of 'us' . . . ?"[62] Curiously, the study never sought to investigate the underlying question of the beginnings of Torah observance among ordinary Judeans. Cohen's "Jewishness" assumes that Torah law was already widely known and observed by the end of the second century BCE; the question that concerned him was not when this first *came to be* but rather when this first *became a central characteristic of Judean identity*.

The Torah itself is placed at the center of John Collins's book *The Invention of Judaism*, published in 2017. This seminal study traces the development of the idea of Torah within the work of Judean writers, from Deuteronomy to the time of Paul. Collins identified a major shift, which he termed a "halakic turn," occurring in the middle of the second century BCE, when for the first time we witness the rise of literature "that was intensely concerned with halakah," a trend seen in such works as the Temple Scroll, Jubilees, and especially 4QMMT. He argued that, prior to this time, no comparable emphasis on legal requirements is at all in evidence—whether in literature belonging to the so-called wisdom tradition, in tales set in the eastern diaspora (such as Esther and the stories in Dan 1–6), in early Enochic literature or other early texts that know of the Genesis narratives (such as the Qumran Genesis Apocryphon and the Aramaic Levi Document), or in Ben Sira. Prior to the middle of the second century BCE, Collins concluded, the Mosaic Torah enjoyed a largely "iconic" status in the sense that it was treated with deference and respect, although it was not necessarily regarded as something that had to be observed in detail.[63]

Collins's study has presented a critical contribution to our appreciation of the profound change in the way Torah was treated in the works of Judean writers following the Hasmonean revolt. It must be stressed that this is decidedly a study of intellectual history rather than social history. Its focus is entirely on investigating the development over time of an *idea* ("the Torah") among several successive generations of Judean literati, all of whom authored highly developed literary works. At no point did this study seek to investigate whether ordinary Judeans were at all aware of what these intellectuals were thinking and writing about, or even whether the idea of a Mosaic Torah was at all well known among the Judean populace at large.

KRATZ'S *HISTORICAL AND BIBLICAL ISRAEL*

In his *Historical and Biblical Israel*, first published in German in 2013 and subsequently in English in 2015, Reinhard Kratz distinguished between "the history of Israel and Judah" and "the biblical tradition." For Kratz, Israelite and Judahite history stands primarily on the epigraphic and archaeological evidence, along with additional information that may be obtained from the biblical tradition by means of both critical analysis and historical analogy.[64] The biblical tradition, on the other hand, may be studied in terms of the formation and history of this very tradition itself.[65] While clearly intertwined, they are not the same thing. In the final section of the book, Kratz revisited and amended Wellhausen's idea regarding the Babylonian exile as a watershed between "ancient Israel" and "Judaism"; while this is an accurate reflection of "the biblical tradition," argued Kratz, from the standpoint of "the history of Israel and Judah" we must recognize that "ancient Israel" actually *coexisted* with "Judaism" both before and after 586 BCE.[66] For the sake of nuance, Kratz introduced the term "biblical Judaism," which represents commitment to the biblical tradition and especially to the Mosaic Torah, as opposed to "non-biblical Judaism," which characterized Israelite and Judean devotees of YHWH who evinced no such commitment. His analysis of the epigraphic corpora from Elephantine, Yāhūdu, Mt. Gerizim, and Qumran (he calls these "Jewish archives") led him to the conclusion that the Hasmonean revolt represented the true *historical* watershed between these two Judaisms: "Up to this point, non-biblical Judaism probably preponderated, with biblical Judaism then having rather marginal historical weight."[67]

Kratz's study was groundbreaking in that it recognized the very real possibility that the biblical tradition, including the Mosaic Torah, may have existed for several centuries only at the margins of Judean society. As far as I can tell, this has been the first study to actively address the evidence (primarily epigraphic) from the Persian and Hellenistic periods that relates to ordinary Judeans—that is, those who were not themselves involved in the creation of biblical literature—in order to inquire whether such rank-and-file Judeans might have even known about the biblical tradition and whether they would have regarded this tradition as authoritative. Like both Cohen and Collins, Kratz viewed the Hasmonean period as formative; for Cohen it was when "Jewishness" as an identity category first emerged, for Collins it was when Judean intellectuals first took a "halakic turn," and for Kratz it was when "the biblical tradition" was first widely disseminated among Judeans at large.

Methods

The present investigation picks up from Sanders's and Kratz's studies, both of which put ordinary Judeans at the center of their historical inquiry. The primary question to be explored is when the Judean masses first came to know about the regulations of the Torah, to regard these rules as authoritative law, and to put these laws into actual practice in their daily lives. In moving toward answering this question, I will follow a novel methodological procedure that will attend to both textual and archaeological evidence. Here I will describe this procedure in detail, after which I will explain how I plan to treat both the written and the material evidence at hand.

The Methodological Procedure

DATA-DRIVEN ANALYSIS: ESTABLISHING A TERMINUS ANTE QUEM

The bulk of the book (chapters 1–6) will be taken up by a data-driven analysis. The procedure to be followed here is quite straightforward. A litany of practices and prohibitions regulated by the Torah will be examined, with each chapter focused on a separate category of laws. We will begin with a historical period from which we possess a preponderance of evidence demonstrating that these laws were generally known and widely observed among ordinary Judeans. As will be seen throughout the book, the first century CE represents just such a time. The first century CE, then, will serve as our benchmark from which we will proceed backward in time in search of evidence indicating that these laws were widely known about and commonly being observed in earlier times, prior to the first century. Our quest will continue until the trail of evidence ends, once we have reached a point in time when we are no longer able to discover any further evidence. The date of the earliest available evidence will be established as our *terminus ante quem*—the boundary of time when or before which the particular element of Judaism under examination must have first emerged. If we encounter a pattern wherein the various rules and regulations investigated present the same terminus ante quem (as will be shown to be the case), we may then claim to have established the terminus ante quem for the emergence of Judaism as a whole.

It bears taking a moment to explain exactly what is meant by the notion of a terminus ante quem, as this is a technical term used widely by archaeologists but not always well understood by nonspecialists. When excavating a site, it is only seldom possible to date a particular layer of excavated material to a precise moment in time. A good example of a well-dated archaeological context is a destruction layer in Jerusalem that contains first-century pottery together with coins dating to the fifth year of the Great Revolt, a stratum that may be confidently dated to the summer of 70 CE. A layer that lies directly above this stratum may be said to date to the year 70 CE *or later*, while a layer which lies directly below this stratum may be said to date to the year 70 CE *or earlier*. In technical jargon, the year 70 CE is the *terminus post quem* for the upper layer and the terminus ante quem for the lower layer. If no other evidence is available to help date these layers, this will be the most we will be able to say about their dating.

In a similar way, the date of the earliest available evidence demonstrating that Judeans knew of something resembling the Torah and were observing its laws will serve as the terminus ante quem for the earliest emergence of Judaism. That is to say, Judaism must have first emerged *at this time or earlier*. Lacking further evidence, this is the most we can determine with any degree of confidence. Absence of evidence is not evidence of absence. It is possible, for example, that Judeans commonly knew of the

Torah and were observing its laws for decades or even centuries prior to our established terminus ante quem, and that for whatever reasons no evidence of this has survived.

It is important to stress here that in our analysis of the data, we will not be seeking evidence suggesting *universal* observance of Torah law. There is no reason to expect that, at any point in history, *all* Judeans strictly adhered to *all* the rules of the Torah. Throughout our investigation, we will seek out evidence not only of observance but also of nonobservance, and any such evidence will be prominently noted.[68] Rather than universal observance, what we will be seeking are patterns of evidence which indicate that familiarity with the Torah and practical adherence to its laws had become commonplace within Judean society at large.

To anticipate the results of this data-driven analysis, in chapter after chapter throughout the book it will be demonstrated that we possess no compelling evidence dating to any time prior to the middle of the second century BCE which suggests that the Judean masses knew of the Torah and were observing its laws in practice. This will establish the middle of the second century BCE as the overarching terminus ante quem for the initial emergence of Judaism.

APPRAISING ORIGINS PRIOR TO OUR
ESTABLISHED TERMINUS ANTE QUEM

The final chapter of the book (chapter 7) will be dedicated to a historical reappraisal of the origins of Judaism during the span of time *prior* to the terminus ante quem established in the previous chapters. By definition, this is a time during which we lack any evidence that the Judean masses were observing the laws of the Torah or even that they may have known of the existence of such laws. As a result, the methodological procedure to be followed in this final chapter will be entirely different from the procedure followed in the data-driven analysis presented in the preceding chapters.

Here we will explore circumstantial and contextual evidence from the Persian and Hellenistic periods which might suggest that something resembling the Torah had already—or had not yet—been adopted as authoritative law among the Judean masses. We will dedicate space here to examine broader textual evidence (not necessarily relating to specific practices) that scholars in the past have regarded as indicators of an existent Judaism. We also will investigate here evidence that particular rules or categories of laws in the Torah were *not* being observed at a certain time. While limited evidence of this sort may be simply anecdotal, a preponderance of such evidence *might* suggest that the Torah itself had not yet become widely re-garded as authoritative. Finally, we will explore here such factors as the sur-rounding political and cultural environments within which Judeans found themselves in order to assess the likelihood that a particular *Sitz im Leben* would have been well suited to the initial emergence of Judaism. Here we will inquire into the historical reasons for *why*, along with the mechanisms for *how*, Judaism might have emerged at a particular juncture in time.

To again anticipate our results, it will be argued that the Persian period appears to be a less-than-favorable era within which to seek the emergence of widespread Torah observance. Instead, it will be posited that the roughly two centuries between the conquests of Alexander the Great circa 332 BCE and the founding of an independent Hasmonean polity in the middle of the second century BCE present a far more conducive epoch within which to seek the origins of Judaism.

Data to Be Consulted

TEXTS

Among the key first-century-CE textual corpora to be consulted are the writings of Philo of Alexandria and of Flavius Josephus, both of which are well dated to this era. Much of Josephus's writings refer to periods that predate his own lifetime, and these will be critically examined to determine their historical value with regard to the earlier periods with which they are concerned. We will also consult New Testament texts, which are commonly dated between the middle of the first century and the beginning of the second century CE. Greek and Latin authors whose writings are well dated circa the first century CE will often provide additional valuable evidence from an "outsider's" perspective.[69]

The Dead Sea Scrolls corpus presents a more complicated situation in terms of dating. On the one hand, these are archaeological artifacts whose *depositional* date may be roughly established in association with the time that Khirbet Qumran was abandoned circa 68 CE. But because our pres-ent interest in the scrolls lies chiefly in the *texts* they provide, what is more important for us is the *compositional* date of the various literary works in question. Although there are exceptions, most of the texts that will concern us here are commonly thought to share compositional dates in the second or first century BCE and therefore will be treated as a group of texts that provide evidence for roughly this period of time.

Texts classified as Apocrypha and Pseudepigrapha are another group of literary works that present formidable challenges in terms of dating. As the bulk of the works that will concern us here are also commonly thought to date to the second or first century BCE, these texts will usually be treated as a group dating roughly to this period. Outliers commonly thought to date to either earlier or later periods will be treated accordingly.

Texts that have come to be included in the Hebrew Bible tend to present even more daunting challenges in terms of dating. As the vast majority of these texts are thought to have been composed prior to the second century BCE, however, these will generally be treated as a group which in the broadest of terms provides evidence for periods of time that predate the turn of the second century. Where there is data that compellingly suggests more precise dates for a particular text, these will be presented and discussed on a case-by-case basis.

By definition, all the ancient literary texts discussed here were the product of intellectuals capable of producing highly sophisticated literature. These texts are excellent sources for the historian engaged in investigating the history of *ideas*, but they present significant challenges for the scholar who seeks to conduct *social* history. The fact that our ancient writers were not only literate but also eminently skilled in composing literature already sets them apart from the Judean masses, most of whom are commonly assumed to have been illiterate. While some of these authors *may* have been influential elites whose ideas and voices affected the societies within which they were embedded, for the most part we simply do not know if this was the case. It seems just as likely that in many if not most cases the authors of these ancient texts were little more than fringe figures with no influence on their surroundings, esoteric intellectuals moving along the outer edges of the societies within which they lived and penned their works. Not only were these ancient texts written by literati who were not *of* the masses; these texts were invariably never written with the intention of providing empirical accounts *about* the behaviors of the masses. The authors of all these texts clearly had other goals in mind, and in fact their writings are for the most part *indifferent* to what the masses were or were not doing. Where a text does refer to behaviors of ordinary Judeans, great care must be exercised to distinguish between the *real* and the *ideal*. For the most part, the authors of these texts were ideologues harboring quite specific agendas, and their writings must be assessed with this basic fact in mind. Among our surviving sources, especially those that have come to be included within the canon of the Hebrew Bible, we find numerous texts that advocate for a practice or against a prohibition in an idealizing manner. When such texts report about the masses engaging in behaviors that the author wished to either promote or castigate, we cannot simply assume that the story reflects some objective historical reality. Such texts must be read critically, against the grain and between the lines, in order to attempt to extract historically useful information about the actual behaviors of ordinary Judeans.

ARCHAEOLOGICAL REMAINS

One of the major advantages of archaeological evidence over texts lies in the fact that the material remains tend to reflect the "real" rather than the "ideal." Archaeology provides one of the most reliable and potent tools for discerning actual human behaviors in the past. The physical remains left over from human activity represent performed actions rather than ideals that remained limited to the realm of thought or speech. This is not to say that archaeological finds represent some kind of simple objective reality, as all archaeological data require interpretation on the part of the archaeologist in order to induce the mute stones and shards to communicate. Nevertheless, that which is reflected in the material finds that we attempt to interpret, at least in their raw form, is actual human behaviors rather than ideal mental constructs. As a rule, materials retrievable through archaeology were created in antiquity primarily to serve functional purposes rather than to propagate ideologically laden narratives. And as a rule, this material was created by and for ordinary people rather than by or for marginal ideologues. Another clear advantage of archaeological remains over textual data is that, to the extent that the material finds are randomly sampled and widely distributed, these may be thought to represent widespread behaviors common among the masses. Compared to literary texts, archaeological remains present a far more direct window onto the actual activities of a sizable population of ordinary people.

THE ELEMENTS OF JUDAISM TO BE EXAMINED

The number of practices and prohibitions that comprise Judaism is certainly too large to allow a comprehensive investigation of them all. For the purposes of the present study, I have chosen several key practical elements of Torah laws for which evidence of widespread practical observance has survived from antiquity to an adequate degree.

Only a limited number of Judaism's practices and prohibitions are cited in the literary works of ancient writers, whose interests usually lay elsewhere. And clearly only a limited amount of ancient Judaism's practices or prohibitions are associated with any sort of material element, and only rarely is this material element of such character that it can be expected to survive in the archaeological record. All of this circumscribes which elements of Judaism are available for study in the present investigation. That said, the practices and prohibitions that *are* attested in both the ancient written sources and the archaeological record provide a sufficiently ample and representative data set to allow our investigation to commence.

How This Book Is Arranged

Each of the following chapters will be devoted to a discrete set of practices or prohibitions that characterized ancient Judaism. Chapter 1 examines the dietary laws, especially the prohibited meats enumerated in Lev 11 and Deut 14:3–21. Chapter 2 investigates the observance of the ritual purity laws, especially those concentrated in Lev 11–15 and Num 19. Chapter 3 examines the Pentateuchal prohibition against the depiction of human and animal forms in artwork in Exod 20:4–5, Deut 4:15–18, and Deut 5:7–9. Chapter 4 investigates the ritual practices of "tefillin" and "mezuzah" through a literal interpretation of Exod 13:9, 16; Deut 6:8–9; and Deut 11:18, 20. Chapter 5 explores six distinct practices that characterized Judaism in the first century CE: circumcision, the Sabbath prohibitions, the Passover sacrifice and the Festival of Unleavened Bread, fasting on the Day of Atonement, the two central rituals of the Sukkot festival (building and residing in booths and taking of the "four species"), and having a continually lit seven-branched menorah in the Jerusalem temple. Chapter 6 will explore the emergence of the synagogue, which, while not directly appearing in the Pentateuch, was the institution through which knowledge of the Torah itself was disseminated among the Judean masses on a regular, weekly basis.

Each of the chapters is arranged in an almost identical manner: the first section of each chapter is devoted to establishing how the practice or prohibition under investigation was manifest in the first century CE, and is followed by a second section that seeks evidence for similar manifestations of the praxis *prior* to the first century CE. Each section is divided into two subsections, the first examining evidence from textual-literary sources and the second investigating the relevant archaeological and epigraphic evidence. As explained above in the section on methods, each of these chapters presents the results of a data-driven analysis aimed at determining a terminus ante quem for the first emergence of the element of Judaism under examination in that chapter.

In chapter 7, we attempt to go beyond the conclusions drawn in the previous chapters by examining evidence deriving from periods of time prior to the terminus ante quem established in the central section of the book. Arranged in forward-proceeding chronological order, this concluding chapter will open with an assessment of the likelihood that Judaism might have first emerged during the Persian period. This will be followed by investigations into the probability that Judaism might have emerged only subsequent to this time, during either the Early Hellenistic period or the Late Hellenistic (Hasmonean) period.

1 Dietary Laws

Numerous dietary restrictions are found scattered throughout the Pentateuch. Foremost among these are the proscriptions against the consumption of certain taxa of animals, fish, birds, and insects as delineated in Lev 11 and in Deut 14.[1] All species of quadrupeds are forbidden to be eaten, with the exception of that which has "divided hoofs and is cleft-footed and chews the cud." Species specially singled out as forbidden because they display only one of the aforementioned criteria are the camel, the hare, and the hyrax (they chew the cud but do not have divided hooves) and the pig (which has divided hooves but does not chew the cud). All aquatic species are forbidden, with the exception of species of fish that have both fins and scales. Birds are forbidden only if they are named on a list of some twenty forbidden species (in Leviticus; in Deuteronomy there are twenty-one). Also forbidden is any species categorized as a "creeping thing" (šereṣ)—apparently including rodents, reptiles, and insects—with the exception of flying insects that have "jointed legs above their feet with which to leap on the ground" (said to include the locust, the bald locust, the cricket, and the grasshopper).

Even among the permitted species, animals that die on their own or that are "torn" by predators are also forbidden.[2] Presumably, an animal must be deliberately killed by a human for its flesh to be permitted as food, although nowhere is this stated explicitly. All blood is forbidden to be consumed, as is fat (ḥēlev).[3] An ox that kills a person and is consequentially stoned may not be eaten.[4] Fruit produced during the first three years after the planting of a tree must not be eaten.[5]

The restrictions on all these foodstuffs appear to be universally addressed to every Israelite, at all times, wherever he or she may be found. Some dietary prohibitions, however, are contingent on the calendar. For the duration of the seven-day holiday called "the Festival of Unleavened Bread" (ḥag hamaṣôt), all "leaven" (śə'ōr) and "leavened bread" (ḥāmēṣ) may not be eaten.[6] Until the day that the sheaf offering is brought, all grain of the new annual crop may not be eaten.[7] Other dietary prohibitions are limited to certain classes of sanctified individuals. For example, wine and other intoxicating beverages are generally permitted, but forbidden to priests entering the sanctum, as also to those who have taken a Nazirite vow (the latter are also prohibited from consuming vinegar or any other grape products).[8] Still other dietary restrictions are focused on the consecrated status of the food. The Passover sacrifice may not be eaten if it is raw or boiled (but according to Deut 16:7 it is *supposed* to be boiled!).[9] Flesh of a peace offering may not be eaten beginning from the third day after the sacrifice was made.[10] Peace offerings and other sacrificial meat may not be eaten by a person who is impure, nor may even a pure person eat peace-offering meat that had itself come into contact with any kind of impurity.[11] Consecrated food may not be eaten by laypeople, nor even by bound or hired servants of a priest, nor by a priest's daughter who is currently married to a layman or who has had children with one.[12] Heave offerings and first fruits given to the priests may be eaten only by ritually pure members of the priestly household.[13] And finally, certain foodstuffs may be eaten only at a very specific location; neither tithes nor animal firstlings nor any votive gifts may be eaten anywhere other than in the sanctum "in the presence of YHWH your God at the place that YHWH your God will choose."[14]

Aside from all these explicit prohibitions, Genesis tells of a taboo said to be practiced among the Children of Israel "until this very day" whereby they avoid eating certain tissue found on the hip (gîd hanāšeh), purportedly because their ancestor Jacob was injured precisely at this anatomical site.[15]

Our investigation will begin by examining evidence that demonstrates the degree to which Judeans in the first century CE actually complied with many of the aforementioned Pentateuchal food prohibitions. We will learn that several first-century writers, Judean and non-Judean alike, were quite explicit in asserting that dietary restrictions based on these laws were observed by Judeans on a widespread basis—claims that will be shown to be in concert with the archaeological data. Following this, we will examine the evidence from periods prior to the first century CE in order to seek the earliest available evidence for the observance of these dietary practices.

First-Century Evidence

We begin by examining the textual evidence composed by writers living in the first century CE which indicates that Judeans adhered to a set of dietary restrictions governed by Torah law. Our survey of the written evidence will be followed by a survey of the archaeological evidence to investigate whether food remains of animal species prohibited in the Pentateuch were found at Judean sites dating to the first century CE.

Textual Evidence

PHILO

In his discussion on the dietary laws of the Pentateuch, Philo expounded at some length on the lessons in discipline and other virtues that he understood to be embedded in the many and various food prohibitions.[16] While it remains unclear to what degree the extensive scope of this exposition may imply that the laws in question were widely observed in actual practice, elsewhere Philo reported two stories from which we might infer not only that Judeans commonly abstained from eating pig but also that Judean avoidance of pork was renowned throughout the Roman world. In the first account, he tells of a "grave and momentous" question that the emperor Gaius Caligula posed reproachfully to Philo and his colleagues who took part in a Judean delegation to Rome in 40 CE: "Why do you refuse to eat pork?"[17] According to Philo, the question was greeted by an outburst of laughter from the Judeans' adversaries who happened to be in attendance. In response, members of the Judean delegation replied to the emperor, "Different people have different customs, and the use of some things is forbidden to us as others are to our opponents." Widespread Judean abstention from consumption of pig is portrayed as having been a matter well known to both the emperor and the Judeans' antagonists, and the Judeans themselves are said to have made no effort to deny the widespread character of the practice.

Another account provided by Philo corroborates the notion that non-Judeans were keenly aware of Judeans' tenacity in avoiding pork. In his account of the anti-Judean atrocities perpetrated in Alexandria during the disturbances of 38 CE, Philo reported that the rioters seized Judean women in the marketplace and theater and forced them to eat swine's flesh.[18] While some of the women tasted the pork out of fear of the consequences they would surely suffer should they refuse, "the more resolute" among them resisted—and were put to torture as a result.

Regardless of the veracity of either account, both stories would have had little resonance among Philo's readers had pork been a food *not* commonly avoided by contemporary Judeans. Although it is difficult to infer from this the degree to which the Judeans of first-century-CE Alexandria might have adhered to the other dietary rules of the Torah, at the very least both stories strongly suggest that this community was widely recognized for its stringent observance of the prohibition against pork.

NEW TESTAMENT

While authors of some New Testament works occasionally did express interest in certain matters relating to foodways, most often their concerns had to do with other problems unrelated to the Pentateuchal dietary prohibitions per se. Of concern were questions such as the propriety of consuming meat offered to idols, dining with Gentiles or sinners, and eating regular food when in a state of ritual impurity.[19] In Romans, Paul writes, "Some believe in eating anything, while the weak eat only vegetables"—which may or may not refer to a conflict within the Christ-following community over observance of the Torah's dietary laws.[20] Further on in the same passage, Paul writes, "I know and am persuaded in the Lord Jesus that nothing is profane [*koinòn*] in itself; but it is profane for anyone who thinks it profane.... Do not, for the sake of food, destroy the work of God. Everything is indeed clean [*kathará*], but it is wrong for you to make others fall by what you eat; it is good not to eat meat or drink wine or do anything that makes your brother or sister stumble."[21] It is unclear whether Paul here is thinking of the Torah's dietary prohibitions (wine would be out of place here), the purity laws, or perhaps both.[22]

Acts provides the only unambiguous references to the dietary laws. The first mention appears in a vision Peter is said to have experienced while under the sway of a trance: "He saw the heaven opened and something like a large sheet coming down, being lowered to the ground by its four corners. In it were all kinds of quadrupeds, and creeping-things of the earth, and birds of the air. Then he heard a voice saying, 'Get up, Peter; kill and eat.' But Peter said, 'By no means, Lord; for I have never eaten anything that is profane or unclean [*hóti oudépote éphagon pān koinòn kaì akátharton*].' The voice said to him again, a second time, 'What God has made clean, you must not call profane [*Hà ho theòs ekathárisen sù mè koínou*].' This happened three times, and the thing was suddenly taken up to heaven."²³ There can be little doubt that the reference here is to the prohibited species of quadrupeds, creeping-things, and birds of Lev 11 and Deut 14. The story continues by reporting that Peter was at first puzzled by the meaning of the vision but eventually came to interpret the heavenly voice as a pronouncement that Gentiles (represented by the menagerie of animals) should be treated as legitimate equals of Judeans rather than as "unclean" or "profane."²⁴ Putting aside the thorny question of whether the author of Acts was necessarily invested in the practical abrogation of the dietary laws, what is important for our purposes is that this author apparently expected his first-century-CE readers to be well aware of the fact that contemporary Judeans commonly abstain from eating certain kinds of animals. If this were not a well-known reality at the time, the story would have lacked resonance.

Another apparent reference to a Pentateuchal dietary prohibition appears in a letter said to have been addressed by a council of apostles and elders of the Judean Christ-following community in Jerusalem to the Gentile Christ-following communities of Antioch, Syria, and Cilicia: "For it has seemed good to the Holy Spirit and to us to impose on you no further burden than these essentials: that you abstain from what has been sacrificed to idols and from blood and from what is strangled [*pniktôn*] and from fornication. If you keep yourselves from these, you will do well."²⁵ The meat of a strangled animal was likely regarded as infused with prohibited blood, as strangling kills the animal without shedding any blood.²⁶ The source for this instruction seems to be God's pronouncement in Gen 9:3–4 addressed to Noah and his sons: "Every moving thing that lives shall be food for you; and just as I gave you the green plants, I give you everything. Only, you shall not eat flesh with its life, [that is,] its blood [*'akh bāśār bənafšô dāmô lō' tō'khēlû*]." This instruction to Noah's family, as the progenitors of all humanity, was apparently taken as applicable not only to Judeans but to Gentiles as well. It would appear that this letter was meant to answer the acute quandary plaguing first-century communities of Gentile Christ-followers as to whether they too should be observing the various dietary restrictions commonly adhered to by Judeans.

FLAVIUS JOSEPHUS
Josephus found numerous occasions to remark on the Judean dietary restrictions.²⁷ Among the specific foods he mentioned as prohibited are the flesh of animals that died on their own; "caul fat" (*epíplou*) and "suet fat"

(*stéatos*) of goats, sheep, and oxen (i.e., the Pentateuchal "*ḥēlev*"); "the broad
sinew" (*tò neûron tò platù*) (i.e., the Pentateuchal "*gîd hanāšeh*"); pork; and
the flesh of other animal species that he did not specify.[28] For Josephus, one
may not consume meat before having taken action "to properly wash away
the blood [*tò haîma kalōs apoplūnai*] and to make the flesh clean [*tàs sárkas
poiēsai katharàs*]."[29] He furthermore claimed that the Judeans of his day,
and the Essenes in particular, were tenacious in their adherence to the food
laws even in the face of torture and death.[30] He also reported that Judeans
"accused by the people of Jerusalem of eating profane food [*koinophagías*]"
would be known to flee and seek refuge among the Samaritans.[31] While
this suggests that at least on occasion some Judeans *did* in fact violate the
food laws, it also informs us that such offenders could expect to endure
harsh social censure from their countrymen. Finally, Josephus went so far as
to claim that all throughout the Roman world one could find non-Judeans
who had adopted many of the Judean dietary restrictions: "The masses have
long since shown a keen desire to adopt our pious observances; and there is
not one city, Greek or barbarian, nor a single nation, to which our custom
of abstaining from work on the seventh day has not spread, and where the
fasts and the lighting of lamps and many of our prohibitions in the matter
of food are not observed."[32]

NON-JUDEAN AUTHORS

That Judeans commonly adhered to the dietary restrictions of the Torah is supported from the writings of several Greek and Latin authors from
the first to the early second century CE, for whom the Judean aversion
to eating certain foods—especially the quintessentially Roman pork—was
frequently cause for comment. For example, the Greek geographer Strabo
(ca. 64 BCE–24 CE) remarked about the Judeans' superstitious "abstinence
from flesh."[33] Josephus reported that the Hellenized Egyptian author
Apion (first half of the first century CE) denounced the Judeans in his
writings for not eating pork.[34] Erotianus, a late first-century-CE writer, advised medical practitioners to ascertain the ethnic identity of their patients
"in order that, if he is a Judean, we should refrain from giving him pig's
flesh."[35] Plutarch (ca. 46–120 CE) cited a debate over whether the Judeans
abstain from pork because of their reverence to the pig or because of their
aversion to it, and also noted that Judeans similarly abstain from eating
hares.[36] Tacitus (ca. 56–120 CE) recorded an alternative hypothesis for the
Judean abstention from pork: it is because the skin of the pig is subject

to scabs which recall a plague that once afflicted the Judeans' ancestors.[37] Juvenal (late first to early second century CE) satirically wrote that Judea is a country "where a long-established clemency suffers pigs to attain old age," and that Judeans "see no difference between eating swine's flesh . . . and that of man."[38] Note that Juvenal must have assumed that his audience was quite familiar with Judean abstinence from pork—otherwise his sarcasm would have been lost on his readers. Sextus Empiricus (second century CE) wrote, "A Judean or an Egyptian priest would prefer to die instantly rather than eat pork"—recalling the above-cited claims of Philo and Josephus about Judeans' willingness to undergo tortures rather than taste forbidden foods.[39] The Stoic philosopher Epictetus (ca. 50–130 CE) reported that the question of whether the act of eating swine's flesh was to be regarded as "holy" or "unholy" was a matter of conflict between Judeans, Syrians, Egyptians, and Romans.[40] Finally, Pliny the Elder (ca. 23–79 CE) apparently knew something about the Judean avoidance of certain kinds of fish, although he seems to have been mistaken as to the details when he wrote that a particular kind of garum "made from fish without scales" was appropriate for Judeans.[41]

Archaeological Evidence

METHODOLOGICAL INTRODUCTION

Of the diverse types of imprints in the archaeological record that bear witness to past human activities, ancient food remains are among the most instructive. While our written records regarding food eaten or avoided by people in the ancient past tend to be limited by the very subjective choices made by ancient writers, archaeological remains provide the opportunity for a far more objective view on actual dietary behaviors in lived reality.

Only some of the Pentateuchal dietary laws lend themselves to archaeological investigation. Animal bones are the primary type of archaeologically retrievable remains that reflect on what ancient humans consumed. If one were to unearth the remains of an ancient meal in the form of animal bones, it would be difficult, if not impossible, to determine whether any efforts were made to avoid eating soft tissues such as fats, sinews, or blood.[42] Although certain marks on the bones may indicate that the animal had been purposefully slaughtered by human hands, lack of such marks does not necessarily imply that the animal had died on its own or was "torn" by predators.

The Pentateuchal dietary prohibitions that are best suited to archaeological inquiry are those involving the prohibited species, as taxonomic
classification of animal bones is the bread and butter of all zooarchaeological work. Here we will limit our discussion to two categories of prohibited
animals: pigs and scaleless fish. This choice is informed by the knowledge
that both these groups tend to be relatively well represented in faunal assemblages at Levantine archaeological levels throughout much of the ancient past. Other taxa forbidden by Pentateuchal legislation (such as dog,
horse, donkey, camel, and various birds of prey) tend to be less common,
and it is often difficult to determine whether remains of such species necessarily represent food consumed by humans or whether they found their way
into the archaeological deposit for other reasons.

As at present faunal assemblages confidently identified as "Judean" are
available only from Southern Levantine sites, the data investigated here
will be culled exclusively from this region.

It is critical to point out here a mistake I have often encountered in the
scholarly literature that has treated zooarchaeological remains as evidence
of ancient dietary "taboos." If the data indicate that the dietary habits of a
certain population did not include a certain kind of food, this does *not necessarily* imply that this group would have regarded their choice as a normative
one—that members of the group believed it to be somehow "wrong" or
"inappropriate" to eat this food. The reasons a group might chose to exploit
one food source over another are many and sundry and, when investigating
ancient populations, oftentimes difficult to ascertain. To posit that a *taboo* is
involved would mean that the group avoided the food because of an implicit
societal *proscription* against its consumption—for whatever reason. Such a
hypothesis *may* be correct, and the fact that a population did not eat the
food in question would be consistent with this hypothesis. What is essential
to remember, though, is that lack of consumption may also be consistent
with many alternative, no less plausible hypotheses that do *not* involve a taboo, and therefore we would still require persuasive evidence before regarding "taboo" as a compelling explanation for ancient dietary choices.

While it will generally prove quite difficult to demonstrate that *absence*
of a certain food in the diet of an ancient society was the result of deliberate *avoidance* for normative reasons, the converse tends to be far easier to
show. To the extent that a certain food is determined to have constituted
a significant part of an ancient society's diet, we may confidently conclude
that this food was *not* widely avoided—whether for normative or any other

reasons. In scientific terms, a hypothesis that a certain food was avoided is falsified to the degree that we uncover remains of that food. In practice, this means that lack of pig or scaleless fish remains in a faunal assemblage from a Judean site cannot be taken on its own merit to indicate that the site's residents regarded these foods as "proscribed" or somehow "inappropriate" for consumption. On the other hand, to the extent that such remains *are* present in a Judean zooarchaeological assemblage, we may safely conclude that at least some people living at the site did *not* regard these foods as something that ought to be avoided.

Having set in order what kind of conclusions we might reasonably expect to derive from the data, we now turn to investigate the degree to which pig and scaleless fish are present or absent in the zooarchaeological record of first-century-CE Judeans.

PIG REMAINS

As we shall discuss in detail below, a considerable amount of scholarly attention has been devoted over the past thirty years to the question of pig consumption in the Southern Levant during the Iron Age. No comparable meta-studies are available regarding the Persian, Hellenistic, and Roman periods, although site reports sporadically do include relevant data from this time frame. Below, I will make ample use of these data as they have been collected in a 2005 study by Liora Kolska Horwitz and Jacqueline Studer and in an unpublished 2011 doctoral dissertation by Ram Bouchnick, and as may be updated with archaeological reports that have appeared in the past decade.[43]

The following table (table 1) presents the frequencies of pig in a presumably representative sample of faunal assemblages from Early Roman (mostly first-century-CE) Judean sites. The collected data on each assemblage include (1) the Number of Identified Specimens (NISP)—which is to say the gross number of bones—identified as pig; (2) the total NISP of all animal bones in the assemblage; (3) pig NISP presented as a percentage of total faunal NISP.[44]

These mostly negligible frequencies at Judean sites should be compared to the considerably higher frequencies of pig bones found in faunal assemblages at roughly contemporary *non-Judean* sites in the region. Because non-Judean sites experienced less destruction or abandonment events during the first century CE than Judean sites (primarily because their inhabitants did not take part in the Judean revolt of 66–70 CE), it is often difficult

Table 1. Frequencies of pig remains at Early Roman Judean sites (note: a letter in parentheses indicates a faunal assemblage at a site that has provided more than one published assemblage)

Site	Pig bones (NISP)	Total NISP	Pig bones as % of total NISP
Qumran (a)	0	6,254	0.0%
Jerusalem, eastern city dump (a)	0	5,701	0.0%
Jerusalem, City of David	0	996	0.0%
Jerusalem, Giv'ati Parking Lot (a)	0	114	0.0%
Jerusalem, eastern city dump (b)	3	5,594	0.1%
Jerusalem, Giv'ati Parking Lot (b)	1	540	0.2%
H. Burnat North	1	329	0.3%
Jerusalem, Mount Zion city dump	2	584	0.3%
Jerusalem, southwest corner of Temple Mount	18	2,982	0.6%
Qumran (b)	6	723	0.8%
H Rimmon	1	107	0.9%
Shu'afat	24	1,584	1.5%
Tell el-Ful	5	129	3.8%

Table 2. Frequencies of pig at Roman-era non-Judean sites

Site	Pig bones (NISP)	Total NISP	Pig bones as % of total NISP
Ibreiktas	1	74	1.4%
Tel Horshan	3	170	1.8%
Tel Michal	4	187	2.1%
Pella (Al Husn)	14	272	5.1%
Tel Hesban	226	3,575	6.3%
Tel Anafa (a)	98	513	19%
Tel Anafa (b)	40	206	19%
Tel Dor	240	1,121	21%
Jerusalem, International Convention Center	29	108	27%
Caesarea	408	706	58%
Jerusalem, eastern cardo	304	494	62%
Umm Qeis (Gadara)	864	1,241	70%

to date first-century faunal remains at non-Judean sites with any degree of precision. Nevertheless, it is instructive to look at the frequencies of pig in faunal assemblages from non-Judean sites dated more generally to the Roman era, presented here in table 2.[45]

Comparing the data in these two tables leads us to the unambiguous conclusion that pig remains are either entirely absent or else quite rare at first-century-CE Judean sites, but invariably present at roughly contemporaneous non-Judean sites—and usually in rather significant frequencies. On the basis of these data, it seems justified to infer that, by and large, Judeans living in the first century CE did not consume pig.

As noted in our methodological preface, the archaeological finds *on their own* do not provide any explanation as to *why* Judeans may have chosen not to eat pig. For this we must turn to the textual sources surveyed above, which allow us to posit a hypothesis according to which Judeans living at this time widely abstained from eating pork deliberately because of the Torah's proscription against pig consumption. The absence of pig in first-century-CE Judean faunal assemblages is fully consistent with this hypothesis, but of course other plausible hypotheses might be proffered as alternatives to explain this archaeological phenomenon. The methodological point here will be particularly crucial for our discussion below, where we will examine earlier periods of time for which textual evidence of the sort we have relied upon here is essentially absent.

It bears pausing for a moment to consider the fact that while pig is largely absent from first-century-CE Judean sites, the data presented above indicate that pig bones are sometimes found in small numbers at such sites. How is this occasional presence of limited quantities of pig remains at Judean sites to be understood? It is of course possible that such finds might be the chance food remains of non-Judean visitors to—or perhaps even ethnic minority residents of—an otherwise predominately Judean site. It is also possible that at least some such anomalous finds might be residual from earlier periods or intrusive from later ones, or else that they were brought to the site from the outside by scavengers. Nevertheless, we certainly should not discount the possibility of occasional noncompliance with the dietary rules of the Torah as an explanation for the presence of pig remains in Judean archaeological contexts. While by all indications these laws appear to have been widely observed among first-century Judeans, adherence to the rules may very well have been less than absolute.

FISH REMAINS

The scaleless fish most common in faunal assemblages from the Southern Levant may be divided into two main taxonomic groups: cartilaginous fish, which include both sharks and rays, and catfish. The term "catfish" refers to a large taxonomic group of fish consisting of numerous families, but in faunal assemblages known from the Southern Levant these include primarily *Clariiadae*, *Bagridae*, and *Mochokidae*. Only the first of these is native to the Levant—where it resides locally in coastal rivers, in the Sea of Galilee, and in other regions of the Jordan River system—while the second two are imports from the Nile. Both cartilaginous fish and catfish have fins but no scales, and consequentially both would have been subsumed under the category of fish prohibited for consumption by the Pentateuch.

In examining whether Judeans in the first century CE regularly consumed sharks, rays, or catfish, we are confronted for the time being with a formidable challenge: only a limited number of ancient fish assemblages dating to this period are available for analysis. The data from these assemblages will be presented here, with the caveat that firm conclusions must await the availability of further data.

Excavations in two sections of the early Roman-period dump on the eastern slopes of the Lower City of Jerusalem unearthed two fish assemblages, both of which included very small amounts of scaleless fish remains. In one assemblage, four catfish bones were identified out of a total NISP of 294 (1.4 percent), and in the other, three catfish bones and one shark centrum were identified out of a total NISP of 114 (3.5 percent).[46] Interestingly, none of the catfish bones in either assemblage were local—they all belonged to the two families native to the Nile. At Masada, 327 fish bones found "in different loci in the fortress" (no precise dates have been provided) were identified as all belonging to taxa of fish with both fins and scales. A small assemblage of fish bones unearthed in Caesarea, in a cesspit adjacent to Herod's hippodrome and found together with early Roman-period remains, included three catfish bones out of a total NISP of 107 (2.8 percent). As at this time Caesarea hosted a mixed population of Judeans and Greek-speaking non-Judeans, it is impossible to know who may have consumed the fish whose remains were discovered here.

It is impossible to draw any compelling conclusions about the fish-consumption habits of first-century Judeans on the basis of this extremely limited set of data. For the time being, we may only note that frequencies of scaleless fish remains among the few available assemblages are quite low, which *may* imply that such fish were not widely consumed at this time. The fact that a very small number of scaleless fish remains *were* unearthed in the Jerusalem dump raises the possibility of at least occasional noncompliance with the Torah's prohibition against consumption of such species.

Conclusions

We began by surveying a large amount of textual evidence which demonstrated that during the first century CE Judeans were in possession of a set of Pentateuchal food prohibitions and were known throughout the Roman Empire for their strict adherence to these rules. This was especially the case for Judeans' avoidance of pork, which was the subject of comments, jokes, and even stinging condemnations in the writings of several non-Judean authors living at this time. The archaeological record from the Southern Levant is in concert with this reading of the literary evidence; whereas pig bones tend to be present in high frequencies in Roman-era levels at non-Judean sites, pig remains are either entirely absent or else quite rare at first-century-CE Judean sites. The evidence provided by fish remains from this period is largely consistent with the hypothesis that first-century Judeans abstained not only from pork but also from other prohibited species such as scaleless fish, although the quantity of such remains is too limited at this stage to allow any firm conclusions on the matter to be drawn.

Early Evidence

We turn now to the period of time prior to the turn of the Common Era in order to seek evidence which might suggest that Judeans in earlier times were observing dietary restrictions of the sort found in the Pentateuchal food rules. We begin with an analysis of the textual evidence, followed by an investigation into the evidence provided by archaeological remains.

Textual Evidence

NON-JUDEAN AUTHORS IN THE FIRST CENTURY BCE

There are several indications that the existence of Judean dietary restrictions had already become well known throughout the Roman world by as early as the first century BCE—although admittedly most of these indications have been preserved only in somewhat later sources. According to a story told by the early fifth-century Latin writer Macrobius, when Augustus heard that his client Herod the Great had ordered the execution of one of his own sons, he exclaimed, "I'd rather be Herod's pig than Herod's son"—satirically implying that, as a Judean, Herod would have never slaughtered a pig.[47] Although it has been suggested that the joke had its origins in Greek—it appears to be a play on the Greek words "pig" (*hûs*) and "son" (*huiós*)—whether it goes back to an Augustan source is impossible to determine.[48]

From a few decades earlier, we have a letter cited by Josephus that was purportedly addressed to the people of Ephesus by the Roman general Dolabella and dated to 43 BCE, wherein the local Judeans were exempted from military service "because they may not bear arms or march on the days of the Sabbath nor can they obtain the native foods to which they are accustomed."[49] Also cited by Josephus is a purported "decree of the people of Sardis" on behalf of the city's Judeans, probably from around the same time, which granted that "the market-officials of the city shall be charged with the duty of having suitable food for them brought in."[50] If either of these documents are authentic, they suggest that non-Judeans in Asia Minor knew of Judean dietary restrictions as early as the middle of the first century BCE.

Also around the middle of the first century BCE, Diodorus Siculus wrote that the "outlandish laws" of the Judeans bid them "not to break bread with any other race" (which may or may not allude to the Pentateuchal dietary restrictions), and furthermore told of Antiochus IV sacrificing a sow on the Jerusalem altar, sprinkling the broth of the meat on the Judeans' holy books, and forcing the high priest and the rest of the Judeans to partake of its meat.[51]

Finally, a quip about Judean avoidance of pork is attributed to the Roman orator Cicero circa 70 BCE, but this is preserved only in the later writings of Plutarch (ca. 46–120 CE).[52]

DEAD SEA SCROLLS

Laws relating to the Pentateuchal dietary prohibitions feature in several of the Dead Sea Scroll manuscripts, some of which may date to as early as the Hasmonean period. The proscription against eating blood is presented in a straightforward manner in the Genesis Apocryphon and in the Temple Scroll, while in the Damascus Document (CD) we find more detailed treatments of legal problems relating to blood in fish and in permitted species of insects (such as locusts).[53] The author of CD came to the conclusion that the blood of fish is strictly prohibited: "And [as for] the fish: they shall not eat [them] unless they were torn while still alive and their blood was poured out." Permitted insects, on the other hand, require no such treatment—probably because their bodies contain nothing closely resembling blood: "And all the locusts in their kinds may be brought into fire or into water [even] while they are still alive, for this is the nature of their physical constitution [*kî hû' mišpāṭ bərî'ātām*]."[54] The Temple Scroll includes the prohibition against carrion, and 4QHalakha A includes a reference to the prohibition against a "torn" animal.[55] Possibly related to one or the other of these two proscriptions is what appears to be a prohibition cited in the latter text against eating the flesh of a fetus that had been removed from the body of a pregnant animal which had been properly killed; the fetus, it seems, was regarded as having not been directly killed by human hands—and is thus regarded as either carrion or "torn."[56] The taboo recorded in Gen 32:33 against eating certain tissue (*gîd hanāšeh*) found "on the thigh socket [*'al kaf hayārēkh*]" is presented more expansively in 4QReworked Pentateuch[a] as applying to the tissue "on both thigh sockets [*'al šətê kapôt hayārēkh*]."[57]

It may be a matter of coincidence that only a limited amount of text has been preserved among the Dead Sea Scrolls which relates to the prohibited species; preserved in the Temple Scroll is the name of a single prohibited bird, "the hoopoe(?)" (*hadûkhîfat*), together with the Pentateuchal criteria regarding the permitted insects.[58] The Damascus Document includes a prohibition against eating any living thing "that swarms in the water [*'ăšer tirmôś bamāyîm*]," along with something (the unfamiliar word "*'eglê*" is used) associated with bees.[59] Perhaps somewhat surprisingly, no surviving texts among the scrolls refer to a prohibition against pork. While none of these texts demonstrate that observance of these laws was *necessarily* widespread among contemporary Judeans, the fact that the authors of so many diverse works actively engaged in legal interpretations surrounding the details of the dietary laws suggests a milieu in which these rules were regarded as worthy of being discussed and perhaps even debated.

APOCRYPHA AND PSEUDEPIGRAPHA

References to the Pentateuchal dietary restrictions appear not infrequently in texts included in the Apocrypha and Pseudepigrapha, many or all of which may date to the final two centuries BCE. The blood prohibition is stressed on several occasions in Jubilees, and severe punishments are threatened for transgressors.[60] Of note, in three instances the author of Jubilees specified as prohibited "any blood of beasts, or birds, or cattle," perhaps with the deliberate intention of permitting the blood of fish (contra the ruling of CD above) and of permissible insects.[61]

The Testament of Asher specified pigs and hares as animals that are "half clean, but in very deed are unclean," alluding to the Pentateuchal verses that singled out these two species as examples of forbidden quadrupeds because they either chew the cud or have split hooves—but not both.[62] Elsewhere in this work, the author pointed out that although stags and hinds might seem to be unclean because they are "in a wild condition," in reality they are "altogether clean."[63] In both instances the dietary rules were referenced as an allegorical device for illustrating vice and virtue in human beings, and therefore it seems likely that these laws would have been well known to the intended readers of this document.

In the Letter of Aristeas, Eleazar the high priest provides the Egyptian delegation sent to Jerusalem with a lengthy (and somewhat rambling) explanation as to why "some animals are regarded as unclean for eating."[64] The excursus mentions among the forbidden species birds of prey and animals that are not cloven-hooved and do not chew the cud.

The three books that narrate the story of the persecutions said to have been perpetrated by Antiochus IV Epiphanes circa 167 BCE all tell of heroic Judeans who willingly gave up their lives to avoid eating forbidden foods. While 1 Maccabees refers to such martyrdoms in a rather succinct manner, the authors of both 2 Maccabees and 4 Maccabees provided lengthy and detailed stories about the martyrdoms of an elderly Eleazar and of seven young brothers who all chose to die rather than taste pork.[65] Whether any of these stories reflect historical events is hard to know, but they certainly may be read as reflections of the importance of the dietary laws to their narrators (1 and 2 Maccabees are both widely thought to date to either the second or the first century BCE, while 4 Maccabees is likely later).[66]

HEBREW BIBLE

Outside the Pentateuch, texts that predate the middle of the second century BCE provide no indications that Judeans might have possessed any set of restrictions on their diet. The very few texts in the Hebrew Bible outside the Pentateuch which involve censuring individuals for eating certain foods invariably refer to cultic or ritual contexts—not to prohibitions that apply to ordinary diet.

In one narrative, Saul's troops are said to have sinned against YHWH when they slaughtered animals from among the spoils they had taken, and proceeded "to eat on the blood [le'ĕkhōl 'al hadām]."[67] The only other instances in the Hebrew Bible where the phrase "to eat on the blood" appears are in Lev 19:26 and Ezek 33:25, and in both cases the act is clearly part of a divination or cultic ritual regarded as a violation of "proper" YHWH worship. Here too, the sin of the troops in eating "on the blood" was apparently cultic in nature, as Saul is said to have rectified the situation by erecting an "altar to YHWH" before which the animals were instead to be slaughtered. Apparently the problem was not that the men had transgressed a dietary prohibition by eating meat that was not sufficiently cleansed of its blood (as Josephus later interpreted the story) but rather that the troops had engaged in "improper" cultic behavior regarded as somehow contravening "correct" YHWH worship.[68]

Similarly, the only two instances in the entire Hebrew Bible outside the Pentateuch which censure the consumption of pig are found in polemics against cultic worship of foreign deities. The first appears in Isa 65, where YHWH accuses Israel of being "a people who provoke me to my face continually, sacrificing in gardens and offering incense on bricks; who sit inside tombs, and spend the night in secret places; who eat swine's flesh, with broth of abominable things in their vessels."[69] The vignette of ritual consumption of swine as part of an idolatrous cultic practice taking place "in gardens" is taken up again in the following chapter: "Those who sanctify and purify themselves to go into the gardens, following the one in the center, eating the flesh of pigs, vermin, and rodents, shall come to an end together, says YHWH."[70] None of this suggests the existence of any kind of prohibition against eating pork as regular food in a noncultic context.

In a passage in Ezekiel containing detailed cultic regulations addressed to the priests serving in the Jerusalem temple, the following instruction appears: "Anything that died of itself or was torn, whether bird or animal, the priests must not eat."[71] The injunction is directed specifically to the priests; nothing suggests that anyone other than priests were under this or any other dietary restriction. When in an earlier chapter Ezekiel exclaims, "Ah! Lord, YHWH! I have never defiled myself; from my youth up until now I have never eaten what died of itself or was torn by animals, nor has detestable flesh [bəśar pīgûl] come into my mouth," this too should be understood as the declaration of a priest of YHWH who has been careful to preserve his cultic purity—rather than as a reflection of some general dietary prohibition.[72]

It seems that the closest we get to the notion that characters found in the Hebrew Bible observed some sort of restriction on their diet is in a narrative about the food that Daniel and his colleagues ate in the palace of Nebuchadnezzar.[73] According to the story, the king assigned the men a daily ration "of the royal portions of food [*mipatbag hamelekh*] and of the wine of his banquets," but Daniel "resolved that he would not defile himself [*'ăšer lō' yitgā'al*]" by consuming these. Daniel furtively requested of the royal official responsible for the men's food that he provision them instead with vegetables and water, to which the latter acquiesced after a successful trial period of ten days which demonstrated that the alternative diet did not cause them malnutrition. It is hard to know what the author of this tale might have considered to be "defiling" about the royal rations of food and wine; perhaps he regarded any food or drink from the table of a Gentile (or of Nebuchadnezzar specifically) as somehow defiling, or else he wished to portray Daniel as practicing an ascetic ideal of sustaining himself on simple food and drink.[74] The fact that not only the royal food but also the king's *wine* was regarded as problematic mitigates against the possibility that Pentateuchal dietary prohibitions might be at stake, as these include no sweeping proscriptions against wine or other beverages (although these might be liable to ritual impurity). Regardless of what might have been deemed objectionable about the food and the wine, there is no compelling reason to think that this story was necessarily composed any time prior to the turn of the second century BCE—and thus can hardly be summoned as especially *early* evidence for the existence of any kind of Judean dietary restrictions.[75]

What about the Pentateuch itself? Nothing in the food regulations explicitly suggests that these were intended to establish already existing dietary taboos. The only long-standing food taboo cited in the Pentateuch (or anywhere else in the Hebrew Bible for that matter) is the one mentioned in the story about Jacob's injury from wrestling at Peniel: "Therefore to this day the Children of Israel do not eat the hip sinew [*gid hanāšeh*] that is on the thigh socket, because he struck Jacob on the thigh socket at the hip sinew."[76] Hermann Gunkel suggested this as an example of an etiological legend, meaning that the story of Jacob's injury was created precisely in order to explain a long-standing practice whose origins had been shrouded in mystery.[77] Aside from this lone attested taboo, there exists no other textual evidence to suggest that Judeans or Israelites were observing a broader set of dietary restrictions any time prior to the second century BCE.

Archaeological Evidence

We now turn to the archaeological record to investigate whether food remains dating to periods of time prior to the turn of the Common Era might suggest that Judeans were already in observance of dietary restrictions of the sort found in the Pentateuch. We start with a survey of the zooarchaeological data regarding pig remains, followed by an investigation of the data regarding scaleless fish remains—in both cases beginning with the first century BCE and continuing backward in time through the Hellenistic, Persian, and Iron Ages.

PIG REMAINS

There have been very few published reports of faunal assemblages from Judean sites that date to the period of Herod the Great or to the Hasmonean era. On the northern slope of Herodium, a faunal assemblage from excavation units thought to be associated with the laborers who built the theater (i.e., in the late first century BCE) contained 83 pig bones out of a total NISP of 1,096 (7.6 percent). As the ethnic identity of the members of Herod's construction team is difficult to determine, it is hard to know to what extent this assemblage reflects on specifically *Judean* dietary habits. At Qumran, four faunal assemblages were found to contain no pig bones at all; these were dated to the first century BCE–first century CE (105 total NISP), the Herodian period (170 total NISP), the first century BCE (45 total NISP), and the Hasmonean period (671 total NISP). At Nebi Samwil, no pig bones were identified in an assemblage containing a total NISP of 415. From Jerusalem, three significant Hasmonean-era faunal assemblages were unearthed in the Giv'ati Parking Lot: Area M1 contained 4 pig bones out of a total NISP of 691 (0.6 percent), Area M2 contained 9 pig bones out of a total NISP of 4,025 (0.2 percent), and Area M4 contained 9 pig bones out of a total NISP of 4,800 (0.2 percent).[78]

The only significant faunal assemblage from an Early Hellenistic-period Judean site that has been published to date is from Jerusalem's Giv'ati Parking Lot (Area M2): it contained 3 pig bones out of a total NISP of 1,327 (0.2 percent).[79] From the period between 586 and 332 BCE, five significant faunal assemblages from Judea have been reported on to date. An assemblage from Ramat Raḥel, dated to the sixth and fifth centuries BCE, contained 5 pig bones out of a total NISP of 252 (2 percent). Another assemblage from Jerusalem's Givʿati Parking Lot (Area M2) contained 3 pig bones out of a total NISP of 2,785 (0.1 percent). No pig bones were identified in an assemblage from Nebi Samwil (NISP 143) or in two assemblages from the City of David in Jerusalem, one of which was dated to the Persian period (NISP 583) and the other to the time of the Babylonian occupation (NISP 663).[80]

Preceding backward in time, we find quantitatively and qualitatively superior faunal assemblages from the Iron and Bronze Ages. A team led by Lidar Sapir-Hen and other researchers has recently published crucial metanalyses on the frequencies of pig remains within these early assemblages and has highlighted the complicated and culturally ambiguous patterns regarding where and when pig tends to be either present or absent.[81] These studies found that during the Iron Age IIC (ca. 680–586 BCE) pig was either absent or else present in extremely small frequencies (2 percent or less) at all analyzed sites in the region: whether within the geopolitical territory of the Southern Kingdom of Judah (Lachish and Aroer), Philistia (Ashkelon, Tel Miqne, and Qubūr el-Walēyideh), or Edom (Ḥorbat Qitmit). Prior to this, in the Iron Age IIB (780–680 BCE), pig was present in moderate to significant frequencies (3.2–7.8 percent) at sites within the lowlands territory of the Northern Kingdom of Israel (Hazor, Megiddo, Tel Yoqneʿam, Beth-Shean, and Tel Ḥamid) and at even higher levels at the Philistine site of Tell eṣ-Ṣafi (15.8 percent), but largely absent or else present in extremely small frequencies (usually less than 1 percent) at sites within the territory of the Southern Kingdom of Judah and at sites such as Tel Dor and Ḥorbat Rosh Zayit (both associated with Phoenician material culture) and Tel Reḥov (where Aramean features have been identified in the material culture). A similar pattern, although somewhat less evident, was found in both late and early phases of Iron Age IIA (950–780 BCE). Previous to this, in the Iron Age I (1130–950 BCE), pig was found to be essentially absent from all sites in the Southern Levant with the exception of Philistine urban centers (Ashdod, Tell eṣ-Ṣafi, and Tel Miqne), where it was found in significant frequencies (6.8–19.5 percent). Complete absence or negligible (mostly less than 2 percent) pig remains were found at highland sites, as well as at small rural sites within the geopolitical region of Philistia (Aphek, Tell Qasile, Qubūr el-Walēyideh, and Tel Jemmeh), at sites in the Shephelah (Beth-Shemesh and Khirbet Qeiyafa) and the Beersheba Valley (Tel Sheba and Tel Masos), and at northern lowland sites that cannot be identified with the highland population or with highland rule (e.g., Tel Dan, Tel Kinrot, and Tel Dor). Prior to this, during the Late Bronze Age IIB–III (1300–1130 BCE), pig was either completely absent or else found in negligible amounts (less than 2 percent) at several sites usually associated with indigenous material culture, it was found in small numbers (2.4–3.0 percent) at several other such sites, but it was found in significant frequencies at Beth-Shean (11.8 percent) and at Timna Site 2 (21 percent)—both sites associated at the time with Egyptian colonization.

How are we to interpret this highly complex picture? Clearly, Judeans were not the only ones who chose cattle and caprines over swine; swine remains are absent at a large aggregate of sites throughout the Southern Levant associated with manifold identity groups throughout the entire Late Bronze and Iron Ages. The possible motivations that may factor into why residents of a certain site or region at any given point in time might or might not have chosen to raise and consume pig are multifarious and complex. Brian Hesse and Paula Wapnish enumerated many of the intricate variables that affect the choice to raise pig, listing eight "pig principles" that they suggested structure the exploitation of swine.[82] They found that pig husbandry and consumption are more likely to be found in (1) wet ecological areas rather than arid regions; (2) permanent settlements rather than nomadic contexts; (3) microeconomies based on domestic consumption rather than those based on intensive agriculture aimed at exchange; (4) economically disengaged or politically autonomous rural settlements rather than economies engaged in politically governed urban markets; (5) settlements founded by new arrivals to a region rather than mature economies; (6) economies where the exchange value of meat is high or the utility of the secondary products of cattle is low rather than those with intensive agriculture where cattle can be exploited for overall higher yields; (7) contexts of nonritual or secular consumption rather than ritual or cultic contexts; and (8) lower-standing social classes rather than socially elite contexts. Fifteen years after Hesse and Wapnish published these principles, Sapir-Hen and other researchers demonstrated that the new data they analyzed sometimes confounded the predictions one might make on the basis of some of the above parameters (e.g., ecology and class), and argued that settlement and demographic processes involving rapid growth in the number and size of settlements may also be a factor in shifting the emphasis of meat production from sheep and goats to swine.[83] Hesse and Sapir-Hen have furthermore shown that the complex matrix of factors that determine whether swine were raised and consumed could sometimes influence husbandry and dietary practices in adjacent communities in divergent ways, and that such discrepancies might even be found within an individual settlement.[84]

Hesse and Wapnish provided an eloquent summary of the place of pig husbandry in the economies of the Southern Levant throughout the Late Bronze and Iron Ages: "Compared to the dependence on sheep, goats, and cattle, the use of swine was both spotty and episodic, never dominant, always supplemental, and enmeshed in the modes of pastoral production in complex ways."[85] It is true that pork was not being (regularly) consumed by the highlanders of the early Iron Age or afterward by the Judeans of the Southern Kingdom, but for the most part pork was concurrently also not being eaten by almost any other group settled anywhere in the region! The reasons for this are most readily sought in the kind of ecological and socioeconomic motivations outlined above; there is no apparent reason to assume that anyone was practicing deliberate *avoidance* of pig consumption because of some sort of cultural *taboo* against the animal.[86]

FISH REMAINS

Two fish assemblages are thought to date to the time of Herod the Great, in the last decades of the first century BCE.[87] At Masada, 1,494 microscopic fish bones were found in an analysis of fish sauce remains ("allec") discovered in a jar fragment thought to date to the time of Herod; no scaleless fish remains were found among these. A small assemblage of 38 fish bones from late first century BCE loci on the northern slope of Herodium also included no scaleless fish remains.

Three small fish assemblages unearthed in Jerusalem's Givʿati Parking Lot represent the only available fish assemblages dating to the Hellenistic period which derive from an unambiguously Judean settlement (fig. 3).[88] The following are the frequencies of catfish bones within each of these assemblages according to date: (1) Late Hellenistic (Hasmonean) period: 1:28 NISP; (2) Late Hellenistic (Hasmonean?) period: 1:9 NISP; (3) Early Hellenistic period: 3:16 NISP.

More substantial fish assemblages are available from Judean contexts from earlier periods. From the Persian period, an assemblage unearthed in Jerusalem's Givʿati Parking Lot included 16 catfish bones (fig. 3), along with one element from a shark or ray, out of a total NISP of 133 (13 per-

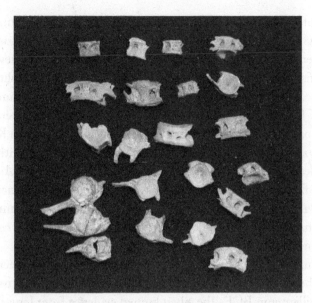

Figure 3. *Catfish vertebrae from Jerusalem's Givʿati Parking Lot, Persian- and Hellenistic-period phases. (From Spiciarich, "Religious and Socioeconomic Diversity," 332, fig. 6.28.)*

cent), while another assemblage from nearby Area G in the City of David included 36 catfish bones out of a total NISP of 195 (18 percent). In a layer found directly below the stratum where this last assemblage was found—dated by the excavator to the time of the Babylonian occupation—an additional fish assemblage included 128 catfish bones out of a total NISP of 467 (27 percent).

Significant frequencies of scaleless fish (especially catfish) have been found in Jerusalem and throughout Judea in all assemblages available for analysis which date to the Iron Age II (ca. 950–586 BCE). These include eight assemblages unearthed in various areas on the eastern hill of Jerusalem—throughout the so-called Ophel, the eastern slope of the City of David, and the Givʿati Parking Lot. Excavations at all these areas unearthed hundreds of catfish bones along with dozens of calcified remains of shark cartilage. These remains all derived from loci dating variously from the late ninth or early eighth century BCE until the Babylonian destruction of the city. Another important assemblage, deriving from a single deposit from the late seventh or early sixth century BCE in a small pit under the floor of the central courtyard of the palatial complex at Ramat Raḥel, included 48 fish bones, of which 23 belonged to catfish. On the basis of the skeletal elements and the size of the bones, there were at least seven individual catfish inside the pit (with a total weight estimated at about 10 kilograms!). Scaleless fish remains were also uncovered outside the immediate vicinity of Jerusalem, at Lachish (17 out of 120 total NISP). Dietary consumption patterns of scaleless fish at all the Iron Age II Southern Kingdom sites analyzed are comparable with those at sites associated with Philistine (Ashkelon) and Phoenician (Acre and Tel Kabri) material cultures. Although far fewer data are currently available from sites associated with the political boundaries of the Northern Kingdom, a small assemblage of fish remains from Tel Megiddo suggests that scaleless fish were consumed at northern sites as well.

In summary, these data indicate that scaleless fish, and especially catfish, were being consumed regularly by Judeans throughout the first half of the first millennium BCE. The albeit limited evidence from Jerusalem that postdates 586 BCE suggests that this pattern continued into the Persian period. Finds from the Hellenistic period until the end of the first millennium BCE are too limited to allow any substantive conclusions to be drawn, although a very small number of scaleless fish remains from Hellenistic Jerusalem may suggest that the trend continued beyond the Persian period.

It bears pointing out that these dietary patterns demonstrate quite clearly that the Pentateuchal writers were capable of legislating a dietary restriction that was not rooted in centuries-old patterns of consumption. If the proscription against scaleless fish could take form in the writings of Pentateuchal authors despite the lack of a long-standing, widespread dietary tradition at its root, this suggests that perhaps other Pentateuchal dietary prohibitions as well were established by these writers quite independently of any preexistent eating habits. This realization supports my argument above that we ought not simply assume that the Pentateuchal proscription against pork necessarily emerged out some kind of early cultural "taboo" against it.

Conclusions

The aim of this chapter was to seek out and identify the earliest evidence indicating that Judeans were observing dietary restrictions of the sort found in the Pentateuchal food regulations. We surveyed an impressive array of textual evidence dating to the first century CE which indicated that Judeans throughout the Roman Empire were in possession of a well-defined set of dietary restrictions that they were quite famously known to have observed meticulously. We found that the archaeological record of pig frequencies in the Southern Levant at this time is consistent with the textual evidence; pig remains tend to be present in high frequencies in Roman-era levels at non-Judean sites, but are either entirely absent or else are very rare at first-century-CE Judean sites. The evidence provided by fish remains from this period, although quite limited, was found to be largely consistent with the hypothesis that Judeans abstained not only from pork but also from scaleless fish. Prior to the turn of the Common Era, textual evidence suggests that the same sort of dietary restrictions widely observed in the first century CE were already in place as early as the first and perhaps even the second century BCE.

Here the trail of evidence ends. Prior to the second century BCE, there exists no surviving evidence, whether textual or archaeological, which suggests that Judeans adhered to a set of food prohibitions or to a body of dietary restrictions of any kind. The only evidence which suggests that a food taboo of any sort was practiced in earlier times is an etiological tale in Genesis aimed at explaining the reason for a long-standing Israelite avoidance of the "hip sinew." Although the archaeological record does suggest that pork did not play a significant role in Judeans' diets from the Iron Age onward, from an archaeological perspective alone there is no compelling reason to think that this was due to some sort of taboo. The presence of substantial quantities of scaleless fish remains in archaeological levels dating from the Iron Age through the Persian period at Jerusalem and at sites throughout Judea suggests that during these periods Judeans were *not* practicing avoidance of fish species that came to be prohibited in the Pentateuch.

The significant conclusion we may draw from all that we have seen in this chapter is that it is only from the Hasmonean period onward that we may claim to know of Judeans adhering to a set of dietary restrictions of any kind.

2 Ritual Purity

Binaries such as "clean"/"dirty," "pure"/"contaminated," and "unpolluted"/"polluted" are extremely widespread (if not universal) throughout human societies, both present and past. An evolutionary explanation for this phenomenon may profitably be sought in disease avoidance, as experience would have taught the dangers of certain contaminants even in prescientific societies wholly oblivious to the biological mechanics of how invisible pathogens generate pathologies. In many languages, today and in the past, some of these same binaries have been borrowed from the physical sphere and applied to the moral realm to describe normative binaries such as "good"/"bad," "right"/"wrong," and "virtue"/"vice." This phenomenon is unsurprising; if physical contaminants are recognized as a cause of *physiological* diseases, moral pollutions may be thought to produce *social* ills. Beyond this, many societies employ binaries such as "clean"/"dirty" and the like to describe phenomena that do not fit so neatly into the simple categories of either physical cleanliness or moral purity—other rules seem to be at play. It is this third, far more abstract and amorphous category that we will refer to here as "*ritual* purity"; its outlines will hopefully become clearer as we progress through the chapter.[1]

As we shall see shortly, by the first century CE Judeans commonly adhered to a highly detailed and complex system of rules that regulated matters relating to ritual purity. This entire system was founded on a large set of Pentateuchal passages that established what it is that causes "impurity" (ṭūmʾāh), how this impurity is transmitted from one physical entity to another, and finally how this impurity is removed from the affected thing and "purity" (ṭāhārāh) is restored. These Pentateuchal passages not only *described* the mechanics of impurity but also *prescribed* detailed rules and regulations regarding how an individual is required to act when impurity has manifested. As our aim in the present chapter is to seek out the earliest evidence for Judean observance of this particular system of rules and regulations, it is critical to briefly review here the specifics of these laws as they appear in the Pentateuch.

The following are presented as persons, fauna, or inanimate objects that are regarded as the *root cause* of impurity: (1) carcasses of quadrupeds, fish, birds, and insects belonging to species that are forbidden to consume; (2) carcasses belonging to eight specified species of "creeping thing" (*šereṣ*); (3) carcasses belonging to species that are permitted to consume but which died on their own or were "torn"; (4) a woman following childbirth; (5) a person suffering specified skin pathologies; (6) cloth or leather upon which specified green or red blotches appeared; (7) a house upon whose walls specified green or red blotches appeared; (8) a man who has experienced a pathological emission from his penis; (9) semen; (10) a woman who has experienced menstrual bleeding; (11) a woman who has experienced abnormal uterine bleeding outside the normal menstrual cycle; (12) a human corpse, bone, or grave; (13) those involved in the slaughtering and burning of the red heifer; (14) the person who collected the ashes of the red heifer; (15) anyone who sprinkled or touched water mixed with these ashes.[2]

Depending on which of the above root causes of impurity are involved, the following are described as *means of transfer* through which a ritually pure person is apt to contract these impurities: (a) undergoing an experience or action that renders the person a source of impurity itself; (b) touching or being touched by the impurity source; (c) carrying the source of impurity; (d) eating the source of impurity; (e) entering into the airspace enclosed by the source of impurity; (f) lying or eating within the airspace enclosed by the source of impurity; (g) touching the bed of an impure person; (h) sitting on a vessel upon which an impure person sat; (i) being spat upon by an impure person; (j) touching anything that is beneath the impure person; (k) having sexual intercourse with the impure person; (l) touching a vessel upon which an impure person sat; (m) touching a person who had become impure from the source of impurity; (n) entering into a tent in which a human had died.[3]

Depending on which root cause of impurity is involved and depending on the manner whereby this impurity was contracted, the Pentateuchal system prescribes that impurity is to be *removed* from a defiled person by either (i) waiting until evening, or (ii) waiting seven days, or (iii) waiting fourteen days, and/or (iv) bathing in water, and/or—where there is a pathology involved—(v) waiting until the pathology clears up.[4] A select few cases require additional actions: (vi) a sacrificial offering in the sanctum itself and/or (vii) a nonsacrificial ritual performed outside the sanctum.[5]

Clothing becomes impure and must be laundered in water if it was worn by a person who was a source of impurity himself, or if it was worn by a person who had come into contact with certain sources of impurity, as also clothing or leather that touched semen.[6] Clothing or leather that is impure because of an impure blotch must be burned.[7] A bed becomes impure if certain human sources of impurity lie on it, as does a saddle.[8] Utensils become impure through contact with certain sources of impurity: if they are sat upon by certain persons who are regarded as a source of impurity, or if they are in a tent where a human had died (but in this last case, only if the vessel is unsealed).[9] Utensils rendered impure from a corpse must be purified through a ritual of sprinkling with water mixed with red heifer ash; those made of metal that can withstand the heat must be passed through fire, while those that cannot be put in fire must be passed through water.[10] As for other impurities, the manner whereby a utensil is purified depends on the raw material from which it is made: wood is "rinsed" or "put into water," as are cloth, leather, and sacking, but pottery is to be broken, and an oven and stove (presumably also of clay) are to be smashed.[11] A house that is impure because of a green or red blotch must be destroyed.[12] Food, beverages, or seeds that were touched by a dead "creeping thing" are rendered impure, but in the case of food and seeds, only if they had been made wet.[13] Water while still in a spring or a cistern is not rendered impure from contact with impurity.[14]

As we shall presently demonstrate, by the first century CE Judean exegetes were actively engaged in interpreting (and debating) the details of this precise set of Pentateuchal regulations, and at the same time regular Judeans were actively involved in observing this complex set of rules in their daily lives. Moving away from the first century CE, we will proceed backward in time to investigate evidence from earlier periods, with the aim of seeking out and identifying the oldest available evidence which might suggest that something closely resembling the Pentateuchal laws of ritual purity were known and observed by Judeans on any kind of wide-scale basis.

First-Century Evidence

We begin by looking at textual evidence dating to the first century CE which indicates that the Pentateuchal purity laws surveyed above were observed by contemporary Judeans on a wide-scale basis. This will be followed by an examination of archaeological evidence that similarly suggests widespread adherence to these regulations among first-century Judeans.

Textual Evidence

PHILO

Among Philo's writings are scattered references to several of the causes of impurity listed in the Pentateuch. On the impurity affecting partners who have engaged in coitus, Philo wrote, "A husband and wife, who have intercourse in accordance with the legitimate usages of married life, are not allowed, when they leave their bed, to touch anything until they have bathed and made their ablutions [*loutroîs kaì perirrhantēríois khrēsthai*]."[15] Other impurities mentioned are "gonorrhea" (*gonorrhuès*) and "scale diseases" (*léprai*); if a priest experienced either of these, he must wait for the pathologies to clear up before he may touch anything consecrated or engage in priestly duties.[16] Similarly, nocturnal emissions and touching anything unclean prevent a priest from partaking in anything consecrated until he has "bathed himself" (*lousámenos*) and waited until the evening.[17] Philo related that "scale disease" is a frequent occurrence in houses and is declared impure upon the inspection of a priest—at which time everything that is in the house becomes impure.[18] People who have gone into a house in which anyone has died are not to touch anything until they have bathed themselves and laundered their clothing, and similarly all the furniture, vessels, and all else in the house are to be regarded as impure.[19] All who have touched a corpse are regarded as impure until they have purified themselves through "aspersions and bathings [*perirrhanámenoi kaì apolousámenoi*]," and even after they are completely pure, they may still not enter the temple within seven days unless they have undergone purifications on the third and seventh days.[20] Elsewhere, Philo described precisely what such purifications involved: branches of hyssop were dipped into a mixture of water and ashes of a red heifer (the ritual of its burning is described in some detail), and the water-ash mixture was then sprinkled over those undergoing purification on the third and seventh days, after which they were to bathe themselves.[21]

It is somewhat difficult to know whether Philo wrote any of this from personal familiarity with these rituals as practiced by Judeans in real life, or whether he was simply paraphrasing and interpreting Pentateuchal regulations whose actual observance he may have never experienced.

NEW TESTAMENT

The accounts found in the four Gospels and in Acts present a far more vivid picture wherein Judeans are portrayed as keenly cognizant of the ritual purity laws and actively putting them into practice in their day-to-day lives. Among these is a story in Mark where contemporary purity practices stand at the center of a debate between Jesus and his interlocutors:

> And the Pharisees and some scribes who had come from Jerusalem gathered with him. And they saw some of his disciples, that they were eating their food with profane hands, that is, with unwashed [hands] [*koinaîs khersín, toût' éstin aníptois*]. For the Pharisees and all the Judeans do not eat unless they wash their hands up to the fist [*pugmḗ nípsōntai tàs kheîras*], holding fast the tradition of the elders [*tền parádosin tỗn presbutérōn*]; and when they return from the market, they do not eat, unless they immerse [*baptísōntai*]. And there are many other things which they receive to hold fast, the immersing of cups and pitchers and copper utensils and dining couches [*baptismoùs potēríōn kaì xestỗn kaì khalkíōn kaì klinỗn*]. And the Pharisees and the scribes asked him, "Why do your disciples not walk in accordance with the tradition of the elders, but eat bread with profane hands?"[22]

The author (or redactor) of this narrative portrayed not only the Pharisees but "all the Judeans" as practicing several purificatory rituals surrounding meals: before eating they wash their hands; if they have returned from the marketplace, they immerse themselves; and they also immerse utensils used for food preparation and table service as well as dining furniture. All of this should almost certainly be understood against the background of the Pentateuchal purification regulations: a visit to the chaotic market would have entailed almost unavoidable contact with impure people and objects, and consequentially one would have had to bathe prior to sitting down to eat in order to avoid ritual contamination of the food. We are told that "cups and pitchers and copper utensils" were regularly immersed as well, undoubtably in adherence to the Pentateuchal requirement that one must "put into water" "rinse in water," or "pass through water" any ritually defiled vessels made of certain materials.[23] Also said to be immersed were "dining couches," probably in compliance with Pentateuchal regulations regarding impurity affecting beds and seats.[24] For now I will only briefly note that the same verb "*baptízō*," which refers specifically to immersion into a liquid, is used here for the action taken to purify both objects and people (below I will expand upon this point further).[25] The notion of "profane hands" that are to be purified through handwashing is presented here explicitly as a "tradition of the elders," which probably means that the idea was understood to be an *expansion upon* Pentateuchal regulations. The Pharisees and scribes are said to complain to Jesus that his disciples are ignoring precisely these unwritten traditions, and Jesus is said to have responded with a counterattack by accusing the Pharisees and scribes of hypocrisy: "Abandoning the commandment of God, you keep the tradition of human beings."[26] Jesus is said to have then turned to the crowds and taught that "there is nothing outside a human being which, by going into him, is able to profane him; rather, it is what goes out of a human being that profanes him," later explaining to his disciples, "Nothing that is outside can profane a human being by going into him, because it does not go into his heart, but into the belly, and it goes out into the latrine." The narrator (or redactor) appended to this last statement of Jesus a dangling participial phrase: "purifying all the food [*katharízōn pánta tà brṓmata*]." For our purposes, it is less important to understand precisely what it was that the writer here intended to convey regarding Jesus's own views on ritual purity practices than it is to note the manner in which "all the Judeans" are depicted as adhering to these rules. Regardless of whether this story actually took place as described (if at all), the writer here clearly believed that it would make sense to readers to have regular Judeans portrayed as actively concerned about the ritual purity of the food they ate, and as commonly practicing purificatory rituals mandated in the Pentateuch—and even expanding upon these rules—in order to ensure the ritual purity of their bodies, utensils, furniture, and food.

Luke presents a different scene in which Jesus himself is said to have sat down to eat without first immersing, which was enough to surprise his Pharisaic host: "While he [i.e., Jesus] was speaking, a Pharisee invited him to dine with him; so he went in and took his place at the table. The Pharisee was amazed to see that he did not first immerse before the meal [*hóti ou prṓton ebaptísthē prò toū arístou*]. Then the Lord said to him, 'Now you Pharisees purify the outside of the cup and of the dish [*tò éxōthen toū potēríou kaì toū pínakos katharízete*], but inside you are full of greed and wickedness. You fools! Did not the one who made the outside make the inside also? So, give for alms those things that are within; and see, everything will be clean for you [*pánta katharà humīn estin*]'."[27] In the scene depicted here, Jesus was expected to immerse himself before sitting down to eat; presumably, as in Mark 7, this would have been standard procedure prior to a meal for any Judean who thought they might have contracted ritual impurity. Jesus replies to the host's apparent sign of surprise by attacking the Pharisees' practice of ritually purifying the outsides of cups and dishes while failing to attend to their own inner *moral* purity. This is followed up by Jesus declaring a series of "woe" pronouncements, among which is one focused on negligent transmission of grave impurity onto unsuspecting victims: "Woe to you! For you are like unmarked graves, and people walk over them without realizing it."[28] Again, the veracity of neither the account itself nor the individual sayings attributed to Jesus here is of much importance for our purposes; what matters is that the author of this text presumably anticipated that a story such as this would at minimum sound *plausible* to contemporary readers at least tangentially aware of first-century-CE Judean practices.

Matthew presents a parallel account to Mark's focus on handwashing and attributes to Jesus a saying parallel to Luke's about the purification of cups and dishes.[29] Matthew also presents a fundamentally different version of the "woe" declaration about grave impurity attributed to Jesus in Luke: "Woe to you, scribes and Pharisees, hypocrites! For you are like whitewashed tombs, which on the outside look beautiful, but inside they are full of the bones of the dead and of all kinds of filth. So, you also on the outside look righteous to others, but inside you are full of hypocrisy and lawlessness."[30]

All three of the Synoptic Gospels include a story about Jesus healing a man who suffered from scale disease and then instructing him to fulfill the Pentateuchal purification regulations for one who has been healed of a skin affliction: "Go, show yourself to the priest, and offer for your cleansing what Moses commanded, as a proof for them."[31] The idea is repeated in a second narrative (appearing only in Luke) wherein Jesus heals a group of ten men afflicted with scale disease who approached him in the region between Samaria and Galilee, and sent them off with the instruction "Go and show yourselves to the priests."[32] Both narratives concern themselves with more than just the healing of a physical malady; the ritual viewing of a priest and the offering of the requisite sacrifice as "Moses commanded" are still necessary in order to complete the full *ritual* purification procedure.

Luke depicts Mary and Joseph ascending to the Jerusalem temple following an undisclosed period of time in order to fulfill the purification

requirements of a postpartum woman in tandem with the redemption ritual for Jesus as a firstborn son: "And when the days were fulfilled for their
purification [*toū katharismoū autōn*] according to the law of Moses, they
went up to Jerusalem to present him to the Lord (as it is written in the law
of the Lord, 'Every firstborn male shall be designated as holy to the Lord')
and to offer a sacrifice according to what is stated in the law of the Lord, 'a
pair of turtledoves or two young pigeons.'"[33]

Another scene at the temple associated with purification is found in
Acts, where the elders of the Christ-following group in Jerusalem adjured
a visiting Paul to demonstrate his fidelity to the Torah by sponsoring the
costs of four members of the group who had undertaken "a vow": "So do
what we tell you. We have four men who are under a vow [*eukhèn ékhontes
eph' heautōn*]. Join these men, be purified with them [*hagnísthēti sùn autoîs*],
and pay for the shaving of their heads. Thus, all will know that there is
nothing in what they have been told about you, but that you yourself observe and guard the law.... Then Paul, having taken the men the next day,
having been purified with them [*sùn autoîs hagnistheìs*], entered the temple,
making public the completion of the days of purification [*tōn hēmerōn toū
hagnismoū*] when the sacrifice would be made for each of them."[34] In the
following verse, it becomes clear that the purification process for the men
who were under the vow took seven days, and that Paul's visit to the temple
took place before the end of the seventh and final day of purification. There
can be little doubt that the narrator here had in mind the purification ritual
for the Nazirite who had accidentally incurred corpse impurity; following a
seven-day purification process, he must shave his head on the seventh day
and bring three offerings to the temple on the eighth day.[35] Paul himself
was not a Nazirite at this time, nor was he corpse-impure, and therefore he
could purify himself already on "the next day" without undergoing the full
seven-day procedure. Why Paul would have had any need to purify himself
at all is not stated; possibly it was common practice for anyone entering the
temple to purify themselves as a precautionary measure.[36]

The Gospel of John also contains several references to practical observance of the purity laws. In the wedding at Cana narrative, the jars in
which the water-to-wine miracle is said to take place are described as being
in accord with the Judean purity regulations: "Now standing there were six
stone water jars in accordance with the purification of the Judeans [*katà tòn
katharismòn tōn Ioudaíōn*]" (more on this below).[37] The disciples of John,
"the Immerser," are said to have gotten into a (legal?) debate with another

Judean over unspecified matters "concerning purification [*perì katharis-moû*]."[38] In the period of time leading up to the Passover, many Judeans are said to have come to Jerusalem "in order to purify themselves [*hína hagnísōsin heautoús*]."[39] And finally when Jesus was arrested shortly before the Passover, it is said that the Judeans who brought him before Pilate refrained from entering into the governor's headquarters "so that they should not be defiled [*hína mè mianthôsin*]" and thus be prevented from subsequently partaking of the Passover offering.[40] Precisely what impurity might have been involved is left unstated; perhaps the writer thought that even just entering into a building belonging to non-Judeans might entail a certain risk of contracting ritual impurity because of Gentiles' lack of concern over such matters.[41]

To remove any doubt, I make no assumptions that any of the stories reported in these accounts actually transpired. What is important for our purposes is that several first-century-CE writers used common, widespread Judean observance of the Pentateuchal ritual purity laws as the setting for various stories they wished to tell about the life and times of Jesus and his followers. Whatever their ideological or literary intentions may have been, in so doing they apparently regarded such portrayals as at least *plausible* depictions of contemporary Judean practices.

JOSEPHUS

The Pentateuchal purity laws are cited on several occasions throughout many of Josephus's works. He reported that those with scale disease and people with gonorrhea are not allowed at all into the city of Jerusalem, that women during their monthly period of menstruation are not allowed into the outer courtyard of the Temple Mount until seven days have passed from the onset of their menses, and that Judeans suffering any other type of impurity are barred from entering into any of the more inner courtyards of the temple.[42] A woman who has given birth may not enter the temple nor touch the sacrifices until forty days have passed if the child is a boy, or until eighty days if it is a girl.[43] Also with regard to the cult itself, Josephus wrote that "purifications for the sacrifices [*hagneías epì taîs thusíais*]" were required by the law after a funeral, childbirth, sexual union with a woman, "and many other [*kaì pollôn állōn*]" such causes of impurity.[44] The Passover sacrifice may not be eaten by those with scale disease, by those afflicted with gonorrhea, by menstruant women, and by "others who were defiled [*toîs állōs memiasménois*]."[45] So convinced was Josephus that Judeans actually adhered to this last rule that, in reporting on the results of a census taken one year in the mid-60s CE by counting the number of Passover animals slaughtered, he claimed that any Judeans who were impure must be excluded from the tally as they assuredly would not have taken part in the sacrifice.

Josephus described the purity regulations as also affecting daily life outside the limited sphere of the temple and Jerusalem. He wrote that those with scale disease are prohibited by the law from "either staying in a city or living in a village [*méte ménein en pólei mét' en kṓmȩ katoikeîn*]."[46] Elsewhere, Josephus reported that Judeans were extremely reluctant to settle in Tiberias when the city was first founded by Herod Antipas (ca. 20 CE) because it had been built over graves: "For he knew that this settlement was contrary to the law and tradition of the Judeans because Tiberias was built on the site of tombs that had been obliterated, of which there were many there. And our law declares that such settlers are unclean for seven days."[47] Antipas, we are told, was forced to use a combination of financial incentives together with coercion to bring in Judean settlers, many of whom he took from among the lowest echelons of society—"a promiscuous rabble" in the words of Josephus.[48]

Josephus provided a rather detailed description of how one particular Judean sect—the Essenes—practiced the purity laws of the Torah, insofar as this group's practices differed somewhat from those of other Judeans. Unlike others, members of the group regarded anointing the skin with oil as ritually defiling, as also defecation (neither of these are included as causes of impurity in the Pentateuch).[49] When they come to purify themselves before sitting down to eat their daily meals, Essenes gird themselves with a linen covering and bathe in cold water (other Judeans apparently bathed in the nude when purifying themselves).[50] Admission of newcomers to the group involved a series of probatory periods; after one year the novice is allowed to "share in the purer waters for purification [*katharōtéron tôn pròs hagneían hudátōn metalambánei*]," and only after two more years does he swear certain oaths admitting him fully into the group and allowing him "to touch the communal food [*tês koinês hápsasthai trophês*]."[51] For the duration of their training, they are divided into a system of four classes within which the newcomers are regarded as so inferior to those with seniority that, should the neophytes touch the more senior associates, the latter "wash themselves off as if they have mingled with a foreigner [*katháper allophúlȩ sumphuréntas*]."[52] It seems that those not fully trained and incorporated as members of the group were regarded as insufficiently knowledgeable and trustworthy with regard to the purity laws as these were understood and practiced by the sect, and as such they were presumed to be ritually impure and their touch was treated as ritually defiling.

It is somewhat unclear if Josephus's reference here to the defiling touch of an actual "foreigner" (i.e., a non-Judean) is simply self-referential, which is to say that only the Essenes would have regarded such contact as imparting ritual impurity, or if this was a matter upon which other Judeans might have been in broad agreement. Regardless of whether Judeans might have commonly regarded non-Judeans as *carriers* of impurity (a question hotly debated within scholarship), it seems likely that they would have at the very least suspected Gentiles of *negligence* in ensuring the purity status of impurity-susceptible objects within their care.[53] For example, Josephus wrote that from the time the Romans took over direct governance of Judea following the removal of Archelaus in 6 CE, the vestments of the Judean high priest were regularly kept locked up and guarded by the garrison commander—presumably a non-Judean.[54] The vestments were delivered by this commander to the priests seven days before each of the three annual pilgrimage festivals and the Day of Atonement, at which time they would be purified before being donned by the high priest. The seven-day period to purify the vestments seems best explained as a precaution in case the vestments had unknowingly contracted the most severe form of impurity—corpse impurity—while under the watch of a Gentile caretaker presumed to be indifferent to such matters. A similar explanation may be behind Josephus's remarks about Judeans' concern to use only "pure olive oil [*élaion . . . katharón*]" procured from other Judeans, as use of oil obtained from Gentiles was regarded as a violation of the ritual "regulations" (*tà nómima*).[55] Gentiles could not be trusted to keep the oil away from impurity (after all, why should they even care!), and hence only oil procured from trustworthy Judeans would have been regarded as ritually pure. An analogous explanation may also be behind Josephus's story about certain Judean priests taken as prisoners to Rome, who supported themselves on figs and nuts out of "piety towards God."[56] Presumably the standard fare in a Roman prison would have been some sort of bread, which like olive oil would have been regarded as ritually impure if it was provided by Gentiles. Leviticus 11:34 states explicitly that only liquids or solid foods which came into contact with water are susceptible to impurity, and thus figs or nuts—

both of which tend to be kept dry to prevent spoilage—would have been regarded as unsusceptible to impurity, and hence permitted even if obtained from Gentiles.

Archaeological Evidence

We now turn to examine archaeological finds from the first century CE which, as will be argued here in detail, are to be viewed as indicative of widespread contemporary Judean adherence to the ritual purity laws. Two archaeological phenomena in particular stand out in this regard: stepped pools and chalk vessels.[57] In presenting each of these, I will open with an argument for why the phenomenon under consideration should be regarded as evidence for Judean ritual purity observance, followed by an examination of what this evidence may inform us regarding the details of this observance.

IMMERSION POOLS

The stepped pool is an exceptionally common type of installation at archaeological sites throughout Judea, Galilee, and Peraea, with over one thousand examples known to date.[58] These pools are fitted with a flight of steps that lead from the rim of the pool to its floor, and in almost all cases the sides and the floor of the pool are covered with a layer of hydraulic plaster. The majority of these pools date to the Early Roman period (from around the middle of the first century BCE until the Bar Kokhba revolt in 132–135 CE), of which hundreds are well dated to before 70 CE. This large group of Early Roman-era pools will be the subject of our discussion presently; below I will focus on installations that are well dated specifically to the period before the turn of the first century CE.

For over half a century, the stepped pools under discussion have been interpreted by scholars as ritual baths, purpose-built and used by Judeans for purificatory immersion.[59] While I wholeheartedly agree with this basic identification, I think it is unfortunate that discussion surrounding these pools has been dominated by scholars' tendency to anachronistically interpret the mostly pre-70 CE finds through the lens of later rabbinic *hălākhāh*. As I shall presently show, there is no need to appeal to rabbinic literature— or any other noncontemporary evidence—in order to demonstrate that these installations were likely used by Judeans precisely for the purpose of purificatory immersions.

That these were *pools* is easily demonstrated by the fact that almost invariably they are found coated with waterproof plaster. In several examples, feeding channels have survived which channeled rainwater into the installation from adjoining rainwater catchment areas (oftentimes shared with adjacent water cisterns). The only installations lacking any plaster are those that have been unearthed at Magdala; these, however, were constructed below the local groundwater table and thus were apparently left without plaster to allow water to seep *into* them—which continues to occur even today (fig. 4).

That these were *immersion* pools is demonstrated by the fact that, without exception, all the pools under consideration here have a flight of steps that lead from the rim of the pool down to its floor. It goes without saying that these steps were designed to allow people to enter the pool and descend to its bottom, and subsequently to ascend from the floor of the pool and exit at its rim. In English, we refer to such descent into water as "immersion." That these pools were designed to permit immersion in water as their *primary* function is suggested by the fact that, as a rule, there is not

Figure 4. *Immersion pool filled with groundwater at Magdala.*
(Photo: Aviad Amitai.)

much space between the bottom step and the far wall of the pool; the tight space at the bottom of the steps seems to imply that no significant activities took place in the pool aside from the simple motion of descending down into the water, turning around, ascending back up, and exiting. An archaeologist encountering a pool like this anywhere in the world—whether in Jerusalem, Rome, New York, or Alaska—could be expected to arrive at the conclusion that the unearthed pool was an *immersion* pool. This verdict is based purely on the kind of functional reasoning employed all the time by archaeologists working throughout the world on archaeological contexts dating to all periods of the human past.

That these were *Judean* immersion pools is demonstrated by the fact that the pools under consideration are found almost exclusively at settlement sites known to have been occupied by Judeans (fig. 5).[60] Conversely, these pools are conspicuously absent from sites known to have been settled predominantly by non-Judeans—such as the cities of the Decapolis, all of Western Galilee, all sites south of Beersheba, and the Greek cities along the Mediterranean coastal plain. An archaeologist encountering an unambiguous distribution pattern along cultural lines like this for any other kind of archaeological phenomenon could be expected to reach the conclusion that the phenomenon in question was a culturally determined one. Again, this verdict is based purely on the kind of culturally attuned reasoning used regularly by archaeologists working across the globe on archaeological contexts dating to all epochs of the human past. Thus, on purely archaeological grounds, we may safely identify these installations as *Judean* immersion pools.

Fortunately, we do not need to go to any great lengths to speculate as to why Judeans—and only Judeans—might have gone to such trouble to construct so many immersion pools virtually everywhere they lived throughout the Southern Levant. Above we had seen the claim in Mark that "all Judeans" immerse (the verb used is "*baptízō*") in order to purify themselves after returning from the marketplace before sitting down to eat, and that they also subject tableware, copper utensils, and dining couches to purificatory immersions. We also saw the story in Luke in which a host is surprised to witness Jesus sitting down to a meal without first immersing (here too the verb used is "*baptízō*") to purify himself. Josephus wrote that a man who ejaculates in his sleep purifies "by plunging himself into cold water [*katheis hautòn eis húdōr psukhròn*]."[61] All these sources suggest that in the first century CE Judeans practiced immersion in water for the purpose of ritual

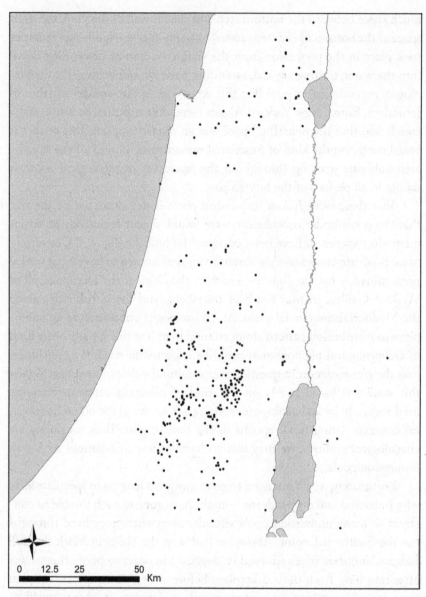

Figure 5. *Distribution of sites in the Southern Levant where immersion pools were unearthed. (From Adler, "The Archaeology of Purity," map 2.)*

purification—doubtless in fulfilment of the Pentateuchal call for "bathing" in water (the Hebrew verb is "*r-ḥ-ṣ*") as the manner whereby various sorts of ritual impurity are to be removed. On the one hand we know that Judeans regularly immersed in water in order to ritually purify themselves, and on the other hand we know that Judeans regularly constructed immersion pools. It stands to reason that the Judean immersion pools we find all over the country were being built and used precisely to accommodate this practice of Judean *ritual* immersion.

If, as seems most likely, all these stepped installations functioned as Judean ritual immersion pools, we might next inquire what these archaeological remains have to teach us about first-century-CE Judean purity practices. The sheer quantity of pools that have been unearthed in total, along with the fact that at practically every sufficiently excavated Judean site dating to this period *several* pools have been uncovered, suggests that ritual immersion was practiced on a regular basis by broad swaths of the Judean population. Had ritual immersion been practiced only occasionally, or only by members of certain groups within Judean society (e.g., priests, Pharisees, or Essenes), we should expect to have found far fewer numbers of these installations—and these probably only at *some* but not at virtually *all* contemporary Judean sites. Furthermore, the fact that these pools are found all throughout the country and not only in Jerusalem or its close environs suggests that Judeans regularly immersed themselves not only before visiting the temple or prior to taking part in sacrificial offerings but also simply for the sake of maintaining ritual purity in their everyday lives.[62]

The varied archaeological contexts within which ritual immersion pools are found is also instructive. Most immersion pools are found within either houses or residential courtyards, which suggests use for everyday domestic purposes. Immersion pools found in public spaces adjacent to synagogues may have been installed for the use of community members.[63] Pools installed in public areas adjacent to gates leading into the Temple Mount were likely used by pilgrims and officiating priests prior to entrance into the various temple courts and before actual participation in the cult.[64] Several pools have been found immediately adjacent to winepresses and oil presses, probably to be used by the agricultural workers employed at these installations in order to ensure the ritual purity of the wine and oil produced at these sites.[65] Similarly, immersion pools unearthed on the grounds of pottery production sites were likely used by workers employed at the kilns in order to ensure the purity of the ceramic vessels manufactured there.[66]

Several ritual immersion pools have been unearthed adjacent to burial caves, and these were likely intended for the use of funeral attendants.[67]

CHALK VESSELS

Chalk vessels are the second phenomenon that, as will be argued, demonstrate widespread Judean adherence to the purity laws throughout the first century CE. These vessels comprise a unique family of tableware and storage containers made of soft chalk which are regularly found at hundreds of first-century-CE Judean sites throughout the Southern Levant. Vessel forms include hand-carved mugs (fig. 6), pitchers, and bowls; various types of lathe-turned bowls and trays; lids and stoppers; and large krater-shaped jars. Over the course of the past three decades, something of a scholarly consensus has formed around the idea that Judeans commonly regarded

Figure 6. *Chalk mugs. (Photo: Meidad Suchowolski; courtesy of the Israel Antiquities Authority.)*

stone to be a material impervious to ritual impurity, and that it was with this ritual concern in mind that Judeans began producing these vessels specifically out of chalk.[68] As with the conversation surrounding immersion pools, here too the discussion has unfortunately tended to focus anachronistically on later rabbinic texts that refer to the ritual status of stone vessels. As I ventured to argue above with regard to the pools, here too I will contend that a very robust case may be made for interpreting the chalk-vessel phenomenon as directly related to Judean ritual purity concerns—and this without turning to the rabbinic literary corpus for support.

Aside from the very brief historical period under discussion, chalk was *never* used in the Southern Levant as a raw material for the large-scale production of tableware or storage vessels to be used with food. This is true of all periods of time throughout the human past, from the arrival of the first hominins in the region tens of thousands of years ago until today. The reason for this cannot be due to a paucity of natural chalk resources or difficulty of access; substantial chalk outcroppings are available at or very near the surface in many locations throughout the region. The soft material is quite easy to quarry, and even easier to work into usable forms. Why, then, was this accessible, easy-to-work natural resource never exploited by humans living in the region? For anyone who has ever handled the material in person, the answer is obvious: chalk is an extremely porous, dusty, and all-in-all highly impractical raw material for vessels meant to be used with food.

In the Early Roman period, an array of materials—especially clay, metals, glass, and wood—were used to produce a wide variety of tableware and storage vessel forms and types. Chalk remained a material completely passed over by local artisans—by all of them, that is, *except for the Judean ones*. Almost without exception, chalk vessels are found only at sites known to have been settled by Judeans, and production sites were found only in Judean regions.[69] Chalk vessels have been unearthed at hundreds of sites within the Judean areas of settlement in Judea, Galilee, Golan, and Peraea, while they are almost completely absent from the non-Judean coastal cities, Western Galilee, Samaria, the cities of the Decapolis, and all sites south of Beersheba. As with stepped pools, when one plots on a map the archaeological sites where chalk vessels have been unearthed, the resultant distribution pattern manifesting along distinct cultural lines could not be more unambiguous (fig. 7). Chalk vessels are a *Judean* phenomenon, and a Judean phenomenon *only*.

Figure 7. *Distribution of sites in the Southern Levant where chalk vessels were unearthed. (From Adler, "The Archaeology of Purity," map 10.)*

The question to be asked is, why did specifically the Judeans, for the first and only time in the entire span of human occupation of the region, decide to take what had always been regarded as a useless material and exploit it for the large-scale production of everyday tableware and storage vessels? What were they up to? And most importantly—why was it *only the Judeans* who did so?

Although none of our surviving, contemporary written sources provide any unequivocal answers to this question, I believe that it is possible to formulate a robust hypothesis that provides a satisfying solution to this conundrum. As seen above, within the Pentateuchal purity rules we find a clear distinction drawn between vessels made of different kinds of raw materials: pottery vessels that have come into contact with impurities are to be broken, while vessels made of other materials—wood, cloth, skin, or sackcloth—are to be purified with water.[70] Metal vessels are to be purified with fire and/or water.[71] Nothing at all is written about vessels made of stone, such as millstones and mortars, and we must presume that ancient Judeans intent on adhering to these laws would have asked themselves how such vessels are to be regarded according to Torah law.[72] I posit that ancient Judeans may well have reasoned that since stone is not listed at all among the materials that can become impure, this must mean that stone does not become impure at all!

If my hypothesis is correct, this would explain why ancient Judeans began to produce vessels from chalk. In the ancient world, clay was by far the most common material used for producing tableware and storage vessels. But Pentateuchal law dictated that pottery which became impure—likely quite a common occurrence—was to be broken. Adherence to the purity rules relating to pottery would doubtless have been experienced as both irksome and costly. My suggestion is that once the purity laws had come to be widely observed among rank-and-file Judeans, the difficulty in observing these laws came to be increasingly felt. At some point, some individual harboring an inventive and entrepreneurial spirit came up with the innovative idea to produce a line of tableware and storage vessels that, like mortars and millstones, were made of a material that is not itemized in the Pentateuchal list of materials that can become impure. The local stones used for grinding and crushing implements (mostly basalt but also coarse-grained beachrock) were completely impractical for the task as they were too heavy, bulky, and difficult to shape into delicate forms. Chalk was also impractical, as it is porous and dusty, but it had the advantage that it was easily quarried and shaped into forms identical to the finest pottery wares. Chalk, while clearly not an ideal material, provided an adequate solution to the ritual problem posed by Pentateuchal law. The earliest producers of chalk vessels would have had to find ways to overcome the porosity and dustiness of the raw material, whether by coating the surfaces of the vessels with some kind of sealant or by some other method of treating the stone to allow its use with liquids and other foodstuffs. As it stands today, we are still not completely sure how this was accomplished by the ancients.

I believe that the theory outlined here presents a robust hypothesis for explaining the stark distribution pattern of chalk vessels along ethnic lines. While the precise contours of the legal argument outlined above are not found in any surviving contemporary texts, one of the passages cited above from the Gospel of John does provide an allusion to the idea that Judeans were using storage jars made of stone specifically in order to comply with the Judean purity laws: "Now standing there were six stone water jars in accordance with the purification of the Judeans [katà tòn katharismòn tōn Ioudaíōn]."[73] Assuming that the parenthetical explanation "in accordance with [or perhaps: for the purpose of] the purification [laws] of the Judeans" is meant to explain the curious choice of material from which the water jars are said to have been made, the explanation that this was in accordance with the Judean purification laws might well allude to the idea that Judeans regarded stone to be outside the purview of Pentateuchal impurities affecting vessels.[74]

It should be noted that in the foregoing explanation, I made no reference at all to the rabbinic legal corpus. Rather than interpreting the early archaeological finds through the lens of later rabbinic legal notions, I would suggest that we approach the matter from precisely the opposite direction—and that we are best off working to infer from earlier practices reflected in the archaeological record how the later rabbis may have come to the ideas that they did. The rabbis clearly assumed the notion that stone vessels (along with vessels made of unfired clay and dung) were unsusceptible to ritual impurity.[75] I posit that the archaeological record suggests that this idea was not one *invented* by the rabbis, but rather was one (like many other ideas) that the rabbis *inherited* from exegetical interpretations of the Pentateuch widely shared by Judeans in previous generations. Regardless, the upshot is that we are in no way dependent on the rabbis for understanding our first-century-CE archaeological finds.

If, as seems to be the case, chalk vessels were being produced and used primarily with a view toward their perceived impermeability to ritual impurity, what then might we learn from the chalk-vessel remains themselves about the manner in which first-century-CE Judeans observed the ritual purity laws? The fact that remains of these vessels are found at practically every well-excavated early Roman-period site located within all areas of Judean settlement in the Southern Levant suggests that adherence to the purity laws was extremely widespread. Alongside their broad geographic distribution, chalk-vessel remains tend to enjoy widespread distribution within individual sites as well. Jonathan Reed has pointed out how these data demonstrate that use of chalk vessels was probably not limited to certain groups, such as the Pharisees or priests, but rather was likely to have been widespread throughout all segments of Judean society.[76]

The fact that remains of chalk vessels are regularly found at peripheral sites in regions as far removed from Jerusalem as the Galilee and the Golan suggests that the temple and its sacrificial cult were most likely not motivating factors for Judeans who accustomed themselves to dining off of these vessels.[77] In recent years I directed several seasons of excavations at two large-scale chalk-vessel production sites in the Lower Galilee where the vessels were produced for local consumption—at 'Einot Amitai and at nearby Reina (both in the vicinity of Nazareth). The sheer scale of production at both sites—we unearthed evidence of thousands of mugs and bowls that had been produced at each workshop—strongly supports the understanding that Galilean Judeans shared with their Jerusalemite brethren a similar market demand for this unique product.[78] This widespread distribution of both production and endpoint use of chalk vessels all throughout the Judean areas of settlement strongly suggests that Judeans of all stripes commonly observed the ritual purity regulations in their everyday lives.

Conclusions

We began by surveying a remarkable amount of textual evidence, especially among New Testament writers and Josephus, which depicts the Pentateuchal purity laws as being put into practice in everyday life by rank-and-file, non-priestly Judeans. Regular Judeans are depicted as carefully adhering to the purity laws not only prior to visiting the Jerusalem temple and participating in its cult but also in regard to day-to-day activities, such as immersing before sitting down to eat their daily meals and regularly immersing cooking utensils, serving dishes, and even dining couches. Corpse impurity, scale disease, gonorrhea, menstruation, childbirth, and seminal emissions are all cited as causes of ritual impurity. It seems, furthermore, that Gentiles may have been commonly suspected of negligence in ensuring the purity status of food and clothing within their care. Observance of the Pentateuchal ritual purity laws was depicted by all these first-century authors as regular, lay, and widespread.

This substantial collection of textual evidence is supported by an equally impressive array of archaeological data which strongly suggest that the Pentateuchal purity laws were observed by South Levantine Judeans on an extremely wide scale. All throughout Judea, Galilee, and the Peraea, Judeans constructed immersion pools in the many hundreds (and likely in the thousands)—apparently in order to practice ritual immersion on a regular basis. In these same areas, Judeans made use of tableware and storage vessels made of local chalk—most likely to avoid the ritual contamination of pottery vessels. Both archaeological phenomena suggest that Judeans of all sorts adhered to the Pentateuchal purity laws on a regular, probably daily basis, and that this commonplace concern surrounding these regulations was not necessarily focused on the temple and its cult, nor was it the reserve of any particular social or ideological groups within Judaism.

Early Evidence

Having demonstrated the widespread character of ritual purity observance among Judeans in the first century CE, we now turn to examine evidence that might indicate adherence to the purity regulations in earlier periods as well. Our aim will be to seek the oldest surviving evidence which might suggest that Judeans were commonly adhering to something closely resembling the Pentateuchal system of ritual purity laws. We will begin by investigating the textual evidence predating the first century CE, and will conclude with an examination of the relevant archaeological data from this earlier period.

Textual Evidence

JOSEPHUS

Josephus cited two stories set in the second half of the first century BCE which relate to ritual purity. In one story, set toward the end of the reign of Herod the Great, Josephus told of a high priest named Matthias who was replaced for a single day when, on the night before the Judean fast (i.e., the Day of Atonement), the man "seemed in a dream to have intercourse with a woman"—an incident that made him unable to serve as a priest the following morning.[79] Clearly this anecdote relates to the notion that a nocturnal emission of semen renders one impure, and—if this story genuinely derives from Herod's day—it suggests that this law was in force in the late first century BCE (at least in the temple). In a second narrative, set circa 43 BCE, Herod is said to have arrived at Jerusalem at the time of a festival leading a troop of soldiers—apparently composed of non-Judeans. The high priest at the time, Hyrcanus II, is said to have sent orders forbidding Herod to bring in foreigners "upon the country-folk while they are purifying [*eph' hagneúontas toùs epikhōríous*]."[80] On its surface, the story seems to suggest that a militia composed of Gentile soldiers would have been regarded as a threat to the purity of Judeans who wished to take part in temple activities associated with a festival. Josephus does not report his source for this narrative, and it remains difficult to assess the degree to which the story might accurately reflect mid-first-century-BCE realities.

Josephus reported that Seleucus I Nicator (312–281 BCE) granted citizenship to the Judeans in the cities he founded in Asia and Syria, adding, "The proof of this is the fact that he gave orders that those Judeans who were unwilling to use foreign oil [*mè bouloménous allophúlǭ elaíǭ khrēsthai*] should receive a fixed sum of money from the gymnasiarchs to pay for their own kind of oil; and, when the people of Antioch proposed to revoke this privilege, Mucianus, who was then governor of Syria, maintained it."[81] Assuming that the Judean reluctance to use oil produced by Gentiles stemmed from their adherence to Pentateuchal purity laws, this report would suggest that Judeans in the Seleucid kingdom were adhering to these laws as early as the late fourth century BCE. It seems unwise to draw any such far-reaching conclusions from Josephus's account here, however, as we do not know if Josephus was relying on original documents from the time or (as seems more likely) on traditions current among Antiochan Judeans of his own day when the matter came to a head under the governorship of Mucianus (ca. 67 CE).[82]

DEAD SEA SCROLLS

Several of the scrolls from the Qumran caves contain detailed regulations regarding the Pentateuchal laws of ritual impurity. While sometimes the Pentateuchal regulations are simply paraphrased, oftentimes the

Qumran texts include substantial interpretative expansions upon these rules. As many of these documents are thought to have been composed some time during the second or first century BCE, they will be surveyed here as a group.

"Bathing" in water is one of the primary methods of purification repeated time and again throughout the Pentateuchal purity laws; the Damascus Document developed this rule by regulating the quality and quantity of the water required for purificatory bathing.[83] Leviticus 15:18 rules that sexual intercourse imparts ritual impurity to both participants; the Damascus Document expanded upon this by ruling that a man may not lie with a woman anywhere within the "temple city."[84] According to Num 19:18, a tent in which a person had died must be purified; the Damascus Document extended this law such that corpse impurity affects also a permanent house—including its stones, wood, dirt floor, and even the nails in its walls.[85] Damascus Document fragments from Qumran also develop and expand upon the Pentateuchal laws on skin diseases in Lev 13.[86]

An entire section of the Temple Scroll is dedicated to the purity laws: unclean animals, birds and "creeping things," skin diseases, semen impurity, pathological male and female sexual discharges, menstruation, and corpse impurity.[87] Like the Damascus Document, the Temple Scroll too contains significant developments and expansions upon the Pentateuchal regulations. For example, Num 19:17–19 instructs that if a person died in a tent, on the third and seventh days of the purification process one must take water mixed with red heifer ashes and sprinkle this "upon the tent, and upon all the vessels and the souls that were there," after which (i.e., on the seventh day after the final sprinkling) one is to launder one's clothing, bathe in water, and wait until the evening. The Temple Scroll presents a far more elaborate procedure, which it applies to a permanent house: on the day when the corpse is removed from the house, the house must be swept clean of "every stain of oil, and wine, and dampness from water"; its floor, its walls and its doors must be scraped; its door bolts, doorjambs, thresholds, and lintels must be washed with water; "the house and all its vessels"—including mills, mortars, utensils of wood, iron, and bronze, "and all vessels for which there is purity"—must be purified; clothing, sacks, and skins must be laundered; and all people who were in the house must bathe in water and wash their clothes.[88] All of this is to take place on the first day of the purification process, a day about which the Pentateuch itself has not a word to say. The Temple Scroll also adds an instruction to bathe and to wash clothing and vessels on the third day of the purification process following the initial sprinkling of water mixed with red heifer ashes—another requirement not explicit in the Pentateuch. Another significant legal elaboration concerns a fetus that had died in utero, not mentioned at all in the Pentateuch, but which the Temple Scroll regards as a corpse that conveys impurity to its surroundings even while still inside the mother's womb.[89]

4QMMT discusses laws relating to skin diseases, impure species and carrion of pure species, the preparation of red heifer ashes, and the impurity of human bones.[90] Here too we find substantial interpretative developments of Pentateuchal laws. For example, Lev 11:34 states that beverages become impure if they are in a vessel into which a creeping thing had fallen, but nothing is said about whether or how an impure beverage might transfer impurity to a pure beverage if one is poured into the other. The authors of 4QMMT argue that "streams" (*mûṣāqôt*) transfer impurity, such that if pure liquid is poured from above into an impure liquid below, the former is made impure from the latter via the stream.[91] This is presented as the legal position of the letter's authors ("we say that . . ."), which implies that the addressee was in disagreement over this matter. On another matter, Num 19:9 requires that "a pure man" collect the ashes of the red heifer after it is burned, and Num 19:18 requires that "a pure man" sprinkle these ashes mixed with water on the corpse-impure; nothing is said of the priest who slaughters the red heifer or of the one who burns it. The authors of 4QMMT argue that all these tasks may be performed only by those who have purified themselves and waited until sunset.[92] Another matter with important ramifications for the purity laws is how the desert encampment of the Pentateuch ought to be translated into the contemporary setting of Judea. For the authors of 4QMMT, the temple is parallel to the desert's "tent of meeting," the city of Jerusalem corresponds to the wilderness "camp," and all areas outside Jerusalem are regarded as equivalent to "outside the camp" of the desert.[93] Once again, the fact that the authors of this letter frame this legal position as specifically their own ("we think that . . .") implies that the addressee held an alternative, perhaps more lenient viewpoint.

Several additional texts from the Qumran caves also discuss the details of various Pentateuchal purity laws, but these are more poorly preserved than the Damascus Document, the Temple Scroll, and 4QMMT, and as a result the precise contours of their regulations are often difficult to decipher. 4QTohorot A (4Q274) discusses the quarantining of the skin-diseased, contact between a female with abnormal uterine bleeding and a male with a pathological sexual discharge, menstruation, semen impurity, corpse impurity, creeping things, impurity affecting foods and juices, how rain and dew affect the susceptibility of foods to becoming impure, and how impurity is conveyed through contact, carrying, sitting, or lying on objects. Methods of purification cited in this manuscript include waiting seven days, sprinkling, bathing in water and laundering clothing, and—in the only surviving appearance of this Hebrew term in any contemporary text—an instruction to "immerse" (*yiṭbôl*) a person or vessel that had touched semen.[94] 4QTohorot Bᵃ (4Q276) and 4QTohorot Bᵇ (4Q277) both include instructions regarding the preparation of red heifer ashes, and the latter text also discusses the sprinkling of water mixed with these ashes and the impurity conveyed by a man with a pathological sexual discharge. 4QTohorot C (4Q278) refers to impurity conveyed via touch and through lying on a bed. 4QPurification Liturgy (4Q284) discusses semen impurity and corpse impurity, and also refers to ritual cleansing through sprinkling of purification water, bathing, and awaiting sunset on the seventh day. 4QRitual of Purification A (4Q414) mentions purification through sprinkling and bathing; refers to the first, third, and seventh (days); and includes the phrase "and after that he shall enter into water [*yāvô᾽ bəmayim*]." 4QRitual of Purification B (4Q512) appears to speak of menstrual impurity and impurity of a male with a pathological sexual discharge, and also refers to a seven-day period of purification, bathing in water, and laundering of clothing. 4QOrdinances B (4Q513) is highly fragmentary but likely refers to impurity as it affects food and drink, perhaps in the cultic sphere. 4QOrdinances C (4Q514) speaks of a person abstaining from eating (certain?) bread while still "with his first impurity [*bəṭūm ᾽ātô harîšônāh*]," and refers to purification through bathing and laundering in water.

Finally, mention should be made here to the Community Rule, which includes regulations for a phased neophyte admission process highly reminiscent of Josephus's description regarding the induction procedures of the Essenes.[95] During the first year after joining, the newcomer must not touch "the purity of the group [*bəṭāhărat hārabîm*]," during the second year he must not touch "the drink of the group [*bəmašqēh hārabîm*]," and only after two full years have passed, if he passes all other requirements, does he fully join "in the purity [*laṭôhārāh*]" of his comrades.

The sum total of this evidence indicates that during the Hasmonean and Herodian periods, when most if not all of these texts were likely first composed, several Judean writers were taking the Pentateuchal purity laws quite seriously. While it is difficult to know from these texts to what degree these laws might have been of common concern to a majority of contemporary Judeans, these writings do suggest that by this time it was possible to find Torah experts who regularly brought highly developed exegetical methods to bear on these laws. The polemical tone found in at least some of these texts suggests that this interpretative activity did not take place in a vacuum, as at times these legal exegeses resulted in polemical encounters between rival exegetes.

APOCRYPHA AND PSEUDEPIGRAPHA

References to Pentateuchal ritual purity laws occasionally appear in works counted among the Apocrypha and Pseudepigrapha, variously dated by most scholars to sometime within the last two centuries BCE. In the Letter of Aristeas, Eleazar the high priest provides the Egyptian mission sent to Jerusalem with a lengthy explanation concerning the "unclean" animals, some of which are forbidden as food and some of which are regarded as impure even just to touch.[96] Unambiguous references are made to the Pentateuchal signs of clean quadrupeds, to the list of unclean birds, and to the list of impure creeping things—with the "weasel" (galē) and "mice" (mûes) singled out. Elsewhere, in a description of the urban layout of Jerusalem, the city's residents are said to practice social distancing when navigating its streets in order to avoid transmission of ritual impurity between one another: "They mostly keep separate on the way, because of those who are in a state of purity [en taîs hagneíais], since they will touch nothing that is forbidden."[97]

Jubilees includes an etiology to explain why a woman is impure for seven days after giving birth to a boy, but for two weeks after giving birth to a girl (Adam was created in the first week of creation, but his wife—formed from Adam's rib—was brought to him only on the second week).[98] An etiological explanation is also given for why a postpartum woman must wait forty days before entering the sanctuary or touching any hallowed thing if she gave birth to a boy, but eighty days if it was a girl (Adam waited forty days "in the land where he had been created" before being brought into the garden of Eden, but his wife was brought into Eden only after eighty days).

In Judith, the heroine is presented as strictly observant of the purity rules as they apply to food. In her preparations before traveling to the camp of Holofernes, Judith has her maid bring along a bottle of wine, a flask of oil, a bag filled with parched grain, a cake of dried fruit, and "pure bread [ártōn katharōn]," along with "all her vessels [pánta tà angeîa autês]."⁹⁹ After Judith meets the Assyrian general, Holofernes commands that Judith be brought into the place where "his silver dishes [tà argurómata autoû]" are kept, and orders that a table be set for her with some of his own food and wine, but Judith refuses these: "I cannot eat it, lest it be an offense; but I will be provided from the things I have brought with me."¹⁰⁰ Holofernes is presented as correctly understanding that Judith will not eat food brought to her by Gentiles and sympathetically asks her, "If your supply runs out, where can we get more like it for you? For none of your people is here with us." In the end, Judith remains in the Assyrian barracks for three days, during which time she left the camp before daybreak each day and "immersed [ebaptízeto]" in a spring, prayed, and then "returned purified [katharà] and stayed in the tent until she ate her food toward evening."¹⁰¹ On the fourth day, when Judith is invited to join Holofernes at his banquet, she is careful to eat and drink only from that which her maid has prepared.¹⁰² There seems little doubt that Judith is being presented here as strictly observant of the purity regulations despite her sojourn in an enemy camp; she carefully prepares her own pure food and utensils ahead of time, and every evening immerses in water and awaits sunset in order to be purified before eating her daily meals. Although it is not made explicit precisely what kind of ritual impurity might have been at stake, perhaps simply living among Gentiles was regarded as jeopardizing one's ritual purity status since Gentiles would certainly not have been careful about avoiding the manifold Pentateuchal causes of ritual defilement.¹⁰³

Judas Maccabaeus's soldiers are said to have "purified themselves according to the custom [katà tòn ethismòn hagnisthéntes]" prior to encamping to observe the Sabbath, but no details are given as what kind of impurity might have been involved or precisely how this act of purification might have been performed.¹⁰⁴

Ben Sira, whose original Hebrew version is widely thought to date to sometime around the first quarter of the second century BCE, refers to immersion as a method of purification after touching a corpse: "If one immerses after [touching] a corpse [baptizómenos apò nekroû] and touches it again—what has been gained by his washing [en tō loutrō autoû]?"¹⁰⁵ While it seems quite possible that what is intended here is the instruction in Num 19:19 to "bathe in water [wərāḥaṣ bamayîm]" at the end of the seven-day process of purification from corpse impurity, this interpretation remains somewhat uncertain.

Finally, mention should be made of several texts that comment on Judeans/Israelites generally keeping separate from Gentiles with regard to food, abstaining from eating the food of Gentiles, or otherwise refraining from sitting down to eat together with Gentiles.[106] While the Pentateuchal ritual purity regulations may have been in the minds of the authors of some or even all of these texts, the possibility remains that other concerns might have been at stake: the dietary laws discussed in the previous chapter, an avoidance of idolatrous sacrificial offerings, or simply a desire to avoid communion with Gentiles.

THE PROCLAMATION OF ANTIOCHUS III

Josephus cited a "proclamation" (*prógramma*) supposedly made by Antiochus III Megas early in the second century BCE which forbade foreigners' entrance into the enclosure of the temple "which is forbidden to the Judeans, except to those of them who are accustomed to enter after purifying themselves [*hagnistheísin*] in accordance with the ancestral law."[107] The edict also forbade bringing into Jerusalem the flesh of horses, mules, asses, leopards, foxes, and hares, or "in general, of any animals forbidden to the Judeans." It was furthermore forbidden to bring into the city the skins of these animals, or even to breed them in the city. The author of this document appears to be aware of something resembling the Pentateuchal laws surrounding impure species and regarded even just the importation of such animals into the city (dead or alive!) as problematic. If this is accepted as a genuine edict dating back to the time of Antiochus III (scholars have rightly questioned the authenticity of the document), it provides evidence that Pentateuch-like ritual purity laws were observed among Judeans to one degree or another as early as the beginning of the second century BCE. (See chapter 7 for a more in-depth discussion about how caution must be exercised before any historical conclusions are drawn from this document regarding realities at the turn of the second century BCE).

HEBREW BIBLE

When we turn to texts generally thought to predate the second century BCE, we find little to no evidence that a system of ritual purity regulations approximating the one found in the Pentateuch might have been known to Judeans—let alone that such a system was commonly observed in practice. Cognates of the adjectives "pure" (*ṭ-h-r*) and "impure" (*ṭ-m-ʾ*) appear quite often throughout the Hebrew Bible, but in many cases these terms are used to describe *moral* categories rather than *ritual* ones.[108] Even when the terms appear in clearly ritual contexts, the few details that are made explicit leave little reason to think that the authors of these texts knew of a system of purity regulations akin to the Pentateuchal purity laws. Socially constructed notions of ritual impurity were to be found in cultures all throughout the ancient Near East, including Egypt, the Levant, Anatolia, Mesopotamia, and Persia, as well as in more distant regions such as Greece and India.[109] While oftentimes different cultures converged on certain notions regarding what things were to be regarded as ritually impure, how this impurity could spread, and how purification is attained, it is also quite common to find divergences on these matters. Biblical writings simply reflect how their authors shared in this common-yet-diverse milieu.

Not infrequently, menstruation is referenced as a metaphor for something either physically repugnant or morally abhorrent, and on two occasions Ezekiel refers to a menstruating woman as ritually impure and sexually off limits.[110] All of this, however, was hardly unique to these texts; the notion that a menstruating woman is in one way or another physically "polluted" or ritually "impure" has been shared over an extraordinarily extensive span of time by a broad range of human societies, both premodern and modern, in the region and indeed throughout much of the entire world.[111] The human corpse also appears as ritually defiling in some Hebrew Bible texts outside the Pentateuch, but this too is a notion widely shared among cultures.[112] Some authors of Hebrew Bible texts outside the Pentateuch also know of a practice of ostracizing those suffering from skin diseases, but again, this too appears to have been a custom widespread throughout the region in antiquity.[113] And finally, the author of Ezekiel regards carrion and "torn" animals as "impure," as did non-Judean authors writing within the Mesopotamian and Persian (Zoroastrian) spheres of influence.[114] None of this suggests that any of these authors knew of any kind of detailed system of impurity regulations akin in any way to the Pentateuchal laws.

Notably, *most* of the causes of impurity found in the Pentateuch are cited nowhere else in the Hebrew Bible. Outside the Pentateuch, the notion of impure species of animals is never mentioned, women who give birth are never said to be impure, sexual intercourse and semen are never spoken of as ritually defiling, nothing is ever said of impure males or females suffering pathological discharges from their genitals, and there is never any mention of impure blotches on clothing or on the walls of houses.[115]

Perhaps even more strikingly, the authors of Hebrew Bible texts outside the Pentateuch display no knowledge at all of anything even remotely resembling the Pentateuchal system for *removing* ritual impurities. As we have seen above, impurities in the Pentateuchal system are eliminated through various means, usually involving the person who had contracted the impurity waiting a certain amount of time (e.g., until sunset or seven days), bathing with water, and laundering clothing. While sometimes *moral* impurities are said to be metaphorically "washed" away with water (often the washing is performed by YHWH himself), and while people are said to literally wash all or parts of their bodies or launder clothing for the sake of physical cleanliness, not once do the authors of the Hebrew Bible ever speak of people bathing or laundering clothing in order to rectify *ritual* impurities.[116] Outside the Pentateuch, no mention is ever made of a person or object remaining "impure until the evening," nor is anybody or anything ever said to require a wait of seven days to be purified.[117] In the Pentateuch, as seen above, utensils are ritually purified through various methods depending on the material from which they are made. Outside the Pentateuch, authors of Hebrew Bible texts never tell of anyone ritually purifying utensils by rinsing them in water, passing them through fire, or (in the case of the ubiquitous pottery) breaking them. And finally, complex rites of purification from corpse impurity and from skin diseases are mentioned only in the Pentateuch, with not even a passing allusion to anyone putting these rites into practice anywhere else in the Hebrew Bible.[118]

To be clear, none of this is to say that the Pentateuchal authors held notions of ritual purity that were radically different from those known to the authors of all other Hebrew Bible texts. It seems doubtless that all these authors held many ideas in common with one another, which they clearly also shared with neighboring societies and even quite distant cultures. My point here is only that in searching for the origins of first-century-CE ritual purity practices, fundamentally founded as they were on the Pentateuchal purity laws, the Hebrew Bible provides little evidence to suggest that anything closely resembling such a system of practices was known among Judeans—let alone widely put into practice—any time prior to the second century BCE.

Archaeological and Epigraphic Evidence

We now turn to archaeological and epigraphic finds that might demonstrate Judean observance of the Pentateuchal ritual purity laws during periods that predate the first century CE. We will begin by looking at the two phenomena shown above to have been so prevalent during the first century CE, and will conclude by examining epigraphic evidence from Elephantine.

IMMERSION POOLS

The archaeological phenomenon of Judean immersion pools is relatively well attested during the first century BCE. From the latter part of this century, immersion pools have been found at every one of the personal palaces of Herod the Great, often in significant numbers. These were usually associated with living quarters, or else were a component of the palaces' heated bathhouses: eight pools at Herodium; six at Masada; four at the Cypros fortress; at Jericho two pools in Herod's First Palace, another two in his Second Palace, and three in his Third Palace; three pools at Machearus; and one pool in the Promontory Palace at Caesarea Maritima.[119] Other pools dated in association with the reign of Herod the Great are those found sealed underneath building projects undertaken during this monarch's rule and which therefore must predate these constructions.[120] From before the time of Herod, about three dozen immersion pools that have been assigned by their excavators to the Hasmonean period (i.e., until the middle of the first century BCE) have been unearthed at the following sites: Keren Naftali, Gamla, Sepphoris, Khirbat Burnat (Southwest), Cypros, Jerusalem in the Jewish Quarter and to the south and to the west of the Temple Mount, Jericho, Khirbat al-Mukhayyat in Jordan, and Qumran.[121] While it is certainly possible that many other pools that have been dated in a rough manner by their excavators to the late Second Temple period might also have been first installed at this early stage, in most cases this is simply impossible to establish archaeologically.

Among the Hasmonean period immersion pools, the earliest assigned dates fall around the beginning of the first century BCE or else the very end of the second century BCE. These include one pool unearthed at Jericho in the Buried Palace, one pool uncovered at the Jewish Quarter in Jerusalem (in Area A), and two pools unearthed at Qumran.[122] No stepped installations of the type under investigation here have been dated to any time earlier than the late second century BCE.

It follows that, as the evidence stands today, we can quite confidently establish the first half of the first century BCE as the rough terminus ante quem for the appearance of the earliest stepped pools. Exactly how much time before this chronological limit the first installations actually appeared is impossible to say at present. Evidence that might help toward answering this question should be sought in Judean sites abandoned prior to this terminus ante quem and in which no stepped pools have been found. For the time being, Nebi Samwil appears to be one such site. Its location in the heart of Judea, right on the outskirts of Jerusalem, strongly suggests that its inhabitants were Judean. The site was apparently abandoned sometime during the first half of the first century BCE, perhaps during the reign of Alexander Jannaeus.[123] The fact that no stepped pools have been found at the site, despite the fact that a large area (about one acre) of an impressively well-preserved residential quarter has been uncovered, might suggest that the advent of immersion pools occurred not much prior to our terminus ante quem. While the negative evidence from Nebi Samwil is suggestive, any final conclusions must be suspended until more data from additional sites become available.

Prior to the introduction of purpose-built immersion pools, it seems highly unlikely that full-body immersion was being practiced by Judeans at any large scale. From a purely practical perspective, full-body immersion is no simple affair. While ordinary washing can be performed virtually anywhere and requires nothing more than a jug or other small utensil capable of holding the requisite amount of water, immersion necessitates a volume of water held in a space large enough to receive the entire body of the person immersing. In a land limited in naturally occurring water resources, access to natural bodies of water large enough to allow full-body immersion would have been quite limited. Which is to say that if Judeans *were* washing themselves for the purposes of ritual purification any time prior to the introduction of the first immersion pools, it seems highly unlikely that they might have been doing so by *immersing* in water. In the past I have posited that the earliest purificatory bathing would most likely have involved a simple form of rinsing the body with water poured from a small utensil or applied to the body with an absorbent material, and that full-body immersion may have developed out of changes in contemporary bathing practices involving the introduction of the Hellenistic hip-bath in the Southern Levant by the late second century BCE.[124] If in fact such simpler forms of washing were being practiced by Judeans for the purposes of ritual purification during the second century BCE or earlier, these have left no identifiable archaeological remains.[125]

CHALK VESSELS

Chalk vessels have been unearthed in a limited number of archaeological contexts dated to the late first century BCE. In excavations at the

Jewish Quarter of Jerusalem (Area E), fragments of chalk mugs and large krater-shaped jars were uncovered in a sealed stratum (Stratum 3) dated on numismatic grounds to a well-defined period between circa 25 and 12 BCE.[126] Fragments of chalk mugs were also found in the stratum immediately below this (Stratum 4), a level dated to the late Hasmonean or early Herodian period. Additional chalk mug fragments were found in a different area of the Jewish Quarter excavations (Area J) in a stratum also dated to the second half of the first century BCE (Stratum 3).[127] At Jericho too, several chalk vessel fragments dating to the second half of the first century BCE were unearthed in the Herodian palace complexes, and a single mug fragment was found in the Hasmonean Twin Palaces, whose destruction has been dated to an earthquake in 31 BCE.[128]

It has recently been reported that chalk bowls were uncovered in Jerusalem's Giv'ati Parking Lot, in a stratum dated to the first half of the first century BCE at the very latest.[129] As none of these finds have been properly published yet, it is difficult to know what to make of this initial report. If the dating is correct, and if the repertoire of bowl types found here can be shown to be precursors to types attested from the Herodian period onward, these would be the earliest Judean chalk vessels discovered to date.

None of the stone vessels produced prior to this time can be shown to have been associated in any way with ritual purity concerns. During the Hellenistic and Persian periods, as well as during the Iron Age, Judeans and others in the region utilized various types of rock—primarily basalt, but also beachrock and hard limestone—to produce a variety of utensils such as millstones, mortars, pestles, and grinding bowls. A certain type of bowl produced from a hard yellow or pink chalk (distinct from the white chalk used in the Early Roman period) is occasionally found in Hellenistic- and Persian-period levels at non-Judean sites such as Tell Keisan (in Phoenicia), Samaria, and Maresha (in Idumea), as well as at Jerusalem.[130] None of these stone vessel types reflect a specifically Judean phenomenon, and accordingly none should be regarded as demonstrating Judean adherence to any kind of purity practices. If Judeans in the second century BCE or earlier regarded stone to be a material impervious to ritual impurity, nothing in the surviving archaeological record demonstrates that such a belief was in existence at this early date.

EPIGRAPHIC FINDS

A fragmentary Aramaic text on an ostracon discovered by Charles Clermont-Ganneau in 1907 at Elephantine and dated on paleographic grounds to the early fifth century BCE has been reconstructed by Bezalel Porten and Ada Yardeni as referring to ritual impurity affecting jars and bread: "[Greetings (to) PN] from [PN. No]w, I [sent (word)] to you, saying: 'Do not dispatch to me bread without it being sealed [*wl' hw ḥtm*]. Lo, all the jars are impure [*kl bqy' ṭm'n*]. Behold, the bread which [yo]u disp[atched] to me yesterday is im[pure] [*ṭ(m')*]. Now, do not [dispatch] to me . . . b[read].'"[131] Porten and Yardeni interpreted this document in light of Num 19:15, writing that a likely reason for the ostracon writer's rejection of the unsealed bread and his observation that all the vessels are impure was "his knowledge that there had been a recent death in the household from which the unsealed vessels with their bread were being dispatched."[132] I am not convinced that such a fragmentary text can bear the weight of such a loaded interpretation. Even assuming that the text is correctly reconstructed (an apparently significant portion of the ostracon is missing, and the handwriting that covers either side of the shard is not easily read), there seems little reason to assume that *ritual* impurity is being referred to here rather than regular, nonritual pollution. Even if it were decided that the word "*ṭm'*" is more likely to mean ritual impurity than it is to mean physical contamination, we would still have no reason to connect this with the Pentateuch. It is also unclear why we should even assume that this particular ostracon was written by or for Judeans, as it contains no mention of Judeans, of any Judean personal names, or of the god YHW—the primary deity of the Judeans at Elephantine. *If* we assume that the text is talking about ritual impurity, *and if* we assume that it is Judean, *and if* we assume that the Judeans of Elephantine held notions of ritual impurity akin to those found in Num 19, *then* Porten and Yardeni's suggestion might be regarded as plausible. It would be an exercise in circular reasoning, however, to take this ostracon as evidence that Judeans at Elephantine practiced ritual purity regulations similar to those found in the Pentateuch.

André Lemaire has pointed out that within the recently published corpus of the Clermont-Ganneau ostraca, the word "impure" (*ṭm'*) appears on two other occasions and the word "pure" (*ṭhr*) appears once.[133] All these texts suffer the same kind of problems as the ostracon text discussed above: it is unclear whether these two Aramaic terms contextually refer to physical pollution/cleanness or whether ritual impurity/purity is meant; it is unknown whether the texts were written by Judeans; and even if it could be shown that the references are to ritual impurity notions held by Judeans, we would still remain almost completely in the dark as to the details of how these ideas might have been put into practice.

Conclusions

The goal of this chapter was to survey the evidence for widespread observance of the Pentateuchal ritual purity laws among first-century-CE Judeans, and to seek out the earliest evidence for such observance prior to the turn of the Common Era. We surveyed a remarkable set of both textual and archaeological evidence that suggested widespread adherence to the ritual purity laws in the first century CE, and a significant amount of evidence indicating that these rules were being followed, discussed, and debated in the first century BCE and perhaps also in the second century BCE. Prior to the second century BCE, we found no evidence which demonstrates that Judeans knew of—let alone practiced—anything closely resembling the Pentateuchal system of ritual purity laws. To be sure, authors of Hebrew Bible texts not infrequently made use of the "pure"/"impure" binary when writing about physical pollution, moral "contamination," and also ritual impurity. But these were simply widely shared cultural constructions; there is little reason to think that the details of the ritual purity notions these writers had in mind looked any more like the Pentateuchal ritual purity system than they might have resembled taboos and practices current among other societies in the Near East and beyond. Lacking earlier evidence, the second century BCE remains our terminus ante quem for the beginning of widespread Judean observance of the ritual purity practices enshrined in the Torah.

3 Figural Art

The Decalogue, as presented in almost precisely parallel versions in Exod 20 and Deut 5, famously opens with a prohibition against veneration of gods other than YHWH: "I am YHWH your God, who brought you out of the land of Egypt, out of the house of slavery; you shall have no other gods before me."[1] First-century Judeans such as Philo and Josephus counted this as the first "commandment" of the Decalogue, while they took the following verses as a *separate* "second commandment": "You shall not make for yourself a graven image [*pesel*] [Exod 20:4 adds: "or"] the form of anything [*(wə)kol təmûnāh*] that is in heaven above, or that is on the earth beneath, or that is in the water under the earth. You shall not bow down to them and you shall not worship them; for I am YHWH your God, a jealous god, punishing children for the iniquity of parents, [Deut 5:9 adds: "and"] to the third and the fourth generation of those who reject me, but showing steadfast love to the thousandth generation of those who love me and those who keep my commandments."[2] Because the more well-known later traditions (Talmudic, Roman Catholic, and Lutheran) counted these two prohibitions as a single "commandment," it is often assumed that graven images are forbidden here *because* they are used in the worship of gods other than YHWH.[3] It seems that on the earlier Judean view—which regarded the prohibition against graven images as a stand-alone "second commandment"—an exegetical route was opened to the understanding that graven images are forbidden *regardless* of whether they were associated with other gods. One could easily understand that the "second commandment" proscribed both the *making* of an image and the *worship* of any such icon, and that neither prohibition was dependant on the other.

Indeed, the prohibition against graven images in Deut 4 is presented in a far more comprehensive manner that may easily be taken to include *any* image of a living creature—insofar as such an image might be taken as a representation of YHWH himself. In his address to the Israelites forty years after the theophany at Horeb/Sinai, Moses reminds the people that no form was seen at the time that YHWH revealed himself and therefore the Israelites are prohibited from creating graven images depicting the forms of any living creature: "YHWH spoke to you out of the fire; you heard the sound of words but saw no form [təmûnāh]; there was only sound. . . . Take care and watch yourselves closely, since you saw no form when YHWH spoke to you at Horeb out of the fire. Lest you act corruptly by making for yourselves a graven image [pesel] in the form of any figure [təmûnat kol sāmel]—the likeness of [tavnît] male or female, the likeness of any animal that is on the earth, the likeness of any winged bird that flies in the sky, the likeness of anything that creeps on the ground, the likeness of any fish that is in the water under the earth."[4] This detailed list presumably leaves no room for mistakes and no place for exceptions: whether male or female, any animal including reptiles or insects, birds, or fish—any living creature in the land, air, or sea—the form of any such figure ("*təmûnat kol sāmel*") must not be fashioned as a graven image. This sweeping prohibition is followed a few verses later by a reminder to make no "graven image in the form of anything [pesel təmûnat kōl]" and a warning that doing so will result in national destruction and exile from the ancestral land.[5] What seems to be at stake here is a concern that any depiction of a living creature is assumed to be a *sacralized* image and therefore—since YHWH himself has no form—the fashioning of any such image is forbidden.

It is precisely the creation of a graven image, independent of idol worship, that appears to be the subject of the curse that is to be declared before the entire nation on Mt. Ebal: "Cursed be the man who makes a graven or cast image ['ăšer ya'ăšeh pesel ūmasēkhāh], abhorrent to YHWH, the handiwork of an artisan [ma'ăśēh yədê ḥārāš], and sets it in a secret place."[6]

The present chapter will begin by surveying the evidence for the widespread acceptance among first-century Judeans of the idea that the Torah prohibited any depiction of living creatures—animals, birds, fish, and humans—in the form of figural artwork. It will be shown that both textual and archaeological evidence point to a common practice among Judeans of eschewing even profane artistic depictions of living creatures—even when these representations were quite evidently not the object of idolatrous worship.[7] Following this, I will proceed backward in time to examine when the earliest evidence for this phenomenon may be found. The bulk of the data surveyed in this chapter has been discussed by other scholars in the past but, as far as I have been able to tell, never with the systematic goal of determining a terminus ante quem for the practice. In the conclusion to the chapter, I will survey interpretations of the data that others have proffered to date, and then outline my own understanding of the conclusions to be drawn.

I should stress at the outset that my interest here is on the observance of a concrete legal prohibition against the depiction of humans and animals *in profane artwork*. I will not seek to investigate questions surrounding the origins of aniconism in the worship of YHWH (the veneration of YHWH as a deity represented in ways that do not include sculptural or pictorial depictions) nor the origins of monolatrism or monotheism in the worship of YHWH (the veneration of YHWH to the exclusion of all other deities, whether these are recognized as existent or not). Notions of both aniconism and exclusivism in the worship of YHWH almost certainly predate the appearance of the Pentateuchal sources and seem to have their roots in exceedingly early West Semitic traditions out of which Israelite and Judean beliefs and practices later developed.[8] There can be little doubt that these early ideas were an integral part of the cultural world into which the Pentateuchal authors had been born, and hence these ideas eventually found their way into the Pentateuch. Rather than investigating the primordial history of these ideas, the present chapter will focus on seeking the earliest evidence of widespread practical implementation of the Pentateuchal prohibition against figural art specifically.

First-Century Evidence

Textual Evidence

PHILO

In his exposition on the Decalogue, Philo asserted that while those who transgress the "first commandment" by venerating multiple deities are certainly in error, their offense is less severe than that of artisans who violate the "second commandment"—"who have given shape to timber and stones, and silver and gold and similar materials, each according to their fancy, and then filled the habitable world with images and wooden figures and the other works of human hands fashioned by the craftsmanship of painting and sculpture, arts which have wrought great mischief in the life of mankind."[9] Their downfall, according to Philo, is that in fashioning these images, the artisans have lost their capacity to see using "the eye of the soul" and have become "blind to the one thing worthy of contemplation, which alone demands keen-sighted vision"—"the rightful conception of the ever-living God."[10] Worshiping other gods (as proscribed in the "first commandment") is bad enough; perversion of the accurate comprehension of *truth itself* by creating artistic images (as proscribed in the "second commandment") is a far worse crime. Repeating this idea elsewhere, Philo maintained that Moses explicitly forbade the visual arts because, like myth-telling, painting and sculpture deceive the soul through false illusions: "And therefore also he [Moses] has banished from his own commonwealth [*ek tēs kath hautòn politeías exélasen*] painting and sculpture [*zōgraphían kaì andriantopoiían*], with all their high repute and charm of artistry, because their crafts belie the nature of truth and work deception and illusions through the eyes to souls that are ready to be seduced."[11] It has been pointed out that Philo's philosophical interpretation of the "second commandment" echoes an idea first proposed by Plato (most fully expounded in books 3 and 10 of *The Republic*) that certain genres of art should be banned from the ideal state since they are deceptive and arouse irrational passions.[12] What interests us here is less Philo's Platonic interpretation of the Pentateuchal prohibition than his apparent allusion to an actual, contemporary reality in which Judeans eschewed certain kinds of painting and sculpture—even when these were unrelated to worship.

JOSEPHUS

Like Philo, Josephus also regarded the fashioning of certain images as a distinct offense to be distinguished from the worship of other gods—although sometimes the two came together in practice. For example, on several occasions Josephus reported incidents where Judeans raised violent objections to the introduction into Jerusalem of images associated with the Roman imperial cult: from busts of the emperor attached to Roman military standards to a statue of Gaius Caligula that was to be set up by imperial decree within the sanctum of the Jerusalem temple itself.[13] On other occasions, however, Josephus explained that Judean law forbade the depiction of living creatures even when these were plainly not meant to represent any foreign gods. For example, in defending against accusations that the Judeans refuse to erect statues of the emperors, Josephus explained,

"The Greeks, with some other nations, think it right to make statues: they delight in depicting the portraits of parents, wives, and children; some even obtain likenesses of persons totally unconnected with them, others do the same for favorite slaves. What wonder, then, to find them rendering this honor to their emperors and masters as well? On the other hand, our legislator, not in order to put, as it were, a prophetic veto upon honors paid to the Roman authority, but out of contempt for a practice profitable to neither God nor man, forbade the making of images, alike of any living creature, and much more of God, who, as is shown later on, is not a creature."[14] Here Josephus made it quite clear that Mosaic law forbade not only the fashioning of actual idols (i.e., the "first commandment") but also the creation of clearly profane images, as in the example of Greek family portraiture (i.e., the "second commandment").

The prohibition against even profane depictions of living creatures appears on several other occasions throughout the works of Josephus. For example, in describing the tapestry that is said to have hung before the gates of the desert tabernacle enclosure, Josephus wrote that the curtain was "beautified with many and divers designs, but with nothing representing the forms of animals."[15] Similarly, in describing the curtain that hung before the tabernacle's Holy of Holies, Josephus wrote, "This curtain was of great beauty, being decked with every manner of flower that earth produces and interwoven with all other designs that could lend to its adornment, save only the forms of living creatures."[16] It is striking that the one design that is actually mentioned in the Pentateuchal prescriptions regarding the tabernacle's hangings—the embroidered cherubim—is completely passed over by Josephus![17] When Josephus came to describe the ark of the covenant, he apparently was unable to suppress all mention of the golden cherubim set upon the ark cover, and so described them in an apologetic manner as "winged creatures, but in form unlike to any that man's eyes have seen."[18]

In another clear example where the ban against graven images was taken to apply to profane figural art, Josephus condemned King Solomon for commissioning the creation of animal images for his "molten sea" as well as for his personal throne: "There had been an occasion on which he sinned and went astray in respect of the observance of the laws, namely when he made the images of the bronze bulls underneath the sea which he had set up as an offering, and those of the lions around his own throne, for in making them he committed an impious act."[19] It should be noted here that the passages in Kings and Chronicles upon which Josephus relied for his reports about Solomon's purported artistic offenses make no allusion themselves to any wrongdoing on Solomon's part (to the contrary, the narratives are quite positive in tone).[20] It was only for Josephus, by whose time a prohibition on images had become part of an authoritative Torah, that Solomon's actions could not be passed over without censure.

One more clear example where Josephus regarded profane figural art as forbidden by the Torah is found in his autobiography, where he relates that the palace that had been erected by Herod Antipas in Tiberias contained (as architectural elements, it seems) representations of animals, adding: "such a style of architecture being forbidden by the laws."[21] Josephus recounts that, as commander of the revolutionary forces in Galilee, he had been commissioned by the Jerusalem assembly to demolish the offending structure. It does not seem that anyone suspected that the animal sculptures built into the Judean tetrarch's palace were *idols* that anyone might have *worshiped*; they most certainly were graven images, however, and as such they were regarded as forbidden by the "second commandment" and by Deut 4.

NON-JUDEAN WRITERS

The Judean avoidance of statuary was sufficiently well known among non-Judeans that around the beginning of the first century CE, the Greek geographer Strabo (ca. 64 BCE–24 CE) could write that Moses had instructed that people "should leave off all image-carving [*pāsan xoanopoiían*]."[22] Around the beginning of the second century CE, the Roman historian Tacitus (ca. 56–120 CE) wrote, "The Judeans conceive of one god only, and that with the mind alone: they regard as impious those who make from perishable materials representations of gods in man's image; that supreme and eternal being is to them incapable of representation and without end. Therefore they set up no statues in their cities, still less in their temples; this flattery is not paid their kings, nor this honor given to the Caesars."[23] Tacitus, it appears, had heard that the Judeans commonly refrained not only from depicting their one and only god in the form of an image, but even refrained from flattering their own mortal kings (and the emperors) with any form of statuary.

Archaeological Evidence

It is fortunate that a substantial quantity of first-century-CE archaeological remains decorated with artwork and clearly associated with Judeans have survived until today. I will survey this evidence here in order to determine the extent to which the avoidance of figural art described by first-century authors might have been widespread. The sizable corpus of evidence to be investigated includes designs on coins minted for Judean use, architectural decoration, funerary art, and artwork on pottery and small archeological finds. Because surprisingly few decorated finds have been found outside Judea which both date to the first century CE and can be compellingly associated with Judeans, the investigation here will focus exclusively on finds from the Southern Levant.[24]

COINS

Throughout the first century CE, coins minted in Judea for Judeans were adorned with images of either inanimate objects or floral forms, but almost never with figural depictions of humans or animals. This phenomenon stands in stark contrast to coinage minted practically everywhere else in the Roman world, where the numismatic imagery usually included a portrait of the emperor on the obverse, or else images of the current emperor's predecessors, his children, the empress, or other members of the imperial family.[25] The reverse of these coins regularly displayed images of additional human (or more rarely animal) forms, oftentimes derived from Roman mythology and its pantheon. In the neighboring independent kingdom of Nabataea, coins displayed portraits of the king and queen and sometimes also images of eagles.[26]

Coins minted by Archelaus, Herod's son and successor as ethnarch over Judea, Idumea, and Samaria (4 BCE–6 CE), displayed nonfigural motifs such as cornucopias, a galley ship, an anchor, a naval ram, a wreath, a military helmet, and a cluster of grapes.[27] Coins minted by Antipas, another of Herod's sons and his successor as tetrarch over Galilee and Peraea (4 BCE– 39 CE), displayed strictly floral motifs: a palm tree, a reed, and a wreath.[28] Whereas not a single example of any of the known coin types minted by either Archelaus or Antipas included figural images, a portrait is featured on every one of the known coin types minted by Philip, the third of Herod's sons and successors (the portrait usually portraying Augustus, the empress Livia, or Tiberius, but sometimes Philip himself).[29] The stark dichotomy in numismatic practices among Herod's three sons is hardly coincidental; while both Archelaus and Antipas ruled over regions whose populations were mostly Judean, Philip ruled over what had been the northeastern territories of Herod—Golan, Auranitis, Trachonitis, Batanaea, and Paneas—

which were populated predominantly by non-Judeans.[30] The circulation of Philip's coins appears to have been limited almost exclusively to the territories associated with his realm; not a single of his coins has been found to date within the region of Judea proper.[31]

The distinction in minting practices between Judean and non-Judean territories continued with Herod's grandson Agrippa I, but here one and the same regent minted coins with figural images for his non-Judean subjects and coins with nonfigural images for his Judean citizens. Agrippa began his reign as king over Philip's former territories, where he minted his first two series of coins (dating to 38 CE and 40/41 CE, respectively). Minted in Paneas for the predominantly non-Judean subjects of this region, every one of the coin types belonging to these series display human portraits: of the emperor Gaius Caligula and members of the imperial family, as well as of Agrippa himself and members of his own royal family.[32] The next series of Agrippa's coins were minted beginning in 41/42 CE—after he was granted reign over Judea, Samaria, and Idumea. These were apparently minted in Jerusalem; most of the coins belonging to this series were found in Jerusalem and its immediate vicinity, with the quantity of finds declining the further the distance from the city.[33] The coins in this group belong to a single type that displays on the obverse a parasol-like royal canopy with fringes, and on the reverse three ears of grain.[34] Scholars have long recognized that the fringed royal canopy on these coins is meant to represent the king himself and acts as a nonfigural substitute for an actual portrait.[35] The final two series of Agrippa's coins (dating to 42/43 and late 43, respectively) were apparently all minted in the predominantly non-Judean coastal city of Caesarea, and all of these display human portraits: of the new emperor Claudius, of Agrippa himself, and of his heir Agrippa II.[36] The pattern described here leaves little room for doubt: Agrippa consciously and consistently avoided figural images when he minted coins in Jerusalem for his Judean subjects, while he displayed no such scruples when he minted coins in non-Judean cities for his non-Judean subjects.

When the Great Revolt broke out in 66 CE, the revolutionary authorities began to mint coins of their own with an array of designs—none of which included human or animal images. Motifs included a chalice, an amphora, a three-branched floral design (possibly pomegranates), a grape leaf and vine, a palm tree with baskets of dates, and the four species associated with the holiday of Sukkot (see chapter 5).[37] The coinage included both bronze denominations as well as silver denominations (sheqels, half-sheqels, and quarter-sheqels). The aversion to figural art represented by these coins was not simply some kind of anti-Roman protest or "nationalistic" cultural identity marker. Agrippa II, who was a Roman client and was certainly opposed to the revolt, minted coins for the Judeans of Sepphoris in the year 67/68 CE (the second year of the Great Revolt) which *also* displayed no figural art. The obverses of these coins display a legend that refers to the emperor Nero but contain no portrait of the man, while the reverses display the legend: "In the time of Vespasian, in the cit[y] of peace [*Eirēnópoli(s)*] Neronias-Sepphor[is]."[38] One of these coin types from Sepphoris displays on the reverse the Latin abbreviation "SC," signifying *Senatus Consultum* (Decree of the Senate), while the second displays a double cornucopia framing a caduceus. Shortly after the war had ended, Agrippa II minted another coin type at Tiberias which again included no figural images, and instead displayed a legend on the obverse that celebrated Vespasian's victory over the Judean rebels with the exclamation "Ki[ng] Agrippa, [the] vic[tory of] Aug[ustus!]."[39] These coins could not be more pro-Roman. It seems almost certain that if he *could* have, Agrippa *would* have displayed the Roman emperors' portraits on all these coins. Agrippa II *did* in fact mint several coin types bearing the images of Nero, Vespasian, Titus, and Domitian, but all these coins—like the coins with figural images minted by his forebears Philip and Agrippa I—were apparently minted in the non-Judean city of Paneas.[40] Undoubtedly, Agrippa II refrained from minting coins bearing the images of the emperors in Sepphoris and in Tiberias because he recognized that figural images would have been regarded as prohibited according to Torah law by the Judeans for whom these coins were minted.

Remarkably, even the Roman prefects and procurators—who in their role as administrators of Judea throughout much of the first century CE minted coins for local use—are found to have exercised great care to avoid images of the emperors and other humans or animals on their coins. These coins, which were minted under the prefects Coponius (6–9 CE), Marcus Ambivulus (9–12 CE), and Valerius Gratus (15–26 CE), as well as under the procurators Marcus Antonius Felix (52–59 CE) and Porcius Festus (59–62 CE), all displayed patently innocuous images such as palm trees and palm branches, ears of grain, floral wreaths, and inanimate objects such as cornucopias, amphoras, weapons, and shields.[41] Coins minted under the prefect Pontius Pilate (26–36 CE) bore images of simpulum and lituus, which, although used as cultic ritual instruments by Roman priests and augurs, apparently did not transgress the prohibition against graven images—as the relevant Pentateuchal passages explicitly forbade only the depiction of living creatures.[42] Yaakov Meshorer has pointed out that while it was not uncommon for Roman provincial administrators throughout the empire to mint coinage for local use, these were always standard Roman coins that, without exception, bore portraits of the emperor and his family.[43] The portraitless coinage produced under the Roman provincial authorities in Judea is without parallel anywhere else in the Roman Empire.

Except for the silver coins minted during the Great Revolt, all the coins discussed until now were made of bronze; neither silver nor gold coins were minted in Judean mints throughout the first century CE. Scholars are divided over whether political, economic, or other reasons might best explain why this was the case, but the unquestionable fact remains that Judean mints did not produce coinage from precious metals.[44] If the Judean economy was to be at all functional, however, there would have certainly arisen a need for silver (and likely also gold) coinage, and so by necessity any silver and gold coins circulating locally would have had to have been imported from foreign mints. Non-Judean mints would have had no compunctions about transgressing Torah laws, and therefore the only silver and gold coins available to Judeans would have been foreign-produced coins bearing figural images. Judging from actual first-century-CE archaeological deposits of silver coins, it appears that the Judean silver-coin market was dominated by the Tyrian mint which produced sheqels and half-sheqels for the entire region.[45] The obverse of all these coins bore the portrait of the Tyrian tutelary god Melqart, identified with the Greek Herakles, and the reverse depicted an eagle. Although less common, coins from other mints were also circulating in Judea, primarily Roman republican and imperial denarii, which invariably depicted images of humans, animals, and Roman deities.[46] Such foreign coins were the only silver coins that were available to Judeans, and therefore these were the coins that Judeans must have used in executing all major financial transactions and in making donations to the Jerusalem temple.[47] As there were simply no alternatives, the fact that Judeans made use of these coins can hardly serve as evidence (as some have claimed) of a general laxity in the observance of a prohibition against graven images.[48] We do not know precisely how first-century Judeans would have rationalized this pragmatic behavior to and among themselves—but clearly they must have found a way.

ARCHITECTURAL DECORATION

The numismatic evidence surveyed above paints an abundantly clear picture of Judean attitudes regarding figural imagery, at least from the perspective of official public policy. In order to provide a more intimate perspective on how individual Judeans and their immediate communities would have regarded figural art, I will survey here archaeological remains of decorative elements found in private homes as well as in more public community structures.

In the surrounding Greco-Roman world within which Judea was situated, figural art was used ubiquitously in adorning architecture both public and private. Throughout the Mediterranean, images of humans, animals, and mythological creatures decorated floor mosaics, paintings and stucco-plaster on walls and ceilings, and carvings on columns, entablatures, roof antefixes, and other architectural elements. It would not be an exaggeration to say that figural images represent one of the hallmarks of Greco-Roman architectural adornment.

First-century Judea presents a striking exception to this otherwise ubiquitous trend. Judean floor mosaics are either unornamented or else decorated with geometric or floral designs—never with human, animal, or mythological images.[49] The most complete first-century-CE examples were found in the private residences unearthed at the Upper City of Jerusalem, where designs include various forms of multi-petaled rosettes, pomegranates, stylized palmette leaves, and chess-board patterns. Borders are rendered in either straight lines or guilloche patterns such as meander, wave-crest, and triangular "saw-tooth" designs. Corners may be decorated with spandrels or simple "gamma" motifs. To date, the only example of a figural image on any mosaic floor dating to the first century CE and plausibly associated with Judean owners is a fragmentarily preserved depiction of a fish (or perhaps a dolphin) on a floor associated with a bathhouse unearthed at Magdala.[50]

The finest examples of first-century-CE painted wall plasters (both fresco and secco) have been found in private homes in the Upper City of Jerusalem, but other examples have been found elsewhere in the country (for example, at Magdala and Iotapata in Galilee).[51] The most common scheme involved the division of the wall into framed rectangular panels painted with alternating colors. Sometimes the panels were adorned with wavy lines and striations meant to give a marble-like appearance. Examples of floral designs have been found which included bunches of apples and pomegranates among tangles of leaves, as well as hanging garlands. An architectural motif in one painting depicts fluted Ionic columns bearing an entablature with a schematic rendering of a Doric frieze divided into triglyphs and plain metopes. As a rule, these paintings lack any depictions of humans or animals. To my knowledge, the only examples of figural art in first-century-CE wall paintings are the depictions of birds found adorning the walls of a single private residence unearthed on Mt. Zion.[52]

Carved stone and molded stucco decoration from Judean contexts dating to the first century CE tend to closely follow Greco-Roman styles but almost never include figural representations. For example, the walls of one reception hall in a private house unearthed at the Upper City of Jerusalem were found decorated with stucco arranged in panels imitating courses of bossed ashlars, while the room's ornamental stucco ceiling was decorated with a pattern of triangles, squares, hexagons, and octagons along with an egg-and-dart motif.[53] A stone carved in relief uncovered in a synagogue at Magdala depicts architectural elements, utensils (including the seven-branched menorah, amphoras, and an oil lamp), and various floral and geometric designs.[54]

FUNERARY ART

Judean funerary art consisted primarily of carved decorations adorning rock-cut tombs, carved and incised decorations adorning ossuaries and sarcophagi, and (more rarely) paintings adorning tombs, ossuaries, and wooden coffins (found in the Judean Desert).

Ornamentation of rock-cut tombs, both the façade and internal spaces, consisted primarily of carving in the rock meant to imitate architecture: ashlar walls, columns (both engaged and detached), entablatures, and (more rarely) pediments.[55] Ornamentation of these pseudo-architectural elements invariably consisted of geometric and floral designs. Some examples of ornamented ceilings have also been found, and again the decoration is invariably either geometric or floral. Although hundreds of first-century-CE Judean tombs have been excavated or surveyed, and many of these contain some amount of carved ornamentation, I know of no examples in which carvings depicting humans or animals were found.

Ossuaries and sarcophagi are also sometimes ornamented with carved or incised designs.[56] The repertoire of motifs involve primarily geometric designs, floral designs, and architectural motifs. Geometric designs include rosettes, discs, concentric circles, half circles, zigzag lines, lozenge patterns, and chess-board patterns. Floral designs include various species of leaves, flowers and fruits, palmettes, wreaths, garlands, grape vines, and palm trees. Architectural motifs include depictions of tomb monuments or façades, tomb entrances, columns, and ashlar walls. Other motifs include vessels such as amphorae, kantharoi, and menorahs. I know of no ossuaries or sarcophagi that were ornamented with figural art. One ossuary known to date includes two schematic outlines of ox skulls (bucrania), but it seems questionable whether any Judeans might have regarded such designs to be prohibited as images of "animals."[57]

Far rarer are paintings adorning tombs, ossuaries, and wooden coffins, as well as graffiti drawn on the walls of tombs.[58] Fragmentary remains of paintings from the Judean Shephela depict geometric and floral designs. The most well-preserved wall paintings have been found decorating the walls of the first-century-CE Judean tomb at Jericho nicknamed the Goliath Tomb; these depict masonry, a wreath, grape vines and clusters, a geometric design that may represent a pergola, and fragments of three birds. Few ossuaries and wooden coffins (preserved only from the Judean Desert) have been found ornamented with paintings, but where these have been found, the designs include garlands, fruit, flowers, branches, rosettes, and simple bands. Graffiti on the walls of Jason's Tomb (in the modern-day Rehavia neighborhood of Jerusalem), which remained in use from the first century BCE into the first century CE, include schematic depictions of three ships, several seven-branched menorahs, a chalice, a palm branch, and a stag with antlers.[59] To the best of my knowledge, the images of the birds on the wall paintings in the Goliath Tomb at Jericho and the graffiti of the stag in Jason's Tomb at Jerusalem are the sole examples of figural images known from any first-century-CE Judean funerary contexts.

POTTERY AND SMALL FINDS

Most pottery and other archaeological small finds at Judean sites consist of functional utensils that were usually left unornamented. When such finds *were* decorated, the ornamentation invariably consisted of simple incised lines, or geometric and floral designs—but almost never figural images depicting humans or animals. Nonfigural ornamentation of this sort is found on certain types of pottery (such as the so-called Pseudo-Nabatean ware), chalk vessels (chiefly tabletops and large jars), ceramic oil lamps (see below), bone implements, and more rarely metal and glass vessels.[60]

Saliently, Judeans appear to have consciously avoided use of contemporary Roman lamps that featured a central discus decorated with human, animal, and mythological images. It is worth citing Renate Rosenthal-Heginbottom's comment on this phenomenon: "The profound transformation that took place in Italy in Augustan times with the production of volute lamps with decorated discus had no impact on consumer behavior in

Jerusalem and Judea until the advent of Roman military and administrative personnel after 70 CE. The subjects depicted on these lamps could not be tolerated by Jews; the introduction of these lamps clearly constitutes a new iconographic trend which in Jerusalem and Judea reflects a post-70 CE development in a non-Jewish society."[61] Instead of importing or imitating Roman discus lamps, Judeans at this time began to produce and widely use wheel-made, knife-pared lamps (often called "Herodian lamps"), which were either completely unadorned or else minimally decorated with incised lines and circles.[62] From the middle of the first century CE, Judeans began producing mold-made lamps with shoulder ornamentations composed of scrolls filled with leaves and rosettes, wreaths of myrtle leaves, myrtle twigs, olive twigs and fruit, oak leaves, and acorns.[63] Slightly later (beginning after 70 CE and continuing into the second century), Judean artisans began to produce a new class of mold-made lamps (often called "Darom-type lamps") decorated with a wide variety of motifs, including geometric designs, scrolls, wreaths, clusters of grapes, pomegranates, rosettes, palm trees, amphorae, menorahs, and the four species associated with the Festival of Sukkot.[64] Examples of this class of lamp bearing *figural* images are exceedingly rare: one example includes an image of a bird in a cage, another shows two birds eating from clusters of grapes, and a third shows two fish.[65] Strikingly, in the latter two cases additional copies of the lamps have been found which were made in the exact same molds—but only after the birds and the fish in the molds had been completely disfigured. Closely placed holes had apparently been added to the molds where the birds and fish had originally been, such that on the later lamps the birds and fish appear instead as schematic clusters of grapes! Varda Sussman, who published these lamps, suggested that the ancient lamp makers, after realizing that they had made something unlawful (or as a result of criticism from others), purposefully disfigured the figural images in the molds by adding holes.[66]

Additional rare examples of figural art on small finds include an engraving of a fish on the side of a stone tabletop, a bronze fitting (for a wooden table leg) in the shape of an animal's paw, a bone gaming piece engraved with a depiction of a human hand (all from the Upper City of Jerusalem), and an etching of two (dead?) sacrificial birds on a chalk core (from near the Temple Mount).[67] Figural images on engraved gemstones used as seals (intaglios), decorative pieces, or amulets are rarely ever found within archaeological contexts that are clearly Judean; salient exceptions are a gemstone depicting Hermes/Mercury, another depicting Demeter/Fortuna, and a third depicting a scorpion—all found in the Upper City of Jerusalem.[68]

Mention should also be made of the images (eagles, sea monsters, and assorted dragons) depicted on the base of the temple's golden menorah visible in the relief on the Arch of Titus in Rome—although several scholars have rightly suggested that the base may be a frame (*ferculum*) constructed by the Roman victors to carry the menorah and was not made by Judeans for Judean use.[69]

Early Evidence

The evidence surveyed until now could not be clearer: with few known exceptions Judeans in the first century CE avoided artistic depictions of humans and animals. Literary sources from this time, especially Josephus, elucidate that such depictions were regarded as forbidden by Torah law. Here we proceed to examine whether this phenomenon is in evidence in earlier periods. It will be shown that compelling evidence for Judean avoidance of figural art has survived from the first century BCE and from the last third of the second century BCE, but not from any time prior to this.

Textual Evidence

THE ERA OF HEROD THE GREAT
(LATE FIRST CENTURY BCE)

Josephus cited a story about how, after Herod the Great had fallen sick toward the end of his life, two Judean scholars (*sophistaì*) incited their followers to cut down a golden eagle that Herod had placed above the "great gate" of the temple in Jerusalem "in defiance of the ancestral laws [*parà toùs patríous nómous*]."[70] According to Josephus in *War*, the reason these scholars objected to the eagle was that it was regarded as "unlawful to place in the temple either images, or busts, or any representation whatsoever of a living creature."[71] While this explanation implies that the prohibition against setting up images applied only to the temple, in *Antiquities* Josephus described the prohibition in more universal terms: "The law forbids those who propose to live in accordance with it to think of setting up images or to make dedications of [the likenesses of] any living creatures."[72] In *War*, Josephus related that about forty young men who were involved in taking down the eagle were caught and, upon being brought before Herod and asked who had ordered them to carry out their deed, replied simply, "The ancestral law [*toû patríou nómou*]."[73] In *Antiquities*, Josephus has the men explain at some length that their actions were in accordance with "the laws that Moses wrote as God prompted and taught him, and left behind."[74] Precisely which precept of the Mosaic law was thought to be transgressed by a golden eagle set above the temple's gate as a donation? In *Antiquities*, Josephus describes the eagle as Herod's "*anáthēma*," a Greek term used to denote a votive offering donated to a temple. Nowhere is it implied that any Judeans regarded the eagle as an idol to be worshiped. By the time this incident took place, the eagle had presumably been hanging above the temple gate for some time, and all would have recognized that this was an ornamental sculpture—one with certain ideological baggage, no doubt—but certainly not an idol that anybody would have thought to worship. It would seem, then, that the eagle would not have been regarded as a transgression of the "*first commandment*" of the Decalogue, which prohibited the veneration of foreign gods, but rather would have been regarded as a violation of the "*second commandment*," which forbade the fashioning of graven images depicting living creatures regardless of whether these were worshiped.[75]

FIGURAL ART IN EARLIER SOURCES

While Judean literary sources predating the Herodian era certainly evince awareness of a commonly accepted Judean aversion to *idolatry*, earlier sources do not appear to provide any unambiguous knowledge of a prohibition against figural art that did not serve as the object of worship.[76] It is unnecessary to adduce here all the biblical sources that deliver sustained invectives against the worship of deities represented in physical form. What concerns us here is that none of these texts seem to be aware of a ban against non-venerated figural artwork—the profane artistic depiction of humans or animals. To the contrary, as we have seen above, the authors of texts in both Kings and Chronicles speak rather approvingly of the twelve molten bulls Solomon had cast as a support for his molten "sea," as also of the sculptured lions adorning his monumental ivory throne.[77] In fact, Solomon's temple is said to have been filled with sculpted and embroidered images of bulls, lions, and winged cherubim—none of which seem to have provoked the ire of the biblical authors.[78]

Archaeological Evidence

THE ERA OF HEROD THE GREAT

The avoidance of figural art so clearly in evidence in the archaeological record of the first century CE is also in evidence during the reign of Herod the Great. Like the coin designers of the first century CE, the minters of

Herod's coins also deliberately refrained from depicting either Augustus and the imperial family or Herod himself and his own royal family. Motifs on Herod's coins included a tripod, a Roman "apex" cap, a military helmet, an aplustre (the ornamental appendage at the stern of Roman ships), a shield, the seed head of an opium poppy, a three-legged table, a diadem, an anchor, cornucopias, and a galley ship.[79] Only one coin type produced by Herod depicts a living creature on its reverse—a standing eagle.[80] It has been suggested that this eagle is meant to represent the golden eagle Herod had set above the "great gate" of the Jerusalem temple according to Josephus's account.[81]

As on his coins, figural art is almost completely absent from every one of the excavated palaces of Herod: at Caesarea Maritima, Jericho, Cypros, Herodium, Masada, and Machearus. Where ornamented mosaic floors have been unearthed in these palaces, all are decorated with geometric designs or with floral motifs (fig. 8).[82] Most of these palaces have yielded remains of fresco fragments as well as relatively well-preserved *in situ* painted walls. These are usually painted in the Second Pompeian Style, but Herod's Third Palace at Jericho has produced fragments resembling examples of the early Third Pompeian Style.[83] While the decorators of Herod's palaces were clearly familiar with original examples of the Second and early Third Styles, so popular in the contemporary Roman world, they refrained from imitating one of these painting styles' most eminent features—the depiction of figural motifs! To date, only two examples of rooms painted with figural images have been found among all the spaces decorated with wall paintings at Herod's numerous palatial estates. Frescoes depicting fowls were uncovered adorning the walls of a bathhouse at Upper Herodium, and additional frescoes adorning the walls of a private royal "theater box" on the slopes below included scenes of humans and animals, including a bull, a crocodile, and a faun.[84] The only other example of figural art unearthed at Herodian palaces was a large, imported marble basin (*labrum*), decorated with winged female figures and Sileni heads.[85] We may be justified in conjecturing that Herod would have regarded his bathhouses at Herodium, along with his royal theater box, as sufficiently intimate spaces where he might securely display prohibited forms of figural art without fear of dissent from his more pious Judean countrymen.

Geometric and floral designs are the sole ornamental features found among all the archaeological remains surviving from Herod's building activities on the Temple Mount in Jerusalem. These include about five

Figure 8. *Mosaic floor in Herod's Western Palace at Masada. (Photo: Bertrand Rieger; Hemis, Alamy Stock Photo)*

hundred carved limestone fragments of architectural elements uncovered at the foot of the southern section of the Temple Mount, all of which likely originated in columns, capitals, friezes, soffits, and carved doorframes that decorated the Royal Stoa and other Herodian structures on the Temple Mount above.[86] Similar designs adorn the richly ornamented *in situ* domes and other architectural elements that survive today in the Double Gate vestibule, most of which likely originate from the original Herodian construction.[87] Not a single figural image has been found among any of these remains.

Small archaeological finds from the late first century BCE also almost universally lack figural images. The predominant oil lamps used by Judeans at this time were mold-made Judean radial lamps decorated with a simple geometric ornamentation of ridges arranged radially on the shoulders.[88] Three unusual specimens of this class of lamp from the Upper City of Jerusalem have been found adorned with what may be a schematic human face incised on the nozzle (although to my mind this interpretation is less than clear).[89] Also dating to this period is an exceptional clay fulcrum medallion decorated with the bust of a woman, apparently belonging to a bed or couch frame.[90] These few examples stand out as extremely rare exceptions to the rule of nonfigural ornamentation among late first-century-BCE Judean remains.

THE HASMONEAN PERIOD

The nonfigural tradition of Judean coinage, so evident in the first century CE and under Herod the Great, traces back to the heyday of the Hasmonean period. Of the many coin types minted by Hasmonean rulers beginning with John Hyrcanus I (134–104 BCE) and ending with Mattathias Antigonus (40–37 BCE), not a single coin type features the image of a human or animal. The most common motif on these coins is a double cornucopia framing what appears to be a pomegranate, but other designs include a flower, a palm frond, a military helmet, an anchor, and a star-shaped design.[91] The last of the Hasmonean rulers, Mattathias Antigonus, innovated a coin featuring vessels from the temple: the seven-branched menorah on the obverse and the table of shewbread on the reverse.[92] Most strikingly, many of these Hasmonean coins feature on their obverse a floral wreath framing a lengthy legend composed of dense text that covers almost every available space on the field. These legends provide the name and title of the Hasmonean ruler, and also cite "the assembly of the Judeans [*ḥever hayəhûdîm*]"—sometimes conferring upon the ruler the title "head of the assembly of the Judeans [*rô'š ḥever hayəhûdîm*]."[93] It seems abundantly clear that the designers of all of these coin types were attempting to display *a virtual portrait* of the Hasmonean leader while avoiding to show *an actual graphic image* of the man. I know of no parallels in coins from anywhere else in the contemporary Hellenistic world where the image of a ruling sovereign is entirely replaced with text.[94] To my mind, the underlying message communicated by the deliberate eschewal of figural art in these coins could not be clearer: the Torah's strict ban on images is endorsed by the highest echelons of the political leadership.

What appears to be the earliest of the "Hasmonean" coins is a type that bears the name not of a Judean ruler but rather of a Seleucid king: Antiochus VII Euergetes (Sidetes). The coins display on the reverse an anchor with the legend "Of King Antiochus Euergetes" together with either the year 181 or 182 of the Seleucid era (= respectively 132/131 and 131/130 BCE); the reverse displays a flower (fig. 9).[95] Scholars are in general agreement that this coin was minted in Jerusalem, a few short years after John Hyrcanus had taken over leadership of the Hasmonean polity. A second type, featuring on the obverse a helmet, and on the reverse an aphlaston (a decorative curving finial of a ship's sternpost) surrounded by the Greek inscription "Of King Antiochus," has recently been identified as also having been minted in Jerusalem around this same time.[96] According to Josephus, Antiochus invaded Judea during the first year of Hyrcanus's rule (135/134 BCE), ravaged the country, and, after besieging Jerusalem, forced Hyrcanus to pay a tribute.[97] The coins in question have been convincingly interpreted upon this historical background as coins minted by Hyrcanus in deference to his Seleucid overlord.[98] The fact that the image of the Seleucid king is replaced by a legend bearing his name and title strikingly underscores the degree to which the Judean aversion to figural images was entrenched by this date. We shall return to discuss these earliest coins in the conclusions presented at the end of this chapter.

Figural art is entirely absent from the Hasmonean palaces at Jericho and the Judean Desert, which prefigure the later Herodian palaces in featuring the first nonfigural mosaic floor found in the country (dating to the mid-first century BCE).[99] Aside from these remains associated with the Hasmonean rulers themselves, I know of no examples of Judean domestic, public, and funerary material culture from this period in which images of humans or animals are featured.

Figure 9. *Bronze coin of Antiochus VII, minted in Jerusalem. (Photo © The Israel Museum, Jerusalem, by Vladimir Naikhin.)*

THE SELEUCID AND PTOLEMAIC PERIODS

The number of archaeological remains associated with Judeans which are well dated to the Seleucid and Ptolemaic periods is far fewer than the amount of such remains from the subsequent Hasmonean and Herodian periods. Although hardly representative, mention should be made here of the monumental structure unearthed at Iraq el-Emir in Transjordan, with its frieze featuring massive sculptures of lions and eagles, together with fountains in the form of sculpted lions.[100] Scholars commonly identify this construction with the "fortress" Josephus described as having been built by the Judean aristocrat Hyrcanus son of Joseph in the early second century BCE, and upon which were said to have been carved "beasts of gigantic size."[101]

Prior to the earliest coins minted by John Hyrcanus I, there is a gap of over one hundred years during which no coins are known to have been minted in Judea. Before this time, Judean coins are known from the reigns of the first two Ptolemaic kings, during the first half of the third century BCE. These coins, all of silver, depict on their obverse the portrait of either the king or the queen, and on the reverse a standing eagle together with a legend in Paleo-Hebrew script reading: "*yəhūd/āh.*"[102] These coins are thought to have been minted by Judeans in Jerusalem, although clearly under the shadow of the reigning Ptolemaic authorities. We cannot know if the Judean minters were at all disturbed by the images they included on their coins.

THE PERSIAN ERA

The earliest Judean coins ever minted are commonly dated to the last phase of Achaemenid rule, in the fourth century BCE. Several coin types from this period are known, all of which feature images of humans and/or animals.[103] The coins are identified as Judean on the basis of their legends in Paleo-Hebrew or Aramaic script which appear on their reverses. All of these legends are composed of either the toponym of the province, "Yehud" (*yəhûd/yəhūd*), or else of the personal name and sometimes also the title of a Judean official: "Johanan the priest" (*yôḥānān hakôhēn*) or "Jehezekiah the governor" (*yəḥizqîyāh hapeḥāh*) (sometimes the title "the governor" is left off). One type features both the names "Yehud" (*yəhūd*) and "Judah" (*yəhûdāh*), the first apparently the toponym of the province and the second likely the personal name of one of its leaders. Many of these types are copies of an Athenian coin that featured on the obverse the head of Athena and on the reverse two of the Greek goddess's attributes: an owl and an olive branch. Other figural motifs on the Judean coins include an eagle with spread wings, the profile of a bearded man wearing a crown, the profile of a clean-shaven and bareheaded man, the frontal portrait of a human face, a human ear, a royal Persian head on a winged lion's body, a horned and winged feline-like beast, a prancing lion above a recumbent bovine, and a facing gorgoneion. One much-discussed coin portrays on the obverse the portrait of a bearded man wearing a helmet and on the reverse a bearded figure sitting on a winged wheel, holding a falcon in his outstretched hand, across from whom (at floor level) appears the face of a bearded, bald man.[104] The only nonfigural images appearing on any of these coin types are a flower and a horn, but in every case where these appear on the obverse, a bird appears on the reverse.

Unlike the Ptolemaic-era issues, which all conform to strict Ptolemaic prototypes, the Persian-era coins minted in Yehud reflect a far freer choice of motifs that mostly do not show any sign of having been prescribed from above by Achaemenid dictates. Accordingly, it seems quite significant that *every example* of the many surviving coin types from Persian-era Yehud displays human and/or animal images. It should be stressed that these issues include coins that feature the names of Judean officials (bearing Yahwistic theophoric elements) who appear to have taken responsibility for the mint, including "the [high] priest" (*hakôhēn*) as well as "the governor" (*hapeḥāh*).

Appearing somewhat earlier than these coins, stamps depicting a lion were regularly used in Judea to mark storage jars, usually on their handles.[105] Over one hundred impressions of these stamps have been found to date, most of them at Ramat Raḥel, but also at Jerusalem (the City of David), Nebi Samwil, and elsewhere in Judea. The common assumption is that these stamps were used to mark agricultural products for administrative purposes, perhaps as taxes. Ephraim Stern, who was the first to study these stamps, dated them to the early Persian period (end of the sixth to beginning of the fifth century BCE), but Oded Lipschits has more recently argued for a slightly earlier dating under Babylonian rule (around the mid-sixth century BCE).[106] Be that as it may, the earlier lion stamps eventually came to be replaced by stamps that feature epigraphic legends naming the Persian province "Yehud" (yəhûd) and/or specific named Judean officials (the title "governor" [paḥāwā'] is sometimes added to a personal name and sometimes replaces it), but without any glyptic elements.[107] There is little reason to think that this development reflects some sort of conscious desire to avoid figural images, however, as—unlike with coins—there was no universal convention at the time to include iconographic images of humans or animals on jar stamps. Furthermore, the later stamps lacking images were in use precisely at the time when Judean officials began to mint coins that, without exception, prominently *did* display figural images.

Terracotta figurines depicting both humans and animals have been found at only a few Judean sites in contexts dating to the Persian period.[108] One of the largest assemblages was found at Tell en-Naṣbeh, where fragments deriving from fifteen anthropomorphic and zoomorphic figurines have been assigned to Persian-period contexts.[109] Similar figurines were found also at Jericho, Gibeon, Jerusalem, Ramat Raḥel, and ʿEin-Gedi.[110] These finds notwithstanding, far fewer terracotta figurines have been found in Persian Judea (or Samaria) compared with other regions of the Southern Levant, a fact that has led Ephraim Stern to hypothesize that Judeans experienced a "religious revolution" wherein "all the pagan-popular elements had undergone purification during the Persian Period."[111] If Stern's assessment is correct, and assuming that the terracotta figurines in question had a specifically cultic function of one sort or another, then the relatively smaller number of figurines found in Judea may reflect a certain movement toward a more exclusivist and aniconic character of YHWH worship among Judeans at this time.[112] It appears far less likely to me, however, that the low number of figurines in Judea relative to other areas of the region reflects adherence to a proscription against *profane* figural art, especially considering the evident lack of any such reservations in relation to the contemporary local coinage.

A small number of figural remains from Persian-era Judean contexts clearly represent foreign deities. Some of the terracotta figurines mentioned above have been interpreted as representing the goddess Astarte.[113] At Gibeon, a bronze Egyptian-style figurine depicting the god Osiris has been dated on stylistic grounds to the fifth to fourth century BCE.[114] Greek deities are depicted on a small number of jar handles with gemstone impressions (intaglios) from Persian-period contexts at Jerusalem (the City of David), Ramat Raḥel, and 'Ein-Gedi.[115] Recent excavations in a Persian-period layer in Jerusalem's Giv'ati Parking Lot unearthed an anthropomorphic vessel (probably a jug) that depicts a finely molded human face thought to represent the Egyptian god Bes.[116] Petrographic analysis has indicated that the vessel is made of local Motza Formation clay, which suggests that it was locally manufactured.

Outside Judea proper, an important assemblage of figural art associated with Persian-period Judeans is found among the seals used in the so-called Murašu archive from Babylonia, dating to 455–403 BCE.[117] Individuals within this archive are identified as Judeans on the basis of their theophoric names, which contain a Yahwistic element. Altogether, nineteen seals have been identified as belonging to named Judeans within the archive, seventeen of which are sufficiently well preserved to allow the identification of their designs. Without exception, all of these Judean seals depict figural motifs including humans, animals (bulls, lions, snakes, and fish), and mythological creatures (monsters, sphinxes and an image of Ahura Mazda).[118] Another Judean seal from Babylonia, found among the Yāhūdu archive and dating to the late sixth century BCE, depicts a worshiper standing before a spade and an eight-pointed star (the symbols of Marduk and Ištar).[119]

Conclusions

The goal of this chapter has been to explore the question of when Judeans began to observe a prohibition against the graphic depiction of humans and animals in profane artwork in fulfillment of what was regarded to be a dictate of Torah law. Throughout the first century CE, Judeans were producing a copious amount of visual art of all sorts, which—with few exceptions—clearly avoided representation of humans or animals. This is seen most strikingly in the designs on coins minted for local use by Judeans, where images of the emperor and of Judean rulers are universally missing. Literary sources from this time, especially the works of Josephus, provide a clear and unambiguous explanation for this archaeological phenomenon: a commonly held belief among Judeans that Torah law forbids the artistic representation of living creatures. Observance of this prohibition is clearly in evidence as early as the first century BCE, as well as in the final three decades of the second century BCE, all throughout which Judeans minted coins that demonstrably avoided figural depictions. Prior to this, we encounter over a century during which time no Judean coins were minted, and almost no well-dated archaeological finds associated with Judeans have been unearthed which display any sort of artistic elements—whether figural or nonfigural. Continuing to proceed backward in time, we again encounter coins minted in Judea for local Judean use in the first half of the third century BCE, but this time the coinage displayed portraits of the Ptolemaic monarchs and the image of an eagle. Prior to Ptolemaic times, Judean authorities in the fourth century BCE minted a wide variety of coins that—without exception—displayed images of animals and humans. The choice of images on these coins (which shows no evidence of having been dictated by Persian demands) stands in stark contrast to Judean practices from the Hasmonean period onward, and suggests that figural art posed no problem for Judeans living in the late Persian period. Figurines from sites in Persian Yehud and Judean seals featuring figural art from Persian Babylonia suggest that figural art was not eschewed during Achaemenid times.

The basic picture that I have painted here is not a novel one; scholars have long recognized that, from the Hasmonean era onward, we begin to encounter widespread evidence for a never-before-seen aversion to figural art among Judeans. Lee Levine has conveniently summarized four theories that have been posited to explain why this phenomenon might have emerged specifically in the mid-second century BCE:[120]

1. It was due to the influence of a stringent position among the Sadducees.[121]
2. It was due to the influence of a stringent position among the Pharisees.[122]
3. It was a reaction against Hellenization and the threat of foreign influences.[123]
4. It was a traumatic reaction to the desecration of the temple by Antiochus IV in 167 BCE, which included the imposition of pagan worship.[124]

Levine himself rejected all of these theories as ultimately lacking evidential support, since we know nothing about either Sadducaic or Pharisaic positions on figural art, and there is no hard evidence to sustain the idea that a putative Hasmonean reaction against Hellenism or response to the events of 167 BCE would have led to a dramatic change in Judeans' "cultural-artistic posture." Instead, Levine suggested that the prohibition against figural art was an initiative of the Hasmoneans, whose political and military policy was shaped in many respects by the book of Deuteronomy—the primary textual source for the ban against all kinds of image-making. The repeated Deuteronomic emphasis on the avoidance of images, Levine suggested, "provided the basis and justification for the Hasmoneans' dramatic move to (re)invent a boundary marker between Jews and non-Jews."[125]

Rather than viewing the ban on figural images in isolation, it bears considering the possibility that adherence to this prohibition might be representative of adherence to Torah laws in general. Rather than regarding the evidence as an indication of stricter interpretation of a long-standing law, perhaps the evidence should be viewed as an indication that the Torah *itself* had only recently become widely known and regarded as authoritatively binding.

The evidence explored in this chapter provides a remarkably precise terminus ante quem for when this turn of events may have occurred: the time when the earliest imageless coins were minted in Judea by John Hyrcanus I. If, as is commonly accepted, Hyrcanus's own coins were preceded by the similarly imageless issue with the legend bearing the name of Antiochus VII and the dates 132/131 and 131/130 BCE, then the year 131 BCE would be our terminus ante quem for when a prohibition against figural images was first put into practice. Prior to this, we simply lack the evidence to determine whether any Judeans were endeavoring to adhere to the Pentateuchal ban on images in one way or another. Over two centuries before this, the Persian-era Judean authorities who were including figural images on all their minted coins exhibited no signs of regard for any such Pentateuchal prohibition.[126]

4 Tefillin and Mezuzot

Following Moses's recounting of the theophany at Horeb in Deut 5:1–6:3, Deut 6:4–9 reads as follows: "Hear, O Israel: YHWH is our God, YHWH is one. Love YHWH your God with all your heart, and with all your soul, and with all your might. These words that I am commanding you today shall be on your heart; recite them to your children and talk about them when you are at home and when you are on the road, when you lie down and when you rise; bind them as a sign on your hand [*ûqšartām lə'ôt 'al yādekhā*], and they shall be as *ṭōṭāfōt* [a difficult word; see below] between your eyes [*wəhāyû ləṭōṭāfōt bên 'ênekhā*]; write them on the doorposts of your house and on your gates [*ûkhtavtām 'al məzūzôt bêtekhā ûvîš'ārekhā*]."[1] Verses 6–9 provide a series of instructions regarding "these words that I am commanding you today," which are to be (1) upon your heart; (2) recited to your children; (3) talked about always (e.g., whether you are at home or traveling, whether you are lying down or arising); (4) bound as a sign on your hand (or arm; "*yād*" can mean both); (5) as "*ṭōṭāfōt*" between your eyes; and (6) written on the doorposts of your house and on your gates. The referent of "these words" is somewhat unclear; the phrase may refer back to the Horeb theophany just recounted, or alternatively to the intervening verses 4–5 ("YHWH is our God . . . Love YHWH . . ."), or else it might refer to the entire paraenesis that forms the bulk of Deuteronomy.

This passage has a close parallel in Deut 11, where it follows immediately upon Moses's exhortation in verses 13–17 about the rewards promised for obeying YHWH's commandments and the punishments threatened for serving other gods: "Put these words of mine on your hearts and on your souls; bind them as a sign on your hands, and they shall be as *ṭōṭāfōt* between your eyes; teach them to your children, talking about them when you are at home and when you are on the road, when you lie down and when you rise; write them on the doorposts of your house and on your gates."[2] The subject here, "these words of mine," appears to refer back to the promises of reward and the threats of punishment in the verses immediately preceding.

The two Deuteronomy passages just cited have two rough parallels in Exod 13. Chapters 12–13 of Exodus are composed of a running narrative about the plague of the killing of the firstborn Egyptians and the subsequent exodus of the Israelites from Egypt, punctuated in a somewhat peculiar manner with several legal pericopes. One of these pericopes is Exod 13:3–10, presented as Moses's instructions to the Israelites about how to observe the annual seven-day Festival of Unleavened Bread. Inserted toward the end of this pericope are the following verses: "Tell your child on that day: 'It is because of what YHWH did for me when I came out of Egypt.' It shall be as a sign on your hand and as a reminder [ûlzikārôn] between your eyes, so that the instruction of YHWH will be in your mouth; for with a strong hand YHWH brought you out of Egypt."[3]

The pericope immediately following is Exod 13:11–16, were Moses instructs the Israelites about how firstborn animals and firstborn children are to be redeemed. Appended to the end of this pericope are the following verses: "When in the future your child asks you: 'What is this?,' say to him: 'By strength of hand YHWH brought us out of Egypt, from the house of slavery. When Pharaoh stubbornly refused to let us go, YHWH killed all the firstborn in the land of Egypt, from human firstborn to the firstborn of animals. Therefore I sacrifice to YHWH every male that first opens the womb, but every firstborn of my sons I redeem.' It shall be as a sign on your hand and as ṭôṭāfôt between your eyes, that by strength of hand YHWH brought us out of Egypt."[4]

In both of these Exodus passages, it seems that the subject which is to be taught to the child and which is to "be as a sign on your hand and as a reminder/ṭôṭāfôt between your eyes" is the rituals surrounding the Festival of Unleavened Bread and the redemption of the firstborn.

The compositional history of these four passages will not detain us here.[5] Our focus in the present chapter will be on two practices, current to one degree or another among first-century-CE Judeans, which were based on practical readings of two of the instructions found among these passages. The first practice involved writing certain Pentateuchal excerpts on small scraps of animal skin, folding these skins and placing them into miniature leather cases, and then affixing these cases to the body—apparently on the hand (or arm) and between the eyes. As will be shown below, this practice likely rose out of a literalist reading of the instruction, repeated in all four passages, that something should be bound as (or "be as") a sign on the hand, and that this same thing should be "as *ṭôṭāfōt*" (or "as a reminder") between the eyes. As it remains unknown how this practice might have been referred to by first-century Judeans, here I employ the terminus technicus "tefillin," which is the term used throughout rabbinic literature for later manifestations of this ritual practice. The second practice involved placing some sort of inscription, likely also Pentateuchal passages, upon doorways. Again, as will be argued below, this practice probably grew out of a literal reading of the instruction repeated twice in the two Deuteronomy passages that "these words" should be written on doorposts of the house and on gates. As here too it remains unknown how this practice would have been referred to in the first century, I will refer to these ritual writings on doorways as "mezuzot" (singular: "mezuzah"), a term borrowed from the Pentateuchal word for "doorposts" and used by the rabbis when discussing this practice in their own times. We begin with an examination of the literary and archaeological evidence for both of these practices in the first century CE, followed by a search for the earliest available evidence which might indicate that these practices were being observed by Judeans in prior centuries.

First-Century Evidence

We begin by surveying the textual evidence for the practices of tefillin and mezuzot among first-century writers. As will be shown, such evidence is admittedly sparse and rather vague. The limited literary evidence, however, is supplemented by archaeological evidence, which—at least as far as tefillin practice is concerned—will be shown to be qualitatively rich.

Textual Evidence

PHILO

The two Deuteronomy passages that give instructions about "these words" were taken by Philo to be speaking about "the [rules] of justice [*tà díkaia*]."[6] Philo paraphrased each of these instructions and then presented an allegorical explanation for each. According to Philo, the hand is a symbol of action, and it is upon this that we are to "fasten and hang for a sign" the rules of justice: "Of what it is a sign he has not definitely stated because, I believe, they are a sign not of one thing but of many, practically of all the factors in human life."[7] As for the commandment "and they shall be as *ṭōṭāfōt* between your eyes," Philo rendered this as an instruction to have the rules of justice "shaking before the eyes [*seiómena prò ophthalmṓn*]," which led him to the following explanation: "Always and everywhere we must have the vision of them, as it were, close to our eyes. And they must have vibration and movement [*sálon d' ekhétō taûta kinoúmena*], it continues, not to make them unstable and unsettled, but that by their motion they may provoke the sight to gain a clear discernment of them. For motion induces the use of the faculty of sight by stimulating and arousing the eyes, or rather by making them unsleepful and wakeful."[8] Philo's curious explanation here seems to be based on the Septuagint's rendering of this commandment as "and they shall be immovable before your eyes [*kaì éstai asáleuton prò ophthalmṓn sou*]"; Philo either had "movable" (*saleutón*) instead of "immovable" (*asáleuton*) as a variant in the Septuagint manuscript before him, or else he misread the text.[9] Be that as it may, it is hard to tell whether behind Philo's allegorical explanations lies some kind of ritual practice involving actually binding a physical object to the hand and placing some sort of dangling object in front of the eyes.

On the other hand, his explanation regarding the instruction to write "these words" on the doorposts of houses and on gates does seems quite clear in envisioning an actual practice of writing something in front of the doors of houses: "He bids them also write and set them forth in front of the doorposts of each house [*grápsantas autà prósthen tṓn phliṓn oikías hekástēs protithénai*] and the gates in their walls, so that those who leave or remain at home, citizens and strangers alike, may read the inscriptions engraved on the face of the gates [*toîs prò tṓn pulṓn grámmasin estēliteuménois entunkhánontes*], and keep in perpetual memory what they should say and do, careful alike to do and to allow no injustice, and when they enter their houses and again when they go forth, men and women and children and servants alike may act as is due and fitting both for others and for themselves."[10] Philo does not detail precisely what of "the [rules] of justice" is to be written, nor does he explain exactly what form such writing is to take, although it seems that he has in mind some kind of engraved plaque that is to be set up *in front of* the doorway. Indeed, both the Hebrew " *'al məzūzôt*" and the Septuagint's "*epì tàs phliàs*" might well be understood as meaning not only "*upon* the doorposts" but also "*before* the doorposts."[11]

THE GOSPEL ACCORDING TO MATTHEW

Matthew provides a statement attributed to Jesus in which the Pharisees and the scribes are rebuked for their ostentatious virtue signaling:

"They do all their deeds to be seen by others; for they make their phylacteries broad [*platúnousin gàr tà phulaktéria autōn*] and their fringes long."[12] The reference to "*phulaktéria*" here raises difficulties if we were to accept the usual understanding of the word as "phylacteries," a type of amulet worn to magically protect the wearer from harm—hardly an object for pious display. This difficulty has led standard commentaries to explain that tefillin is meant, and that these were dubbed here "*phulaktéria*" primarily because of the outward resemblance of tefillin to small amulets that are similarly worn on the body. Yehudah Cohn has argued that the tefillin ritual itself originated as an apotropaic practice, an idea that would find support if we were to accept the identification of Matthew's "*phulaktéria*" with tefillin.[13]

To my mind, the correlation between tefillin and amulets seems rather forced. As we have understood it above, the ritual practice of tefillin was directed toward fulfilling a literalist interpretation of a Pentateuchal commandment, whereas amulets are strictly functional devices designed to ward off harm through magical means. It seems to me that any apotropaic interpretations some Judeans *may* have invested in the practice would have been quite ancillary. The identification of Matthew's "*phulaktéria*" with tefillin may still be salvaged, however, if we interpret the word not as "phylacteries" but rather as "protective cases." The noun "*phulaktērion*" derives from the verb "*phulássō*," meaning "protect," "guard," "preserve," or "maintain." Its original connotation as a "fortified post" developed later into the more abstract sense of "that which protects," a meaning that eventually came to be used with reference to protective amulets.[14] It does not seem at all implausible to me that the "*phulaktéria*" of Matthew may have been the leather cases that *housed and protected* the inscribed tefillin slips, and that it was their broadening by Pharisees and scribes which was regarded as an ostentatious display of piety. If the word would have had any unfavorable associations with Matthew's readers because of its usual association with amuletic practices, calling the enlarged protective cases of the tefillin used by these groups "*phulaktéria*" may have only added potency to the stinging critique.[15]

JOSEPHUS

In his summary of the Mosaic law that Josephus provided right before narrating the death of Moses, the following regulations are included: "They shall inscribe also on their doors [*epigráphein dè kaì toîs thurómasin autōn*] the greatest of the benefits which they have received from God and each shall display them on his arms [*én te brakhíosin hékaston diaphaínein*]; and all that can show forth the power of God and His goodwill towards them, let them bear a record thereof written on the head and on the arm [*phérein engegramména epì tês kephalês kaì toũ brakhíonos*], so that men may see on every side the loving care with which God surrounds them."[16] Josephus diverges here from a simple paraphrase of Deut 6 and Deut 11 by adding several important details not found in the Pentateuch. For Josephus, "these words" that are to be bound to the hand, that are to be as "*tōṭāfōt*" between the eyes, and that are to be written on the doorposts describe God's strength and his benevolent and all-enveloping affection toward Israel. Precisely what Josephus might have meant by all of this is unclear, although it seems reasonable to assume that he had in mind references to the exodus from Egypt and perhaps also to the giving of the Torah at Sinai.[17] Be that as it may, in portraying "these words" as being written down (*engegramména*) and borne on the arm and head—and in so doing concretizing the far more abstract language of the Pentateuch—Josephus appears to reveal familiarity with a contemporary practice quite reminiscent of tefillin. That the practice would have involved tangible objects that were physically worn on the arm and head is further supported by his comment about how these inscriptions were visible to others.

Archaeological and Epigraphic Evidence

We now turn to survey a significant assemblage of archaeological finds from caves in the Judean Desert which reflect how tefillin was practiced among first-century-CE Judeans. Unfortunately, because artifacts associated with this ritual were apparently made only from organic materials (primarily animal skins), no such remains have ever been found outside the arid and climatically stable conditions of the Judean Desert caves. Because of this, we find ourselves quite limited in terms of our ability to draw meaningful conclusions regarding the quantity or the geographic distribution of these remains within settled regions of the country. What the assemblage is missing in quantity and distribution, however, is made up for in *qualitative* terms by the opportunity these artifacts provide us to analyze the intricate exegetical thought processes that lie behind the details of their designs.

The bulk of this assemblage was found in caves in the vicinity of Khirbet Qumran and has been assigned a depositional date around the time when the settlement site is thought to have been destroyed—in 68 CE. A smaller number of finds within the corpus were discovered in caves elsewhere in the Judean Desert, such as at Wadi Murabbaʿât and Naḥal Ṣeʾelim (Wadi

Seiyal), and these might share slightly later depositional dates—perhaps from the time of the Bar Kokhba revolt in 132–135 CE. Because the entirety of this assemblage represents a single phenomenon, it will be addressed here as a unit representing first-century-CE practices. Below, when we turn to investigate evidence predating the first century CE, we will reexamine whether any of the various exemplars within this corpus might have been manufactured in an earlier period.

The identification of the assemblage under discussion as remains of an ancient tefillin practice dates back to the time of the initial discovery of these artifacts in the mid-twentieth century.[18] In previous publications, the rationale for this identification has been the apparently close resemblance between the archaeological finds and later rabbinic prescriptions regarding tefillin. Here I will argue that interpretation of our archaeological assemblage should be approached from the opposite direction; the first-century artifacts are to be identified as tefillin independently of the rabbinic corpus, which itself should be studied as a product of earlier praxes represented by the finds.

THE FINDS AND THEIR INTERPRETATION AS TEFILLIN

The assemblage is composed of two kinds of artifacts: small leather cases and thin slips made of animal skin (parchment or thin leather) inscribed with Pentateuchal passages. The collection includes five leather cases that were discovered with tightly folded and bound slips still in place inside the casings (fig. 10). Aside from these, an additional twenty-two leather cases were found with no slips inside, and another twenty-five slips were found independent of cases (fig. 11).[19] It seems quite likely that all the cases found empty were originally meant to contain slips, and that all the slips found without a case were originally made to be put into a case; the slips had simply either fallen out of their cases or else were not yet put into one.

The leather cases are constructed from a single, rectangular piece of leather. At one of the long ends of the rectangle, either a single indentation or else a row of four indentations was pressed into the skin, creating either one or four cavities on the inner side of the leather into which the inscribed slips were to be placed. One end of the rectangle was then folded over to meet the opposite end, creating the closed casing, and this was subsequently sewn shut in a manner that left a hollow space along the width of the case into which a leather strap was inserted.[20] The presence of such

Figure 10. *Tefillin case with folded slips (XQPhyl 1–4) (Photo © The Israel Museum, Jerusalem, by Yigael Yadin.)*

Figure 11. *Tefillin slip from Qumran (4Q140, recto). (Photo: Najib Anton Albina; courtesy of the Leon Levy Dead Sea Scrolls Digital Library; Israel Antiquities Authority.)*

a strap leaves little room for doubt that all of these cases were meant to be affixed to something else—perhaps to be worn somewhere on the body of a person.

The inscribed slips all contain Pentateuchal passages excerpted from Exodus and/or Deuteronomy, written on small scraps of skin in miniscule script. The diminutive dimensions of the slips and of the writing, along with the fact that these slips were folded up, bound, and placed into sealed leather cases, clearly indicate that these texts were never meant to be read. While the precise scope of the passages contained among the various slips is somewhat diverse, it is far from arbitrary; without exception, every slip contains (a) one or more of the four passages which instruct that something should "be as," or that one should "bind as," a "sign" upon the hand, and that this should "be as a reminder/as ṭōṭāfōt" between the eyes (Exod 13:9, 16; Deut 6:8; 11:18) and/or (b) a large selection of verses in passages adjacent to these four verses.[21] This is the only shared characteristic readily demonstrable among all these texts, and this seems unlikely to be accidental.

Why would these specific texts have been copied and sealed inside cases affixed with straps? The most plausible explanation seems to be that these four verses had come to be interpreted as a commandment to write down the scriptural passages within which these four verses themselves appear and to physically strap these texts to the hand (or arm) and between the eyes. This would reflect a close, quite literal interpretation of the instruction in the two Deuteronomy verses to "bind" "these words" on the hand. This manner of interpreting the Pentateuchal verses was apparently later inherited by the rabbis, for whom the practice was known as "tefillin."[22] The material remains from the Judean Desert clearly demonstrate, however, that this way of reading and implementing this particular Pentateuchal instruction was not the rabbis' own invention.

"REVERSE ENGINEERING" TEFILLIN TO REVEAL ANCIENT EXEGETICAL PATHWAYS

Once we have accepted that these artifacts represent physical manifestations of how a particular Pentateuchal instruction was interpreted by ancient Judean exegetes, we may begin to appreciate the vast potential these remains offer for deepening our understanding of the inner workings of ancient Torah law. By carefully examining some of the detailed features of these artifacts, we may attempt to "reverse engineer" the exegetical pathways that might have led to the tefillin having been designed as they were.

Here I will only briefly outline some of the kinds of information that may be gleaned from a close examination of the Judean Desert assemblage.

A perfunctory examination of the tefillin cases reveals two main typological forms: (1) cases that have a single cavity for holding a tefillin slip (or slips) and (2) cases that feature four distinct compartments, each meant to hold an individual slip. Recalling that the Pentateuch instructs the binding of words "as a sign" upon the hand and also having them "as a remembrance/*ṭōṭāfōt*" between the eyes, we may conjecture that perhaps one type was to be worn on the hand while the other type was to be worn between the eyes. If this supposition is correct, we may further speculate as to which type might have been intended for which part of the body. That which is to be bound to the hand is referred to in the singular as "a sign" (*'ôt*), whereas that which is to be placed between the eyes is usually referred to in what was likely read as the plural term "*ṭōṭāfōt*."[23] It seems plausible that the single-compartment tefillin cases might have been meant to be bound to the hand or arm, while the multiple-compartment cases were meant to be worn between the eyes.[24] Exactly this kind of exegesis is recorded in a Tannaitic midrash halakhah, and our analysis of the Judean Desert finds suggests that the rabbis did not devise this exegetical maneuver themselves but rather inherited it from earlier generations of Judean legal specialists.[25]

As noted above, all the tefillin texts discovered in the Judean Desert contain exclusively one or more of the four constitutive verses and/or a large selection of verses found preceding these four verses such as were probably understood as the referent of "these words." To this extent, the choice of texts included in tefillin was quite uniform. Beyond this, however, there seems to have been a substantial range of options as to the selection of verses that might be included in the tefillin from among the passages preceding the four constitutive verses. While the diversity of texts found among the Judean Desert tefillin exemplars confounds any simple effort to classify all the slips comprehensively into a limited number of clearly defined taxonomic groups, the corpus can be viewed roughly in terms of two distinct types of tefillin slips:[26]

1. Slips that contain exclusively the four entire scriptural sections (as delineated in the medieval Masoretic division of the Pentateuch) in which the verses understood as mandating the practice of tefillin are found—namely, (1) Exod 13:1–10, (2) Exod 13:11–16, (3) Deut 6:4–9, and (4) Deut

11:13–21. This type includes slips that contain either one or more (usually all four) of these sections.

2. Slips that contain verses from the scriptural sections which immediately precede the scriptural sections delineated above—namely, (1) Exod 12:43–51, (2) Deut 5:1–6:3, and (3) Deut 10:12–11:12. Tefillin slips of this type often (although not always) also include verses from the scriptural sections delineated for the first type.

The two types appear to represent two distinct approaches to interpreting what was meant by "these words" that are to be affixed to the hand and placed between the eyes. The first type apparently represents an understanding that "these words" is a self-referential phrase, meaning the words which themselves instruct this practice, along with the entire scriptural pericope within which these words occur. This type appears to reflect a strict, literalist exegetical approach, focused more on a rigidly narrow interpretation of the phrase "these words" than on any broader rationale that might be sought for the commandment.[27] The second type, conversely, seems to reflect more of an interest in gauging "original authorial intent" for the Pentateuchal commandment, as slips of this type include what appear to be more meaningful pericopes that were apparently interpreted as the logical referents of "these words": the commandment regarding the Passover sacrifice in Exod 12:43–51 (preceding the two Exod 13 verses), the theophany at Horeb including the Decalogue in Deut 5:1–6:3 (preceding Deut 6:8), and the sweeping historical survey found in Deut 10:12–11:12 (preceding Deut 11:18). Whether these two exegetical approaches reflect a diachronic development or a synchronic dispute between competing contemporary exegetes, the variety within the Judean Desert tefillin assemblage highlights the rich and varied ways Judeans were actively engaging in the interpretation and implementation of Torah law in the first century CE.

MEZUZOT

Maurice Baillet published a miniature scroll from Qumran Cave 8 (8Q4), which he identified as a "mezuzah" (fig. 12).[28] It is written on a "rather thin" rectangular skin (6.5 × ±16 cm) and preserves text from Deut 10:12–11:21. It seems that the identification of this artifact as a mezuzah stemmed primarily from the textual content, which generally resembles the contents of the rabbinic mezuzah (Deut 6:4–9; 11:13–21) except that Deut 6:4–9 is missing and Deut 10:12–11:12 was added. It seems likely that the

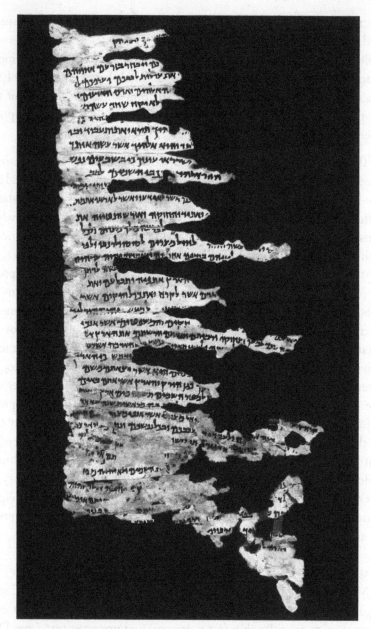

Figure 12. *"Mezuzah" from Qumran (8Q4). (Photo: Shai Halevi; courtesy of the Leon Levy Dead Sea Scrolls Digital Library; Israel Antiquities Authority.)*

dimensions of the skin, the quality and size of the script, the size of the spaces between the lines, and the presence of small margins all suggested to Baillet that the text was too large to be a tefillin slip and yet still too small to be a scriptural excerpt meant for reading.[29]

József Milik subsequently published another seven texts from Qumran Cave 4 (4Q149–155), which he identified as additional examples of mezuzot.[30] The content of these texts resembled that found in tefillin (including Exod 13:1–16), but Milik explained that it was the quality of the skins, especially their thickness, that served as his main criterion for distinguishing mezuzot from tefillin.[31] Although these were found to resemble tefillin with regard to the dimensions of the skins, the tiny size and shapes of the letters, and the absence of dry rulings to guide the scribe, Milik's "mezuzot" were written on the same kinds of thicker and higher-quality skins as were used for ordinary manuscripts—and hence Milik regarded these as unlikely to be tefillin.

As a commandment to write "these words" on doorposts appears only in Deut 6:9 and Deut 11:20, it seems safe to assume—judging from how the intimately related tefillin instruction was practiced—that the textual content of mezuzot would have included Deut 6:9 and Deut 11:20 themselves along with a selection of verses preceding these two constitutive verses such as would have been understood as the referent of "these words." It seems to me rather far-fetched that anyone would have regarded verses from Exod 13:1–16 as appropriate text to place on a doorpost. Since two of the slips that Milik identified as "mezuzot" (4Q154, 4Q155) are composed of text from precisely these verses, it seems far more reasonable to assume that these would have been tefillin rather than mezuzot. A consequence of identifying these two slips as tefillin is that the identification of the rest of Milik's "mezuzot" is now called into question; since his only criterion for distinguishing between tefillin and mezuzot was the thickness of the skin upon which they were written, if we accept that 4Q154 and 4Q155 are tefillin written on somewhat thicker skins, this raises the possibility that the other five slips from Cave 4 with textual content from Deuteronomy appropriate for tefillin (4Q149–153) may *also* have been tefillin. This leaves 8Q4 as the only anomalous artifact; it seems too small for a manuscript meant for reading, but too well written and profligate in terms of unused spaces for it to be easily identified as a tefillin slip. It remains unclear, however, whether these factors are enough to require that this diminutive manuscript was necessarily a mezuzah rather than simply a somewhat larger and more handsome tefillin slip.[32]

Aside from this small assemblage of texts on skins which have survived in the Judean Desert, I know of no archaeological remains from the first century CE that might readily be associated with the observance of a mezuzah ritual. No archaeological remains from this period are identifiable as mezuzah housings, no niches for mezuzot are known from the remains of doorposts, and no mezuzah inscriptions have been found on either stone or plaster. Despite this complete lack of evidence, however, it still seems quite possible that the commandment to write "these words" on doorposts was being observed in one way or another without leaving any surviving trace in the archaeological record. Certainly, if texts were being inscribed on perishable writing materials and affixed to doorposts, no identifiable remains of the practice would be expected to survive outside the desert. But even if texts were being engraved or written in ink directly onto doorposts, we would still be left with no material traces of the practice if the inscriptions were made on wooden doorjambs. At most, we may reasonably conclude that a mezuzah ritual that involved engraving scriptural verses on *stone* was unlikely to have been practiced among Judeans in the first century CE, as inscriptions in stone—had there been any—could be expected to have survived and to be archaeologically retrievable.

Summary

The finds from the Judean Desert caves provide incontrovertible evidence that the ritual practice of tefillin was observed by Judeans living in the first century CE. Josephus likely referred to this practice, and both Philo and the author of Matthew may also have been familiar with such an observance—although the opaque character of their comments makes this somewhat difficult to ascertain. Considering the rather limited textual evidence, and because tefillin were made entirely from perishable organic materials that could not survive outside the arid climate of the Judean Desert, it remains difficult to determine how widespread the practice might have been at this time. What the sum of this evidence lacks in quantity, however, is duly compensated for by the treasure trove of information the archaeological data contribute toward elucidating the complex exegetical thought processes that lie behind many of the intricate details that composed the ritual.

Evidence for the observance of a mezuzah ritual is less clear. Philo may have known of a concrete practice of setting up inscriptions in front of doorways which could be read by all who entered and exited, and Josephus may have been familiar with a similar practice. Considering how the instruction to inscribe "these words" on doorposts is intimately linked with the instruction to bind these same words on the hand and to have them as "*ṭōṭāfōt*" between the eyes, the fact that the latter was being implemented through the concrete practice of tefillin suggests that the former was also likely being observed through a similar ritual practice of mezuzah. Although some of the inscribed slips from the Judean Desert may represent just such a practice, this remains uncertain.

Early Evidence

We turn now to texts and to archaeological remains that predate the first century CE and that might be taken to indicate the existence of ritual practices resembling tefillin and mezuzah during this earlier time.

Textual Evidence

LETTER OF ARISTEAS

In earlier chapters, I referred to the excursus in the Letter of Aristeas where Eleazar the high priest provides the Egyptian delegation sent to Jerusalem with a lengthy explanation about the dietary and purity laws.[33] Inserted into this somewhat rambling speech is the following passage: "And indeed also he has given us a symbolic reminder on our clothes, just as also on gates and doors [*epì tōn pulōn kaì thurōn*] he has prescribed that we set up the sayings [*tithénai tà lógia*] to serve as a reminder of God. And also he has commanded us expressly to fasten the sign upon our hands [*kaì epì tōn kheirōn dè diarrhēdēn tò sēmeîon keleúei periēphthai*], showing clearly that every activity must be accomplished with justice, keeping in mind our own constitution and above all the fear of God."[34] The "symbolic reminder on our clothes" is likely a reference to the instruction in Num 15:37–41 regarding the "fringes" (*ṣîṣīt*) and blue thread that are to be placed on the edges of clothing. The speaker here then turns to paraphrase the suite of instructions featured in Deut 6:5–9 and repeated in Deut 11:18–20 (the following paragraph speaks of studying God's provisions "when sleeping and rising"). It seems noteworthy that the author diverges from the Pentateuchal instructions on several points. "The sayings [*tà lógia*]" (compare LXX: "*tà rĕmata*") are to be put on "doors [*thurõn*]" rather than on "doorposts" (Hebrew: *məzūzôt*; LXX Greek: *tàs phliàs*). Rather than an instruction to "write them" (Hebrew: *ûkhtavtām*; LXX Greek: *grápsete autà*), the instruction is "to set up [*tithénai*]" these sayings. It is also noteworthy that the author speaks only of fastening a sign on the hands but omits mention of anything that is to be "between [or: before] the eyes." It is hard to tell if these divergences from a more direct paraphrase of the Pentateuch might allude to the author's familiarity with any ritual practices akin to mezuzot and tefillin.[35] The insertion of the passage within the larger context of a discussion about the dietary and ritual purity laws, together with its placement immediately adjacent to a reference about the "fringes" commandment, may imply that the author understood the instructions to set up sayings on doors and to bind signs on hands as concrete ritual practices rather than merely as metaphorically couched abstractions. Beyond this general observation, I question whether we may reasonably infer from here any further details about precisely what these practices might have entailed.

If the passage is accepted as referring to a concrete material practice, it would be our earliest surviving textual evidence for tefillin and mezuzah. Although the work itself purports that it was written during the reign of Ptolemy II Philadelphus (ca. 285–246 BCE), most scholars claim a middle to late second-century-BCE date for the work.[36]

SEPTUAGINT

The Septuagint provides mostly unremarkable translations of Exod 13:10, 16; Deut 6:8–9; and Deut 11:18, 20, and is of interest only for its rendering of the enigmatic phrase "as *ṭōṭāfōt* between your eyes." An examination of how the Septuagint translator chose to render this phrase may be instructive for whether a concrete ritual practice might have been understood.

Most textual witnesses to the Septuagint read "and it shall be immoveable before your eyes [*kaì éstai asáleuton prò ophthalmõn sou/humõn*]." This rendering would seem to reveal a metaphorical understanding of the phrase; the divine words are to be a permanent fixture, as it were, always within focus of the mind's eye. However, a textual variant drops the alpha privative in the adjective "immoveable [*asáleuton*]" and instead reads "movable [*saleutón*]."[37] As we saw above, Philo seems to bear witness to this variant, as does the Vulgate translation of the phrase in Deut 6:8: "they will be and they will move between your eyes [*eruntque et movebuntur inter oculos tuos*]." It is hard to know whether the variant "movable" suggests a metaphorical understanding of the commandant or whether perhaps a tangible, dangling object might be meant—a difficulty with which Philo had already struggled. As it is difficult to know which variant might have been the original reading, and as the precise sense of the alternative variant is anyway unclear, it would be unsafe to draw any firm conclusions about whether the Septuagint translator knew anything of a practice similar to tefillin.

HEBREW BIBLE

The Hebrew Bible outside the Pentateuch includes no allusions to any ritual practices akin to tefillin or mezuzah. The closest one gets is Prov 6:20–22, whose author clearly knew of a text resembling, if not identical with, Deut 6:6–8 and Deut 11:18–19: "My child, keep your father's commandment, and do not forsake your mother's instruction. Bind them [*qāšrēm*] on your heart always; fasten them [*āndēm*] on your neck. When you walk, it will lead you; when you lie down, it will watch over you; and when you awake, it will converse with you."[38] The author of this passage is almost certainly speaking figuratively; he is essentially saying that if you have securely internalized the ethical teachings of your parents, binding them on your heart and fastening them on your neck, as it were, you may be assured that their moral instruction will remain with you everywhere and always. What matters for us here is that there is no indication that this author read his source, whether Deuteronomy or some similar text, as instructing any kind of ritual practice akin to tefillin.

Archaeological and Epigraphic Evidence

JUDEAN DESERT FINDS PREDATING THE FIRST CENTURY CE?

Tefillin and "mezuzot" uncovered in the vicinity of Qumran were all found in caves together with other finds whose latest depositional dates are commonly associated with the abandonment of Khirbet Qumran circa 68 CE. Tefillin from caves located elsewhere in the Judean Desert were found together with finds dating to as late as the Bar Kokhba revolt. Although it is certainly possible that some of these artifacts might have been produced earlier than the first century CE, this has yet to be established. None of these remains have been subjected to radiocarbon analysis because of their small dimensions and the destructive nature of the tests. Paleographic analysis of the letter forms on the inscribed slips remains the only method to date the production of these remains, but unfortunately hardly any of the tefillin texts have been subjected to comprehensive paleographic analyses. For now, we may refer only to perfunctory remarks by the original publishers of the finds. While some of the Qumran finds (e.g., 8Q3, XQ1–3) have been assigned first-century-CE paleographic dates, Milik has noted that the semi-cursive forms characteristic of the assemblage closely relate to the cursives of the second and first centuries BCE, which continued without discernible signs of change until the middle of the first century CE.[39] If Milik's assessment is correct, it would *allow*—but certainly not *require*— that some of the tefillin and "mezuzah" slips were prepared as early as the Hasmonean period.

THE NASH PAPYRUS

A text known as the Nash Papyrus, purchased from an Egyptian antiquities dealer who claimed that it was found in the Faiyum, is composed primarily of a harmonized version of the Decalogue (from Exod 20 and Deut 5), to which is appended a Hebrew version of Deut 6:3b, which appears in the Septuagint but is missing from the Masoretic Text, followed by Deut 6:4ff. (the bottom portion of the papyrus is missing).[40] Because its textual content and physical dimensions resemble the Qumran tefillin and "mezuzot," it has been identified by some as either a tefillin slip or a mezuzah.[41] The papyrus has been assigned a paleographic date from the mid-second century BCE until the mid-first century BCE. If both this date and the papyrus's identification as a tefillin or mezuzah are accepted (both are far from certain), the Nash Papyrus would represent one of the earliest artifacts representing either of the two practices.

EVIDENCE PREDATING THE SECOND CENTURY BCE

No artifactual remains predating the second century BCE have been reasonably associated with tefillin or mezuzah practices. Although some scholars have attempted to identify possible precursors to both rituals in various amuletic practices found in the Near East during the Iron Age, the correlations are quite tenuous.[42] Perhaps the closest we get are two silver plaques found at Ketef Hinnom which contain apotropaic formulae resembling the priestly blessing found in Num 6:24–26.[43] But aside from their being small objects inscribed with words resembling what came to be a Pentateuchal text and which may (or may not!) have been worn on the body, there seems little reason to regard these singular artifacts as early evidence of any sort of common Judean ritual observance akin to either tefillin or mezuzah.

Conclusions

The present chapter opened with a survey of the evidence demonstrating that tefillin and mezuzah existed as Judean ritual practices in the first century CE. Although it is difficult to know how widespread these practices were, it was shown that the tefillin remains from the Judean Desert provide invaluable data concerning the details of the practice, data that may be "reverse engineered" to reveal the exegetical pathways taken in the development of the ritual. The fact that different types of tefillin were found among the caves suggests that Judean legal experts were actively debating the minutiae of the ritual, an insight that contributes to our understanding of how Torah as a legal system was developing at this time. Texts and archaeological remains pointing to tefillin or mezuzah observance prior to the first century CE are rather less certain, and in any event these date to no earlier than the second century BCE. No evidence for the observance of any practice resembling either tefillin or mezuzah is available from any time before the middle of the second century BCE.

5 Miscellaneous Practices

Unlike the previous chapters, which focused on a single category of practices or prohibitions, the present chapter will examine successively six distinct practices that (as will be shown) characterized Judaism in the first century CE: (1) circumcision, (2) the Sabbath prohibitions, (3) the Passover sacrifice and the Festival of Unleavened Bread, (4) fasting on the Day of Atonement, (5) the two central rituals of the Sukkot festival (residing in booths and taking the "four species"), and (6) having a continually lit seven-branched menorah in the Jerusalem temple. In each case we will begin by examining evidence for the practice or prohibition in the first century CE and continue by seeking the earliest available evidence prior to the turn of the first millennium.

Circumcision

First-Century Evidence

Circumcision appears in the Pentateuch as one of the few commandments whose origins are said to predate the events at Sinai, having been ordained already to Abraham as God's "covenant" (bərît) to be kept by Abraham's offspring "throughout their generations."[1] The Pentateuchal instruction is quite straightforward: every eight-day-old male is to be circumcised, along with "the slave born in your house and the one bought with your money from any foreigner who is not of your offspring." The threat of punishment for those who do not comply is severe: "Any uncircumcised male who is not circumcised in the flesh of his foreskin shall be cut off from his people; he has broken my covenant." Not only are infants and purchased slaves (and *their* infants) to be circumcised, but also the "*gēr*" (often rendered as "resident alien") must circumcise himself and all the males of his household if he wishes to partake of the Passover sacrifice.[2]

In the writings of first-century-CE writers, Judeans and non-Judeans alike, the Judean practice of male circumcision was one of the primary identity markers of a Judean.[3] For first-century Judeans, however, the practice of circumcising every eight-day-old male child was much *more* than just a cultural or ethnic identity marker—the act was a fulfilment of a divine *commandment* enshrined in Torah law. Philo, for example, wrote of "the law laid down for circumcising [*tòn epì tȇ̄ peritomȇ̄ tethénta nómon*]," referred to circumcision as a "commandment of the law" ordained by "the Divine legislator," and spoke of Isaac as "the first of our nation who was circumcised by law."[4] For Paul, circumcision was a central component of the Judean "law" (*nómos*) that he insisted was not to be applied to Gentiles.[5] The author of Acts spoke of the practice of circumcision as being "according to the custom of Moses [*tȇ̄ éthei tȇ̄ Mōüséōs*]" and cited a current rumor about Paul that he was teaching the Judeans living among the Gentiles "apostasy from Moses [*apostasían . . . apò Mōüséōs*] and not to circumcise their children or observe the customs [*mēdè toîs éthesin peripateîn*]."[6] The author of the Gospel of John has Jesus tell a crowd in the temple, "Moses gave you circumcision [*Mōüsȇ̄s dédōken humîn tèn peritomḗn*]," and that this circumcision is to be performed even on the Sabbath "in order that the law of Moses may not be broken [*hína mè luthȇ̄ ho nómos Mōüséōs*]."[7] And finally, Josephus recounted that King Izates of Adiabene had adopted the Judean way of life except for circumcision and was consequently admonished by a Galilean Judean named Eleazar, who was known for being exacting in the ancestral laws: "In your ignorance, O king, you are guilty of the greatest offence against the law and thereby against God [*tà mégista toùs nómous kaì di' autōn tòn theòn adikōn*]. For you ought not merely to read the law but also, and even more, to do what is commanded in it. How long will you continue to be uncircumcised? If you have not yet read the law concerning this matter, read it now, so that you may know what an impiety it is that you commit."[8]

The upshot of all this is that, for first-century-CE Judeans, circumcision was first and foremost a *commandment of the Torah*, and one whose abrogation was regarded as a most serious *legal* infraction. While the Judeans were not the only group to practice circumcision—Egyptians, Arabs, and Ethiopians were also said to do so around this time—Judeans were certainly unique in that they were the only ones known to have practiced circumcision out of deference to a statutory law.[9]

Early Evidence

The mid-first-century-BCE author Diodorus Siculus is the first non-Judean writer to provide an unambiguous reference to the Judean practice of circumcision.[10] Earlier yet, Judean sources tell of the practice taking place in the second century BCE; Josephus relates that when Hyrcanus I conquered the Idumeans and when Aristobulus I conquered the Itureans, both of these Hasmonean rulers forced the conquered peoples to be circumcised and henceforth live in accordance with "the laws of the Judeans."[11]

Turning now to texts widely thought to have been composed in the Hasmonean period, Jubilees described circumcision in starkly legal terms.[12] Also probably from this period, a Judean writer named Theodotus (some think he was Samaritan) cited the story in Gen 34 about the circumcision of the men of Shechem, describing the rite as mandated by divine law: "The command remains unshaken, since God himself spoke it [*astemphès dè tétuktai, epeì theòs autòs éeipe*]."[13] From these texts alone, it is difficult to know how widespread such notions may have been at the time. On the other hand, circumcision as a quintessential practice of Judean law followed by the masses features prominently in the narratives surrounding the reign of Antiochus IV Epiphanes in both 1 and 2 Maccabees. The author of 1 Maccabees tells of "renegade" Judeans who, in the early days of Antiochus's reign, built a gymnasium in Jerusalem "according to Gentile custom," undid their circumcision (literally: "they made foreskins for themselves [*epoíēsan heautoîs akrobustías*]," and "abandoned the holy covenant [*apéstēsan apò diathēkēs hagías*]").[14] When Antiochus later made his decrees, a death penalty was declared upon "anyone who adhered to the law [*eí tis suneudókei tǭ nómǭ*]," including prominently "the women who had their children circumcised, and their families and those who circumcised them."[15] After the Maccabean rebellion broke out, Mattathias and his companions "forcibly circumcised all the uncircumcised boys that they found within the borders of Israel," and thereby "rescued the law [*antelábonto toû nómou*] out of the hands of the Gentiles and kings."[16] Similarly, when the author of 2 Maccabees narrated about the king's decrees "to compel the Judeans to forsake the laws of their ancestors [*tôn patríōn nómōn*] and not to live by the laws of God [*toîs toû theoû nómois mè politeúesthai*]," he presented as a prime anecdotal example a story about two women who were punished with death for having their infants circumcised.[17]

The Antiochene decrees against circumcision described in 1 and 2 Maccabees may be alluded to already in Dan 11, where it is foretold that the "king of the north" "will be enraged against the holy covenant [bərît qôdeš] and take action."[18] While some Judeans at this time are regarded as "the people who are loyal to their God [ʿam yōdəʿê ʾelōhāyw]," others are described disparagingly as "those who forsake the holy covenant" [ʿōzvê bərît qôdeš]" or "those who violate the covenant [maršîʿê bərît]."[19] Although set in the Persian period, this text is widely thought to allude to the reign of Antiochus IV and to have been written between 167 and 164 BCE.[20] If "the holy covenant" in fact refers to circumcision, we would have an indication that the practice was at least somewhat common by this time—otherwise it would be difficult to understand a Seleucid king "raging" against the practice. Alternatively, however, Sylvie Honigman has suggested that the phrase may be referring to "the components of the divine covenant, namely the people and the temple."[21]

Closer to the beginning of the second century BCE, Ben Sira wrote about the patriarch Abraham: "He kept the commandment of the Most High [šāmar miṣwat ʿelyôn], and entered into a covenant with him; in his flesh he incised a statute [bivśārô kārat lô ḥōq]."[22] While clearly envisioning circumcision as required by "law," we do not know how widespread the notion might have been among the Judean populace at large at this time.

Prior to the second century BCE, I know of no evidence—outside the Pentateuch—for the notion of circumcision as fulfillment of a divine commandment, as in any way legally mandated, or otherwise as associated with any framework of law. That early Israelites were generally thought to be circumcised we learn tacitly from numerous passages in the Hebrew Bible that disparagingly refer to Philistines as "the uncircumcised," thereby implying that Israelites were conversely imagined to usually be circumcised.[23] There is no indication, however, that any of the biblical writers harbored a notion that Israelites were the *only* group to regularly practice circumcision; as a matter of fact, the practice appears to have been common concurrently among other West Semitic groups as well as among Egyptians.[24] And outside the Pentateuch, there is no indication that any of the biblical authors entertained any ideas as to *why* Israelites practiced the procedure. While scholarly theories abound as to when, where, and why the practice of circumcision might have first arisen, there is no evidence that any of the groups that practiced it—including the Israelites—ever viewed circumcision as somehow commanded by force of any sort of law. It appears that much like the taboo against the consumption of the "hip sinew" (*gîd hanāšeh*) discussed in chapter 1, circumcision was an early cultural practice whose origins are lost in the mists of time, and which may well predate the formation of any kind of distinctly "Israelite" identity. And like the "hip sinew" taboo, this primordial West Semitic practice eventually came to be taken up into Pentateuchal legislation—and only some time thereafter came to be adopted by Judeans as a salient component of Torah law.

Sabbath Prohibitions

First-Century Evidence

The Pentateuch prohibits "all manner of work" (*kōl məlākhāh*) on the seventh day of the week—the "Sabbath" (*šabāt*)—but provides only incidental examples of forbidden work: plowing, reaping, kindling fire, gathering wood, and leaving one's "place."[25] In the writings of first-century-CE authors, Judean and non-Judean alike, observance of the Sabbath prohibitions had become one of the hallmarks of the Judean way of life among Judean communities throughout the Mediterranean world. Contemporary Judean writers contended with questions regarding the boundaries of exactly what qualified as "work" that was prohibited on the Sabbath, and under what extenuating circumstances might normally prohibited "work" be permitted.

Philo, as may be expected, expounded at great length on the symbolic and ethical values manifest in the idea of Sabbath rest.[26] Simultaneously, he also unambiguously advocated the actual, practical compliance with the "laws laid down [*tà . . . nomothetēthénta*]" for the Sabbath, taking issue with certain individuals who emphasized only the allegorical meaning of the Sabbath while treating the practical observance of its laws "with easy-going neglect," "handling the matter in too easy and off-hand a manner."[27] As concrete examples of activities conventionally regarded as prohibited on the Sabbath, Philo cited lighting fires, tilling the ground, carrying loads, instituting court proceedings, acting as jurors, demanding the restoration of deposits, and recovering loans. From his presentation of the matter, one gains the impression that most Judeans did not fall in with the extreme allegorists against whom Philo polemicized. To the contrary, elsewhere he presents Judean adherence to the Sabbath laws as so widespread that even

Augustus paid deference to Judean practice by ordering that the Judeans' portion out of the monthly doles of money and corn to the people of Rome was to be reserved until Sunday if the dole happened to fall out on a Saturday, "when no one is permitted to receive or give anything or to transact any part of the business of ordinary life, particularly of a lucrative kind."[28] Philo furthermore told a story about a governor of Egypt in his time who tried to compel the Egyptian Judeans to do work for him on Sabbaths, "thinking that if he could destroy the ancestral rule of the Sabbath it would lead the way to irregularity in all other matters, and a general backsliding." The attempt met with widespread resistance, according to Philo, as those pressured to break the Sabbath refused "and that the rest of the population instead of taking the matter calmly were intensely indignant and shewed themselves as mournful and disconsolate as they would were their native city being sacked and razed, and its citizens being sold into captivity."[29]

The parameters of certain aspects of the Sabbath prohibitions are explored in numerous stories spread throughout the New Testament Gospels. Jesus is said to have permitted the healing of the sick on the Sabbath, against his interlocutors who prohibited it.[30] In one anecdote, Jesus is said to have defended his followers who on the Sabbath plucked grain in a field, again in opposition to his interlocutors who opposed the act.[31] In another story, Jesus allows a man to carry a mat in a public space on the Sabbath, while other Judeans are said to have deemed the act forbidden.[32] On the other hand, Jesus is said to have taken for granted that certain actions would have been permitted by all Judeans even on the Sabbath: the cultic activities of the priests in the temple, the untying of an animal in order to give it water, the rescuing of a child or a domestic animal from a pit, and the performance of circumcision.[33] Following his crucifixion, which is said to have taken place on a Friday, Jesus's followers who tended to his body are reported to have taken care of all necessary arrangements either prior to the onset of the Sabbath or else after the Sabbath ended, while "on the Sabbath they rested according to the commandment."[34]

The prohibition against engaging in work on the Sabbath is cited on numerous occasions throughout the works of Josephus, especially as this prohibition affected warfare and other martial activities.[35] Josephus's portrayal of the problem of Sabbath warfare is somewhat complex: while he claimed that it is permitted to break the Sabbath in order to fight "whenever it becomes necessary [ei pote deēseien]," the boundaries of what precisely "necessity" entailed was something that Josephus grappled with time and again in various ways.[36] For Josephus, this was no theoretical matter; as commander of the Galilean front at the start of the Great Revolt, he surely would have regularly been forced to decide precisely what kinds of military activities he could permit his men on the Sabbath. (See below for Josephus's depictions of Judean views on dispensations for Sabbath combat *prior* to the first century CE). Aside from discussing the permissibility of waging war on the Sabbath, Josephus also mentioned that it is forbidden for Judeans "to travel" (*hodeúein/hodoiporeîn*) on the Sabbath.[37] Josephus also told of a legal debate surrounding the Sabbath laws—the only one of its kind that he cites—between members of the Essene sect and other Judeans: "[The Essenes] are stricter than all Judeans [*Ioudaíōn hapántōn*] in abstaining from work on the seventh day; for not only do they prepare their food on the day before, to avoid kindling a fire on that one, but they do not venture to remove any vessel or even to go to stool."[38] Josephus related that at the corner of the temple enclosure opposite the Lower City of Jerusalem was a place where "it was the custom for one of the priests to stand and to give notice, by sound of trumpet, in the afternoon of the approach, and on the following evening of the close, of every seventh day, announcing to the people the respective hours for ceasing work and for resuming their labors."[39] Finally, as we have already cited in chapter 1, Josephus went so far as to claim that all throughout the Roman world one could find non-Judeans who had adopted many of the Judean ritual practices—including abstention from work on the Sabbath: "The masses have long since shown a keen desire to adopt our pious observances; and there is not one city, Greek or barbarian, nor a single nation, to which our custom of abstaining from work on the seventh day has not spread."[40]

Several non-Judean authors writing in the first century cited Judean abstinence from work on their "Sabbath," but often in less than complimentary terms.[41] The fact that the Sabbath prohibitions are cited in the works of non-Judean authors broadly substantiates the picture drawn from the Judean sources and points to the remarkably widespread scope of the practice.

A recent study has investigated Sabbath observance among the small Judean community at Edfu in the south of Egypt on the basis of ostraca containing tax records dating to the reigns of Vespasian until Trajan (69–117 CE).[42] The study showed that while regular taxes were often collected from Judeans on Sabbaths, the special "Judean tax" (*fiscus Iudaicus*) imposed after the Great Revolt was almost never collected on a Sabbath. The authors of the study hypothesized that the regular taxes were collected by non-Judeans, whereas the special Judean tax was collected by the Judeans themselves, and these refrained from doing so on Sabbaths.

Early Evidence

An abundant amount of surviving evidence from the first and second centuries BCE indicates not only that the Sabbath prohibitions were widely observed throughout the Judean world but also that the precise contours of the Sabbath laws were being debated at this time by various individuals and groups.

From the first century BCE, Josephus cited several letters and decrees that he claims were promulgated by Roman officials directing cities around the Mediterranean basin to allow the local Judean communities the freedom to observe their Sabbath laws.[43] Specific activities cited as forbidden on the Sabbath include giving bond (i.e., appearance in court), bearing arms, and marching. Josephus also recounted that when Pompey attacked Jerusalem (in 63 BCE), the Roman general took advantage of the Sabbath in order to raise earthworks against the walls of the city: "for on the Sabbaths the Judeans fight only in self-defense"; "the Law permits us to defend ourselves against those who begin a battle and strike us, but it does not allow us to fight against an enemy that does anything else."[44]

The Sabbath prohibitions feature not infrequently in numerous works whose composition is generally thought to date to the last two centuries BCE. Jubilees cites specific prohibited actions, including bringing in and taking out items from one house to another; preparing food and drink; drawing water; riding an animal or traveling by ship; catching animals, birds, or fish; slaughtering animals or birds; waging war; engaging in sexual intercourse; and even just speaking about work.[45] Even more detailed treatments of Sabbath prohibitions feature in the Damascus Document, where the following are forbidden (already from the time on Friday afternoon when the setting sun has reached a certain point in the sky): speaking disgraceful and empty words; demanding payment from a neighbor; engaging in legal proceedings for financial gain; speaking about work to be done the following day; walking in a field "to do one's work"; walking a thousand cubits outside one's town; eating food that had not been prepared or that was not in "the camp" prior to Sabbath; drawing water in a vessel while on the way down to bathe; sending a Gentile to attend to one's business; wearing soiled or lint-filled(?) clothing; willfully intermingling (pure things with impure?); grazing an animal more than two thousand cubits outside one's town; raising a hand to strike one's animal; driving a wayward animal out from one's home; carrying things into or out of a house or a booth; opening a sealed vessel; carrying spices on one's person into and out from (a house?); picking up a stone or dirt inside a dwelling; (for a nurse) carrying an infant into and out from (a house?); provoking(?) one's servant or hired laborer; birthing an animal; raising an animal out of a pit it has fallen into; staying the Sabbath near Gentiles; desecrating the Sabbath for financial gain; using a ladder, rope, or other utensil to save a person who has fallen into water; and offering any sacrifices on the altar aside from the Sabbath burnt offering.[46] Fragments of other compositions found at Qumran include some of these restrictions along with additional prohibitions, such as studying and reading in a book and (for a priest) sprinkling purification water.[47]

The Judean author Aristobulus, writing perhaps in the mid-second century BCE, referred to the seventh day as a day of rest commanded by God in the Judean code of law: "And the legislation has shown plainly that the seventh day is legally binding [*énnomon*] for us as a sign of the sevenfold principle which is established around us, by which we have knowledge of human and divine matters."[48]

The Sabbath prohibitions feature also in narratives found in both 1 and 2 Maccabees. The author of 1 Maccabees tells of a group of pious Judeans who, when attacked on the Sabbath by a Seleucid military contingent during the persecutions of Antiochus IV, refused to profane the Sabbath by engaging in self-defensive combat and were killed as a result.[49] When the rebels under Mattathias heard of this, they concluded that abstention from self-defensive warfare on the Sabbath is simply unsustainable: "'If we all do as our kindred have done and refuse to fight with the Gentiles for our lives and for our ordinances, they will quickly destroy us from the earth.' So they made this decision that day: 'Let us fight against anyone who comes to attack us on the Sabbath day; let us not all die as our kindred died in their hiding places.'"[50] Later, when Mattathias's son Jonathan and his men were attacked by the Seleucid general Bacchides on a Sabbath, the Judean leader ordered his men to fight for their self-preservation.[51] What appears striking in both of these narratives is that the exemption to engage in self-defensive warfare on the Sabbath is presented as a novel innovation of the Hasmonean rebels; apparently Judeans had no trouble getting along (and indeed surviving) prior to the middle of the second century BCE without worrying about their enemies taking advantage of Saturdays as ideal times to attack the Sabbath-observing Judeans![52] The author of 2 Maccabees tells a similar story about certain Judeans who attempted to evade the Seleucid persecutions in caves in order to observe the Sabbath in secret, but were discovered and subsequently burned alive "because their piety kept them from defending themselves, in view of their regard for that most holy day."[53] Unlike the author of 1 Maccabees, however, the author of 2 Maccabees appears to have been entirely unaware of (or else was tacitly opposed to) a Hasmonean dispensation for self-defensive fighting on the Sabbath.[54]

The earliest non-Judean author who is said to have mentioned the Judean observance of Sabbath is the mid-second-century-BCE Agatharchides of Cnidus, as cited by Josephus: "The people known as Judeans . . . have a custom of abstaining from work every seventh day; on those occasions they neither bear arms nor take any agricultural operations in hand, nor engage in any other form of public service, but pray with outstretched hands in the temples until the evening."[55] Thereafter the Judean observance of Sabbath prohibitions becomes a common trope among Greek and Latin authors writing in the first century BCE onward.[56]

A somewhat enigmatic reference to the Sabbath appears among the Zenon papyri, in a document thought to date to around the time of Ptolemy II Philadelphus in the middle of the third century BCE. The papyrus contains an account of bricks received by the unnamed writer of the document, which were delivered to him by a certain Phileas, a certain Demetrios, and unknown persons from Tanis. The account provides the number of bricks delivered from the fifth to the eleventh of the Egyptian month of Epeiph (no year is cited), but on the seventh of the month—instead of writing a sum of bricks—the author of the account wrote only "*Sábbata*" (Sabbath).[57] It seems that either the one who delivered the bricks, the one who received the bricks, or else the bricklayers for whom the bricks were intended took vacation from work on "Sabbaths." Whether or not those involved (presumably Judeans) would have regarded work on the Sabbath to have been *forbidden* by dint of something like Torah law is difficult to know from this singular document.[58] Possibly, the term refers to a traditional Judean holiday, weekly or otherwise, when Judean workers would have taken a break from their normal labors as others would have on their customary holidays.

The only surviving account that relates to widespread Judean observance of concrete Sabbath prohibitions prior to the second century BCE is found in the continuation of Josephus's quotation from Agatharchides, where the pagan author claims that Ptolemy I Soter succeeded in capturing Jerusalem in the late fourth century BCE because the Judeans refused to engage in combat on their day of rest: "Consequently, because the inhabitants, instead of protecting their city, persevered in their folly, Ptolemy, son of Lagus, was allowed to enter with his army; the country was thus given over to a cruel master, and the defect of a practice enjoined by law was exposed. That experience has taught the whole world, except that nation, the lesson not to resort to dreams and traditional fancies about the law, until its difficulties are such as to baffle human reason."[59] If we were to rely on Agatharchides, we should deduce that strict adherence to the prohibition against fighting on the Sabbath was in place even before the start of Ptolemaic control over Judea in the late fourth century BCE. Ben Zion Wacholder and others, however, have suggested that Agatharchides's report may be wholly unhistorical and inspired by events known to him from the clash between Antiochus IV and the Hasmoneans.[60] Agatharchides wrote his composition around the middle of the second century BCE—at precisely the time when massacres of Judeans who refused to fight on the Sabbath were said to have taken place—and it would not be at all surprising if a story about the fall of Jerusalem 150 years prior was reinterpreted anachronistically by a Greek writer in light of currently circulating anecdotes about contemporary Judean practices.

It is remarkable that, outside the Pentateuch, the Hebrew Bible contains no narratives at all about Judeans or Israelites who abstained from this or that activity in deference to a prohibition against engaging in "work" on the Sabbath. The majority of passages that refer to the Sabbath do not even seem to know anything at all of a notion that certain activities are prohibited on the Sabbath, and display no indication that Sabbath is something that requires "guarding" or that it can be "profaned."[61] A common explanation for this is that the entire notion of Sabbath prohibitions is a late innovation that post-dates the Babylonian exile. It is posited that prior to this the "Sabbath" (šabāt) was regarded as an essentially cultic institution, characterized by its own special sacrificial rites, with some scholars even questioning whether this holy day would have been commemorated on a regular, weekly basis.[62]

Even once we first encounter the notion of Sabbath prohibitions in a relatively small number of late texts, we still find no evidence that the prohibitions were actually put into practice by any population of Judeans or even that the very notion was widely known and circulating in any way. To the contrary, the three passages outside the Pentateuch that refer explicitly to Sabbath prohibitions are all presented against a backdrop where the general populace is in fact said *not* to be observing these prohibitions. One passage is Neh 10:32, where Judean dignitaries are said to invoke "a curse and an oath" in ratifying a pledge that includes the following clause: "And if the peoples of the land bring in merchandise or any grain on the Sabbath day to sell, we will not buy it from them on the Sabbath or on a holy day." That the people were regularly engaging in commerce and agricultural work on the Sabbath is even more evident in Neh 13:15–22, where the narrator (i.e., Nehemiah) recounts how he had discovered Judeans "treading wine presses on the Sabbath and bringing in heaps [of grain] and loading them on donkeys; and also wine, grapes, figs, and all kinds of burdens, which they brought into Jerusalem on the Sabbath day," and how certain Tyrians who lived in Jerusalem "brought in fish and all kinds of merchandise and sold them on the Sabbath" to the Judeans. Nehemiah responded to this "profaning" (*məḥaləlîm*) of the Sabbath by warning the people how such behavior brought evil to the city in the past and would serve only to increase divine wrath upon Israel in the present. He consequently is said to have had the gates of the city shut every Sabbath to prevent entry of the merchants, and from that time onward the peddlers stopped coming.[63] The third passage is Jer 17:19–27, where the prophet cites YHWH's instruction to him to stand in the gates of Jerusalem to admonish the kings of Judah and all the people not to "bear a burden on the Sabbath day, bringing it in by the gates of Jerusalem," and not to "carry a burden out of your houses on the Sabbath or do any work [*kōl məlā'khāh*]." The prophet then reveals that the people ignored his call: "And they did not listen or incline their ear; they stiffened their necks and would not hear or receive reproof." This is followed by a promise of reward (a prosperous Davidic monarchy together with thriving cultic worship in YHWH's temple) should the listeners heed the admonition, and a threat of punishment (the palaces of Jerusalem will be incinerated with an unquenchable fire) should the warning be ignored.[64] The authors of all three passages appear to have been quite cognizant of a reality in which Judeans *were in fact* engaging in commerce on the Sabbath, behavior that they could hope to stop only by invoking cataclysmic threats.

It is unclear if the passages in Ezekiel that decry those who "profaned my Sabbaths [*šabtôtay ḥiləlû*)]" and "disregarded my Sabbaths [*mišabtôtay he'lîmû*]" had in mind engagement in certain prohibited activities, or if instead they meant to denounce neglect of the cultic sphere.[65] A similar problem obtains in Isa 56, where various forms of prosperity are promised for all those who "guard the Sabbath from profaning it," including eunuchs and foreigners who "join themselves to YHWH."[66] Even more cryptic is the notion of the Sabbath in Isa 58:13, where blessings are promised for one who "honors" the Sabbath to wit: "If you refrain from [trampling?] the Sabbath [under?] your foot, from pursuing your own interests on my holy day; if you call the Sabbath a delight and the holy [day] of YHWH honorable; if you honor it by not going your own ways, serving your own interests, or speaking about a [self-serving?] matter." Whatever the precise intention of all these texts, it seems clear that in each case the author is decrying rampant "profanation," or at least disrespect, of his own idea of the Sabbath, and the objective of the author is to counter such behavior.

Anecdotal support for the notion that Persian-period Judeans were regularly engaging in commerce on the Sabbath may be adduced from a Judean ostracon from Elephantine that mentions a delivery of goods on the Sabbath: "Greetings Islaḥ! And now, I am sending you vegetables tomorrow. Meet the boat tomorrow on Sabbath [bəšabāh] lest they get lost/spoiled. By the life of YHH! If not, I shall take your lif[e]! Do not rely upon Meshullemeth or upon Shemaiah. Now send me barley in return.... By the life of YHH! If not, you will be responsible for the [bi]ll."[67]

Sacha Stern has pointed out that three Elephantine documents from the middle of the fifth century BCE and one from the end of this century, all written for (and mostly by) Judeans, were signed on dates that are reckoned as having fallen on Saturdays.[68] Yigal Bloch has adduced further anecdotal evidence of this sort from the documents associated with Judeans living in Babylonia in the sixth and fifth centuries BCE.[69] If signing on legal contracts would have fallen under the sort of commerce regarded as forbidden by the authors of the late biblical passages cited above (which is questionable), we would then have further evidence from fifth-century-BCE Elephantine and from sixth- to fifth-century Babylonia that Judeans were not observing a prohibition of this kind at this early date.

Recently, Ilaria Bultrighini and Sacha Stern have compellingly argued that—outside the Pentateuch and Ezek 46:1—the earliest surviving attestations of the seven-day week itself date to the late second century BCE, in calendrical and liturgical texts from Qumran and in the Septuagint version of Psalms.[70] They stressed that prior to the second century we lack any evidence that the seven-day week was ever used as a unit for reckoning time, whether among Judeans or among any other groups. Events in the Hebrew Bible are dated according to the day of the month and/or a specified year, but never according to the day of the week. Similarly, documents from Elephantine are often dated precisely according to the Babylonian or Egyptian calendars, but never according to days of the week. [71]

The upshot of this entire investigation is that, starting at the earliest in the mid-second century BCE, a plethora of evidence begins to emerge attesting to the Sabbath prohibitions being widely (if not universally) observed by Judeans in Judea and throughout the Mediterranean world. Prior to this time, there is simply no reliable evidence that the notion of certain activities being forbidden on the Sabbath was widely observed—or even commonly known of—among the Judean masses. Until the second century, there is even little reason to suppose that time was ever reckoned according to a seven-day week, whether among Judeans or anyone else. While the word "Sabbath" is found among a small number of earlier epigraphic remains (in a papyrus from the Zenon archive and in ostraca from Elephantine), the term here may simply refer to a Judean holiday of some sort; how and at what frequency such a holiday might have been marked are matters that remain essentially unknown. While the authors of certain late biblical texts clearly advocated observance of Sabbath *prohibitions* (weekly or otherwise), their own writings together with anecdotal evidence from Elephantine and Babylonia suggest that the masses were not heeding their call. In fact, there is little reason to suspect that the general populace was even aware that anybody was sounding such a call in the first place. [72]

Passover and the Festival of Unleavened Bread

First-Century Evidence

In Exod 12 we find YHWH instructing Moses and Aaron on the eve of the exodus from Egypt to direct Israel to set aside a year-old male lamb or kid on the tenth day of the first month, to slaughter it on the fourteenth day, to place part of the animal's blood on the lintel and doorposts of the houses where the meat of the animal is to be consumed, and then at night to eat the roasted meat together with "unleavened breads" (*maṣôt*) and "bitter herbs" (*mərôrîm*). [73] YHWH further instructs that this rite of the "Passover sacrifice" (*zevaḥ pesaḥ*) is to be practiced in every generation "as an ordinance" (*ləḥāq*) for all time. Extraordinarily detailed instructions are given as to when the animal should be taken and by whom, when it should be slaughtered, precisely how the blood is to be placed on the doorways, precisely how the meat should (and should not) be prepared, how it is to be handled (it is not to be removed from the house), precisely who should (and who should not) eat of the meat, precisely in what manner it should be eaten, and what should be done with the leftovers. Less extensive instructions are given again elsewhere in the Pentateuch, with some additional instructions added: Num 9:1–14 adds a dispensation for those who were impure or "on a distant journey" to prepare the sacrifice one month later, and Deut 16:1–2, 5–7 stipulates that the Passover must be slaughtered only at "the place that YHWH your God will choose to cause his name to dwell there" and not "within any one of your gates that YHWH your God is giving you."[74] Associated with the Passover sacrifice, and also said to commemorate the exodus from Egypt, is a seven-day holiday called the Festival of Unleavened Bread (*ḥag hamaṣôt*) from the fifteenth to the twenty-first day of the first month.[75] During this holiday, "leaven" (*śə'ōr*) and "leavened bread" (*ḥāmēṣ*) may not be eaten or even be found in the home, and instead unleavened bread is to be eaten. The first and last days of the holiday are to be "a holy convocation" (*miqra' qōdeš*) when no work is to be done. Numbers 28:19–24 adds detailed instructions about special sacrifices and libations that are to be offered on all seven days of the festival.

A plethora of literary evidence attests that both the Passover sacrifice and the Festival of Unleavened Bread were practiced by first-century-CE Judeans on an impressively widespread scale. Philo, apparently reporting on the manner whereby the Passover was practiced in his own day, wrote that "many myriads" of sacrifices are offered from noon until the evening, with "the whole people [*ho leòs hápas*]" / "the whole nation [*súmpan tò éthnos*]," young and old alike, taking the place of the priests in conducting the rite.[76] Philo then describes how "every dwelling-house is invested with the outward semblance and dignity of a temple," and how the guests—following purification—assemble for the banquet "to fulfil with prayers and hymns the custom handed down by their fathers [*pátrion éthos*]."[77] Rather than simply paraphrasing the Pentateuchal prescriptions, Philo appears to be describing contemporary practices with which he was intimately familiar. While it may be possible that the practices Philo depicts here were those current at Jerusalem, some have suggested instead that Philo was describing practices he knew from Alexandria.[78]

That massive numbers of Judeans participated in the Passover rites is apparent from the story Josephus told of the population census taken in his own time at the behest of Cestius Gallus, legate of Syria in the mid-60s CE.[79] In order to assess the population of Jerusalem, the priests counted the number of animals slaughtered for the Passover sacrifice on a single occasion, and the sum amounted to 255,600 animals. Josephus further explained that "a little fraternity, as it were, gathers round each sacrifice, of not fewer than ten persons (feasting alone not being permitted), while the companies often include as many as twenty"—bringing the sum total of those participating in the sacrificial feast that year to over two and a half million! Josephus noted that the estimated number of participants he provided includes a large number of Judeans who "assemble from abroad," and that non-Judeans and Judeans who were impure and hence could not participate in the sacrifice are excluded from the count. Even if we discount the numbers Josephus furnished here as grossly exaggerated, his account still provides compelling support to Philo's report of "many myriads" of animals slaughtered for the Passover sacrifice every year, and creates an impressive picture of extremely widespread Judean observance of the rite in the middle of the first century CE. This is only one of several accounts provided by Josephus that feature first-century-CE events occurring on Passover feasts and which tell of untold numbers of Judean throngs assembling in Jerusalem in honor of both the Passover sacrifice and the subsequent Festival of Unleavened Bread.[80] In another story meant to highlight the degree to which the Judeans adhere to their laws, Josephus tells that shortly before the war a very large quantity of "flour" (áleuron) was brought to Jerusalem during the Festival of Unleavened Bread to relieve the people during a dire famine, but that—apparently since it was regarded as forbidden "leavened"—not one of the priests ventured to consume a crumb "from fear of the law and of the wrath wherewith the Deity ever regards even crimes which elude detection."[81]

While Josephus painted a panoramic vista that depicted millions of Judeans gathered in small groups of ten to twenty to sacrifice and consume hundreds of thousands of Passover offerings, the Synoptic Gospels home in on how one such group—Jesus and his twelve disciples—prepared and reclined to eat their own individual Passover sacrifice at a festive meal.[82] According to this account, the Passover itself was accompanied with "bread" (unleavened bread is not stipulated but may be implied), and Mark (followed by Matthew but not Luke) describes a hymn being sung at the end of the banquet.[83] In all versions of this account, it seems implicit that observance of the Passover was a ubiquitous practice among contemporary

Judeans. The widespread observance of Passover and the Festival of Un-leavened Bread is also implied elsewhere in the Gospel accounts and in Acts, where both feasts appear as quite prominent time markers within the Judean calendar.[84] The pervasive character of the practices associated with both feasts may also explain how Paul was able to effortlessly exploit one of the salient regulations connected with these feasts—the prohibition against leaven—for his own allegorical purposes: "Your boasting is not a good thing. Do you not know that a little leaven leavens the whole batch of dough? Clean out the old leaven so that you may be a new batch, as you really are unleavened. For the anointed, our Passover, has been sacrificed. Therefore, let us celebrate the festival, not with the old leaven, the leaven of malice and evil, but with the unleavened bread of sincerity and truth."[85]

That these laws were known by non-Judeans even outside the commu-nity of Paul's Christ-following addressees we learn from the slightly later Tacitus, who, in describing the expulsion of the Judeans' ancestors from Egypt, mentioned as an aside that "the unleavened Judean bread is still employed in memory of the haste with which they seized the grain."[86]

Early Evidence

Josephus related an incident that is said to have occurred in 4 BCE at Passover and the Festival of Unleavened Bread, when "a vast crowd" of Ju-deans assembled at Jerusalem to offer "a multitude of sacrifices."[87] From the days of Hasmonean rule, the only Passover-related incident conveyed by Josephus is set at the time when Aristobulus II was besieged in the temple by Hyrcanus II and when, we are told, the besieged lacked the requisite animals for sacrifices and were tricked by the besiegers into paying an ex-orbitant price for animals that in the end were never supplied.[88] Josephus writes that the incident took place at Passover, "at which it is our custom to offer numerous sacrifices to God," but this description cannot be taken as a reliable portrayal of practices in the mid-first century BCE—and in any event it is possible that he meant festal sacrifices other than the Passover offering itself.

While some compositions widely thought to have been written during the Hasmonean period engage with various details relating to the laws of Passover and Unleavened Bread, it is hard to gain a sense from these texts of how widespread the observance of these practices might have been at this time.[89] On the other hand, some legal texts do provide important evidence for the way Judean exegetes in the second and first centuries BCE were actively interacting with the Pentateuchal laws in order to derive detailed rulings on these matters not explicit in the foundational text of the Pentateuch itself. Jubilees, for example, specifies that the Passover must be slaughtered in the last third of the day on the fourteenth of the month and then eaten in the first third of the night of the fifteenth.[90] Jubilees also specifies that the animal must not only be slaughtered but also be *eaten* "in the sanctuary of your God before the Lord," a regulation that is found in the Temple Scroll as well.[91] Both Jubilees and the Temple Scroll allow the sacrifice to be eaten only by those twenty years and older, a requirement that may find expression also in another Qumran fragment.[92] This latter fragment specifically excludes women from eating the Passover, and this restriction may also be implied in Jubilees and in the Temple Scroll.[93]

Prior to the second century BCE, the Hebrew Bible is our almost exclusive source of evidence for the observance of practices resembling the Passover sacrifice and the Festival of Unleavened Bread. (The epigraphic evidence from Elephantine is the exception and will be discussed below). Aside from the prescriptions concentrated in the Pentateuch, extra-Pentateuchal texts relate narratives about four purported large-scale observances of the Passover offering (and in some cases the Festival of Unleavened Bread as well):

1. Joshua 5:10–11 reports tersely that the Israelites, encamped at Gilgal immediately after crossing the Jordan, "performed the Passover [*waya'aśû 'et hapesaḥ*]" on the evening of the fourteenth of the first month, and that on the following day they ate "the produce of the land, unleavened bread and parched grain." Nothing is said of a seven-day festival.

2. Second Chronicles 30:1–27 provides an extensive account of Hezekiah's observance of the Passover offering in Jerusalem on the fourteenth day of the *second* month, of a (subsequent) seven-day Festival of Unleavened Bread, and of *another* seven-day period of festivities that followed. The reason given for these observances taking place in the second month is that the priests had not sufficiently sanctified themselves and the people had not assembled in Jerusalem on time. The king sent out messengers throughout the land, including the territories of the northern tribes, to persuade the people to come to Jerusalem to offer the Passover, warning them not to be "stiff-necked" as their ancestors had been. Although the northern tribesmen scoffed at the messengers, it is said that "many

people [ʿam rāv]" / "a very large assembly [qāhāl lārōv məʾōd]" did in fact heed the call, including both Judeans and some northerners—although many of the latter are said to have offered their sacrifices in impurity. Of the great joy that accompanied these festivities it is said, "Since the time of Solomon son of David, King of Israel, there had been nothing like this in Jerusalem."

3. Second Kings 23:21–23 provides a very brief account of Josiah, in the eighteenth year of his reign, instructing "all the people" to perform the Passover "as is written in the book of the covenant" (that had just been discovered by Hilkiah in the House of YHWH). No description is given other than the assertion that "no such Passover had been performed since the days of the judges who judged Israel, and during all the days of the kings of Israel and the kings of Judah." Nothing is said of unleavened bread or of a seven-day festival. Second Chronicles 35:1–19 (followed in both content and form by 1 Esd 1:1–22) provides a far more detailed account: Josiah's offering takes place on the fourteenth day of the first month, the precise roles of the priests and Levites are described, we are told that burnt offerings accompanied the Passover, we are given the precise numbers of slaughtered animals (sheep or goats, and cattle) and are informed of exactly who provided for these, and finally we are told that "they cooked the Passover in fire [wayəvašəlû hapesaḥ bāʾēš]" while the other offerings were cooked in three types of cooking pots. Of this event we are told, "No Passover like it had been performed in Israel since the days of the prophet Samuel; none of the kings of Israel had performed such a Passover as was performed by Josiah, by the priests and the Levites, by all Judah and Israel who were present, and by the inhabitants of Jerusalem." Observance of this Passover, we are informed, was accompanied by a seven-day Festival of Unleavened Bread.

4. Ezra 6:19–22 (with a parallel in 1 Esd 7:10–15) tells briefly of the performance of the Passover by the returnees from the Babylonian exile. The offering is said to have been slaughtered on the fourteenth of the first month by the priests and Levites, all of whom had purified themselves, and was eaten by all the returnees from the exile "and all who separated from the impurity of the peoples of the land." This was accompanied by celebration of a seven-day Festival of Unleavened Bread.

The Pentateuchal instructions, along with these four narratives, have provided scholars ample fodder for speculating about the origins of both the

Passover offering and the Festival of Unleavened Bread. Theories abound, with most hypotheses envisioning two distinct springtime agricultural/ shepherding festivals harkening back to premonarchic or even Canaanite beginnings, with the two eventually coming together in association with a later exodus narrative.[94] As a rule, these theories assume from the outset that the prescriptions surrounding these holidays in the Pentateuchal sources derive from practices already widespread in Israelite society for generations. Actual evidence for any of these supposedly widespread practices is nonexistent, however, which is of course the precise reason why so many divergent theories have been proposed over the years and why none have ever been falsified.

Putting aside unfalsifiable hypotheses, we might inquire whether any of the narratives outlined above provide evidence for the actual widespread observance of the Passover or the Festival of Unleavened Bread as early as the so-called Return to Zion, the reign of Josiah, the reign of Hezekiah, or the supposed time of the entry into Canaan. The answer, of course, is no; the fact that later writers presented narratives about mass Passover observances in earlier times is no reason for us to assume that anything resembling these events ever actually took place. The real question that should concern us, rather, is whether any of these narratives should be taken as reflecting actual practices common *at the time these stories were first composed*. Must we presume a *Sitz im Leben* wherein these practices had already become common on an annual basis? I see no reason to make any such assumptions. To the contrary, it is quite easy to imagine how a detailed narrative that tells of an important ritual that had been completely "forgotten" for generations but was "reintroduced" by a cherished leader from the past might have been written precisely at a time when this ritual was widely unknown or otherwise ignored.[95]

While the biblical texts inform us only about what their authors thought their readers *ought to be doing*, the corpus of epigraphic material from Elephantine provides evidence for the *actual observance* of something called "Passover" as well as of a seven-day period likely coinciding calendrically with the biblical Festival of Unleavened Bread.[96] Two letters on ostraca refer succinctly to "Passover" (*pisḥā*) but provide no details as to what this "Passover" might have looked like: who observed the rite, what was involved, when it took place, where it was practiced (in a temple? at home?), or why (e.g., was it associated with an exodus narrative?). Both ostraca have been dated on paleographic and other grounds to the first quarter of the

Figure 13. *Papyrus letter from Elephantine (TAD A4.1, recto). (© Staatliche Museen zu Berlin—Ägyptisches Museum und Papyrussammlung, Inv. Nr. P. 13464.)*

fifth century BCE. A third fragmentary letter on papyrus, dated internally to 419/418 BCE, makes no mention of "Passover" but *does* refer to a period of time between the fifteenth and the twenty-first days of a certain month, possibly the springtime Nisan (fig. 13).[97] In the surviving portions of the letter (the body of the letter has been preserved only partially), there is no mention of any sort of sacrifice or of unleavened bread. Although scholars have reconstructed the missing parts of the letter such that it includes explicit instructions relating to the Passover sacrifice, the Festival of Unleavened Bread, a prohibition against drinking beer, and the hiding away of leaven, such reconstructions are completely founded on the assumption that the Pentateuchal (and rabbinic!) regulations surrounding Passover were known and observed at Elephantine already in the late fifth century BCE. The extant portions of the letter provide no unambiguous details about the character of the seven-day period between the fifteenth and the twenty-first of Nisan (if this is indeed the month intended). While it is certainly striking that this period of time cited in the letter appears to coincide precisely with the same seven-day period known from the biblical prescriptions and accounts as the Festival of Unleavened Bread, any further attempt at correlating the two can remain no more than conjectural. The evidence from Elephantine, in sum, is simply too fragmentary to allow any reconstruction of what either "Passover" or a seven-day period coinciding with the Festival of Unleavened Bread might have looked like. While the Judeans at Elephantine *might have* practiced something very much resembling the practices called for by the biblical authors (albeit far from Jerusalem), we have no reason to simply assume this to be the case. It seems just as easy to imagine that the Judean garrison stationed near the Nubian border was observing springtime rituals inherited from their early Israelite or Canaanite ancestors, rituals that may have borne very little resemblance to the practices prescribed in the Pentateuch.

In conclusion, the earliest evidence for widespread observance of the Passover and the Festival of Unleavened Bread is found in the accounts provided by Josephus regarding violent incidents at the Temple Mount on these occasions from the end of the first century BCE and into the first century CE. Compositions from the Hasmonean period provide evidence for exegetical activity surrounding the details of the holidays' laws, but the extent to which these laws were actually observed at this time remains unknown. The biblical accounts about mass observance of the Passover and of the Festival of Unleavened Bread inform us only about how individual biblical writers envisioned the ideal way these two feasts *should be* celebrated, but provide no evidence regarding the character of these festivals *in reality* or of the extent to which they were at all well known and commonly practiced at the time of their writing. The epigraphic material from Elephantine *does* provide evidence for actual practice, but the character of the practices recorded is too opaque to allow any conclusions to be drawn about the existence of something at all recognizable in terms of Pentateuchal prescriptions.

Excursus: Passover at Elephantine

As noted above, two letters written on ostraca from Elephantine include brief references to Passover. The first is addressed to a certain Hoshaiah and includes, along with instructions regarding looking after children whose mother was away, the following request: "Send [word] to me when you will make the Passover [*ʾēmat tə ʾavdūn pisḥā*]."[98] The second ostracon is fragmentary but preserves the following request: "If you can d[o] [or: pas(s) by)] . . . on the Passover [*bəpisḥā*] then stand w[ith . . .]."[99] Further on, the letter mentions the name "Hosea" and possibly also "Micayah" (the critical last two letters "*y-h*" are missing)—which may both be Judean names. Neither of these letters provide any details as to what this "Passover" involved, although the first may imply that the date for the Passover was not fixed.

A third letter, on papyrus, preserves no mention of "Passover" at all, but does refer to a period of time between the fifteenth and the twenty-first days of the month, possibly Nisan.[100] The letter is sent by a certain Hananiah to "Jedaniah and his colleagues, the Judean garrison," on the fifth year of a King Darius, and refers to something sent by the king to "Arsa[mes]." It is usually understood that the king is Darius II, which would date the letter to 419/418 BCE, and Arsames would have been the current Achaemenid satrap of Egypt. After invoking "the gods" (*'elāhayā'*) to ensure the welfare of the addressees, the critical portion of the fragmentary letter reads as follows:[101]

Recto [...](?) Now, you thus count fou[r(?)[102] ...]
[...](?) and from the 15th day until the 21st day of [...]
[...](?)[103] you shall be, and take heed. Work (?)[...]
[...](?) drink, and anything which is fermented[104] (?)[...]
Verso [...] from sunset until the 21st day of Nisa[n(?) ...]
[... b]ring into your chambers and seal between [these(?)] day[s ...]

The letter has been preserved only partially, as the text at both the beginnings and the endings of every line (on both recto and verso) is missing, and consequentially the original lengths of the lines are essentially unknown.[105] Because the letter (on the recto) refers to a period of time "from the 15th day until the 21st day of" some unknown time frame, and because (on the verso) "the 21st day of Nisa[n]" is reasonably reconstructed as referring to the Babylonian name of the biblical "month of the *'āvîv*," scholars have assumed that the content of the letter relates to the Passover and to the Festival of Unleavened Bread—despite the fact that neither of these two terms appears in the extant portions of the letter.[106] After deciding that the letter is focused on these two feasts, scholars used the Pentateuchal injunctions regarding these festivals both to reconstruct the missing segments of the letter and to explicate opaque words and phrases in the surviving portions. The missing parts of the letter were thus *imagined* to contain injunctions to observe the Passover on the fourteenth of Nissan at twilight, to eat unleavened bread for seven days during the Festival of Unleavened Bread, to maintain ritual purity during these festivals, to abstain from work on the first and last days of this holiday, to refrain from consuming leavened food and beverages made from grains, to ensure that no leaven is seen in the house, and to seal up any existing leaven. To be clear: none of these instructions appear in the extant portions of the letter; they are all conjectural reconstructions of the missing segments at the beginnings and endings of the lines. While some of these reconstructions are based on explicit Pentateuchal instructions, others are known only from rabbinic regulations in late antiquity. For example, the missing portion of the final line on the recto, which speaks of "drinking," has been reconstructed as a prohibition against drinking *beer* during the Festival of Unleavened Bread, a notion known only from rabbinic legislation.[107] The preserved segments also have been translated and interpreted entirely in line with biblical and rabbinic language and notions surrounding the Passover laws. For example, the phrase *"kōl minda ʾam zî ḥāmîr,"* appearing on the same line that mentions *drinking*, is most straightforwardly translated as "anything that is *fermented*." Instead, scholars anachronistically exploited an Aramaic term attested only in rabbinic literature from late antiquity onward, and translated the word *"ḥāmîr"* as "leaven" (i.e., fermented *dough*).[108] Many of these scholars then conjectured that the word "eat" must be missing, and reconstructed the entire phrase as "anything of leaven [do] n[ot eat]"!

My purpose here is not to dismiss this or that reconstruction or interpretation of the Elephantine epigraphic material as more or less plausible. It is only to point out that reconstructions and interpretations that are based entirely on biblically and rabbinically prescribed practices cannot be adduced as evidence independent of these same sources. To do so would require an undue amount of circular reasoning.

Day of Atonement Fast

First-Century Evidence

The Pentateuch legislates a "Sabbath of Sabbaths" (*šabat šabātôn*) to be observed on the tenth day of the seventh month, during which time work is forbidden and some form of self-torment is mandated: "and you shall afflict yourselves [*wa ʾînîtem/tə ʾanû ʾet nafšôtêkhem*]."[109] The consequence for one who does not practice this self-affliction is that "he will be cut off from his people." The day is characterized as a "Day of Atonements" (*yôm kîpūrîm*) upon which the people are purified of their sins before YHWH.

By the first century CE, a consensus seems to have formed among Judeans that the Pentateuchal call for self-affliction is to be carried out specifically through fasting. Observance of this fast among Judeans is described by both Philo and Josephus as universal. Philo writes, "On the tenth day is the fast [*hē nēsteía*], which is carefully observed not only by the zealous for piety and holiness but also by those who never act righteously in the rest of their life. For all stand in awe, overcome by the sanctity of the day, and for the moment the worse vie with the better in self-denial and virtue."[110] Josephus too, in describing the vestments worn by the high priest on the Day of Atonement, speaks of this holiday as "the day on which it was the universal custom to keep fast to God [nēsteúein . . . pántas tǭ theǭ]."[111] The author of Acts cites "the fast" as an apparently common chronological reference to this day, which suggests that he would have expected the practice to be completely familiar to his readers.[112] The unique Judean day of fasting was also well known to pagan Greek and Latin authors, some of whom apparently confused the Day of Atonement with the weekly Sabbath and thought that Judeans engaged in fasting every Saturday.[113]

Early Evidence

In chapter 2 I cited Josephus's anecdote about Matthias, a high priest serving in the final years of Herod the Great, who was replaced for a single day when, on the night prior to that day "which the Judeans observe as a fast," the man "seemed in a dream to have intercourse with a woman"—an incident that made him unable to serve as a priest the following morning.[114] There can be little doubt that the story refers to the Day of Atonement, and if this story, at least with regard to the fast, truly derives from Herod's day, it may suggest that this fast was observed toward the end of the first century BCE.

Pesher Habakkuk presents the only explicit reference among the Dead Sea Scrolls to a fast on the Day of Atonement, and may in fact present the earliest surviving reference to this practice.[115] The scroll tells of "the Wicked Priest" who pursued "the Teacher of Righteousness" on the Day of Atonement and attacked his men on their holy day: "He appeared to them to consume them and make them fall on the day of fasting [bǝyôm ṣôm], the Sabbath of their rest." The scroll is written in Herodian characters, but the date of its initial composition is difficult to determine.[116] Many scholars have conjectured that the Wicked Priest should be identified as one of the Hasmonean rulers (all of whom also served as high priests), but this cannot be ascertained with any degree of confidence.[117]

The Damascus Document speaks of a "day of the fast" (yôm hata 'anît) which, although not explicit, is likely a reference to the Day of Atonement.[118] Other compositions commonly dated to the Hasmonean period mention the Day of Atonement but make no explicit mention of fasting. The Temple Scroll paraphrases the Pentateuch in calling for "self-affliction" on this day.[119] Jubilees states that the Israelites "should be distressed" on the Day of Atonement, also without explicating that fasting is meant.[120] The Melchizedek fragment from Qumran Cave 11 cites the Day of Atonement as the time of the Jubilee call to freedom (as per Lev 25:9), but no self-affliction is mentioned.[121]

Outside the Pentateuch, these compositions are the earliest surviving references we have to the notion of a Day of Atonement. Not only is the Day of Atonement nowhere attested prior to the Hasmonean period, there is in fact good reason to believe that several biblical authors writing in the Persian period or later *knew nothing at all* of any such holiday. For example, the author of 2 Chr 7:8–10 depicted Solomon celebrating a seven-day "dedication of the altar" in the seventh month in the days immediately preceding what we know of as the Festival of Sukkot; this would have the celebrations begin on the eighth of the month and carry on through until the fourteenth—with no awareness of a Day of Atonement taking place on the tenth.[122] The author of Neh 8:13–18 also appears to have been unaware of any such day, as he portrays a "rediscovery" of the Sukkot festival occurring on the second day of the seventh month, followed by the people going out to build booths and celebrate the seven-day holiday. Regardless of precisely when this "Sukkot" festival was celebrated (the dates are not made explicit), the author of this passage seems to know nothing at all of any Day of Atonement occurring on the tenth of the month.[123] Similarly, the author of Ezra 3:1–6 reported that Zerubbabel and his colleagues built an altar in Jerusalem on the first of the seventh month and then offered sacrifices daily from then on, including the special sacrifices indicated for the Festival of Sukkot. Here, too, we would have expected something to be said about the intervening Day of Atonement had the author of our pericope known of such a day. Finally, the author of Ezek 45:18–25 instructs certain purgation offerings to take place on the first and seventh days of the first month, and also provides instructions for Passover, for a seven-day Festival of Unleavened Bread, and for a seven-day festival beginning on the fifteenth of the seventh month. Nothing is said of a Day of Atonement occurring during this time, and one senses that the author of this passage was not aware of any such holiday. While it may be possible to proffer ad hoc apologetic explanations for why each of these pericopes ignores the Day of Atonement,

understanding that such a holiday was still unknown to these authors provides a far more satisfying solution to explicate the phenomenon.[124]

In summary, the practice of an annual fast on the Day of Atonement
appears to have been universal among Judeans in the first century CE. The
holiday, including the practice of fasting or "self-affliction," is attested in
writings commonly thought to date to the Hasmonean period. Prior to the
Hasmonean period, the Day of Atonement is completely unattested anywhere outside the Pentateuch. Furthermore, biblical sources dating to the
Persian period or later provide clear indications that nothing like a Day of
Atonement was known among certain biblical writers at this time, let alone
among the Judean masses.

Sukkot: Booths and the Four Species

First-Century Evidence

While the autumnal Festival of Sukkot ("the Festival of Booths" [ḥag
ḥasūkôt] or "the Festival of Ingathering" [ḥag hā 'āsîf]) is mentioned several times throughout the Pentateuch, instructions regarding two practices
peculiar to this holiday are concentrated in Lev 23:40, 42–43:[125] "On the
first day you shall take the fruit of a majestic tree [pərî 'ēṣ hādār], branches
of palm trees [kapōt təmārîm], and the bough of a leafy tree [wa 'ănaf 'ēṣ
'āvōt], and willows of the brook [wə 'arvê nāḥal]; and you shall rejoice before YHWH your God for seven days.... You shall abide in booths [basūkōt
tēšvû] for seven days; all that are citizens in Israel shall abide in booths, so
that your generations may know that I set the Children of Israel in booths
when I brought them out of the land of Egypt: I am YHWH your God."
The first instruction involves "taking" the fruit of a certain tree (the term
"majestic tree" is difficult to decipher) together with branches of three other
species ("palm" and "willow" are easily identified, while "a leafy tree" is not).
Precisely what is to be done with these floral elements once they are "taken"
is unclear. The second instruction involves abiding in "booths," which presumably means some kind of impermanent structure.

There is good reason to believe that both of these Pentateuchal ordinances were widely observed by Judeans in the first century CE. Philo,
for instance, when relating an event that took place in Alexandria around
38 CE, mentioned in passing that "the Judeans were holding then the national feast of the autumn equinox, in which it is the custom of the Judeans
to live in booths [en skēnaîs]."[126] Josephus referred to this custom as a ubiq-

uitous practice; when reporting on an incident from 62 CE that happened to take place on Sukkot, he described the holiday as "the feast at which it is the custom of all [Judeans] to erect booths [*en hẽ̜ skēnopoieîsthai pántas éthos*] to God."[127] Taking of the four species is also described by Josephus as a universal practice: ". . . it being a law among the Judeans that at the festival of booths everyone holds wands made of palm branches and citrons [*ékhein hékaston thúrsous ek phoiníkōn kaì kitríōn*]."[128] It should be noted that while only two species are mentioned here, previously, in his account of the Mosaic legislation regarding Sukkot, Josephus wrote that the people were commanded to offer sacrifices in the temple while "bearing in their hands a bouquet [*eiresiōnēn*] composed of myrtle and willow with a branch of palm, along with the Persian apple [*mẽlou toũ tẽs perséas*] [i.e., the citron]."[129] Josephus's description entails very precise interpretations of what had been left rather opaque in the Pentateuchal instructions in Lev 23:40: (1) "the fruit of a majestic tree" is interpreted to mean a citron, (2) "a leafy tree" is understood to mean myrtle, and (3) the three leafy species are to be bound together as a "wand/bouquet" (*thúrsos/eiresiōnē*) and held in the hands with the citron.[130] To "take" these four species appears to have been interpreted as a directive that they be held in the hands of all the pilgrims visiting the courtyard of the temple while the festal sacrifices were being offered; it is difficult to tell whether Josephus knew of the ritual being practiced outside the temple.[131]

That the ritual of the four species was a practice that must have been extremely well known among Judeans in the first century CE one may also infer from the fact that all three denominations of the bronze coins minted in the fourth year of the Great Revolt (69/70 CE) featured variations on the "four species" motif (fig. 14).[132] The motif included two elements: (1) a lemon-shaped fruit depicted with rows of bumps on the surface of its rind and a prominent nipple at its apex—evidently a citron; and (2) an array consisting of a tall branch, almost certainly a palm frond, tied in a bundle at its bottom with other leafy branches belonging to at least one other species. While it is impossible to definitively identify what species is or are bundled with the palm, the presence of small berries scattered among the branches (indicated by small dots) may suggest myrtle. It seems quite likely that the designs on these coins reflect precisely the practice described by Josephus, who, we may note, may well have handled these coins himself while touring Judea in Titus's legionary camp toward the end of the revolt. The fact that this practice was granted such a prominent position on the revolutionary

Figure 14. *Bronze coin from the fourth year of the Great Revolt with "four species" motif on the reverse. (Photo © The Israel Museum, Jerusalem, by Yair Hovav.)*

coinage clearly suggests the great symbolic value it possessed in Judean minds in the year leading up to the destruction of Jerusalem.

The two central practices associated with Sukkot were known to Plutarch, who, writing shortly after the close of the first century CE, described the Judean rites thus: "When they celebrate their so-called Fast, at the height of the vintage, they set out tables of all sort of fruit under booths and huts plaited for the most part of vines and ivy. They call the first of the days of the feast 'Booths.' A few days later they celebrate another festival, this time identified with Bacchus not through obscure hints but plainly called by his name, a festival that is a sort of 'Procession of Branches' [*kradēphoría*] or 'Thyrsus Procession' [*thursophoría*], in which they enter the temple each carrying a thyrsus. What they do after entering we do not know, but it is probable that the rite is a Bacchic revelry, for in fact they use little trumpets to invoke their god as do the Argives at their Dionysia."[133] Plutarch's is of course an outsider's account that, while clearly muddling rites associated with two or three of the autumnal festivals, is valuable in showing how word of these Judean practices had attained such reach that it succeeded in garnering the interest of a non-Judean writer living in mainland Greece.

Early Evidence

The two primary practices associated with Sukkot, residing in booths and carrying the four species, may have been known as early as the last two centuries BCE, although the evidence is somewhat limited and problematic. The four-species ritual features in a story recorded by Josephus about a rebellion raised against Alexander Jannaeus early in the first century BCE: "As for Alexander, his own people revolted against him—for the nation was aroused against him—at the celebration of the festival, and as he stood beside the altar and was about to sacrifice, they pelted him with citrons, it being a custom among the Judeans that at the festival of Booths everyone holds wands made of palm branches and citrons—these we have described elsewhere."[134] While the parenthetical explanation about the "custom among the Judeans" may simply reflect the experience of Josephus in his own day, the narrative of the crowds pelting the king with their citrons features in the main body of the story and, if taken at face value, would indicate that the practice was in place in the early first century BCE. The value of this evidence is unfortunately limited, however, as we do not know what Josephus's source was, and therefore the possibility remains that the tale derives from a later period and reflects rituals current at this later time.

Other texts that are widely thought to have been composed during the Hasmonean period provide more reliable evidence for how the central rituals associated with Sukkot were understood and put into practice. The author of Jubilees, for example, imagined that the patriarch Abraham celebrated Sukkot by building booths for himself and his servants, sacrificing animals and offering incense for seven days, and taking "branches of palm trees and fruit of good trees and each day of the days he used to go around the altar with branches." The remaining two species appear in the previous verse that speaks of the obligation for future generations: "It is ordained forever concerning Israel so that they should observe it and they should dwell in tents and that they should place crowns on their heads and so that they should take branches of leaves and willow from the stream."[135]

The Temple Scroll prescribed that skeleton structures be built on the roofs above the third stories of certain buildings in the outer court of the temple and that every year "booths" (*sûkôt*) be built upon these: "Every year on the Festival of Sukkot, for the elders of the congregation, for the leaders, for the heads of the fathers' houses of the Children of Israel and for the commanders of the thousands and for the commanders of the hundreds who will come up and abide there until the sacrificing of the festival burnt offering—that of the Festival of Sukkot; [thus they shall do] every year."[136] It seems unlikely that the author of this text would have envisioned these as the *only* booths to be built, since Lev 23:42 instructs that "all that are citizens in Israel shall abide in booths." Be that as it may, neither Jubilees nor the Temple Scroll necessarily depicts a reality of large-scale observance of the central Sukkot rituals in Hasmonean times (but they also in no way suggest *against* such a possibility).[137]

The author of 2 Maccabees claimed that Judas Maccabaeus and his men cleansed the temple on the twenty-fifth of the month of Kislev and celebrated the event for eight days just like the Festival of Sukkot: "They celebrated it for eight days with rejoicing, in the manner of the Festival of Booths, remembering how not long before, during the Festival of Booths, they had been wandering in the mountains and caves like wild animals. Therefore, carrying wands [*thúrsous*] and beautiful branches [*kládous hōraíous*] and also fronds of palm, they offered hymns of thanksgiving to him who had given success to the purifying of his own holy place."[138] It is difficult to assess what to make of this passage for our understanding of the four-species ritual in Hasmonean times. On the one hand, the author of this text seems to be aware of a well-known custom to carry something *like* the four species in the temple during Sukkot. On the other hand, what Judas's men are said to have carried does not correspond precisely with the species listed in Lev 23:40. Of course, the procession is said to have taken place almost two months after the proper time of Sukkot, and therefore the Maccabean celebrations may be intended to only *approximate* the actual Sukkot ritual.

Prior to the second century BCE, the sole evidence for the existence of either of the two central rituals of Sukkot is found in a single passage in Neh 8:13–18. Aside from this passage, neither of these two rituals are attested anywhere in the Hebrew Bible outside the Pentateuch.[139] Because this is our lone testimony regarding the central Sukkot rituals any time prior to the Hasmonean period, I will cite it here in full. On the day following Ezra's public reading from the "book of instruction of Moses," Ezra is said to have reconvened the heads of the people to study the "words of instruction" further:

> And it was found written in the instruction which YHWH had commanded through Moses, that the Children of Israel should abide in booths during the festival of the seventh month, and that they should publish and proclaim in all their towns and in Jerusalem as follows: "Go out to the hills and bring foliage of olive [*'ălê zayit*], oil-wood [*'ălê 'ēṣ šemen*], myrtle [*'ălê hădas*], palm [*'ălê təmārîm*], and leafy trees [*'ălê 'ēṣ 'āvōt*] to make booths, as it is written." So the people went out and brought them, and made booths for themselves, each on the roofs of their houses, and in their courts and in the courts of the house of God, and in the square at the Water Gate and in the

square at the Gate of Ephraim. And all the community that had returned from the captivity made booths and abided in them; for from the days of Jeshua son of Nun to that day the Children of Israel had not done so.[140]

While the correspondence between this passage and Lev 23:40–43 is striking, so are the divergences. First, the number and identity of the species do not cohere; olive, oil-wood, and myrtle do not appear at all in Lev 23:40, while Neh 8:15 does not include willows or a "fruit" of any sort. Second, the Nehemiah passage has the people collect the foliage *in order to build booths from them*, while the plants in Lev 23:40 (which include a fruit!) are not depicted as building materials for the booths prescribed only two verses later (in Lev 23:42–43). As many scholars have already suggested, it seems likely that the author of the Nehemiah passage knew of a source that included a passage somewhat similar to Lev 23:40 (note the matching "leafy tree" and "palm") but not identical to it.[141]

Be that as it may, the real question that interests us is whether this narrative provides any evidence for the wide-scale observance among Judeans of the Sukkot "booths" ritual—and perhaps also of a rite somehow resembling the ritual of the four species—as early as the Persian period. Certainly, we have no reason to presume that the narrative given here ever actually took place; there is simply no independent witness to corroborate the story. More importantly, there seems little reason to assume that these rituals were widely observed—or even commonly known of—in the contemporary reality within which the author of this passage lived. This author was apparently familiar with a copy of a "book of instruction" attributed to Moses which included a commandment to build booths on the holiday of Sukkot. He evidently believed that this commandment should be followed, and he clearly wanted his readers to think the same. We simply have no way of knowing whether his contemporaries were in agreement. To the contrary, as I argued above with regard to the Passover narratives, it is quite easy to imagine how a narrative that tells of an important ritual that had been completely "forgotten" for centuries but was "rediscovered" and "reintroduced" by a revered leader from the past might have been written precisely at a time when this ritual was widely unknown or otherwise ignored. A pattern emerges wherein writers living in the Persian period—or perhaps somewhat later—have depicted the Judeans as living their lives blithely unaware of various Mosaic laws, until a cherished figure comes along to discover the laws and the masses happily follow this leader in submissive obedience. This common trope of a law having been "forgotten" since the days of Joshua, the Judges, Samuel, or Solomon certainly provided a convenient explanation for why contemporary listeners had never heard of the law under discussion. I see little reason why we should read these narratives as anything other than idealized portraits of how these authors *wished* that their own contemporaries—who may well have also lived their lives merrily unaware of the Mosaic laws at hand—would themselves discover these laws and put them into practice. The earliest evidence we have for this actually occurring derives from no earlier than the second century BCE.

The Seven-Branched Menorah

First-Century Evidence

The Pentateuch prescribes the construction of a golden lampstand, called a "*mənôrāh*," designed with seven branches and decorated along its central shaft and branches with stylized cups (*gəvîʿîm*), calyxes (*kaftōr*), and flower petals (*peraḥ*).[142] This menorah is to be set up in the tabernacle, and its lamps are to be lit "continually."

There is no doubt that a menorah closely corresponding with this Pentateuchal prescription stood in the Jerusalem temple during the first century CE. Josephus, who was a Jerusalem priest and likely saw the menorah himself when it was still in the temple, described the lampstand in some detail.[143] He also reported that when the temple was destroyed in the summer of 70 CE, the Romans took this lampstand among the spoils and paraded it in the triumphal procession at Rome, after which it was placed on display in Vespasian's Temple of Peace.[144] Josephus's descriptions of the menorah and his narrative about its procession through Rome are both graphically corroborated by the famous bas-relief on the Arch of Titus which depicts the menorah carried on the shoulders of the Roman victors. A recent study employing ultraviolet-visible spectroscopy to detect color on this marble relief revealed traces of yellow ocher on the arms and base of the menorah, confirming that the lampstand was originally depicted as golden.[145]

In the first century CE, the Pentateuchal commandment regarding the menorah was manifest not only in the form of a physical artifact in the temple itself but also as a mental impression upon the consciousness of lay Judeans living outside the direct sphere of the temple. Josephus described the setting up and continual lighting of the menorah as "obedience to the law [*akoloúthōs tǭ nómǭ*]," and presumably regular Judeans would have learned about the laws regarding the menorah when the relevant Pentateuchal passages were publicly read and taught in synagogue gatherings (see chapter 6).[146] That this was likely the case we may infer from the fact that the menorah is depicted in popular artwork decorating archaeological artifacts from the first century CE: incised on a sundial found in Jerusalem; engraved on chalk ossuaries (one found at Jericho and two others unprovenanced); scratched on the side of a chalk vessel found in Jerusalem; carved in a relief decorating a stone unearthed in a synagogue at Magdala; featured on a certain type of oil lamp (the *Darom* type) that became popular during the 70–132 CE interwar period; incised as graffiti on the lintel and doorjamb of an olive press at Ḥ. Beit Loya; and in several examples of graffiti scratched or painted on the walls of a Jerusalem home, a burial cave near Jerusalem (Jason's Tomb), a refuge cave at Naḥal Mikhmas in the Judean Desert, and an immersion pool south of Jerusalem.[147] In toto, these finds suggest that awareness of the menorah ritual mandated by Torah law was quite widespread among first-century Judeans.

Early Evidence

Widespread awareness regarding the temple menorah in the mid-first century BCE may be adduced from the fact that Mattathias Antigonus (ca. 40–37 BCE) included a depiction of the seven-branched menorah on the reverse of one of his bronze coins (the obverse has been identified as depicting the table of shewbread).[148] The appearance of this coin type is our earliest evidence for the notion of a seven-branched lampstand outside the Pentateuch.

Josephus reported that Pompey and his men encountered the "sacred lampstand" (*lukhnías hierãs*) upon their entering the sanctuary, although it is difficult to determine if this detail might have appeared already in Josephus's source.[149] Reporting on an event that is said to have taken place a century prior to this, the author of 1 Maccabees claims that Antiochus IV also entered the sanctuary and took away the "lampstand of light," but a new one was later fashioned by Judas Maccabeus's men.[150] None of these sources indicate what the "lampstand" spoken of might have looked like, and therefore it is difficult to know to what degree it might have comported with Pentateuchal prescriptions. A similar problem obtains when Ben Sira writes metaphorically of beauty: "A lamp burns upon a holy lampstand [*nēr ṣōrēf ʿal mənôrat qōdeš*]."[151] While it sounds as if Ben Sira's lampstand has only one lamp upon it, there is reason to question whether his "holy lamp-stand" refers specifically to something that he thought stood in the temple.

The author of a passage in Kings (with a parallel in Chronicles) tells of ten lampstands in Solomon's temple, and Jeremiah similarly speaks of Nebuzaradan taking as spoils from the Jerusalem temple "lampstands" (*mənōrôt*) in the plural.[152] No description is given of any of these lamp-stands, and as their number does not tally with the single lampstand of the Pentateuchal prescriptions, there seems little reason to think that these au-thors would have imagined an artifact resembling the seven-branched Pen-tateuchal menorah. The author of a different passage in Chronicles clearly envisioned something very different from our Pentateuchal prescriptions of a single seven-branched, golden menorah, as he writes that, of the numer-ous lampstands planned for Solomon's temple, some were made of gold and others of silver.[153] On the other hand, a third passage in Chronicles *does* depict a single golden lampstand in the Jerusalem temple under Solomon's grandson Abijah—although here, too, no description is provided which might allow us to know whether this author would have envisioned specifi-cally a seven-branched menorah.[154] It should be noted that in the book of Ezra there is no mention of a menorah (nor of multiple menorot) among the gold and silver vessels that Cyrus is said to have repatriated to Jerusa-lem from the spoils taken by Nebuchadnezzar.[155]

The only instance where a single golden lampstand with seven lamps is mentioned anywhere in the Hebrew Bible outside the Pentateuch is in Zechariah, where the prophet recounts how an angel initiated a conversa-tion with him concerning a vision he beheld: "He said to me, 'What do you see?' And I said, 'I see a lampstand of gold [*mənôrat zāhāv*], with its bowl [*gūlāh*] on the top of it; there are seven lamps on it, with seven lips [*mûṣāqôt*] on each of the lamps that are on the top of it. And by it there are two olives [olive trees?], one on the right of the bowl and the other on its left.' I said to the angel who talked with me, 'What are these, my lord?' Then the angel who talked with me answered me, 'Do you not know what these are?' I said, 'No, my lord.'"[156] The angel is then said to have proceeded with an allegorical interpretation of the vision. There is no indication that Zechariah's lampstand was thought to have anything at all to do with the Jerusalem temple, and in any event the description of this lampstand—with its bowl, forty-nine lips, and no branches—looks nothing at all like the Pentateuchal prescriptions for the tabernacle menorah. When Zechariah admits to the angel that he has no idea what it is that he is looking at, it seems that the prophet had never before encountered the strange artifact that stood before him in his vision.

In summary, a single golden, seven-branched menorah as prescribed in the Pentateuch certainly stood in the temple prior to its destruction in 70 CE, and both texts and archaeological finds suggest that Judeans living in both the first century CE and the first century BCE were well aware of both its existence and its general appearance. Prior to the mid-first century BCE, not a single example has been found of a seven-branched menorah depicted in Judean (or Israelite) art, and earlier texts that speak of either a single or multiple golden or silver lampstands in the temple provide little correspondence with Pentateuchal prescriptions.

Conclusions

In this chapter we investigated several practices that comprised important elements of the Judean way of life in the first century CE. We saw how circumcision was widely practiced among first-century Judeans, for whom the rite not only served as an identity marker that distinguished Judean from Gentile but also—and perhaps even more importantly—was regarded as a central commandment of the Torah. Laws surrounding the Sabbath prohibitions were also widely observed at this time by Judeans both in Judea and throughout the Mediterranean world, and the precise parameters of these regulations were concurrently being discussed and debated by exegetes of the Torah. A plethora of literary evidence attests that both the Passover sacrifice and the Festival of Unleavened Bread were practiced by first-century-CE Judeans on an impressively wide scale. The main ritual associated with the Day of Atonement was observed at this time through fasting, a practice described by first-century authors as universal among contemporary Judeans. There is good reason to believe that both of the two central rituals associated with the Festival of Sukkot, residing in booths and taking the four species, were observed by Judeans in the first century CE on a very broad scale. And finally, a seven-branched menorah as prescribed by Torah law undoubtedly stood in the temple in the first century CE, and both texts and archaeological finds suggest that Judeans living at the time were well aware of both its existence and its general appearance.

All these elements of first-century-CE Judaism are attested in the first century BCE, and some also in the second century BCE, but none are clearly attested to prior to this. Circumcision was regarded as required by

Torah law as early as the second century BCE, but prior to this time no evidence outside the Pentateuch points to circumcision being practiced as fulfillment of a divine commandment or as in any way legally mandated. Like the "hip sinew" taboo explored in chapter 1, circumcision was likely an early cultural practice whose origins are lost in the mists of time, and which may have even predated the formation of any kind of distinctly "Israelite" identity; only from the second century BCE onward does the practice manifest as a commandment required by Torah law. Similarly, observance of Sabbath prohibitions is attested as early as the second century BCE, but prior to this time we have no reliable evidence suggesting that the notion of certain activities being forbidden by law on the Sabbath was widely observed—or even commonly known about—among the Judean masses. While the authors of certain late biblical texts advocated observance of Sabbath prohibitions, their own writings (together with anecdotal evidence from Elephantine and Babylonia) suggest that the Judean masses living in the Persian period were not heeding their call. The extent to which Passover and the Festival of Unleavened Bread were observed in the last two centuries BCE is not well attested, although compositions from the Hasmonean period provide evidence for exegetical activity surrounding details of the festivals' laws. Prior to this time, we lack any reliable evidence that could allow us to gauge the extent to which the rituals surrounding these festivals might have been observed or even known about. Evidence for observance of the Day of Atonement as far back as the Hasmonean period is quite limited. Prior to the Hasmonean period, however, the Day of Atonement is completely unattested anywhere outside the Pentateuch, and biblical sources dating to the Persian period or later indicate that nothing like a Day of Atonement was at all known about outside the writings of Pentateuchal authors. The two primary practices associated with Sukkot, residing in booths and taking the four species, appear to have been known in the last two centuries BCE, although the extent to which they were observed by the general public is difficult to gauge. Prior to the second century BCE, however, the sole evidence for the existence of either of these two rituals is found in a single passage in Neh 8:13–18, but there seems little reason to read this narrative as anything other than as an idealized portrait of how its author hoped that his contemporaries would come to observe this festival. And finally, while the seven-branched menorah is attested as early as the first century BCE, it is completely unattested prior to this in both ancient Judean art and earlier texts outside the Pentateuch.

The sum of this evidence is clear. As with the practices investigated in the previous chapters, all the practices examined here characterize Judaism in the first century CE and are attested to one degree or another in the first century BCE and in some cases also in the second century BCE. As with all the practices analyzed until now, the trail of evidence ends once we reach beyond the second century BCE. Prior to this time, we have good reason to think that certain practices (most saliently, the practice of fasting on the Day of Atonement) were completely unknown. This conclusion should cause us to reconsider the quite common notion within scholarship since the time of Wellhausen that at least some of the observances analyzed here had become widespread beginning already with the Babylonian exile and the early days of the so-called Return to Zion.[157] It is certainly true that all the practices examined in the present chapter appear in portions of the Pentateuch commonly identified as "Priestly" sources (P and H), and in several cases they appear *exclusively* in such passages. But while most scholars date the so-called Priestly material to the "exilic" or "postexilic" periods, we must be exceeding careful not to confuse the date assigned to a document's *composition* with the time when it came to be *widely accepted as authoritative or legally binding among the masses of ordinary Judeans.* The evidence we have investigated in this chapter simply does not support the contention that any of the practices examined here were commonly observed—or even widely known of—as early as the Babylonian or Persian periods.

6 The Synagogue

Unlike the subjects of previous chapters, the focus of the present chapter—the synagogue—represents neither a practice nor a prohibition regulated by Torah law. Despite the fact that the concept of the synagogue was apparently never thought to derive from a Pentateuchal source, by the first century CE it had become the preeminent Judean institution aside from the Jerusalem temple. It earned this status because, as I will demonstrate below, the synagogue served as the principal vehicle for the dissemination of the Torah, without which Judaism itself may have never taken root and spread. Accordingly, it would be impossible to conduct a proper investigation into the origins of Judaism without also exploring when evidence for the synagogue first begins to emerge.

Much ink has been spilled over the question of the origins of the synagogue, especially the question of how and why this institution emerged when it did.[1] It is not my intention to rehash the problem here, as my interest in the present chapter is far narrower. Following the approach pursued in previous chapters, I will begin by attempting to characterize the synagogue as it was known in the first century CE on the basis of the available contemporary evidence. It will be shown that the synagogue functioned primarily as a kind of *educational* institution, where members of the local Judean community would assemble on a weekly basis to listen to a formal public reading of the Pentateuch (perhaps along with other sacred texts), accompanied by a more dynamic explanation or learned address presented orally. I will furthermore show that this institution was extremely widespread, appearing throughout the Judean homeland and its diaspora. It was through the synagogue, therefore, that Torah was disseminated widely among the Judean masses. Having characterized the function and prevalence of the synagogue in the first century, I will proceed to seek out the earliest available evidence for the existence of something closely resembling this institution in the centuries prior to the first century CE.

First-Century Evidence

Textual Evidence

PHILO

Throughout his writings, Philo made frequent reference to locations where Judeans would assemble communally for public readings of the law, places that he usually referred to using the term "(place of) prayer" (*proseukhē*) or, less frequently, "(place of) assembly" (*sunagōgē*). It seems that, for Philo, both terms referred to one and the same institution, which for our purposes here I will refer to simply as the "synagogue."[2] At this point what is important for our purposes is the function and character of the institution (below we will attend to a possible explanation for the enigmatic use of the term "[place of] prayer").

Philo credited Moses with instituting the public dissemination of the law among the masses on a weekly basis: "He [Moses] considered that they . . . should have expert knowledge of their ancestral laws and customs [*tōn patríōn nómōn kaì ethōn*]. What then did he do? He required them to assemble in the same place on these seventh days, and sitting together in a respectful and orderly manner, hear the laws read so that none should be ignorant of them. And indeed they do always assemble and sit together. . . . Some priest who is present or one of the elders reads the holy laws [*toùs hieroùs nómous*] to them and expounds them point by point [*kath' hékaston exēgeîtai*] till about the late afternoon, when they depart having gained both expert knowledge of the holy laws and considerable advance in piety."[3] Note that Philo described these weekly sessions as being composed of two distinct activities: (1) *reading* of the sacred laws followed by (2) detailed *oral explanation* meant to clarify the finer points of the subject of instruction. What Philo appears to describe here is a public reading of the written text of the Pentateuch, followed by an oral elucidation of how the Pentateuchal laws are to be properly understood. In other words, this was not merely a ceremonial or ritual reading of the Pentateuch but rather a didactic activity aimed at disseminating knowledge of Torah among the Judean public at large. According to Philo, this educational program was so successful that any Judean whom one might encounter, when asked about details of the laws, would have been able to answer readily and easily: "And so, they do not resort to persons learned in the law with questions as to what they should do or not do, nor yet—by keeping independent—transgress in ignorance of the law, but any one of them whom you attack with inquiries about their ancestral institutions can answer you readily and easily. The husband seems competent to transmit knowledge of the laws to his wife, the father to his children, the master to his slaves."[4] Another clear indication that synagogues functioned primarily as educational institutions may be found in the places where Philo refers to synagogues as "schools" (*didaskaleîa*), as when he rhetorically asks, "For what are our [places of] prayer [*proseuktēria*] throughout the cities but schools of prudence and courage and temperance and justice and also of piety, holiness and every virtue by which duties to God and men are discerned and rightly performed?"[5]

Notwithstanding their principal purpose as institutions for the dissemination of the Torah, synagogues were also portrayed by Philo as the place where Judeans would collect "the annual first fruits" to be sent via envoys to the Jerusalem temple to pay for the sacrifices.[6]

Synagogues are depicted by Philo as a ubiquitous feature in Judean communities everywhere, to be counted in the "thousands" and to be found "in every city."[7] Of his native city, Alexandria, he wrote, "There are many in each section of the city."[8] Philo mentions a multiplicity of synagogues outside Egypt, in Rome as well as in the Roman province of Asia.[9]

NEW TESTAMENT

The institution of the synagogue features prominently and frequently in the narratives of the Gospels and Acts, where it is invariably referred to as the "*sunagōgē*." As in the writings of Philo, these stories depict Judeans assembling in synagogues specifically on the Sabbath. Time and again we are told that Jesus visited synagogues on the Sabbath, and no other days of the week ever appear as occasions when synagogue assemblies are said to have taken place.[10] Paul and his companions are similarly portrayed in Acts as visiting synagogues in Asia Minor and Greece specifically on the Sabbath.[11]

The Gospel narratives, like Philo, imply that the primary function of the synagogue was educational. When Jesus visits synagogues, he does so to "teach [*didáskō*]."[12] In one account, upon standing up to read in the synagogue of Nazareth, Jesus is handed a scroll of Isaiah from which he read a certain portion (the exact length of the reading is unclear), after which he rolls up the scroll, sits down, and delivers an oral explanation of what he has just read.[13] Other narratives tell of Jesus lecturing in the synagogue on the permissibility of healing the sick on the Sabbath, and one source tells of Jesus engaging in a legal debate on this topic in a synagogue with the "head of the synagogue [*arkhisunágōgos*]."[14] Widespread dissemination of the Torah on a weekly basis as a central function of the synagogue is encapsulated in a saying attributed to James, a leader of the Christ-following Judeans in Jerusalem: "For in every city, for generations past, Moses has had those who proclaim him, for he has been read aloud every Sabbath in the synagogues."[15] Acts also tells of Paul and his companions visiting a synagogue in Pisidian Antioch, where it is said that "the law [*toū nómou*]" and "the prophets [*tōn prophētōn*]" were read, followed by an oral "word of exhortation [*lógos paraklēseōs*]."[16] A dynamic discussion session following the formal readings of Scripture seems to be the likely setting for the sometimes heated exchanges Paul and his colleagues are said to have engaged in upon visiting synagogue after synagogue in their travels throughout the eastern Mediterranean.[17]

While New Testament texts portray communal teaching of the Pentateuch and the Prophets as the primary activity associated with the synagogue, these sources also tell of other, apparently ancillary activities that sometimes took place in synagogues. Several texts speak of the synagogue as a place where corporal punishment in the form of public flogging is said to have been meted out.[18] And some synagogue-goers are said to have engaged in almsgiving and prayer, although Jesus purportedly scolded such individuals as "hypocrites" for their ostentatious performance of good deeds in a space as public as the synagogue.[19] In all these cases, it seems that the synagogue was simply exploited as a public forum where many members of the local Judean community would be expected to be in regular attendance. None of these extracurricular activities can be said to define the *purpose* of the institution.

The Gospels relate several stories about Jesus visiting synagogues "throughout Galilee," in "all the cities and villages," as well as "in the synagogues of Judea."[20] From these narratives one gains the impression that synagogues were located throughout the Galilean countryside and that these were to be found even in backwater villages such as Nazareth and Capernaum. Acts tells of at least one synagogue in Jerusalem (the implication is that there were more), of multiple synagogues in Damascus, and of synagogues throughout Asia Minor and Greece: in Pisidian Antioch, Iconium, Thessalonica, Beroea, Athens, Corinth, and Ephesus.[21] Emerging from these narratives is an image of a ubiquitous institution spread throughout the Judean homeland and its diaspora, recalling the above-cited claim attributed to James that synagogues wherein "Moses has had those who proclaim him" were to be found "in every city."

JOSEPHUS

Like Philo and the New Testament authors we have just reviewed, Josephus too asserted that ordinary Judeans regularly participated in weekly assemblages in order to study Torah: "He [Moses] left no pretext for ignorance, but instituted the law [*tòn nómon*] as the finest and most essential teaching material; so that it would be heard not just once or twice or a number of times, he ordered that every seven days they should abandon their other activities and gather to hear the law, and to learn it thoroughly and in detail [*toûton akribôs ekmanthánein*]."[22] As above, here too the weekly sessions are depicted as composed of two parts: (1) *hearing* the law and (2) *learning* the law "thoroughly and in detail." Again, what seems to be described is a public reading of the written *text* of the Pentateuch, followed by a detailed *interpretation* of this text presented orally. Josephus asserted that this institution was so effective at disseminating knowledge of the Torah among the masses that every Judean knew the laws of the Torah by heart: "Were anyone of us to be asked about the laws, he would recount them all more easily than his own name. So, learning them thoroughly from the very first moment of consciousness, we have them, as it were, engraved on our souls."[23]

A Josephean narrative set in 66 CE involving a synagogue in Caesarea Maritima generally supports this picture of an institution centered on weekly dissemination of Torah.[24] According to Josephus's account, a dispute arose between Judeans and Greeks regarding the construction of workshops directly adjacent to the local synagogue (*sunagōgē*). Josephus recounts that one Sabbath, when the Judeans assembled in their synagogue, a "mischief-maker" from among the pagans placed an overturned pot near the synagogue's entrance and sacrificed birds on it. The two factions came to blows over the incident, and the violence ended with the Judeans fleeing the city with a rescued copy of "the laws" (*toùs nómous*)—apparently a reference to the community's scroll of the Pentateuch that was taken from the synagogue.[25]

CONCLUSIONS

In summary, a rather coherent portrait of the first-century synagogue emerges from a holistic reading of the writings of Philo, the Gospels and Acts, and Josephus. It is an institution to be found throughout the Judean homeland and diaspora, wherein regular Judeans would gather on a weekly basis to listen to formal readings from the Pentateuch and other sacred texts, followed by a more dynamic oral exposition. Its primary function was educational, aimed at the widespread, public dissemination of the Torah and its associated traditions among the Judean masses. Aside from this principal purpose, the synagogue could also function—probably on more of an ad hoc basis—as a space where other communal functions requiring large public assemblies might take place, such as collections of dues for the temple (Philo) and floggings (the Synoptic Gospels and Acts).

Epigraphic and Archaeological Evidence

EPIGRAPHIC EVIDENCE

Several inscriptions dating to the first century CE refer to a Judean "(place of) assembly" (*sunagōgē*) or "(place of) prayer" (*proseukhē*). The "Theodotos inscription" is perhaps the most important of these for the crucial details it provides regarding the character of the institution during this period (fig. 15).[26] Unearthed in a water cistern on the southeastern spur of Jerusalem (the City of David) during excavations conducted by Raymond Weill in 1913–1914, this Greek inscription carved onto a rectangular limestone slab was found discarded among debris from the destruction of 70 CE. Dated paleographically to the late first century BCE or the early first century CE, the inscription commemorates the founding of a synagogue and opens by stating the purpose for which the synagogue had been built: "Theodotos, son of Vettenos, priest and archisynagogos, son of an archisynagogos, grandson of an archisynagogos, built the synagogue for the reading of the law [*eis aná(g)nō|s(i)n nómou*] and teaching of the commandments [*eis (d)idakh(è)n entolōn*]." Supporting what first-century authors repeated time and again, this inscription provides direct epigraphic attestation to the two primary activities carried out in the synagogue: (1) the "reading of the law" and (2) the "teaching of the commandments." What is perhaps most striking about the inscription is its assertion that public dissemination of the Torah served as the raison d'etre for the construction of the synagogue in the first place.[27]

Figure 15. *Theodotos inscription. (Photo © The Israel Museum, Jerusalem, by David Harris.)*

Other inscriptions dating to the first century CE offer valuable evidence regarding the widespread distribution of the synagogue. One inscription, discovered in Berenice (Cyrenaica, Libya) and dating to 55 CE, commemorates a lengthy list of donors who contributed to the restoration of the community's synagogue building (*sunagōgē*).[28] Another inscription, from an unknown site in Egypt and dated on paleographic grounds to the first or second century CE, commemorates a single individual who had "built the [place of] prayer [*proseukhē*] on behalf of himself and his wife and children."[29] An inscription from Acmonia (Asia Minor) commissioned by the local Judean community (*sunagōgē*) honors a female non-Judean aristocrat named Julia Severa for erecting "the building" (*oīkon*), along with one "archon" and two "synagogue heads" who are said to have donated to the restoration and ornamentation of the structure.[30] From the Bosporus, at the time a kingdom vassal to Rome, eight inscriptions mentioning Judean communities and their communal buildings have been found dating to the first and early second centuries CE. All these inscriptions refer to the manumission of slaves; the procedure of freeing the slave is said to take place in the "(place of) prayer" (*proseukhē*), the Judean community (*sunagōgē*) would take legal responsibility for the freedman or freedwoman, and the latter bears the responsibility of continuing to regularly attend the "(place of) prayer."[31]

ARCHAEOLOGICAL EVIDENCE

The first building to be identified as a first-century-CE synagogue was unearthed at Masada during the course of Yigael Yadin's excavations at the site between 1963 and 1965 (fig. 16).[32] The structure measures approximately 15 × 12 meters and consists of a main hall with a small room (ca. 5.7 × 3.5 meters) protruding into its northern corner. Four tiers of benches surround the interior walls of the main hall on all four sides, and a single bench abuts the wall of the northern room. Five columns originally supported a roof. The sizable dimensions of the structure indicated to Yadin that this was a public building, and the benches clearly pointed to its function as an assembly hall where a large number of individuals could be seated. This alone probably would have been enough for Yadin to have identified the building as a synagogue, but what ultimately clinched the identification was the remains of scrolls from the books of Deuteronomy and Ezekiel found in two pits dug into the floor of the northern room.

In the half century since the discovery of the structure at Masada, several similar buildings dating to the first century CE have been identified by their excavators as synagogues: in the north at Gamla, Magdala (two buildings), and Tel Rekhesh and in the Judean heartland at Khirbet Di'ab, Qiryat Sefer, Umm el-'Umdan, Herodium, and Khirbet 'A-Taw'ani.[33] At all these sites, the excavated structure was regarded as a public building

Figure 16. *Synagogue at Masada. (Photo courtesy of the Madain Project.)*

because of its size and, most significantly, because it featured benches lining its interior walls.[34]

There are good reasons to equate the building at Masada, and those like it, with the institution reflected in the literary sources surveyed above. Putting aside these textual sources for the moment, it bears asking how we would have interpreted these structures from a purely archaeological perspective. Let us imagine one were excavating in China, or in Ireland, or in Peru, and a structure composed primarily of a sizable space surrounded by benches was unearthed. How would such a building be interpreted? From a strictly functional perspective, we would likely conclude that a space of this sort would have been intended to accommodate a gathering of people. The arrangement of the seating indicates that the focal point of the space—the direction toward which everyone seated physically faced—was toward the center of the room. At the same time, everyone seated could easily see, hear, and communicate through speech and body language with all the others assembled on the benches surrounding the room. An archaeologist excavating such a structure would likely identify it as an "assembly hall," a "meeting house," or else something quite similar. Again, it matters little where in the world a building like this might have been unearthed, nor does it matter what historical period it might date to—the interpretation from a strictly functional perspective would likely be the same. When buildings like this are unearthed at Judean sites dating to the first century CE, we can proceed one step further. The contemporary literary sources surveyed above know of a Judean institution centered on an assembly hall: the synagogue. One of the primary names for the institution in Greek—"*sunagōgē*"—very literally means "(place of) assembly." And what was probably at the time the primary name for the institution in Hebrew and Aramaic—"*bêt kəneset*" and "*bê kənîštā* "—carries the even more direct meaning of "house of assembly." These texts locate the institution in Judean communities of all sizes throughout the Southern Levant—and this is precisely what we find with our archaeological assembly halls. Furthermore, none of these literary sources report about any other type of common Judean institution that would fit the description of the archaeological assembly halls. Using Occam's razor, the most straightforward explanation would be that the assembly halls known from archaeology are in fact one and the same as the synagogues described in the literary sources.

The above argument is strengthened by the fortuitous discovery of fragments of a Deuteronomy scroll and an Ezekiel scroll in the building excavated at Masada. While Yadin's notion that the room functioned as a "genizah" annex is rather anachronistic, it seems too much of a coincidence that precisely these artifacts—upon which the primary activity of the synagogue is known to have centered—were found within the walls of a first-century Judean assembly hall.[35] If, as I would argue, the discovery of these fragments strongly supports the identification of the structure at Masada as a synagogue, then buildings discovered at other sites that resemble the Masada building should by analogy also be rightfully regarded as synagogues.

Summary

A copious volume of evidence—literary, epigraphic, and archaeological—allows us to characterize the first-century synagogue as an institution whose raison d'être was the dissemination of the Torah and associated sacred texts through public readings and oral lectures before assemblies of local Judean communities which were held every Sabbath inside purpose-built structures. While it stands to reason that differences in detail were to be found from one community to another, it seems likely that the general portrait painted here in rather broad strokes represents an institution common to Judean communities spread throughout the ancient world. Aside from the Jerusalem temple, no other institution appears to have held a more central role in the communal lives of Judeans at this time.

Early Evidence

Having characterized the first-century synagogue, my interest now turns to the question, What is our earliest evidence for the existence of something resembling an institution so defined? As usual, I begin with an examination of the literary evidence, followed by an investigation of the evidence provided by physical remains—epigraphic, papyrological, and archaeological.

Textual Evidence

PHILO AND JOSEPHUS
Philo claimed that in the time of Augustus there were multiple "[places of] prayer" in Rome in which the city's Judeans would meet together, "particularly on the sacred Sabbaths when they receive, as a body, a training in their ancestral philosophy."[36] According to Philo, Augustus permitted the

Judeans of Rome to so assemble, and furthermore sent a letter to the governors of the provinces in Asia ordering that there too the Judeans should be permitted to assemble in synagogues (*tà sunagṓgia*).[37] These claims appear in Philo's *Embassy to Gaius* in a clearly apologetic context, and if only for this, there would certainly be good grounds to treat with suspicion his assertions of benevolent treatment toward synagogues on the part of Augustus.

Interestingly, however, Josephus also cited a letter sent by Augustus to the provincial governors of Asia, in which he is said to have ordered, "And if anyone is caught stealing their sacred books [*tàs hieràs bíblous*] or their sacred monies from a Sabbath-hall or a banquet-hall [*ék te sabbateíou ék te andrṓnos*], he shall be regarded as sacrilegious, and his property shall be confiscated to the public treasury of the Romans."[38] The "*sabbateîon*" here most likely refers to a synagogue and was probably called a "Sabbath-hall" out of consideration for the time when such a building would have been in use. What one would expect to find in such a building was "sacred books" along with "sacred monies," collected and apparently stored in the synagogue prior to being sent to Jerusalem. The reference to a "banquet-hall" (*andrṓn*) is more problematic; it has been suggested that the word should be amended to "*aarṓn*," a transliteration from the Hebrew " *ārṓn*," a term meaning "Torah ark" in later rabbinic literature.[39] Be that as it may, Josephus here apparently agrees with Philo in having Augustus writing to the governors of Asia to ensure that the Judeans of the province be unmolested in using their synagogues. As with Philo, however, the reason for Josephus's citation of this alleged letter from Augustus is evidently apologetic and should be read with more than a modicum of skepticism.

The institution that Augustus is said to have protected is depicted by both Philo and Josephus in terms quite reminiscent of the later first-century-CE synagogue—an institution whose primary function was communal assemblies for the public reading and teaching of Torah on a regular, weekly basis. That such an institution existed already in the Augustan age is also implied elsewhere, where Josephus cited an address purportedly made by Nicolaus of Damascus on behalf of the Judeans of Ionia before Marcus Agrippa (died 12 BCE): "We give every seventh day over to the study of our customs and law."[40] If these depictions are not simply anachronisms on the part of Philo and Josephus, they may represent some of the earliest literary evidence we have for the existence of the institution of the synagogue as it was known in the mid to late first century CE.

Relating to the time prior to Augustus, on three occasions Josephus referred to a Judean communal institution that may or may not have functioned in a manner resembling the first-century-CE synagogue. In the first instance, Josephus asserted that plunder taken from the Jerusalem temple by Antiochus IV in the early second century BCE was restored by his successors to the Judeans of Antioch "to be laid up in their synagogue [*tèn sunagōgèn*]."[41] Nothing is said of how this "synagogue" of Antioch functioned under these later Seleucid rulers. On another occasion, Josephus claimed to cite a "decree of the people of Halicarnassus," which declared that the local Judean community was permitted to "build the [places of] prayer [*tàs proseukhàs*] near the sea in accordance with their native custom."[42] Again, it is difficult to know what kind of activities might have gone on in any such "*proseukhai*." Finally, Josephus cited a purported "decree of the people of Sardis" regarding the city's Judeans which instructed that "a place [*tópos*] be given them in which they may gather together with their wives and children and offer their ancestral prayers [*tàs patríous eukhàs*] and sacrifices [*thusías*] to God. . . . Permission shall be given them to come together on stated days to do those things which are in accordance with their laws, and also that a place [*tópon*] shall be set apart by the magistrates for them to build and inhabit, such as they may consider suitable for this purpose."[43] In all three cases, nothing is said of communal assemblies on a weekly basis for the purpose of reading and teaching Torah. While in the first two instances (Antioch and Halicarnassus) Josephus used terms commonly applied to the first-century synagogue—"*sunagōgē*" and "*proseukhē*"—in the last instance (Sardis) he used a rather vague term: "a place" (*tópos*). Furthermore, the manner in which this "place" is to be used—"in which they may gather together with their wives and children and offer their ancestral prayers and sacrifices"—is quite different from all that is known of the first-century-CE synagogue.[44] Again, while it is certainly possible that in some or all of these instances the actual institution that stands behind Josephus's words is one that very much resembled the first-century-CE synagogue, it is difficult to be sure of this.

DEAD SEA SCROLLS

There are no references to a "house of assembly" (*bêt kəneset* or *bê kəništā'*) akin to a synagogue in the Dead Sea Scrolls. Perhaps the closest we get to the institution of regular public readings of the Torah is in the Community Rule (1QS), except that here the study sessions are prescribed to take place on a nightly rather than weekly basis: "And the many [*hārabîm*] shall be diligent together for one-third part of every night of the year, to read from the book [*liqrô᾿ basēfer*], and to study law [*lidrôš mišpāṭ*], and to bless together [*ləvārēkh bəyāḥad*]."⁴⁵ While the public reading and studying of the law prescribed here recalls to a certain extent the synagogue activities described in later sources, this hardly necessitates that at the time this text was composed (probably during the Hasmonean period) an institution like the synagogue had already come into existence outside the narrow sectarian community addressed by the author of this work.⁴⁶

APOCRYPHA, PSEUDEPIGRAPHA, AND THE HEBREW/ARAMAIC BIBLE

Reference to anything that might reasonably be construed as a synagogue are completely absent from the Apocrypha, the Pseudepigrapha, and the Hebrew/Aramaic Bible, and these contain no references to a building or to an institution termed a "*sunagōgḗ*," "*proseukhḗ*," "*bêt kəneset*," or "*bê kənîštā᾿*." An extremely opaque reference to a Judean "place of prayer [*tópon proseukhês*]" appears in 3 Maccabees, but there is certainly little compelling reason to assume that anything like a first-century-CE synagogue was meant here.⁴⁷

Epigraphic and Archaeological Evidence

DEDICATORY INSCRIPTIONS

Several dedicatory inscriptions on limestone plaques that refer to a "(place of) prayer" (*proseukhḗ*) have been found in Egypt dating to the Ptolemaic era. No buildings associated with any of these inscriptions have been identified to date. The two earliest of these inscriptions state that the dedication was accomplished "on behalf of" (*hupèr*) a King Ptolemy and Queen Berenice, commonly identified as Ptolemy III Euergetes and Berenice II Euergetis, co-regents from 246 to 221 BCE. The importance of these inscriptions lies in their early dates, and accordingly they both deserve to be cited here in full: "On behalf of King Ptolemy and Queen Berenice his sister and wife and their children, the Judeans [dedicated] the [place of] prayer [*tèn proseukhèn hoi Ioudaîoi*]."⁴⁸ "On behalf of King Ptolemy, son of Ptolemy, and Queen Berenice his wife and sister and their children, the Ju[dean]s in Croc[o]dilopolis [dedicated] the [place of] pra[yer] [*tèn pro(seukhēn)*]."⁴⁹ The first inscription was discovered in Schedia (southeast of Alexandria), and the second inscription was purchased from an antiquities dealer in Medinet el-Faiyum near the site of ancient Crocodilopolis referenced therein. Aside from informing us that both of these cities hosted a Judean "(place of) prayer" sometime around the third quarter of the third century BCE, neither inscription betrays any details about how such an institution may have functioned at this early date.

Other Ptolemaic-era *proseukhē* inscriptions provide precious few additional details surrounding the character of the institution at this time. One inscription dated 140–116 BCE states that "the Judeans of Xenephyris [dedicated] the gateway of the [place of] prayer [*tòn pulōna tēs proseukhēs*]."⁵⁰ Another inscription dating to this same period states that "the Judeans in Nitriai [dedicated] the [place of] prayer and its appurtenances [*tēn proseukhēn kaì tà sunkúronta*]."⁵¹ The precise character of the "gateway" (*pulón*) in the first inscription is unclear, and that of the "appurtenances" (*tà sunkúronta*) subsidiary to the *proseukhē* in the second inscription is even less certain.⁵²

An inscription from Athribis, dated to sometime during the second or first century BCE, states that the Judeans of the city dedicated the *proseukhē* "to the most high god [*theōi huphístōi*]."⁵³ Another inscription, from the same site and sharing the same chronological range for its date, states that a certain individual, together with his wife and children, donated "this exedra to the [place of] praye[r] [*tēnde exédran tēi proseukhē(i)*]."⁵⁴ Were it possible to confidently identify the form or function of the "exedra" here, we might have a hint as to the character of the Ptolemaic *proseukhē*; unfortunately, the term has a wide range of meanings in the Hellenistic and Roman periods, and consequently its meaning in the present context remains elusive.⁵⁵

Finally, two inscriptions that may date to the end of the Ptolemaic period refer to the *proseukhē* but add little to our understanding of the institution. An extremely fragmentary inscription from Alexandria has been reconstructed as honoring a benefactor who built a *proseukhē* "for the [gr]eat god who l[istens to prayer] [*theōi (me)gálōi e(pēkó)ōi*]."⁵⁶ If the rather speculative reconstruction here is correct, this may imply a central role of prayer in the institution—as the name "*proseukhē*" itself would indeed suggest. Another inscription of unknown origin purports to replace an earlier plaque upon which a "King Ptolemy Euergetes" (i.e., either Ptolemy III, 246–222 BCE, or Ptolemy VIII, 145–116 BCE) is said to have granted to the *proseukhē* the right of asylum (*ásulon*)—a privilege usually granted to temples.⁵⁷

PAPYROLOGICAL EVIDENCE

A small number of papyri predating the first century CE refer to Judean *proseukhaí*. One is addressed to a "King Ptolemy" and contains a charge brought by a woman in Alexandrou-Nesos (in the Faiyum) against a man named Dorotheos: "My cloak . . . caught Dorotheos' eye, and he made off with it. When I saw him [he fled] to the Judean [place of] prayer [*en têi proseukhêi*] [holding] the cloak, [while I called for help]. Lezelmis, a holder of 100 arourai, came up to help [and gave] the cloak to Nikomachos the verger [*tôi nakórōi*] to keep till the case was tried."⁵⁸ It is difficult to ascertain why Dorotheos may have fled into the *proseukhé*; possibly he sought refuge in a "holy place" that enjoyed the right of asylum (as in the roughly contemporaneous inscription just discussed).⁵⁹ Nikomachus appears as a caretaker (*neōkóros*) of the *proseukhé*, a title known from neighboring pagan cults as a member of a temple's personnel.

Another papyrus, with no internal date but thought to have been written in the late second century BCE, describes a land survey in Crocodilopolis that mentions a "Judean [place of] prayer [*proseukhês Ioudaíōn*]."⁶⁰ A "consecrated garden [*hierâs para(deísou)*]" appears as adjacent to the Judean "(place of) prayer," but it remains unclear whether this was part of the estate of the *proseukhé*.

One final papyrus, of unknown provenance and dated on paleographic grounds to the second half of the first century BCE, seems to refer to a meeting held in a *proseukhé* of an "association" (*súnodos*) of some sort—perhaps one concerned with assisting the community with the burial of its members.⁶¹ The fragmentary state of the document does not permit more information to be gleaned about the character of the *proseukhé* involved.

ARCHAEOLOGICAL EVIDENCE

With one exception, none of the excavated first-century-CE synagogue buildings discussed above have earlier construction phases.⁶² The sole exception is the synagogue unearthed at Umm el-'Umdan, where an earlier Hasmonean period phase (dated as "late second century or early first century BCE") was identified beneath the remains of a subsequent phase assigned to the period of Herod's reign (fig. 17).⁶³ The earlier phase features a single masonry bench (possibly the foundation of a system of multi-tiered benches) arranged along three of its walls, while the Herodian phase features two or three stepped benches that encompassed the hall on all four sides. The existence of benches in what appears to be a public

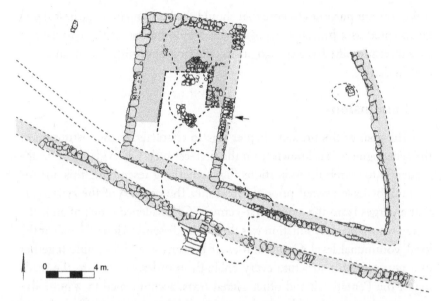

Figure 17. *Plan of Hasmonean phase of the synagogue at Umm el-ʿUmdan. (From Onn and Weksler-Bdolah, "Khirbet Umm el-ʿUmdan," 2062. Courtesy of the IES.)*

structure makes the identification of the building as a synagogue in both phases quite likely.

The identification of a roughly contemporaneous structure unearthed on Delos as a Judean synagogue remains a far more contentious matter. The building (GD 80) was excavated in 1912–1913 by André Plassart and has been the subject of intense debate over the ensuing years, with various phases assigned to the structure and various functions suggested for each of these phases.[64] The earliest phase seems to predate 88 BCE, when the island was sacked by Mithridates VI of Pontus. While some scholars identified this earliest phase as a synagogue, others have identified the building in this early stage as a private domicile or as a meeting hall for a pagan association, with a synagogue identified only in a later phase. Still other scholars have rejected the identification of the building as a synagogue in *any* of its phases of construction. Finally, even among the scholars who have identified the building as a "synagogue," whether constructed as such or transformed into one, debate has arisen over whether the structure might have been associated with the Judean community of Delos or else with a community of Samaritans known to have been living on the island. The problem is far too complex to be addressed in any detail here. It will suffice for our purposes to note that should the building in its earliest stages be accepted as a Judean synagogue, this would be one of the two earliest structures identified as a synagogue to date (together with the one at Umm el-'Umdan).

Conclusions

The goal of the present chapter was to characterize the institution of the synagogue as it is known from the first-century-CE evidence and subsequently to search for indications that something resembling this institution might have existed prior to this time. The portrait of the synagogue that emerges from the ample first-century-CE evidence is one of an institution whose primary function was the public dissemination of Torah at the local, communal level. Communities of Judeans would assemble together in a purpose-built structure every Sabbath in order to listen to the reading of the Pentateuch and other sacred texts, accompanied by a more dynamic explanation or address presented orally. Assemblies of this sort were to be found throughout the Judean heartland—even in rural towns and villages—and in cities scattered throughout the Judean diaspora. The synagogue appears as the central public institution in many Judean communities, and as such the synagogue space was used at times for other communal or public functions that required the community at large to be assembled in a single place (e.g., public floggings and collections of dues for the temple). Its role as a multipurpose "community center" of sorts, however, appears to have been ancillary to its primary purpose as a center for communal learning. The synagogue would have been the primary vehicle for the widespread dissemination of the Torah among Judeans wherever they might have been found living in a communal setting.

What is the earliest evidence for the existence of an institution of this sort? Prior to the first century CE, the evidence is rather sparse. We have reports of synagogues under Augustus and in late Republican and late Seleucid times (from around the middle of the second century through the first century BCE), but these are thin on details and anyway these accounts are wholly reliant on the first-century-CE writings of Philo and Josephus. One building identified as a synagogue (at Umm el-'Umdan) has been dated to the late second or early first century BCE, and another from Delos, whose identification as a Judean synagogue is a matter of contention, dates to around the same time. Epigraphic and papyrological evidence from Egypt clearly demonstrates the existence of a Judean institution called a "(place of) prayer" (*proseukhē*) beginning as early as 246–221 BCE and continuing throughout the Ptolemaic period, but there is little evidence that at this early date the institution that went by this name functioned anything like the first-century-CE synagogue.

It bears pausing here to explore this problem for a moment. As we have seen, two terms were used in the first century CE to refer to Judean places of communal assembly: "(place of) assembly" (*sunagōgē*) and "(place of) prayer" (*proseukhē*). Both terms appear to refer to one and the same institution—that which we have been calling here the "synagogue." From the vantage point of the twenty-first century, it seems hardly surprising that a synagogue might be called a "place of prayer," but this is not the case for the first century CE. The evidence suggests that prayer was *not* a regular feature in first-century synagogues.[65] Of all the many references to activities that took place in first-century synagogues, only two make any mention of prayer. One is Josephus's account of an assembly held in the *proseukhē* of Tiberias on a random Monday that had been declared a public fast day, during which time—apparently as part of the special regimen customary on such fast days—those assembled engaged in prayer.[66] The second is Matthew's account of Jesus scolding as "hypocrites" those who were so ostentatious in their performance of good deeds that they chose to pray in public spaces like street corners and synagogues.[67] This source, it seems, assumed that prayer was decidedly *not* a regular feature of the synagogue—any more than it was of street corners! It seems somewhat strange, then, that an institution whose primary function was as a meeting place for public Torah readings and communal learning, and where prayer was likely a rare activity at best, might be referred to not infrequently as a "(place of) prayer."

A possible solution—and a plausible one, to my mind—is that in the first century CE the term *proseukhē* was little more than an heirloom from an earlier time when there existed a Judean institution dedicated specifically to prayer.[68] This conjectural earlier institution may well be that which is represented in the inscriptions and papyri from Ptolemaic Egypt which speak exclusively of a Judean "*proseukhē*" and never of a Judean "*sunagōgē*." Such an institution may also be behind the "place" (*tópos*) the Judeans of Sardis were to be given "in which they may gather together with their wives and children and offer their ancestral prayers [*tàs patríous eukhàs*] and sacrifices [*thusías*] to God."[69] It is difficult to say precisely how "prayer" might have been conducted in such an institution, whether it might have been performed communally, or whether Judeans might have visited such an institution to pray on any kind of regular basis. Anders Runesson has suggested that early *"proseukhai"* of Egypt were essentially temples, where Judeans accompanied their prayers with offerings of incense and vegetable sacrifices (as at Sardis).[70] Be that as it may, we know from the inscriptions that the early *"proseukhē"* was located in a purpose-built structure (which at least sometimes had a "gateway" and an "exedra" annexed to it). Eventually, this early institution would have been replaced by what we might regard as a completely *new* institution in terms of its novel function—the *"sunagōgē."* Rather than a "(place of) prayer," the new institution was a "(place of) assembly" where Judeans would gather on a weekly basis for the purpose of communal learning. The name *"proseukhē"* carried over, however, and was sometimes used to refer to this new institution as well. The simple fact that both were Judean institutions located in a purpose-built structure may have been enough to provide for such a carryover of names. If the hypothesis is accepted as plausible, it follows that we ought to exercise extreme caution in adducing Ptolemaic-era epigraphic and papyrological evidence as a reliable indicator for the existence of something closely resembling the first-century-CE synagogue as early as the late third or second century BCE.

In summary, evidence for the existence of the synagogue prior to the first century CE is spotty at best. If we choose to accept the testimonies of Philo and Josephus regarding synagogues in the time of Augustus, we would have evidence for the institution as early as the late first century BCE or early first century CE. Assuming that the "assembly hall" excavated at Umm el-'Umdan (and more problematically at Delos) is interpreted as a gathering space for communal readings and learning, we would have a synagogue from as early as the Hasmonean period. If it is not wholly anachronistic, supporting evidence might be sought from Josephus's references to a synagogue in Antioch at this time. Epigraphic and papyrological references to *"proseukhai"* in Egypt would pull our earliest evidence as far back as the late third century BCE, but only if we take for granted the highly problematic proposition that the institution reflected in these inscriptions closely resembles the first-century-CE synagogue.

7 The Origins of Judaism Reappraised

In each of the preceding chapters, we investigated practices and prohibitions legislated in the Torah which had come to be widely observed by the first century CE as integral components of a commonly followed Judaism. In chapter after chapter, we sought textual and material evidence that might indicate if these practices and prohibitions were being observed by regular Judeans in the centuries prior to the first century. In each and every case, we learned that the trail of the available evidence ends in the second century BCE at the earliest. In the preceding chapter, we learned that the second or first century BCE provides the earliest available evidence that regular Judeans were gathering in synagogues in order to read and interpret the Torah communally. The entirety of this evidence clearly establishes the second century BCE as the terminus ante quem for the initial widespread dissemination of the Torah among the Judean masses and its common acceptance as authoritative law. In simpler terms, Judaism as it is defined in this book must have emerged either sometime in the middle of the second century BCE or earlier.

The present chapter will be devoted to going beyond this data-driven terminus ante quem and will explore when it would have been *most likely* for the Torah to have been adopted as authoritative law among the Judean masses. We will begin by investigating the likelihood that this might have occurred as early as the Persian period, an idea that many scholars take for granted (as we saw in the section "The History of Scholarship" in the introduction). As it will be shown that there are good reasons to think that at this time many Judeans knew nothing of the existence of anything resembling the Pentateuch, or at the very least were not adhering to its laws, we will proceed to assess the likelihood that Judaism may have emerged in the subsequent Early Hellenistic period. We will conclude this chapter with a cautious assessment of the proposition that the Torah came to be widely known to the masses and regarded as authoritative law only in the Late Hellenistic period, following the cataclysmic events surrounding the Hasmonean revolt toward the middle of the second century BCE.

The Persian Period (539–332 BCE)

Cyrus the Great (ca. 559–530 BCE), scion of the Teispid-Achaemenid royal dynasty of Persia, conquered Babylon in 539 BCE and consequently took hold of the vast territories that made up the Neo-Babylonian Empire of the time. Several communities of self-identifying Judeans are known to have flourished in various parts of this realm throughout much of the period of Persian rule, an era that ultimately ended with the conquests of Alexander the Great in the 330s BCE.

The present section seeks to assess the likelihood that the Torah might have come to be accepted by Judeans as their authoritative law and widely put into practice sometime during the Persian period. We will begin by examining the biblical narratives that are set in the days of the Teispid-Achaemenid kings and that tell the story of a Judean official named Ezra publicly disseminating "the *tôrāh* of Moses" among the populace of Judea. Following this, we will examine the "theory of Persian imperial authorization," which has posited that the Pentateuch came to be regarded as an authoritative source of law among Judeans through the mechanism of Achaemenid imperial sponsorship. Lastly, we will analyze the primary evidence from archaeological and epigraphic remains deriving from three Judean areas of settlement within the Persian realm—Judea proper (Yehud), Elephantine, and Babylonia—with the aim of assessing the degree to which these communities' ritual and cultic practices aligned with, or diverged from, Pentateuchal rules and regulations.

Ezra-Nehemiah on the Promulgation and Widespread Adoption of "the *Tôrāh* of Moses"

The canonical version of Ezra-Nehemiah is an apparently composite text, composed of several sources that were likely written by different authors at various times.[1] Several of these sources include tales about a public promulgation of "the *tôrāh* of Moses" among the residents of Judea during the Achaemenid period and its widespread adoption as binding law among the masses. Following an overview of these stories, we will attempt to assess whether any of these narratives reflect an actual historical reality wherein the Torah came to be widely accepted as authoritative law among the Judean masses as early as the Persian period.

AN OVERVIEW OF THE EZRA-NEHEMIAH TÔRĀH NARRATIVES

Ezra 7 tells about a certain priest named Ezra, described as "an agile scribe skilled in the instruction of Moses [sōfēr māhîr bətôrat mōšeh] that YHWH the God of Israel had given," who comes to Jerusalem from Babylon in the seventh regnal year of the Persian king "Artaxerxes" ('artaḥšast').[2] The purpose of this figure's arrival in Jerusalem is described as follows: "For Ezra had set his heart to inquire into the instruction of YHWH [lidrōš et tôrat YHWH], and to do it, and to teach in Israel statute and ordinance [ḥōq ûmišpāṭ]."[3] The author of this narrative then cites a copy of an Aramaic letter that Artaxerxes is purported to have given to Ezra, which included the following royal injunction: "And you, Ezra, according to the wisdom of your God that you possess, appoint magistrates and judges who may judge all the people in the province Beyond the River who know the laws [decrees?] of your God [dātê 'elāhākh]; and you shall teach those who do not know them. All who will not obey the law [decree?] of your God [dātā' dî 'elāhākh] and the law [decree?] of the king, let judgment be strictly executed on them, whether for death, or for banishment, or for confiscation of their goods, or for imprisonment."[4]

Following Ezra's arrival in Jerusalem, upon being told that the people have behaved treacherously by intermarrying with the "people of the lands," Ezra fasts and confesses their sins before YHWH: "For we have forsaken your commandments, which you commanded by your servants the prophets, saying, 'The land that you are entering to possess is a land unclean with the pollutions of the peoples of the lands, with their abominations. They have filled it from end to end with their uncleanness. Therefore do not give your daughters to their sons, neither take their daughters for your sons, and never seek their peace or prosperity, so that you may be strong and eat the good of the land and leave it for an inheritance to your children forever.'"[5] One of the pious bystanders, Shecaniah son of Jehiel, responds by suggesting to Ezra that the sinners remove their foreign wives and their children: "according to the counsel of my lord and of those who tremble at the commandment of our God; and let it be done according to the instruction [*wəkhatôrāh yē 'āśeh*]."[6]

An account of how Ezra's educational mission is ultimately carried out appears only in Neh 8, where a mass gathering ("all the people as one man") assembles in a square before the Water Gate of Jerusalem and requests that Ezra bring forth "the book of the instruction of Moses [*sēfer tôrat mōšeh*], which YHWH had commanded Israel."[7] Ezra then stands on a wooden platform, specially built for the occasion, and reads from the book before the assembled crowd from dawn to noon, while several named assistants "helped the people to understand the instruction [*məvînîm et hā 'ām latôrāh*], while the people remained in their places. So they read from the book, from the instruction of God [*bətôrat hā 'elōhîm*], with specification [*məfōrāš*]; and they gave the sense, so that the people understood the reading [*wəśôm śekhel wayāvînû bamiqrā '*]."[8]

The response of the people upon hearing "the words of the instruction [*divrê hatôrāh*]" is to weep. On the morrow, the "heads of the families of all the people" reconvene, together with the priests and Levites, to again "learn from the words of the instruction [*ləhaśkîl 'el divrê hatôrāh*]," upon which "it was found written in the instruction which YHWH had commanded through Moses [*batôrāh 'ăšer ṣiwāh YHWH bəyad mōšeh*], that the Children of Israel should abide in booths during the festival of the seventh month, and that they should publish and proclaim in all their towns and in Jerusalem as follows: 'Go out to the hills and bring foliage of olive, oil-wood, myrtle, palm, and leafy trees to make booths, as it is written.'"[9] Fulfilling this proclamation, the people go out and build for themselves booths on their rooftops, in their courtyards and in public areas, of which it is said that "from the days of Jeshua son of Nun to that day the Children of Israel had not done so."[10] Ezra continues to read "from the book of the instruction of God [*bəsēfer tôrat hā 'elōhîm*]" daily, until the last day of the seven-day holiday, which is followed by an assembly on the eighth day "according to the ordinance [*kamišpāṭ*]."[11]

Following this account, we find an extended speech addressed to YHWH, said to be made by a group of eight Levites (according to the Hebrew; in the Greek version it is Ezra who makes the speech), which recounts several of the narratives found in the Pentateuch, starting from creation and continuing through the covenant made with Abraham, the enslavement in Egypt, the exodus, the wandering through the desert, and the theophany on Mt. Sinai: "You came down also upon Mount

Sinai, and spoke with them from heaven, and gave them right ordinances [*mišpāṭîm yəšārîm*] and true instructions [*wətôrôt 'emet*], good statutes and commandments [*ḥuqîm ûmiṣwōt ṭôvîm*]. And you made known your holy Sabbath to them, and commandments and statutes and instruction [*ûmiṣwōt wəḥuqîm wətôrāh*] you commanded them through your servant Moses."[12] The speech ends with the text of a compact, to be ratified by a long list of Judah's dignitaries, in which these, along with the rest of the people loyal to the "instruction of God," pledge to "enter into a curse and an oath, to follow God's instruction [*lālekhet bətôrat hā'elōhîm*], which was given by Moses the servant of God, and to observe and do all the commandments of YHWH our lord and his ordinances and his statutes."[13] Among the specific commandments the people pledge to observe are abstention from inter-marriage with "the peoples of the land" and from conducting commerce with them on the Sabbath and on "a holy day," observance of the Sabbatical year remittance (of debts?), payment of an annual one-third-of-a-sheqel levy toward the upkeep of the temple, the bringing of a regular "offering of wood" for the altar's pyre, the annual bringing of the first fruits of crops to the temple and firstborn of both sons and livestock to the priests, and the bringing of tithes and heave offerings to the Levites and priests.[14]

Finally, Neh 13 relates how it was publicly read "from the book of Moses [*bəsēfer mōšeh*]" that an Ammonite and a Moabite were forever restricted from entering the congregation, and how immediately "upon hearing the instruction [*kəšām 'ām 'et hatôrāh*]," the people separated themselves from the prohibited "admixtures."[15] The narrator (i.e., Nehemiah) then recounts how Judeans were publicly desecrating the Sabbath by treading wine presses, by purchasing fish and "all kinds of merchandise" from Tyrians who lived in Jerusalem, and by loading donkeys with grain, wine, grapes, figs, "and all kinds of burdens" and bringing these into Jerusalem.[16] To all of this activity, described as "profanation of the Sabbath," Nehemiah responds by instructing that the gates of the city be shut every Sabbath day—a response that is said to have succeeded for the time in putting an end to the Sabbath desecration.

THE HISTORICITY OF THE EZRA-NEHEMIAH
TÔRĀH NARRATIVES

The anthology of stories cited here focuses on the concerted efforts of Judean leaders, chiefly Ezra, to promulgate a Mosaic "book of instruction" (*tôrāh*) as authoritative law among rank-and-file Judeans. Regardless of how exactly we might understand the character of this "book of instruction"—whether it was something closely resembling our canonical Pentateuch or whether it was an earlier version of this work which we might think of as a "proto-Pentateuch"—what is important for our purposes is that the sort of laws that the authors of these texts ascribe to this Mosaic "book" *do* seem to more or less resemble the kinds of laws found in the finalized Pentateuch.[17] The "instruction" (*tôrāh*) found in this book is portrayed as being read and explained to the people, perhaps even together with some exegetical explanations: "They read from the book . . . with specification [*məfōrāš*]; and they gave the sense, so that the people understood the reading [*wəśôm śekhel wayāvînû bamiqrā*]."[18] And most importantly, the Judean masses are portrayed as having accepted this law upon themselves as authoritatively binding. The central question that concerns us here is whether these tales reflect to one degree or another any sort of historical reality.

To begin, we must concede that almost nothing is known about the authors of any of these texts. We are ignorant, for example, as to whether these writers were active in the Persian period—the time when the plots in these stories are set—or if they lived and wrote their narratives only in later centuries.[19] One thing we know for sure about these authors is that they were literate and capable of compiling somewhat sophisticated narratives. Their purview of interests suggests that they were Judeans. And finally, we may infer from the gist of their writings that they believed that the Mosaic "*tôrāh*" was something that their fellow Judeans *ought to* observe diligently.

This last inference suggests that we are well advised to apply the technique of "*Tendenzkritik*" when analyzing the historicity of these texts. There can be little doubt that these narratives are best classified as ideological stories about the past. The stories surrounding Ezra's ascent from Babylon by imperial decree to teach and enforce the Mosaic *tôrāh*, and the subsequent dramatic public acceptance of this *tôrāh* by the masses of Jerusalem, are all aimed at staking the normative claim that the Mosaic *tôrāh* is something that *should* be accepted by all Judeans as binding. This seems to be a central motive for why these narratives were put into writing in the first place. There is nothing in the texts themselves which suggests that these stories were written with the intent of conveying historically accurate details about the past. These are idealized portraits of earlier times, aimed at communicating an unambiguously ideological agenda. These are stories; they are not histories. If anyone wishes to stake the claim that these stories reflect some kind of historical reality, the burden of proof lies squarely on his or her shoulders to demonstrate that such is likely to be the case.[20]

Even if we *were* to accept the narratives relayed in Ezra-Nehemiah at face value and naively assume without compelling evidence that they necessarily represent some historical reality, it should be noted that the stories themselves never stake the claim that Ezra's promulgation of the Mosaic book of instruction had any lasting effects upon the Judean masses. Although the people are said to have initially accepted the Torah as binding law and immediately put some of its rules into practice, this purported widespread acceptance of the Torah is also said to have been ephemeral. According to the usual understanding that Ezra is depicted as having arrived prior to Nehemiah, when we read in Neh 13:15–31 that the latter found the Judeans desecrating the Sabbath and marrying foreign women, it appears that the internal story line itself seeks to portray Ezra's previous efforts as having had little long-term consequences.[21]

In summary, the collection of tales about the promulgation and widespread acceptance of a Mosaic Torah in Achaemenid Jerusalem by an Ezra figure, in and of itself, provides little compelling reason to think that anything of the sort actually took place. To be sure, none of this is to say that these stories are *necessarily* wholly fictious; it is only to demand compelling evidence demonstrating the likelihood that these narratives reflect some sort of historical reality before they are accepted as credible witnesses for the emergence of Judaism as early as the Persian period.[22]

THE THEORY OF PERSIAN IMPERIAL AUTHORIZATION

In the introduction to this book, I briefly mentioned an idea, first propounded by Eduard Meyer in 1896, that the promulgation of the Pentateuch among rank-and-file Judeans was a direct result of Achaemenid interests in legislating a local law code for the province of Yehud. This hypothesis came back into vogue following an influential study published in 1984 by Peter Frei, a Swiss scholar of ancient history, which argued that Persian imperial policy sought to guarantee local customs and legal norms through a process of "imperial authorization" (*Reichsautorisation*).[23] Frei adduced a number of examples of codification of local Egyptian regulations under Darius I, Achaemenid involvement in the founding of local cults at Elephantine and in Asia Minor, and claims in the books of Ezra-Nehemiah and Esther that Persian kings had authorized the legislation of certain Judean customs and laws. In his treatment of the biblical materials, Frei never took for granted that the narratives presented by the biblical authors are in any way *histori-cal*. To the contrary, he assumed that in many cases they are fictional. He argued only that when it can be shown that the author of a story was familiar with details of the real historical environment within which his plot unfolds, we must assume that the setting within which he placed his narrative accurately reflects situations, conditions, and institutions typical of the time within which his story is set. For Frei, the biblical narratives relating to the Persian period retain their worth in this manner even if they were written in the Hellenistic period, as accurate knowledge of Achaemenid conditions was likely retained for some time even into the third century BCE.

Within a few years after Frei's study was published, biblical scholars began to use his thesis by flipping it on its head; whereas Frei had cited Ezra 7 as a possibly *fictive* narrative that supported his more general claims about Persian policies, biblical scholars now took the notion of Achaemenid imperial authority as a likely historical framework wherein the Pentateuch became legally binding upon the general populace of Persian Yehud.[24] Many of these scholars posited that in order to present the Persian authorities with a unified document for official ratification, the various groups in Yehud were forced to come to an agreement tolerable on the majority. This they accomplished by combining disparate "Priestly" and "non-Priestly" compositions into a single document that looked something very much like the Pentateuch we have today. With the official authorization of this document by the central Persian government, the Pentateuch became the normative law of the residents of Yehud, and perhaps also of Judean communities elsewhere throughout the empire.

The hypothesis, which came to be known as the "theory of Persian imperial authorization," might have been regarded as providing circumstantial support for the idea that Judaism emerged as early as the Persian period. If indeed the central Persian government authorized the Torah as the official code of law to govern Yehud, we might have had good reason to suspect that the Judean masses on their part would likely have acceded to this legal mandate by putting into practice in their daily lives the rules and regulations of the Torah. As it stands today, however, the hypothesis has few remaining adherents. The first flurry of studies in the early 1990s by biblical scholars favorable to Frei's hypothesis was met by a barrage of counterarguments beginning in the second half of the same decade.[25] The pushback came from two main directions. The first relates to Frei's hypothesis itself.

Scholars questioned whether the evidence Frei adduced really does point to any kind of concerted, unified Achaemenid policy of granting imperial authorization to local legal norms. The documents presented by Frei are often ambiguous in meaning, and the individual cases they tell of, when viewed together, present a rather incongruous picture of how the Persian authorities dealt with local matters. The second problem lies in the fact that even if we accept Frei's hypothesis of a general Achaemenid policy of authorizing local norms, we still have little reason to think that the local code the Persians would have ratified for the province of Yehud would have been *the Pentateuch*. Why, for example, would the central Persian authority have been interested in including a large amount of *narrative* material in their officially authorized *law code*? And how could they have allowed material that would have been at odds with imperial interests, such as God's promise to Abraham's seed of all the land stretching from the "river of Egypt" to the Euphrates (Gen 15:18), or the various injunctions throughout Deuteronomy to wage war against—and to utterly annihilate—the nations occupying the land? Even if we were to assume that the Persians authorized a local law for Yehud, these scholars argued, it is highly unlikely that the law code would have looked anything like the Pentateuch as we have it.

Archaeological and Epigraphic Evidence of Judean Ritual and Cultic Practices

In what follows, we will seek to investigate the archaeological and epigraphic remains that reflect ritual and cultic practices associated with Persian-period Judeans. The question to be considered is the degree to which this assemblage of primary evidence may or may not be suggestive of widespread familiarity and compliance with Torah law. To date, a significant volume of relevant archaeological and epigraphic data is available from three distinct geographical locations in which communities we know to have self-defined as "Judean" thrived during the Persian period: Judea proper, Elephantine in Egypt, and Babylonia. The evidence from each of these areas will be examined here separately.

JUDEA

We have already seen in chapter 1 that certain limited evidence suggests that at least some people in Persian-era Jerusalem were eating catfish, a scaleless fish prohibited in the Pentateuch. In chapter 3, we saw that all the surviving coin types minted in fourth-century-BCE Yehud under the auspices of local Judean authorities displayed human and/or animal images. We furthermore saw there that figural art is present in the sporadic finds of terracotta figurines at several sites in Yehud and in a locally manufactured anthropomorphic vessel depicting a finely molded human face (perhaps the Egyptian god Bes) recently unearthed in Jerusalem. These findings would appear to suggest behaviors discordant with apparent Pentateuchal regulations.

In the cultic sphere, it seems quite certain that Judeans in Persian-era Yehud had inherited from their Iron Age forebears veneration of a deity named YHWH. Most saliently, this is reflected in the frequent use of theophoric elements deriving from YHWH in personal names found within the region of Yehud on coins, ostraca, stamp impressions, bullae, and a lone papyrus document.[26] Unfortunately, the archaeological record has preserved precious few remains that might indicate how local Judeans might have worshiped this deity. It seems that the most we can say with any degree of certainty is that a hierarchical order of Yahwistic priests was to be found in Jerusalem by the late fifth century BCE. A papyrus found at Elephantine refers to a letter sent by the Elephantine Judeans circa 410 BCE to a certain "Jehohanan the high priest [kāhănā᾿ rabā᾿] and his colleagues the priests [kāhănayā᾿] who are in Jerusalem," together with another named official and "the nobles of the Judeans [ḥōrê yəhûdāyē᾿]."[27] From this we learn that by the end of the fifth century, there was a serving "high priest" in Jerusalem whose authority was of sufficient stature that he was (so it seems) the chief addressee of a letter of supplication sent by Judeans in distant Egypt, and seemingly of superior status to "the nobles of Judea." Presumably such a high priest would have had a cultic role of some sort—almost certainly in the cult of YHWH, judging from Jehohanan's Yahwistic name and from the context of the letter. As "high priest," he presumably would have served at the head of a hierarchy of lesser priests. This probably implies the existence of a functioning temple dedicated to the cult of YHWH in Jerusalem at this time and, if so, it would be our most direct evidence for the existence of such a temple in Persian-period Jerusalem outside of the biblical texts. No archaeological remains from a Persian-period temple in Jerusalem have been identified to date, but probably this is only because any such remains would have been covered over with the Herodian-era temenos that forms the Temple Mount and would therefore be currently inaccessible to archaeological investigations. One other find that likely

Figure 18. *Persian-period silver coin bearing the Paleo–Hebrew legend "Johanan the priest" (yôḥānān hakôhēn). (Photo © The Israel Museum, Jerusalem, by Yair Hovav.)*

relates to this temple is a silver quarter-obol coin dated to the Persian period that contains the Paleo-Hebrew legend "Johanan the priest" (*yôḥānān hakôhēn*) (fig. 18); if not identical to the high priest Jehohanan mentioned in the Elephantine letter, this individual very likely held the same position in the cult of YHWH.[28] At the very least, the high standing of this Johanan and his office is implied by the fact that a coin was minted with his name and title. None of this limited evidence suggests that the cultic activities carried out by this priestly hierarchy in this presumed temple necessarily conformed with anything resembling the rules and regulations outlined in the Pentateuch. If, as seems likely, a temple dedicated to the cultic worship of YHWH flourished in Jerusalem (among other places) throughout much of the Iron Age, it would not be a stretch to imagine that the cultic regime carried out in a subsequent Persian-period temple in Jerusalem might have simply followed earlier priestly practices.

The character of ritual and cultic practices that may have taken place in Judea *outside* the sphere of a central Jerusalem temple may be examined by seeking out the presence or absence of certain material finds that may be regarded as "ritual" artifacts. Ephraim Stern has noted that while many assemblages of figurines and several sanctuary structures have been unearthed in parts of the Southern Levant known to have been inhabited by non-Judean ethnic groups (i.e., in Idumea, Phoenicia, and Galilee), none have been found in Judea itself: "In areas of the country inhabited by Jews during the Persian Period, ... not a single cultic figurine or sanctuary has been found! This, in spite of the many excavations and surveys that have been conducted, and the same is true of Samaria. Archaeologists have also failed to locate any sanctuaries for this period within Judah and Samaria, while many have been found outside their borders, with two exceptions: the new Temple of Jerusalem, which was never excavated, and the Samaritan Temple on Mount Gerizim."[29] According to Stern, this lack of "cultic figurines" and sanctuaries in Persian-period Yehud stands in stark contrast not only to the plethora of such finds elsewhere in the region contemporaneously but also to the many figurines and local sanctuaries found in Judea itself at the end of the Iron Age. This understanding led Stern to hypothesize that Yehud underwent a "religious revolution" wherein "all the pagan-popular elements had undergone purification during the Persian Period" and no longer had any role within the "religious" expression of common Judeans.[30] If Stern is correct, such a revolution might be explained by hypothesizing the widespread adoption of Torah as authoritative among local Judeans at this time—although such an explanation is hardly the only plausible one available.

Stern's assessment has come under increased scrutiny in recent years, perhaps most saliently in the 2014 volume of essays dedicated to explicitly challenging his thesis and titled in the form of a question: *A "Religious Revolution" in Yehûd?*[31] On the one hand, Stern's claim that "not a single cultic figurine" has been unearthed in Achaemenid Yehud has been shown to be less than accurate; a small number of terracotta figurines *have* been identified in Persian-period strata within the presumed boundaries of Yehud.[32] On the other hand, scholars have also questioned the *significance* of the relative lack of figurines in Persian-period Yehud when compared to the large number of such finds in contemporaneous neighboring regions and in Iron Age Judea itself. Stern's argument has force only if the "cultic figurines" found outside the geographic boundaries of Yehud and in Iron Age Judea are assumed to represent deities—a presumption many scholars reject.[33] Furthermore, a large percentage of the Persian-era figurines found outside Yehud are votive objects unearthed in favissae located within the enclosures of sanctuaries; lack of parallels from Yehud may be due to the simple fact that no shrine dedicated to YHWH and located within the boundaries of Yehud has (yet?) been identified and excavated.[34] At most, the fact that a relatively smaller number of figurines were found in Persian-period Judea compared to other parts of the country and compared to early periods of time may reflect a certain degree of aniconism that had taken root in local contemporary YHWH worship, although clearly not in any kind of universal way.

To what degree might Judeans in Yehud have practiced their veneration of YHWH to the exclusion of other deities? In chapter 3, we encountered sporadic examples of figurines representing foreign deities (Astarte, Osiris, and Bes) unearthed in Persian-era Judea. Beyond these, coins minted in fourth-century Judea (also discussed in chapter 3) present what may be the most significant data suggestive of a certain degree of openness toward the recognition of deities other than YHWH among Judeans living in Persian Yehud. Perhaps the clearest examples are the coins that imitate an Athenian prototype that displayed the helmeted head of the goddess Athena on the obverse, with her sacred owl and olive branch on the reverse, accompanied by a legend in Paleo-Hebrew reading *"Yəhūd"* in place of the Greek *"Athe[natōn]"* ([of the] Athe[nians]) on the original Athenian coins.[35] Many scholars have downplayed the significance of these coins as simple imitations whose iconography was copied but whose "religious" meaning was ignored.[36] This may be, but we should not discount the possibility that many Judeans who used these coins would have recognized the image as that of the Greek warrior goddess. There are good reasons to believe that the Greek Athena was identified among easterners with the West Semitic goddess Anat, whom, as we shall see below, appears to have been venerated by the Judeans at Elephantine.[37] Is it at all unlikely that also in Yehud Judeans may have viewed Anat/Athena as a deity to be recognized, if not revered, alongside the primary cult of YHWH? Aside from Athena, additional divine beings appear to be represented on other coins minted for use in Yehud, including a winged lynx figure, a royal head on a lion's body, and a possible depiction of the nymph Arethusa.[38] Another much-discussed coin bearing the legend *"Yəhūd"* displays on its reverse a bearded figure holding a bird and seated on a winged wheel, with the head of a bearded male facing the seated figure's shins.[39] If, as many scholars have suggested, the seated figure represents YHWH himself, the head of the bearded male facing him may be identified as a different deity. Alternatively, the seated male has been identified as a deity other than YHWH, with numerous identifications suggested. Either of these two possibilities would have a deity other than YHWH represented on this Judean coin as well. If any of these interpretations are accepted, the numismatic remains would appear to suggest either wholesale ignorance of the manifold Pentateuchal injunctions against the veneration of "foreign gods" or else largescale flouting of these interdictions.[40]

In summary, while it seems quite likely that the ancestral Judean deity YHWH was widely venerated among the residents of Persian Yehud, the archaeological record is largely silent regarding the details of *how* Judeans might have worshiped their god at this time, and the degree to which either popular or official forms of YHWH veneration might have been at all exclusivist. Even if the data are interpreted as suggesting the prevalence of a monolatrist/monotheistic and aniconic cult, the archaeological remains on their own provide no indication that during the Persian period the ritual and cultic practices associated with YHWH worship might have resembled anything like those legislated in the Pentateuch.

ELEPHANTINE

A large corpus of papyri and ostraca associated with a Persian-era Judean community has been unearthed on the island of Elephantine (and at the neighboring mainland settlement of Syene) in the Upper Nile region of Egypt.[41] Many of the texts within this assemblage contain precise dates ranging from close to the beginning of the fifth century BCE to the end of that century. The community associated with this epigraphic corpus self-identified as "Judeans" (*yəhûdāyē'/yəhûdîn*) in their own writings, its members worshiped a deity named YHW or YHH (shortened forms of YHWH), and many individuals bore Hebrew names containing Yahwistic theophoric elements.[42] As we have seen above, members of the Judean leadership at Elephantine were in written correspondence with fellow Judeans in Judea proper, including with the provincial governor of Yehud and with a "high priest" and his subordinate priesthood in Jerusalem.

We have already encountered material from Elephantine in previous chapters, where I cited scholarship that has consistently sought to read Pentateuchal laws into the epigraphic remains. Three poorly preserved ostraca that employ the terms "impure" (*ṭm'*) and "pure" (*ṭhr*) have been assumed to belong to Judeans and have been interpreted in light of Pentateuchal rules of purity. Two letters on ostraca that refer pithily to "Passover" (*pisḥā'*)—apparently an observance of some sort with no set date or time—have been interpreted through the lens of biblical sources that relate to the springtime Passover sacrifice. Famously, a fragmentary papyrus letter refers to a period of time between the fifteenth and the twenty-first days of a certain month, possibly Nisan. The preserved portion of the papyrus speaks only of drinking fermented beverages (whether as a prescription or as a prohibition), but scholars have filled in the missing portions of the letter in lockstep with Pentateuchal and rabbinic laws about the Festival of Unleavened Bread. And finally, an ostracon that implores its addressee to engage in commerce "on Sabbath" (*bəšabāh*) has been explained away as implying "some extraordinary situation," and therefore indirectly attesting to the *regular observance* of the Sabbath. All these interpretations *assume from the start* that the Judeans of Elephantine knew about and observed the laws of the Torah; to take the data in question *as evidence of such* is to commit the fallacy of circular reasoning.

Indeed, none of the Elephantine documents make any mention of "*tôrāh*" (or an Aramaic equivalent), of the name Moses, or of any kind of document that might be thought to otherwise resemble the Pentateuch. Neither do any of the Elephantine documents cite any verses that might be thought to resemble any Pentateuchal verses. As far as the surviving evidence indicates, the Torah was simply not known at Elephantine.[43] In fact, numerous epigraphic remains within the Elephantine corpus seem quite hard to square with the assumption that the Judeans living at this location regarded the Pentateuch as an authoritative source of law—or even that they knew anything of its existence at all. While these Judeans worshiped YHWH as their primary deity, several documents indicate that they concomitantly venerated multiple deities other than YHWH—in direct violation of the many Pentateuchal proscriptions against polytheism. A document from Syene dated to 440 BCE tells of a Judean woman named Mibtahiah, daughter of Mahseiah, son of Jedania (all Yahwistic names), who, upon her divorce from her (apparently Egyptian) husband, swore an oath by Sati "the goddess ['*elāhatā* ']."[44] Another document, dated to 401 BCE tells of a Judean bearing an oath to Herembethel "the god ['*elāhā* ']."[45] And yet another (undated) document tells of an oath taken by one Judean to another in the name of "H[erem?] the [god] in/by the place of prostration [*bəmisgādā* '] and by Anathyahu [*ûva ănātYHW*]."[46] The meaning of the name Anathyahu is not at all self-evident, but a plausible interpretation is that it means "Anat of YHW" and refers to the Semitic goddess Anat as the female consort of YHW.[47] As we have seen in chapter 5, the Judean author of the so-called Passover Letter began his message to his "brothers" of the Judean garrison with a salutation invoking "the gods" ('*elāhayā* ') to ensure the welfare of the addressees.[48] Another letter, sent from one Judean to another, opened with the salutation "May all the gods ['*elāhayā* kōl*] seek after your welfare at all times."⁴⁹ And in yet another document, a servant by the name of Giddel (or Gaddal) blessed his Judean lord Micaiah "by YHH and by Khnum [*ləYHH ûləḤnûm*]"—invoking the Judean deity together with the Egyptian ram-headed god.⁵⁰

Most telling, perhaps, is a papyrus scroll from Elephantine that is usually dated to either 419 or 400 BCE and which contains a lengthy accounting of the names of individual members of "the garrison of the Judeans" who "gave silver to YHW the god [*zî yəhav kəsaf ləYHW 'elāhā*]."⁵¹ Although the surviving list is fragmentary, it appears that it included over one hundred names of Judeans who contributed two sheqels of silver each. Following this accounting, it is noted that the entire sum was collected by a certain Jedaniah b. Gemariah, who divided the silver among three deities: 126 sheqels for YHW, 70 sheqels for Eshembethel, and 120 sheqels for Anathbethel.⁵² It is something of a mystery why the prologue of the document claims that the monies were given to YHW, while the epilogue states that the monies were subsequently distributed to YHW along with two other gods. Regardless of the solution to this problem, the fact remains that the Judean Jedaniah took the contributions collected from over one hundred fellow Judeans and distributed them—unproblematically to the donors, it seems—between YHW and two other Semitic deities.

To all of this evidence of polytheistic veneration among the Judeans of Elephantine we may add that there are several instances within the corpus where a person with a non-Hebrew name bearing a theophoric element of a deity other than YHWH is said to be either the child of or the father or grandfather of someone with a Hebrew, Yahwistic name.⁵³ All of these cases imply that a Judean had chosen to name his or her son in a manner that acknowledged a deity other than YHWH.

One more reason to think that the Judeans of Elephantine knew nothing of the Pentateuch—or else that they ignored it—is that a temple to YHWH operated on the island throughout the course of much of the fifth century BCE, in clear violation of Deuteronomic proscriptions against the offering of sacrifices outside "the place that YHWH will choose" in Cisjordan.⁵⁴ One document refers to this temple as "the altar-house [*bêt madbəḥā*]," and an altar associated with this shrine is also attested elsewhere.⁵⁵ The temple was operated by "priests [*kāhǎnayā*]" as well as by male and female staff holding the enigmatic title of "servitor [*ləḥēn/ləḥēnāh*]."⁵⁶ The temple's cultic worship apparently included a regular set of "meal-offering, incense and burnt-offering [*mîḥātā' ûlvôntā'*] *wə ʿalwātā ʾ*]" together with other forms of "sacrifices [*dīvḥīn*]."[57] Two of-ficial documents (apparently drafts of the same letter) dated to 407 BCE and sent by "Jedaniah and his colleagues, the priests [*kāhănayā ʾ*] who are in the fortress of Elephantine," to Bagohi, the governor of Yehud, tell of the destruction of this temple in the year 410 BCE at the hands of troops from Syene and priests of Khnum.[58] Noting that they had previously sent a letter on the matter to "Jehohanan the high priest and his colleagues the priests who are in Jerusalem," together with another named official and "the no-bles of the Judeans," but did not receive a reply, the Elephantine Judeans requested that the governor of Yehud himself intercede on behalf of the rebuilding of this temple.[59] The letter concludes with a note claiming that a similar request had been sent also to "Delaiah and Shelemiah, the sons of Sanballat the governor of Samaria." Fortuitously, an undated memorandum recording the joint reply of Bagohi and Delaiah in support of the rebuild-ing of the temple has also survived.[60] One more undated document written by Jedaniah and his colleagues and probably addressed to a Persian official contains what appears to be a negotiation regarding the conditions for the rebuilding of this temple.[61] None of these documents—including the re-ported correspondence with Judean officials in Yehud—suggest that the Judeans of Elephantine ever entertained the notion that a temple located outside Jerusalem might be viewed as in any way problematic.[62]

In summary, the Torah seems to have been unknown to the Judeans of Elephantine. The well-documented ritual and cultic practices of the Ju-deans at Elephantine appear to have been quite different from what the Pentateuch would have allowed, apologetic attempts to interpret this data in line with Pentateuchal norms notwithstanding. Importantly, there is little reason to think that the ritual and cultic practices followed by the Judeans at Elephantine differed in any substantial way from those followed by the average Judeans one would have encountered elsewhere within the Persian realm.[63]

BABYLONIA

A significant corpus of cuneiform tablets dating to 572–477 BCE has been associated with a Judean presence in Babylonia.[64] About one-third of the tablets were written at a site that bore the toponym "*Yāhūdu*" (Judah-town) or "*ālu ša Yāhūdāya*" (Town of the Judeans), while others were writ-ten at sites named "*Ālu ša Našar*" (or "*Bīt Našar*") and "*Bīt Abī-râm*."[65] A large proportion of the individuals mentioned in documents from these sites bear names that are in Hebrew and/or that bear Yahwistic theophoric elements. Yahwistic names are also found among another large collection of texts known as the "Murašû archive," which dates to a slightly later time within the Persian period (455–403 BCE).[66]

Nothing in these documents suggests that Babylonian Judeans in the sixth and fifth centuries BCE knew of the existence of the Pentateuch, let alone that they observed any of its rules and regulations. To the contrary, in chapter 5 we noted that the dates found on these documents reveal no conscious effort on the part of Judeans to refrain from participating in transactions conducted on Saturdays. Perhaps even more significantly, theophoric names associated with deities other than YHWH are found among Judean families both in the Yāhūdu documents (although in very small numbers) and in the Murašû archive.[67] One of the more interesting deities found among these names is "Bīt-il," apparently identical with the theonym "Bethel," which, as we have seen, featured so prominently among the Judean documents from Elephantine.[68] Another indication that Judeans in Babylonia may have venerated various gods alongside YHWH may be found in the iconography on seals they used for signing documents, which sometimes included divine symbols or images of deities such as Marduk, Ištar, Sîn, and Ahura Mazda.[69] Furthermore, some examples of marriage agreements pertaining to Judeans summon the Babylonian deities Marduk, Zarpanītu, and Nabu to punish the violator of the agreement.[70] The general impression one gains from all of this is that the Judeans of Babylonia, like their ethnic brethren at Elephantine, did not see an inherent incompatibility between veneration of YHWH and openly displayed reverence toward other deities.[71]

Conclusions

The literary, epigraphic, and archaeological evidence surviving from the Persian period provide little reason to think that large numbers of ordinary Judeans adhered to the precepts and prohibitions of the Pentateuch at this early date. Furthermore, this evidence provides little reason to think that even the *existence* of a compilation resembling the Pentateuch—or indeed any of its constituent parts—was at all known about among anyone outside a small circle of Judean literati. The Ezra-Nehemiah narratives that tell of mass acceptance of the Torah among the populace of Judea are best classified as ideological stories about the past rather than as anything akin to accurate accounts about real events. There is nothing in these narratives themselves which suggests that the stories reflect any kind of historical reality. Even if we *were* to accept the anthology of tales in Ezra-Nehemiah about the promulgation of a Mosaic Torah in Persian-era Jerusalem at face value, the stories themselves suggest that Ezra's promulgation of the Torah had no lasting effects on the Judean masses. Furthermore, the by-now largely discredited "theory of Persian imperial authorization" fails to provide a compelling reason to assume that the Achaemenids would have sponsored the Pentateuch as the local law of Yehud. And finally, much of the surviving archaeological and epigraphic finds from Judea proper, from Elephantine, and from Babylonia suggest that Judean ritual and cultic practices during the Persian era diverged significantly from fundamental rules and regulations found in the Pentateuch. Most saliently, Judeans in Elephantine, Babylonia, and perhaps even Judea seemed to have at least tolerated the veneration of deities other than YHWH—much as the Judeans' Iron Age forebears did—in violation of clear Pentateuchal proscriptions against polytheistic worship. Similarly, a temple dedicated to YHWH at Elephantine blatantly contravened the centralization of the cult in Cisjordan as prescribed in Deuteronomy.

Taken together, the popular ritual and cultic practices of the Judean masses during the Persian period may well be reconstructed as largely resembling those of the Judeans' Iron Age ancestors, with the possible exception that cultic figurines (if that is indeed what they were) may have no longer remained in large-scale use in Yehud. Like Egyptians, Phoenicians, Babylonians, Medes, and others, Judeans living under Persian dominion likely shared with one another certain unique cultural practices that were distinct to one degree or another from those found among neighboring cultures. These probably would have included the celebration of festivals, the practice of rites of passage, the observance of dietary conventions, the commemoration of the dead through rituals of burial and mourning, and more. It seems likely that many of these unique cultural practices might have been passed down to the Judeans of the Persian era from their Iron Age progenitors, who themselves might have inherited much of this cultural baggage from their own Bronze Age forebears. Significantly, however, none of this presupposes anything resembling what would eventually manifest as "Judaism": a distinct way of life *governed by a legal system* composed of commandments, prohibitions, and assorted regulations founded on the Pentateuch.

Certainly, none of the evidence explored here demonstrates in any conclusive manner that the Torah had *not* emerged sometime during the Persian period as the authoritative law of the Judeans. Much if not all of the evidence signaling practices at odds with the Pentateuch may well be interpreted as dating to the time *immediately before* the Torah might have come to be known and regarded as authoritative by the masses. Alternatively, this evidence may be thought to reflect a minority of Judeans who had not (yet?) come to accept the rules of the Torah, despite its authority having already begun to be widely acknowledged among most Judeans. Nevertheless, the fact remains that *no evidence* has survived from the Persian period that necessarily indicates familiarity with Torah observance, while *copious evidence* has survived that reveals noncompliance with Torah laws. While this means that we cannot rule out the possibility that Judaism emerged as early as the Persian period, the sum of the evidence suggests that we would be better advised to seek the origins of Judaism in a later era.

The Early Hellenistic Period (332–167 BCE)

The Persian Levant fell to the forces of Alexander the Great of Macedonia in 332 BCE, and following the death of Alexander in 323 BCE, Judea passed hands several times between various generals who had served under the Macedonian conqueror (the so-called Diadochi). In 301 BCE, Judea finally came under the steady dominion of the Macedonian general who ruled out of Alexandria, Ptolemy I Soter (ca. 305–282 BCE). Judea subsequently remained under Ptolemaic rule until around 200 BCE, when Antiochus III Megas (222–187 BCE), scion of the Seleucid dynasty ruling out of Antioch on the Orontes, wrested the Southern Levant from Ptolemaic hands. Judea stayed under uncontested Seleucid dominion until a Judean revolt broke out under the leadership of the Hasmonean family under the reign of Antiochus IV Epiphanes (175–164 BCE), probably around 167 BCE.

The present section seeks to assess the likelihood that the Torah might have been adopted by rank-and-file Judeans as their authoritative law sometime during the 165-year period between the conquests of Alexander and the outbreak of the Hasmonean revolt. We will begin by critically examining several literary sources that might be thought to suggest that the Torah was widely known among regular Judeans and regarded by them as authoritative during this time. This will be followed by an exploration of a hypothesis, first forwarded some years ago by Michael LeFebvre, which posits that the Pentateuch was recharacterized from a *descriptive* collection of laws to a *prescriptive* code of law during the Early Hellenistic period on the basis of contemporary Greek ideas surrounding the notion of written law.

The Literary Evidence

ALLEGED CITATIONS FROM HECATAEUS OF ABDERA

The Mosaic law is described quite explicitly as the authoritative law of the Judeans in two sources that have been thought to cite the now lost writings of the late fourth-century-BCE Hecataeus of Abdera. The first is Josephus's first book *Against Apion*, but as the citation there that Josephus attributed to Hecataeus is widely rejected by modern scholars as pseudepigraphic (it is thought to actually have been written by a Judean at a much later time), it will not detain us here.[72] The second source is the ninth-century-CE *Bibliotheca* of Photius, the Byzantine Patriarch of Constantinople, who cited directly from a now lost book of the mid-first-century-BCE author Diodorus Siculus.[73] In this citation, Diodorus prefaces his report about Pompey's war against the Judeans in the 60s BCE with a brief historical overview of "both the foundation of this nation from the beginning, and the customs [*nómima*] among them." According to Diodorus's account, the Judeans were aliens driven out of Egypt, and they subsequently established a colony in Judea and founded the city of Jerusalem under the leadership of Moses. In Jerusalem, Moses built a temple and "established the offices and rites for the divinity, codified and arranged the things relating to the constitution [*tà katà tèn politeían enomothétēsé te kaì diétaxe*]. . . . He established sacrifices and modes of conduct for everyday life [*tàs katà tòn bíon agōgás*] differing from those of other nations." Moses entrusted "guardianship of the laws and customs [*tōn nómōn kaì tōn ethōn*]" to the priests, with a high priest who is believed to act as "a messenger to them of the commandments of the god [*tōn toū theoū prostagmátōn*]." This high priest "proclaims the commands in the assemblies and other gatherings," and the Judeans are so obedient that they "immediately fall to the ground and make obeisance to the high priest interpreting [the laws] to them." Diodorus claims to cite directly from the Judeans' law in what may represent a paraphrase from one of several possible Pentateuchal verses: "There is appended even to the laws, at the end: 'Moses having heard these things from the god says [them] to the Judeans."[74] The citation from the work of Diodorus concludes with the following remark: "But during the [foreign] rules that happened later, out of mingling with men of other nations—both under the hegemony of the Persians and of the Macedonians who overthrew this [hegemony]—many of the traditional customs of the Judeans [*tōn patríōn toîs Ioudaíois nomímōn*] were distorted." After presenting this citation from Diodorus, Photius accuses Diodorus of "telling lies about most things," adding that Diodorus "distorted the truth" by falsely attributing his description to another author: "Using a cunning device as a refuge for himself, he attributes to another [author] the above said things, which are contrary to history. For he [i.e., Diodorus] adds: 'As concerns the Judeans, this is what Hecataeus of Miletus relates about the Judeans.'"[75] Whereas Photius tells us that Diodorus claimed that his knowledge about the Judeans was indebted to the work of Hecataeus of Miletus, Photius himself believed that this claim on the part of Diodorus was nothing less than a deliberate fabrication.

Most scholars today reject Photius's skepticism regarding Diodorus's assertion that he had gleaned his knowledge about the Judeans from an earlier Hecataeus.[76] Not only do these scholars believe that Diodorus truly was informed by this earlier work; most have gone one step further in asserting that almost the entire citation from the work of Diodorus presented to us by Photius is actually *a direct citation* from Hecataeus![77] Furthermore, most scholars have emended the word "*Milésios*" with "*Abdērítēs*," arguing that Diodorus would have most likely meant Hecataeus of Abdera (ca. 300 BCE) rather than the earlier Hecataeus of Miletus (ca. 500 BCE).[78]

On the supposition that we have here before us a direct citation from Hecataeus of Abdera, one might view the description of how the Judeans as a group treated the Mosaic laws as evidence which demonstrates that, by the turn of the third century BCE, widespread knowledge of the Torah and its common observance among the Judean masses had already become the norm.[79] This conclusion is hardly compelling, however, as it rests entirely upon extremely shaky assumptions. First, we do not know if Diodorus had an authentic work of Hecataeus of Abdera from which he learned his information about the Judeans.[80] Even if he did, there is little reason to think that Diodorus's account represents a *direct citation* from Hecataeus. From what Photius tells us, Diodorus does not seem to have ever made any such claim; according to Photius, Diodorus simply informed his readers from where he had gleaned his knowledge about Judeans. I see no reason to assume that Diodorus would have been informed *only* from the alleged work of Hecataeus and not from any later sources of information. And I certainly see no reason to assume that we have here anything resembling a *direct citation* from Hecataeus. To the contrary, scholars today understand that, in compiling his histories, Diodorus regularly drew from several sources and routinely mingled the information he elicited from these sundry informants into his own historical constructions.[81]

Because of these serious uncertainties, we should conclude that the description of the Judeans found in the work of the first-century-BCE Diodorus provides no compelling reason to think that the Judean masses knew of the Torah and regarded it as legally binding as early as the turn of the third century BCE.

THE LETTER OF ARISTEAS AND THE SEPTUAGINT

The Letter of Aristeas presents itself as a written, eyewitness account conveyed by a certain Aristeas, courtier of Ptolemy II Philadelphus (ca. 285–246 BCE), to his brother Philocrates. The writer portrays himself as part of a delegation from Ptolemy's court sent to Jerusalem in order to recruit a group of seventy-two Judean elders who were to be tasked with translating the Judean law into Greek. This law is described as given by God and as "legislation ... established for all Judeans [*tēs gàr nomothesías keiménēs pāsi toîs Ioudaíois*]," while the Judeans themselves are described as "men who have lived—and are living—in accordance with [*tôn kat' autà pepoliteuménōn kaì politeuoménōn andrôn*]" this law.[82] Ptolemy sends an epistle to Eleazar, the Judean high priest, requesting that he send to Alexandria elders "who are well-versed in your law and able to interpret it [*empeirían ékhontas toū nómou, kaì dunatoùs hermēneûsai*]."[83] The elders who were subsequently chosen are described as those who "possessed a great facility for lectures and questions connected with the law [*tàs eperōtēseis tàs dià toū nómou megálēn euphuían eîkhon*]."[84] The account also specifies certain regulations said to be found in the law—including some of the dietary prohibitions and purity laws, as well as the injunction to place certain "symbols ... on our garments ... on our gates and doors ... and on our hands"—all paralleling Pentateuchal commandments.[85]

Were this account to be regarded as both historical and accurate, it would imply the existence of a Judean law that governed the lives of regular Judeans as early as the 270s BCE.[86] However, scholars today almost unanimously agree that the story is a fiction written much later than the time of the events it narrates. While most scholars claim a mid to late second-century-BCE date for the work, others have suggested that the text may date to the first century BCE or even to as late as the beginning of the first century CE.[87]

What does seem quite beyond doubt is that by the time the Letter of Aristeas was authored, the Pentateuch had already been translated into Greek. When exactly this translation was accomplished is not known, although many scholars claim that a third-century-BCE date is likely.[88] Does the very fact that the Pentateuch had been translated into Greek indicate that by the time of its translation the Pentateuch had already attained authoritative status as the foundational text of a prescriptive Torah, recognized by the Judean masses as legally binding? I see little reason why this should necessarily be the case. While theories abound, as far as any actual evidence informs us, we know close to nothing about the historical circumstances surrounding the translation of the Pentateuch into Greek or about the earliest reception of this translation among Greek-speaking Judeans. Even if it could be demonstrated convincingly that a Greek translation of the Pentateuch existed as early as the third century BCE, there would be little reason to surmise anything about the *status* that such a translation—or its Hebrew *Vorlage*—might have enjoyed among ordinary Judeans living at the time.[89]

Another matter that should be taken into consideration is the fact that the translators of the Septuagint almost consistently made the choice to translate the Hebrew "*tôrāh*" wherever it appears in the Pentateuch with the Greek "*nómos*" rather than with potential alternative Greek words that mean "instruction" (such as "*didakhḗ*" or "*didaskalía*"). Does the decision to render "*tôrāh*" as "*nómos*" suggest that the Pentateuch necessarily had become recognized as normatively authoritative among the Judean masses by this time? Such an inference, I believe, would be reading too much into the evidence at hand. The word "*tôrāh*," after all, appears not infrequently in biblical works together with words unquestionably associated with law, such as "*ḥōq*" (statute), "*mišpāṭ*" (ordinance), and "*miṣwāh*" (commandment). Each of these words was consistently rendered with what was considered a sufficiently close Greek equivalent, and the Greek "*nómos*" was apparently taken to adequately approximate the translators' understanding of the Hebrew "*tôrāh*" as legal instruction.[90] We certainly cannot make any determinations on this basis as to whether the Pentateuch had already come to be widely recognized as normatively binding among ordinary Judeans.

PENTATEUCHAL NARRATIVES IN FRAGMENTS OF
DEMETRIUS THE CHRONOGRAPHER

Fragments of writings attributed to a certain Demetrius (known as "the Chronographer" or "the Chronicler") are commonly dated to the reign of Ptolemy IV Philopator (ca. 221–204 BCE) and therefore are thought to represent the earliest surviving literary texts penned by a Judean author writing in Greek.[91] Demetrius's preserved writings are concerned chiefly with chronologies of the Israelite patriarchs otherwise known from Genesis, as well as brief accounts about Moses otherwise known from Exodus (up until shortly after the drowning of the Egyptians in the Reed Sea). Despite reflecting a certain familiarity with these Pentateuchal narratives, the fragments preserve no reference at all to any Mosaic (or otherwise Judean) body of law, and as a result it is difficult to know how Demetrius might have regarded such a law—or indeed if any such law was even known to him. Even if we were to assume that Demetrius was familiar with the existence of the entire Pentateuch, we would still remain in the dark as to whether ordinary Judeans who were not intellectuals like Demetrius might have known about the Pentateuch or whether they would have recognized the binding authority of its rules and regulations.

THE "ANCESTRAL LAWS" IN THE LETTERS AND
PROCLAMATION OF ANTIOCHUS III

The "ancestral laws" are mentioned in a letter Josephus cites as sent by Antiochus, almost certainly meaning Antiochus III Megas, to a certain Ptolemy (identified with Ptolemy son of Thraseas, governor of the province), probably shortly after the Seleucid king had wrested Judea from Ptolemaic control circa 200 BCE. After acknowledging the Judeans' support for the Seleucid king in his fight against the Ptolemaic garrison in Jerusalem, Antiochus proclaimed certain privileges to be granted to the Judeans, which included the following clause: "All who belong to the people are to be governed in accordance with their ancestral laws [*politeuésthōsan dè pántes hoi ek toū éthnous katà toùs patríous nómous*]."[92]

After citing this letter, Josephus quotes a "proclamation" (*prógramma*) made by this same Antiochus which reads as follows: "It is unlawful for any foreigner to enter the enclosure of the temple which is forbidden to the Judeans, except to those of them who are accustomed to enter after purifying themselves in accordance with the ancestral law [*katà tòn pátrion nómon*]. Nor shall anyone bring into the city the flesh of horses or of mules or of wild or tame asses, or of leopards, foxes or hares or, in general, of any animals forbidden to the Judeans. Nor is it lawful to bring in their skins or even to breed any of these animals in the city. But only the sacrificial animals known to their ancestors and necessary for the propitiation of God shall they be permitted to use. And the person who violates any of these statutes shall pay to the priests a fine of three thousand drachmas of silver."[93] Finally, Josephus cites a third document, a letter said to have been sent by Antiochus to the governor of Lydia ordering the transportation of two thousand Judean families from Babylonia to Phrygia, where they are to be allowed to "use their own laws [*nómois autoùs khrẽsthai toîs idíois*]."[94]

Elias Bickerman conducted in-depth studies on the first two of these documents, both of which he viewed as authentic.[95] Regarding the first letter, Bickerman asserted, "Historically speaking, the most important affirmation which we may infer on the basis of this document is that the Seleucid king confirmed the Mosaic law shortly after his conquest, following the example of Artaxerxes (and certainly also of Alexander and the Lagids). Accordingly, Torah was a royal law on the eve of the Maccabean period."[96]

Some scholars have accepted the authenticity of only the first document while rejecting the other two as spurious, and other scholars have questioned the authenticity of all three documents.[97] Even if some or all of these documents are not deemed complete forgeries, the fact that their contents may have been tampered with during the course of the almost three hundred years prior to being recorded for posterity by Josephus is enough of a reason to exercise caution before drawing conclusions of the sort proposed by Bickerman regarding any widespread recognition of the normatively binding authority of a "Mosaic law" circa 200 BCE.

THE LAW AND COMMANDMENTS IN BEN SIRA

The work known as the Wisdom of Joshua Ben Sira makes frequent reference to "*tôrâh*" (in the fragments that survive in Hebrew) or "*nómos*" (in the Greek translation of the work). The compositional date of the original Hebrew version of Ben Sira is widely accepted to fall sometime around the first quarter of the second century BCE, while its Greek translation—purportedly by the author's own grandson—is recognized as having been completed toward the end of the same century.[98] Only about two-thirds of the original Hebrew are now extant (mostly in medieval fragments found in the Cairo Genizah but also in ancient fragments from Masada and Qumran), but the Greek translation has survived apparently in its entirety.

There is substantial debate within scholarship over precisely what Ben Sira meant when he wrote about law. On the one hand, the work makes somewhat frequent reference to a divine "*tôrāh*" or "*nómos*," to a divine "commandment" (*miṣwāh* or *entolē*), and to other similar terms.[99] The author is also very familiar with narratives known to us from the Pentateuch.[100] On the other hand, very little attention is paid to any *specific* commandments known from the Pentateuch. This ambiguity has led to a debate as to what exactly Ben Sira may have had in mind when he extolled the "*tôrāh*"/"*nómos*" and the "commandment(s)"; while some scholars assume these terms to mean Mosaic legislation as found in the Pentateuch, others have argued that the author intended a more universal kind of natural law.[101]

Even if the Mosaic law as found in the Pentateuch is meant, it is hard to find in Ben Sira any kind of dynamic, exegetical interaction with the Pentateuch for the derivation of practical legal conclusions as we find in later works. John Collins has described Ben Sira's use of the Mosaic law as "iconic": "It is a formal acknowledgement of the superiority of Mosaic wisdom, but it is far removed from the kind of obsession with the details of Mosaic law that we will find in some of the Dead Sea Scrolls. Halakic Judaism, the view that Judaism is defined primarily by Mosaic law, as law, had not yet become dominant in Judah when Ben Sira wrote."[102] On this nuanced view, Ben Sira provides evidence as early as the first quarter of the second century BCE for the existence of a didactically edifying Mosaic "*tôrāh*," although perhaps not yet for a legally prescriptive Torah.

Regardless, for our purposes it must be recognized that Joshua Ben Sira was an intellectual, and as such hardly representative of the Judean masses. Whether or not any regard for a Mosaic instruction might have been shared by ordinary, non-elite (and for the most part nonliterate) Judeans is impossible to determine from the writings of Ben Sira on their own.

CONCLUSIONS

The small assemblage of ostensibly relevant literary texts well dated to the Early Hellenistic period provides no compelling evidence which might indicate that the Torah was regarded as authoritative—or even known of at all—among the Judean masses at this time. Signs of a widely known and accepted Torah in what is often thought to be a citation from Hecataeus of Abdera, in the Letter of Aristeas, and in the purported letters and proclamation of Antiochus III all may date to later periods of time. The translation of the Septuagint, and the apparent familiarity of Demetrius the Chronographer and Joshua Ben Sira with at least parts of the Pentateuch, together indicate that at least some Judean literati in the Early Hellenistic period were familiar with the Pentateuch and held the work in high regard—but this says nothing of common knowledge or interest in the Torah.[103] There is little reason to assume that the Judean intellectuals who showed interest in the Pentateuch were particularly influential among the masses or even that they may have been representative of most Judean thinkers at the time. Other Judean intellectuals may never have heard of the narratives and laws recorded in the Pentateuch, and many of those who did may have regarded these stories and legal material as of little concern. The author of a work like Ecclesiastes, if he lived during the Early Hellenistic period, may represent Judean literati of just this sort.

Written Law among the Greeks as a Model for the Torah

Despite the lack of compelling evidence for the Torah's acceptance among the Judean masses during the Early Hellenistic period, certain developments within the history of law suggest that this epoch, characterized by Greek political and cultural hegemony, may have been particularly well suited to the widespread promulgation of the Pentateuch as law. Many scholars of legal history credit the Greeks with the innovation of a distinctive category of rules—written laws—that are both prescriptive and formal. These laws covered not only the categories of civil and criminal law but also what scholars refer to as "sacred law," with legislation regulating matters such as mortuary rites, cultic rituals, and festivals. While Mesopotamian societies had been producing written collections of laws for well over a thousand years prior to the first emergence of written law among the Greeks, the written law codes developed by Greek-speaking societies can be shown to have functioned in a completely novel manner. In what follows, I will examine a hypothesis first offered by Michael LeFebvre which posits that the initial contact of Judeans with these new conceptions of law during the Early Hellenistic period may have laid the groundwork for the widespread adoption of the Pentateuch as prescriptive Torah.[104]

In order to highlight the novelty of Greek legislation, I will begin by describing how the earlier Near Eastern law collections are conventionally viewed by modern scholarship as nonprescriptive in nature. This will be followed by a discussion about how the emergence of written law among the Greeks beginning around the middle of the seventh century BCE was revolutionary in creating what might be regarded as the first examples of true *prescriptive* legislation. Finally, I will discuss the hypothesis posited by LeFebvre that it was only with the exposure of the Judeans to the Greek notion of written law that the Pentateuch was recharacterized as a prescriptive law binding on all Judeans as Torah.

LAW COLLECTIONS PRIOR TO THE EMERGENCE
OF WRITTEN LAW

In our modern world, it is common to assume that all collections of law are inherently *prescriptive* in nature. Today, a law code legislates how a society is to behave by *prescribing* specific rules and regulations. In a way, a society's law code embodies for that society "the law" *itself*.

Law writings in ancient Mesopotamia appear to have functioned in a very different way from this commonplace, modern-day conception. On the one hand, we know of over half a dozen extensive law collections such as the so-called "codes" of the Mesopotamian kings Hammurabi, Ur-Namma, and Lipit-Ishtar, and the ostensible "code" of the city of Eshnunna. On the other hand, we have thousands of law-practice documents that record how law was actually applied in various real-life situations. In many cases, these two sources of legal material do not coincide, with prices, fines, and penalties in the records of actual court cases often contradicting those set down in the law collections. Furthermore, the court records as a rule do not cite the law collections as their rationale for adjudication.

Since the early 1960s, many scholars have come to recognize that the ancient law collections were never regarded as *prescriptive* law—they were not themselves "the law." Such a concept as legislation did not even exist at such an early date. Jacob Finkelstein, for example, wrote, "It is probably well to stress first of all that the purpose of the Lower Mesopotamian 'law codes' was decidedly not legislative, if indeed it is not altogether anachronistic to speak of 'legislation' in the ancient Mesopotamian context. These 'law codes' . . . must be viewed in the first instance as royal apologia and testaments. Their primary purpose was to lay before the public, posterity, future kings, and, above all, the gods, evidence of the king's execution of his divinely ordained mandate."[105]

Along somewhat similar lines, Meir Malul has suggested that the legal collections were compiled as literary exercises: "We are dealing here with a *literary tradition* rather than with a *practical legal tradition*."[106] Others have argued that these compilations were written in the form of contemporary Mesopotamian scientific lists and reflect scholastic exercises in jurisprudence.[107] According to Raymond Westbrook, "the nearest modern analogy would be a legal text-book."[108]

Westbrook suggested that actual legal rulings in ancient Mesopotamian societies were likely adjudicated on the basis of unwritten custom "derived not from known cases but from timeless tradition."[109] Here it is crucial to stress the distinction between a system that settles disputes on the basis of traditional or customary rules of conduct and one that adjudicates on the basis of an authoritative body of "law" distinguished from other societal rules. Michael Gagarin has argued that Mesopotamian societies did not possess "true legislation," and that formal "laws" distinct from traditional or customary rules of conduct did not emerge until the advent of written legislation among the Greeks in the middle of the seventh century BCE (as will be described presently).[110]

THE EMERGENCE OF WRITTEN LAW AMONG THE GREEKS

Like Mesopotamian and other ancient societies, the early Greeks had orally preserved customs and traditions that included normative rules to guide behavior, along with well-developed procedures for resolving disputes and regulating conflict. And like their Mesopotamian counterparts, the early Greeks had no authoritative body of rules that could be considered "the law" as distinct from other, nonauthoritative customs and traditions.[111]

A significant amount of both epigraphic and literary evidence indicates that, beginning around the middle of the seventh century BCE, cities scattered widely throughout the Greek world began to enact written laws. Inscriptions containing written legislation appear for the first time in the mid or late seventh century BCE at Dreros (on Crete), followed by inscriptions at several other sites such as Chios (in the northern Aegean), Eretria (in Euboea), and Gortyn (on Crete).[112] This inscriptional evidence is supplemented by several literary sources (albeit from later periods) that tell of famous early "lawgivers" (*nomothétai*) who enacted written laws for various cities from the middle of the seventh century onward: Zaleucus for Epizephyrian Locri (in southern Italy), Draco and Solon for Athens, and Charondas for Catana (now Catania, in Sicily).[113] Lawgivers were often idealized; the antiquity and authority of these legendary figures conferred legitimacy and permanence on the laws attributed to them, and provided a sense that the laws associated with a founding lawgiver formed a coherent unity.[114] Some fabled lawgivers were said to have been given their laws by a god, thus adding to the authority of their legislation.[115]

For Michael Gagarin, it was precisely in *writing down* their laws that the Greeks became the first to establish "true legislation":

> The availability of writing led the Greeks to the crucial step of differentiat-ing from the mass of their stated and unstated norms, including customs, traditions, maxims, fables, proverbs and previous judicial decisions, a body of rules specifically to be used in the judicial settlement of disputes. It mat-tered not whether this legislation was the product of a single legislator or of an anonymous body, or whether laws were enacted singly or in a set. What mattered was that the act of legislation, essential to the existence of a true legal system, had been invented. Henceforth, the laws of a polis would be a separate, recognizable body of norms, differentiated from all the other rules of the society.[116]

> Not until the invention of writing and its subsequent use in the process of writing legislation did the Greeks create laws for their community that were distinct from their customs and traditions.[117]

Gagarin has argued that the movement to enact written legislation which swept over Greek-speaking lands beginning around the middle of the sev-enth century BCE was so revolutionary that "it is legitimate to speak of the 'invention' of legislation in Greece" at this time.[118]

Critically, these laws not only were written but also were made pub-licly available through prominently placed inscriptions, often on or near temples. Fragmentary inscriptions that have been uncovered are inscribed in large and clearly formed letters, and sometimes the inscribed letters were colored with red ocher in order to attract an audience and to make their texts easier to read.[119] Laws were also inscribed and publicly displayed on bronze plaques and probably also (so we are told with regard to the Athe-nian laws of Draco and Solon) on wooden pillars.[120] It seems that temples were chosen not only because these were highly public places but also be-cause display in a sanctum would have implicitly added a sense of divine authority to the laws, reinforcing the notion that the gods both supported and supervised the laws.[121]

Gagarin considered the public nature of the Greek laws revolution-ary when considering the private nature of the earlier, Near Eastern law collections, which had been written down only for academic purposes or propaganda but were not intended to be accessible to most members of the community and had relatively little effect on the actual operation of the legal system:

> In contrast, the early Greek codes were true legislation, embodying the fundamental notion that the actual rules, both substantive and procedural, governing the operation of a community's judicial system should be made publicly available for all to read and to employ in a legal action, or indeed in their everyday lives. . . . The public nature of Greek laws has no parallel in the law codes of the Near East.[122]

> Among the most important creations of this unique political entity, the polis, was the rule of law. . . . Although laws and legal procedures were known in various forms in other parts of the world, the Greeks created something different. For the first time the law was made available to and was intended to be used by the entire citizenry. In most other "advanced" cultures law came to be controlled by a relatively small group of lawyers or jurists, often rather removed from the majority of citizens.[123]

For the first time ever, one could point to a set of rules as "the law" itself, formally encapsulated in writing, prominently published, and freely available to the public at large.

Significantly, Greek legislation covered not only civil and criminal categories of law but also ritual and sacred matters such as mortuary rites, cultic rituals, and sacred festivals.[124] Scholars today often categorize these laws under a special class of "sacred laws," but the ancient Greeks themselves enacted and displayed these laws in exactly the same way as other public laws, tort laws, family laws, and procedural laws. The important point here is that while earlier societies regulated such matters on the basis of traditions and custom, the emergence of written law among the Greeks brought these customary norms under the purview of true legislation for the first time ever.

Following its initial emergence in Archaic Greece, the critical place of written law in Greek society continued to expand into the Classical period and beyond. It was precisely the existence of formal written law that provided the basis for Classical and Hellenistic philosophers to deliberate over more abstract ideas such as a cosmic "law of nature" (*nómos phúsōs*), various notions of "unwritten law" (*ágraphos nómos*), and an embodied "living law" (*nómos émpsukhos*)—all of which were contrasted with the by-now well-established idea of written law.[125] Ironically enough, these philosophical musings about how such notions of "higher law" excel over the apparent inadequacies of written law were made possible only because positive written law had by this time already come to reign supreme among the Greeks. While the Hellenistic world following the conquests of Alexander the Great differed in many critical ways from the world of Classical Greece that preceded it, the central role of written laws in the practical regulation of society only grew in significance.[126]

THE EMERGENCE OF TORAH AS THE JUDEAN LAW

In a study published in 2006, Michael LeFebvre argued that in biblical sources that predate the Hellenistic era, the Mosaic *tôrāh* was conceptualized as a descriptive collection of laws and as "a preeminent description of Yahwistic ideals as practiced by Moses," but it did not function as a prescriptive law code. He argued that this conception of the biblical "*tôrāh* of Moses" accords well with scholarly understandings of law collections elsewhere in the ancient Near East, especially in Mesopotamia as discussed in detail above. LeFebvre suggested that the Pentateuch was reconceptualized as prescriptive law only in the Hellenistic period, and posited two mechanisms that may have contributed to this recharacterization.

The first mechanism was the administrative structure of the Ptolemaic court system—in particular, court reforms instituted by Ptolemy II around 275 BCE.[127] Earlier studies by Hans Julius Wolff had demonstrated that Ptolemy II organized the judiciary in his realm under a hierarchy of laws that subordinated Greek and Egyptian law to royal law, while also creating separate courts to hear cases of Greek-speaking parties (*dikastēria*) and native Egyptians (*laokritai*)—each according to their own laws.[128] The Greek-speakers, which included the Judeans, were adjudicated on the basis of the so-called civic laws (*politikoì nómoi*), which at least theoretically referred to the laws of the litigants' homeland. There is some evidence that Judeans living in Egypt adjudicated in *dikastēria* under "Judean law" as their own form of *politikoì nómoi*.[129] Although the epigraphic remains from the third century BCE are silent as to the content and character of this Judean law, LeFebvre hypothesized that the reforms of Ptolemy II may have served as the catalyst for a recharacterization of the Pentateuch from descriptive to prescriptive law, and for the adoption of this law code as the Judean *politikoì nómoi*.[130] Although a paucity of evidence from Judea proper makes this difficult to demonstrate, LeFebvre believed it reasonable to expect that such a shift would have taken place around the same time in both Egypt and Judea.

A second mechanism posited by LeFebvre was the cultural impetus posed by Hellenistic presuppositions that prescriptive law is a necessary mark of civilization.[131] In the writings of several ancient Greek authors, all of humanity is oftentimes presented as a binary between Greeks and others, characterized as "civilized" versus "barbarian." For these writers, the "rule of law" was upheld as one of the key features that set the Greeks apart as a "civilized" race in contrast to "barbarian" peoples ruled by "lawless" despots. LeFebvre posited that once Judeans came under the direct sway of Greek culture following the conquests of Alexander the Great, they felt compelled to advance a defense of their native culture as "civilized" by re-characterizing the Pentateuchal collection of laws in alignment with the Greek model of a prescriptive code of law.

If LeFebvre is correct, the recharacterization of the Mosaic *tôrāh* from a didactic collection of laws to a prescriptive code of law may have had repercussions far beyond any small circle of intellectuals who would have known of the Pentateuch and who might have held the compilation in high regard. If the Ptolemaic court reforms induced Judean authorities in Egypt and Judea to adopt the Pentateuch as the textual foundation of the prescriptive law they were to enforce, the Torah would certainly have become binding henceforward on *all* Judeans living under Ptolemaic rule. But even if a scenario of direct administrative fiat from the Ptolemaic authorities is rejected, the more diffuse cultural impetus of Greek notions about law might still be regarded as a plausible catalyst for the promulgation of the Torah as written law among the Judean populace at large. Such a process might have begun at the level of the Judean leadership, who would likely have had at least some familiarity with the surrounding Hellenistic cultural milieu, including its legal culture. For these leaders, the Greek narratives about ancient lawgivers and their codes of law may have sounded quite similar to the Pentateuch with its stories about Moses and his laws.[132] Taking their cues from the manner whereby Greek cities made their law codes widely known among their citizenries, the Judean leaders may have similarly decided to publicly promulgate the Pentateuch among the Judean masses as the foundation of a prescriptive law that was henceforth to govern the Judeans' communal way of life. Surely the Hellenistic period is the most reasonable time to imagine the unfolding of such a scenario, as it was at this time that Judea proper, along with practically all other locations where Judeans are known to have lived, first came under the direct sway of Greek cultural norms.[133]

Conclusions

On the one hand, we have seen that the literary sources that are firmly dated to the Early Hellenistic period provide no compelling evidence regarding the degree to which the Torah might have been known or regarded as authoritative among the Judean masses of the time. On the other hand, the Hellenistic era does present a plausible *Sitz im Leben* for when the Pentateuch may have first risen out of obscurity as a little-known legal collection to become the authoritative law code of the Judeans at large. Although lacking any direct evidence, the hypothesis that the Greek paradigm of written law served as a model for the emergence of the Torah as the prescriptive law of the Judeans presents some intriguing possibilities. Whether such a scenario might have unfolded because of direct Ptolemaic administrative reforms or as a consequence of more general cultural influences, the Early Hellenistic era presents a plausible time for when the Judean masses began to regard the Torah as an authoritatively binding prescriptive law akin to the Greek model.

The Late Hellenistic (Hasmonean) Period (167–63 BCE)

A complex series of events that unfolded throughout the middle of the second century BCE led to the Judeans' gaining independence from the Seleucid Empire and their establishing an autonomous polity under the rule of the priestly Hasmonean family. The books of 1 and 2 Maccabees attribute the catalyst for these events to official policies of Antiochus IV Epiphanes (175–164 BCE) that transformed the cult in the Jerusalem temple and forbade the Judeans from adhering to their native laws. A popular uprising is said to have broken out around 167 BCE, first under the leadership of a priest named Mattathias, scion of the Hasmonean clan, and later successively by his sons Judas Maccabaeus, Jonathan Apphus, and Simon Thassi. The last of these brothers is said to have established in 142 BCE an independent polity under his own rule as "the great high priest, and commander and leader of the Judeans."[134] The hereditary dynasty founded by Simon remained in power until the fall of the Hasmonean state to the Roman general and statesman Pompey in 63 BCE.

In what follows, I will seek to assess the likelihood that the Torah might have been adopted by the Judean masses as their authoritative law sometime during the period when the Judeans had broken free from Seleucid rule under the leadership of the early Hasmoneans. We will begin by surveying the literary evidence preserved in the book of Daniel and in 1 and 2 Maccabees which might suggest that the Torah already existed as the established law of the Judeans *prior* to the Antiochene persecutions that purportedly sought to forbid its practice. Our analysis of these texts will lead us to consider the possibility that the accounts of Antiochene decrees against Torah observance and of the ensuing deliverance wrought by Mattathias and his sons may have all been created ex post facto as political propaganda meant to legitimate the Hasmonean regime and its hegemony over the Jerusalem temple. Finally, we will explore the possibility that it was only following the uprising of 167 BCE that the Torah came to be widely disseminated and regarded as the authoritative law of the Judean populace at large as a result of proactive Hasmonean policies toward this end.

The Literary Evidence

THE ANTIOCHENE PERSECUTIONS IN DANIEL

The second half of the book of Daniel, although set in the Babylonian and Persian periods, is widely thought to allude to the reign of Antiochus IV and to the events that led to the outbreak of the Hasmonean revolt. Scholars commonly believe that the bulk of this material was penned during a narrow time frame between 167 and 164 BCE, and therefore these writings may be valuable for assessing whether widespread adherence to the Torah is in evidence at this time.[135]

In Dan 7, Daniel has a cryptic vision of four beasts, the last of which is particularly frightful; it has ten horns and another little horn that sprouts among them, upon which are "eyes like human eyes . . . and a mouth speaking arrogantly."[136] Daniel is then provided the interpretation that this little horn represents an evil monarch who will arise after ten other kings: "He shall speak words against the most high, shall wear out the holy ones of the most high, and shall attempt to change times and law [*wəyisbar ləhašnāyāh zimnîn wədāt*]; and they shall be given into his power for a time, two times, and half a time."[137]

In Dan 8, Daniel receives another vision, which features a unicorn he-goat whose horn breaks and is replaced by four new horns, one of which sprouts an additional small horn that grows upward to the sky: "It grew as high as the host of heaven. It threw down to the earth some of the host and some of the stars, and trampled on them. Even against the prince of the host it acted arrogantly; and it took the regular burnt offering away from him [*ûmimenû hērîm/hûram hatāmîd*] and overthrew the place of his sanctuary. Because of wickedness, the host was given over to it together with the regular burnt offering; it cast truth to the ground, and kept prospering in what it did."[138] This second vision is also provided with an interpretation: the small horn is explained as a king who will "destroy the powerful and the people of the holy ones [*'am qədōšîm*]."[139]

In Dan 9, the angel Gabriel tells Daniel that a future period of distress will come to Jerusalem and its temple: "The troops of the prince who is to come shall destroy the city and the sanctuary. Its end shall come with a flood, and to the end there shall be war. Desolations are decreed. He shall make a strong covenant with many for one week, and for half of the week he shall make sacrifice and offering cease; and on the corner shall be an abomination that desolates [*wə 'al kənaf šîqûşim məšômēm*], until the decreed end is poured out upon the desolator."[140]

Daniel 11 foretells about a "king of the north" who, upon returning to his land from (a military) engagement with the "king of the south," will attack "the holy covenant": "He shall be enraged against the holy covenant [*bərît qôdeš*] and take action; he shall turn back and pay heed to those who forsake the holy covenant [*'ōzvê bərît qôdeš*]. Forces sent by him shall occupy and profane the temple and fortress. They shall abolish the regular burnt offering [*hatāmîd*] and set up the abomination that makes desolate [*hašîqûş məšômēm*]. He shall seduce with intrigue those who violate the covenant [*maršî'ê bərît*]; but the people who are loyal to their God [*'am yōdə'ê 'elōhāyw*] shall stand firm and take action."[141] Daniel continues to prophesize that during this time the "wise among the people [*maśkîlê 'ām*]" will endure martyrdom "by the sword and flame" and will suffer captivity and plunder. The removal of "the regular burnt offering" and its replacement with "a desolate abomination [*šîqûş šōmēm*]" is referred to one final time in Dan 12:11.

Traditional and modern academic readers alike have long recognized that these prophecies closely resemble the general narrative line found in both 1 and 2 Maccabees surrounding persecutions perpetrated by Antiochus IV. While the Daniel texts are often interpreted through the lens of the books of Maccabees, which tell of Antiochene decrees against the Torah (see below), *on their own* the Daniel texts make no clear allusions to any assaults upon Torah observance per se. The focus clearly seems to be on the disruption of the traditional cult in the Jerusalem temple. While the multiple references to a "holy covenant [*bərît qôdeš*]" and the single mention of the evil king's intention "to change times and law [*ləhašnāyāh zīmnîn wədāt*]" may well refer to the Torah, on their own they might just as well be speaking of a foreign corruption of the traditional cultic rites in the temple of YHWH—rites that would not necessarily have been associated with any Mosaic Torah. Likewise, while those who "forsake the holy covenant" or "violate the covenant" may perhaps allude to Judeans who according to 1 and 2 Maccabees neglected circumcision—or even practiced its surgical reversal—the phrase may just as well refer to Judeans who supported the royally enforced changes to the traditional temple cult. One can easily read all these texts without assuming that Torah was regarded as authoritative among the Judean masses by 167–164 BCE.

THE "LAW" IN THE PERSECUTION NARRATIVES IN 1 AND 2 MACCABEES

Unlike in Daniel, in both 1 and 2 Maccabees "the law" (*ho nómos*) (also "the regulations" [*tà nómima*]) plays a critical role. In 1 Maccabees, Mattathias and his sons are portrayed as heroes of Israel for recovering the law from obliteration at the hands of Antiochus IV and the "wicked men" of Israel who supported him in his persecution of those loyal to the law. It is related that books of the law that were found were torn to pieces and burned, and "anyone found possessing the book of the covenant [*biblíon diathḗkēs*], or anyone who adhered to the law [*suneudókei tǭ nómǭ*]," was condemned to death by decree of the king.[142] Pentateuchal laws singled out as targets of Antiochus's persecution included circumcision, observance of the Sabbath and festivals, and prohibitions against sacrificial offerings to "idols" and partaking of impure foods (especially pig).[143] These decrees are portrayed as abolishing the law that, prior to the persecutions of Antiochus, had been the norm among the Judean populace at large.[144] "Many in Israel" refused to submit and chose to die rather than abrogate the law's regulations.[145] Open rebellion ensued under the enlistment slogan of Mattathias: "Let everyone who is zealous for the law and supports the covenant [*pâs ho zēlȭn tǭ nómǭ kaì histȭn diathḗkēn*] come out with me!"[146] Specific Pentateuchal laws the rebels are cited as observing include separation of first fruits and tithes, Nazirite vows, turning back from battle "those who were building houses, or were about to be married, or were planting a vineyard, or were fainthearted," using whole stones for constructing the temple's altar, and abstention from agricultural work on Sabbatical years.[147] The dynamic character of the law is portrayed in a narrative regarding a group of rebels who died because they refused to do battle and defend themselves on a Sabbath; when Mattathias and his company hear of this, they reinterpret the law in such a way as to permit defensive fighting on the Sabbath.[148]

A rather similar portrayal of the law appears in 2 Maccabees. Here too it is said that in the days leading up to the reign of Antiochus IV "the laws were strictly observed [*tôn nómōn hóti kállista suntēroumênōn*]."[149] Thereafter, Antiochus sent an emissary "to compel the Judeans to forsake the laws of their ancestors [*tôn patríōn nómōn*] and no longer to live by the laws of God [*toîs toû theoû nómois*]."[150] As in 1 Maccabees, the laws of the Pentateuch cited specifically as those abrogated by the Seleucid king are observance of Sabbath and festivals, circumcision, and bans against prohibited foods—particularly pig and idolatrous sacrifices.[151] The book contains several narratives about martyrs who willingly underwent torture and ultimately gave up their lives rather than transgress these prohibitions.[152] One of these martyrs is said to have proclaimed, "I will not obey the king's command, but I obey the command of the law that was given to our ancestors through Moses [*toû nómou toû dothéntos toîs patrásin hēmôn dià Mōuséōs*]."[153] The hero of the book is Judas Maccabaeus, who time and again invokes defense of the law when rallying his warriors before combat—and in one instance even appoints his brother Eleazar to "read aloud the holy book [*paranagnoùs tèn hieràn bíblon*]" prior to battle.[154]

There is some question as to when all these stories were first penned. The plot in 1 Maccabees ends with the reign of John Hyrcanus I (134–104 BCE), and while many scholars date the work to sometime during his rule, some have argued for a date during the reign of Alexander Jannaeus (103–76 BCE).[155] The line of narrative in 2 Maccabees ends in the days of Judas Maccabaeus, and a broad range of dates have been suggested both for the work as we have it and for the now-lost work that 2 Maccabees is said to be a condensed version of; suggested dates range from the mid-second century BCE until the first century CE.[156]

Is the portrait of Antiochene persecutions targeting the Torah historically accurate, or is there something else behind these narratives—penned as it seems at a time when the Hasmonean dynasty was firmly in power? Most modern scholars have taken the explanation for the revolt provided in 1 and 2 Maccabees as reflecting a historical reality, accepting that Antiochus in fact issued royal decrees abolishing observance of a previously entrenched Judean law. Against this, Sylvie Honigman has recently argued that the revolt was motivated primarily by economic factors, and that no "religious persecution" ever actually took place.[157] According to Honigman, the persecution accounts reflect the atrocities of the military suppression of this revolt, which is to say that they were a *result* rather than a *cause* of the revolt. All the narratives surrounding Seleucid prohibitions against Judean observances she interpreted as the employing of a set literary pattern of the "wicked king" as "cult disrupter," while stories of martyrdom she explained as use of the narrative pattern of the "suffering servant"; neither of these reflect historical reality. Honigman's thesis has been subject to extensive critique, both for its literary analysis of 1 and 2 Maccabees and for its treatment of parallel historical sources that arguably provide independent evidence for the Antiochene persecutions claimed by the authors of these works.[158]

Assuming the standard scholarly view that the revolt was in fact precipitated by oppressive decrees issued by Antiochus, we are justified in questioning precisely what these persecutions might have entailed. As we have seen above, references to the blasphemous actions of Antiochus in the second half of the book of Daniel focus almost exclusively on the corruption of the temple cult. Recalling that all the narratives about Antiochene decrees against *Torah observance* are recorded in texts penned only at a somewhat later date, we might question the degree to which these stories reflect a historical reality. Could these be an invention of the later authors of 1 and 2 Maccabees who, at a time when the Torah had already come to be regarded as the authoritative law of the Judeans, wished to present the leaders of the Hasmonean revolt as saviors and restorers of this Torah?

Hasmonean Sponsorship of the Pentateuchal Laws

THE TORAH AS AN INSTRUMENT OF UNIFICATION

We have seen throughout this book that we possess no compelling evidence suggesting that Judeans were observing the laws of the Torah any time prior to the second century BCE. We further learned in chapter 6 that the institution of the synagogue, the central vehicle that spread knowledge of the Torah among the Judean masses, is nowhere in evidence prior to this same time. Because of the adage "the absence of evidence is not evidence of absence," our analysis of the data could not establish that the laws of the Torah took hold specifically during the second century. Rather, our resolute conclusion has been that some point around the middle of the second century should be regarded as our terminus ante quem, the time during *or before* which we ought to seek the emergence of Judaism. This having been clearly said, we would be remiss not to regard as at least suggestive the fact that all of the many practices and prohibitions analyzed throughout this book first come into historical and archaeological focus precisely during the course of the Hasmonean period. Is it possible that Judaism as a way of life followed by Judeans at large first emerged only around this time?

Reinhard Kratz has posited just such a bold conjecture: "Much in the relevant literary sources points to the second century BCE as the time frame in which the Torah of Moses and the rest of biblical tradition gained considerable influence at the sacred sites in Jerusalem and on Mount Gerizim. To avoid any misunderstanding, the question does not revolve around the formation of biblical tradition—which is, of course, much older—but rather the dissemination and status of biblical tradition: the impact of biblical tradition, not its very formation, would date to the second century BCE. . . . Admittedly, however, this conclusion comes from only indirect evidence."[159] Kratz envisioned that, prior to this time, commitment to the Mosaic Torah (and indeed to the entire "biblical tradition") remained limited to certain marginal circles of "literate and well-educated individuals."[160] These fringe groups may have first emerged at the end of the fourth or beginning of the third century BCE, but they came to exert significant political influence only during the Hasmonean uprising. The Hasmonean leaders availed themselves of these ideological groups and exploited them politically for their own cause, although their alliance with these circles was short-lived. According to Kratz, "such circles eventually merged into the Qumran community or the faction later called the 'pious' (*Hasidim*)," and soon after the uprising of 167 BCE these groups broke away from their Hasmonean allies.[161] Even after this rupture, however, "the Torah of Moses was and remained the religious foundation of the Maccabean revolt and the Hasmonean dynasty."[162]

Approaching the matter from a somewhat different direction, John Collins came to a similar conclusion regarding the Hasmoneans' novel use of the Torah as a political tool. His interest in the intellectual history of the Torah's reception among ancient Judean writers led him to identify a major shift occurring in the middle of the second century BCE, when for the first time we witness the rise of a literature "that was intensely concerned with halakah" and with "the detailed interpretations of the laws of the Torah." Collins suggested that this major shift (he dubbed this "the halakic turn") should be attributed to official Hasmonean political policy: "When the Maccabees came to power . . . they did not simply revert to the status quo. Wherever they ruled, they imposed observance of key features of the law of Moses, such as circumcision and Sabbath observance, that served as markers of Judean identity. . . . The Hasmoneans, who were not especially known for their piety, sponsored the Torah as an instrument for the unification of their people, and indeed succeeded in fostering a 'common Judaism,' marked by certain practices and beliefs."[163]

Building on the work of Kratz and Collins, the following conjectural reconstruction may be proposed. After their successful revolt, the early Hasmonean leaders decided to solidify their position vis-à-vis both their subjects and their enemies by officially ratifying a document that might serve to codify the core Judean narratives of origin together with the officially sanctioned Judean laws. Here I am envisioning a single, composite work that would have served the Hasmoneans in a way roughly akin to an amalgamated American Declaration of Independence and the Constitution of the United States. The Pentateuch would have served such a role magnificently. Although it is quite likely that this document (or its constituent parts) had already been circulating for years if not centuries in a limited manner among certain members of Judea's literati, this would not necessarily entail that it was in any way known to the Judean masses. We may speculate that it was precisely the Hasmonean leaders who saw to change this. In adopting the Pentateuch as the formal legal foundation of the newly emergent Judean state, the Hasmonean rulers provided a rallying point around which the people of Judea might unite. With this, *Judaism* itself would have been born.

When recalling the origins of this newly formed polity in 1 and 2 Maccabees, the authors of these works retroactively and anachronistically portrayed the Seleucid persecutions against the traditional Judean cult and culture as persecutions against the *Pentateuchal laws*. They furthermore portrayed the Hasmoneans' legislation of the Torah as the new law of their newly founded state as the *restoration* of the Pentateuchal laws to their *former position of authority*. In this way, the novelty of the authoritative status now granted to the Pentateuchal laws would have been downplayed in the eyes of the Judean public for whom these laws had until now been largely unknown. It was not a *new* system of law that the Hasmoneans had adopted—thus the authors of 1 and 2 Maccabees would have their readers believe—but rather it was an *ancient*, original law that the Hasmonean leadership was simply reviving. The trope of the "restoration" of the Mosaic Torah first used by the authors of the Josiah and Ezra stories is repeated here—to powerful effect—by the narrators of the Maccabean revolt stories.

Greek culture would have surely posed an alluring option for the Judean populace at large even after the initial slew of Hasmonean successes. At the same time, any large-scale trend of Hellenization among the Judean population would have undoubtedly posed an existential threat to a newly autonomous Hasmonean state founded on opposition to Seleucid hegemony and still surrounded by two larger and far more powerful Hellenistic kingdoms. In adopting the Pentateuch as the foundation of the Judeans' law, the Hasmoneans would have created a solidly defined "Judaism" that could pose as a viable and attractive alternative to "Hellenism." Judaism was the powerful ideological glue that would have sustained the fledgling Hasmonean state as a unified body.

LATER HASMONEAN TERRITORIAL AND CULTURAL EXPANSION

The proposal that the sons of Mattathias were responsible for sponsoring and disseminating the Pentateuch as the official law of the Judeans is admittedly a conjectural one. Nevertheless, we may find supporting evidence for this hypothesis in the far-better-documented actions of the direct heirs to these early Hasmonean leaders.

According to Josephus, Simon's son and successor John Hyrcanus I conquered the neighboring region of Idumea and coerced the Idumeans to follow "the laws of the Judeans [*toîs Ioudaîōn nómois*]" in a campaign that included circumcising all the males.[164] This essential account is already found in the writings of Strabo and another ancient author named Ptolemy (identity and date uncertain).[165] Similarly, Josephus related that John Hyrcanus's son and successor Aristobulus I conquered part of the region of Iturea (to the north of Judea) and forced the Itureans there to be circumcised and "to live in accordance with the laws of the Judeans [*katà toùs Ioudaîōn nómous zên*]."[166] Strabo, drawing on the first-century-BCE historian Timagenes, also reported on Aristobulus having annexed a portion of Iturea and having the resident Itureans circumcised.[167]

While scholars have debated the degree to which the implementation of the Judean law among the Idumeans and Itureans was compulsory (as alleged by Josephus and Ptolemy) or voluntary (as suggested by Strabo), what seems clear is that both John Hyrcanus and his son Aristobulus were heavily invested in instituting Torah as authoritative law among the Semitic peoples who had come under their dominion.[168] In doing so, both of these Hasmonean leaders might not have been innovating any radically new policy, but rather may well have been following in the footsteps of their predecessors who had begun the project of promulgating the Torah as law *among the Judeans themselves* only one or two generations earlier.

Around the time that John Hyrcanus conquered Idumea, his army also subdued Samaria and destroyed the Samaritan temple on Mt. Gerizim.[169] Many scholars view the demolition of this temple as a decisive moment in the "parting of the ways" between the Samaritans and the Judeans.[170] It is generally assumed that the Samaritans would have accepted some version of the Pentateuch as binding at some point in time prior to this, when relations between Samaritans and Judeans would have still been reasonably amicable.[171] Recently, however, Jonathan Bourgel has argued that rather than viewing Hyrcanus's actions in Samaria as leading to the decisive *separation* of the Samaritans *away from* the Judeans, Hasmonean policy should on the contrary be regarded as designed to bring about a forced *incorporation* of the Samaritans *into* the Hasmonean state.[172] This model understands the integration of the Samaritans into the Judean polity along very similar lines to the almost precisely concurrent incorporation of the Idumeans and the Itureans into the Hasmonean realm and into the Judean way of life. According to the hypothesis we are exploring here, the policy of disseminating the Torah among all three of these non-Judean groups may have constituted a direct continuation of the initial policy instituted by the earlier Hasmonean leaders who sought to actively promulgate the Torah among the Judeans themselves.[173]

As discussed in the introduction, Shaye Cohen argued that the late second century BCE marked a seismic change in what it meant to be a "Judean": what had once been a strictly "ethno-geographic" term had now developed into an "ethno-religious" category of identity.[174] Behind this semantic shift, for Cohen, was the opening up of the Judean *éthnos* to the incorporation of outsiders and the emergence of the notion that an ethnic outsider could convert to become a Judean as a matter of will. According to the hypothesis we are positing here, this novel idea may well have come about as a direct result of the Judeans *themselves* having had only recently adopted the Torah as the authoritative basis of a newly emergent Judaism. It was only with the advent of this novel Judaism that being a Judean became increasingly associated with what one *does* rather than simply with what one *is*. While being born into a Judean family would still have meant that one would be regarded as a nominal Judean, the *practice* of Judaism itself became far more paramount in the self-definitions of Judeans. With the emergence of Judaism, for the first time one could be regarded as a properly *practicing* Judean or as an improperly *practicing* Judean (and Judeans certainly came to learn how to accuse one another of being the latter!).[175] Along with Judeanness increasingly coming to be associated with the proper observance of the Torah came the notion that by *adopting* these practices, an outsider could in fact *become* a full-fledged Judean.

THE RISE OF SECTARIANISM

Another factor that may lend support to the idea that Judaism first emerged under Hasmonean aegis is the rise of sectarianism specifically at this time. Many scholars have recognized that the splintering of the well-known late Second Temple–period sects (Pharisees, Sadducees, Essenes, the Qumran community, etc.) was triggered primarily by legal disputes over practices enjoined by the Torah rather than by differences over matters of belief. Morton Smith, for example, has argued that the major sects arose as "groups for the observance of peculiar legal interpretations," and that, once formed, such factions would have tolerated among their members all sorts of eschatological speculations and a variety of ideas surrounding personal piety. Such beliefs would have been nonessential to the structure of these sects and secondary in their development: "They could be changed or even removed, and the sect would go on, as a peculiar community defined and held together by its peculiar legal observances. But touch the Law, and the sect will split."[176]

Various lines of evidence have led many scholars to date the initial splintering of some if not all of these sects in the mid to late second century BCE.[177] The reason for the initial rise and flourishing of the sects at precisely this time, however, remains a difficult historical problem. If the hypothesis we are exploring here is correct, and the widespread adoption of the Pentateuch for the first time as the foundation of a newly authoritative Torah dates to sometime soon after the Maccabean revolt, it becomes readily understandable why sectarian groups splintering over legal matters would have arisen precisely at this time. As I defined it in the introduction, the Torah is best envisioned as a dynamic interplay between the Pentateuch and its interpretation. Contingent as such a Torah would have been on human interpreters, it was entirely inevitable that disagreements would have arisen regarding the "proper" interpretation of the opaquely worded Pentateuch almost immediately after it was first widely adopted as a foundational legal text. There could have been no other way if such a text was taken seriously as the preeminent source of divine law binding on all Judeans. It is more than reasonable to expect the development of substantial schisms surrounding legal matters between rival interpretive communities very soon after the Pentateuch had attained its new authoritative status among the Judean masses.

Had the Pentateuch been widely accepted as the authoritative law of Judea in the third, fourth, or fifth century BCE, we would hardly expect a lull of hundreds of years before Judeans began to actively contend with one another over the "correct" exegesis of the laws' minutiae. If the Pentateuch had indeed attained authoritative status so early, and if sectarian factions vying over its accurate interpretation did in fact arise soon afterward and flourish in the subsequent centuries, all historical knowledge of such sects has since been lost to us.[178]

Summary

Did Judaism emerge only sometime during the second century BCE, under the direction of the powerful Hasmonean priestly family? The hypothesis is fully consonant with the fact that all our earliest surviving evidence for widespread Judean adherence to the Torah dates to this time or later. We have explored here the hypothesis that the Pentateuch first came to be known and adopted among the Judean populace at large as a result of the proactive backing of the early Hasmonean leadership. These revolutionary leaders would have legitimized their sponsorship of the Pentateuch as the authoritative law of their newly autonomous polity by fashioning themselves as the "restorers" of an ancient system of divine law. While the suggestion that early Hasmonean leaders were responsible for the promulgation of the Torah among the Judeans remains conjectural, we *do* know that the direct heirs to these leaders devoted themselves to precisely such a promulgation of the Torah among the Semitic peoples that they conquered. The splintering of sectarian groups over legal interpretations of the Torah during exactly this period of history may suggest that the widespread promulgation of this Torah had been a relatively recent development.

Summary and Conclusions

Throughout this book, in chapter after chapter, it has been shown that the earliest surviving evidence for a widely practiced Judean way of life governed by the Torah never predates the second century BCE. The aim of the present chapter has been to go beyond the data surveyed and analyzed throughout the book and to assess the likelihood that Judaism may have first emerged during one or another specific historical period of time.

Our analysis in the present chapter has led us to conclude that the Judean way of life during the Persian period was more likely governed by cultural norms and traditions inherited from the Iron Age than by anything resembling some kind of Torah law. A central element of what it meant to be a Judean at this time was veneration of YHWH and participation in the cultic worship of this deity, although it remains unclear to what degree this might have excluded the possibility of veneration and worship of other deities. It does not seem unlikely that at least some of the practices that came to be legislated in the Pentateuch were part of Judean culture already in the Persian period, possibly including a taboo against eating the "hip sinew" and perhaps also circumcision. The origins of practices such as these may reach back to extraordinarily early epochs, possibly to before the emergence of any kind of distinct "Israelite" identity. The evidence from Elephantine that points to a Judean practice of some form of "Passover" ritual, as well as of a seven-day period probably coinciding in time with what we know of as the Festival of Unleavened Bread, may also reflect very early practices whose origins remain opaque. In all these cases, however, there is little reason to interpret the evidence as reflecting practices that were somehow *legally* mandated by anything akin to a Mosaic law. A conjectural Persian-period Judean way of life thus reconstructed, bereft of any sort of Torah as its regulating principle, can hardly be said to resemble *Judaism* in any meaningful way.

The roughly two centuries between the conquests of Alexander the Great circa 332 BCE and the founding of an independent Hasmonean polity in the middle of the second century BCE remain a far more conducive epoch in which to seek the origins of Judaism. Various hypotheses may be proffered to explain how and why something recognizable as Judaism may have first emerged during this particular historical era. Here I have explored the possibilities that the Pentateuch came to be adopted as authoritative Torah by Judeans either during the Early Hellenistic period, when Judea found itself under foreign domination by the two great Hellenistic kingdoms, or during the Late Hellenistic period, after the Judeans had gained autonomy under the leadership of the priestly Hasmonean family. Both hypotheses identify the emergence of Judaism at a time when practically all Judeans—both in their homeland and throughout their diaspora—were deeply embedded in a world dominated by Hellenistic culture. In either case, it would not be wrong to view *Judaism* as having emerged out of the crucible of *Hellenism*, which dominated the cultural landscape of the time. In a poetic way, it seems only fitting that our English word "Judaism" itself is the result of a Hebrew/Greek hybrid, rooted etymologically in the Greek rendering of the Hebrew "*yəhûdāh*" merged with the Greek suffix "*-ismós*."

With this, we have come to the end of our journey. Stepping backward to gain perspective, we appreciate that this is by no means the final chapter in the story of Judaism—it is only its preface and introduction. From its earliest origins, Judaism emerged and developed in manifold directions. Rabbinic Judaism was one pathway by which Judaism continued to thrive and expand, but the centuries have witnessed the emergence of other, parallel and no-less-influential byways. Indeed, the roots of both Christianity and Islam are well sought in the Judaism whose origins we have explored throughout these pages. Viewed in this way, the emergence of Judaism was the catalyst for setting the course of much of world history over the past two thousand years—and probably also for centuries if not for millennia to come.

Notes

Introduction

1. Already at the end of the first century CE, Flavius Josephus (*Ag. Ap.* 2:156) described Moses as having "encompassed the whole structure of their [i.e., the Israelites'] life with the law." Further on (2:173–174), Josephus explained how Moses, as the supreme lawgiver, left no sphere of life unregulated: "Rather, starting right from the beginning of their nurture, and from the mode of life practiced by each individual in the household, he did not leave anything, even the minutest detail, free to be determined by the wishes of those who would make use of [the laws], but even in relation to food, what they should refrain from and what they should eat, the company they keep in their daily lives, as well as the intensity in work and, conversely, rest, he set the law [*tòn nómon*] as their boundary and rule, so that, living under this as a father and master, we might commit no sin either willfully or from ignorance." All translations here follow Barclay, *Against Apion*.

2. Although modern-day scholars often use the term "*hălākhāh*" to also refer to legal notions that obtained outside the rabbinic sphere (as when they speak of "Qumranic *hălākhāh*" or "Josephus's *hălākhāh*"), historically the term has no clear surviving attestations prior to the time of the formation of early rabbinic literature (see Meier, "Is There Halaka"). Some have suggested that the expression "*dôrəšê hălāqôt*" (speakers of smooth things) found among the Dead Sea Scrolls (1QH ii, 15, 32; 4Q163 23 ii, 10; 4Q169 3–4 i, 2, 7; ii, 2, 4; iii, 3, 6–7; 4Q177 ii, 12) is a thinly veiled polemical designation for the Pharisees, reflecting a play on "*dôrəšê hălākhôt*" (interpreters of *hălākhāh*) (see, e.g., Hoenig, "Dorshé Halakot"). Even if it might be argued that the Pharisees used the term "*hălākhāh*" before the rabbis, this should hardly give license to make use of the term with reference to those who *rejected* Pharisaic legal ideas. In this book, the term "*hălākhāh*" will be used only with relation to rabbinic legal writings.

3. For the idea that these sects split precisely over matters related to the implementation of legal interpretations of Torah, see Smith, "The Dead Sea Sect," 360; Sussmann, "The History of the Halakha," 61–64.

4. A good example of non-Karaite deviance from rabbinic *hălākhāh* may be found in the medieval Jewish communities that adhered to the Torah regulations surrounding menstrual impurity, but in ways that conflicted with rabbinic interpretations (and sometimes in ways that were more *stringent* than the rabbis' interpretations; see S. Cohen, "Purity, Piety, and Polemic"; S. Miller, *At the Intersection*, 297–306; Krakowski, "Maimonides' Menstrual Reform."

5. Gove, *Webster's*, s.v. "Judaism" (def. 2–3). I have not cited the first definition provided here, which appears to be deeply indebted to a Christian mindset: "the religion of the Jews, characterized by belief in one God and in the mission of Jews to teach the Fatherhood [*sic!*] of God as revealed in the Hebrew Scriptures." It appears to me that something reminiscent of this first definition—with its focus on *religion* specifically—lies at the base of the arguments put forward by Steve Mason ("Jews, Judaeans, Judaizing, Judaism," 460–488) and Daniel Boyarin ("No Ancient Judaism"; *Judaism*) against any use of the term "Judaism" when discussing antiquity. It is unclear to me why Mason and Boyarin ignore the non-"religious" usage of the word in current English and insist that "Judaism" can only have a "religious" sense.

6. So as not to be misunderstood, I have no interest here in staking the claim that "Judaism," whether today or anytime in the past, is essentially focused on practical behaviors rather than on beliefs. I have no interest in making any essentialist claims, nor do I wish to argue for a "correct" definition of "Judaism." My point is simply that the Jewish way of life has historically been characterized by practical adherence to the laws of the Torah, and that a useful one-word term for this phenomenon is "Judaism." Readers who would prefer a different technical term for the Jewish way of life as regulated by the Torah are invited to replace "Judaism" where it appears throughout the book with any other term of their choosing.

7. 2 Macc 2:21; 8:1; 14:38; Gal 1:13–14; 4 Macc 4:25. For the inscriptions, see citations and discussion in Mason, "Jews, Judaeans, Judaizing, Judaism," 476–480. For Christian writers from the third century onward, see ibid., 471–476.

8. Thus Boyarin, *Judaism*, 38–48. Contra Mason, who assumed that "*Ioudaïzō*" (as the verb behind "*Ioudaïsmós*") must have taken the transitive sense of "to Judaize"—that is, the action of winning over other people to the side of the Judeans. For Mason, the noun does not denote a static "Judaism" as a way one lives one's own life, but rather an active "Judaizing" of others. For critiques of Mason's reading of "*Ioudaïsmós*," see S. Schwartz, "How Many Judaisms," 224–226; D. Schwartz, *Judeans and Jews*, 91–112.

9. For Boyarin, "*Ioudaïsmós*" in the early Jewish sources has the sense of "acting like a Judean," which he argues is not reducible to being a member of a religion that we now call "Judaism." In his provocatively titled *Judaism: The Genealogy of a Modern Notion*, Boyarin has compellingly demonstrated that none of the languages used by Jews throughout their history ever had a word for

"Judaism" in the sense of a religion, and that this state of affairs continued until the eighteenth century when the word "Judenthum" entered into the language of German Jews as a consequence of their adoption of standard German for both speech and writing. The notion of "Judaism" as a religion was thus born, a Christian (or more precisely Protestant) child of the Enlightenment brought into the Jewish household through the backdoor of the Jewish adoption of a "Christian language." On the one hand, I fully agree with Boyarin's assessment that "Judaism" as a religion is a modern innovation. (For more on this see Batnitzky, *How Judaism Became a Religion*). On the other hand, there can be no doubt regarding the antiquity of Judaism as a way of life characterized by the observance of Torah. It seems to me that it was precisely because of the *embeddedness of Judaism in the very fabric of Jewish life* throughout most of Jewish history that Jewish languages almost never employed a single word to describe this "Judaism." Precisely because Judaism permeated everything, because it was so completely enmeshed within the matrix of Jewish living, it should be unsurprising that the concept had never become reified into the form of a single word. The notion *does* become concretized into single, specialized words precisely at times and places where these practices had become disengaged to one extent or another: as "*Ioudaïsmós*" within the narrative worlds of the authors of 2 Maccabees and 4 Maccabees and among the non-Judean but Christ-following communities addressed by Paul, and then centuries later as "Judenthum" in post-Enlightenment Germany. It seems that it was precisely when and where a very real option of *not* observing Judaic practices emerged that a specialized word for "Judaism" suddenly became necessary.

10. Jacob Neusner ("Preface," xi–xii) has argued for speaking of "a Judaism" as "the world view and the way of life that characterize the distinctive system by which a social group of Jews works out its affairs"; when discussing the sum of such systems, he posited that we should instead speak of "Judaisms" in the plural. Judging from Neusner's own voluminous work which regularly makes use of the singular "Judaism" to refer to a commonly shared Judaic way of life, it seems to me that his inconsistent and peculiar insistence on the plural "Judaisms" should be viewed more as an occasionally recurrent rhetorical flourish rather than as any kind of substantive critique of the standard use of the singular form. While a minority of scholars have picked up Neusner's idiosyncratic insistence on a pluralized "Judaisms," the initiative appears to have never really struck roots in the scholarly community, and therefore I have chosen to hold to the standard, singular form of "Judaism" throughout this book. For a critical assessment that takes Neusner's "Judaisms" far more seriously than I do (yet which agrees with my assessment that the term never gained any kind of wide acceptance), see S. Schwartz, "How Many Judaisms," 208–221.

11. Seth Schwartz has made this essential argument in his *Imperialism and Jewish Society*, 66.

12. An investigation into what non-Jewish writers in antiquity wrote about ancient Jews supports my contention here that practices are far more accessible to the view of an outsider than are beliefs. A thorough survey of what Greek and Latin authors had to say about Jews and Judaism (a convenient task utilizing Menahem Stern's corpus *Greek and Latin Authors on Jews and Judaism*) reveals that non-Jews oftentimes made special note of the Jews' distinct practices. Recurrent topics include circumcision, the dietary restrictions (especially abstention from pork), the prohibition against work on the Sabbath, and fasts (probably referencing the Day of Atonement). As far as I can tell, abstract beliefs are never described or even mentioned. Even when speaking about Jewish monotheism, the descriptions always revolve around concrete practices—particularly the notable fact that the Jews placed no icon of their god in his own temple (see citations referred to in the index provided in *GLAJJ*, s.v. "God, Jewish, God of the Hebrews; anonymous, uncertain, nameless and incorporeal").

13. For a still valuable investigation into the meaning and etymology of "*tôrāh*" in the Hebrew Bible, see Östborn, *Tōrā in the Old Testament*.

14. For example, Exod 13:9–10; 18:16, 20; Lev 7:36–37; 26:46; Num 15:15–16; 19:2; 31:21; Deut 4:8, 44–45; 17:8–11; 30:10; 33:10; 2 Kgs 17:13, 34, 37; Isa 24:5; 42:4; 51:4; Jer 44:10; Ezek 43:11; 44:5, 24; Amos 2:4; Hab 1:4; Mal 3:22; Ps 89:31; 105:45; 119 (on this psalm, see Levenson, "The Sources of Torah"); Ezra 7:10; Neh 8:18; 9:13–14, 29; 1 Chr 22:12–13; 2 Chr 19:10. When the term "*tôrāh*" appears without any accompanying legal terms, we are often left wondering whether any statutory content is meant at all, or whether perhaps some other kind of "instruction" is to be understood: moral guidance, ethical instruction, or perhaps just useful wisdom or good advice; see, e.g., Isa 1:10; 2:3; 5:24; 8:16, 20; 30:9; 42:21, 24; 51:7; Jer 2:8; 6:19; 8:8; 9:12; 16:11; 18:18; 31:32; Ezek 7:26; 22:26; Hos 4:6; 8:12; Amos 2:4; Mic 4:2; Zeph 3:4; Zech 7:12; Mal 2:6–9; Ps 1:2; 37:31; 40:9; 78:1, 5, 10; 94:12; Lam 2:9; 2 Chr 6:16; 12:1; 15:3; 17:9; 35:26. For "*tôrāh*" used in clearly nonlegal ways, see, e.g., Prov 1:8: "Hear, my child, your father's teaching, and do not reject your mother's instruction [*tôrat 'imekhā*]"; see also elsewhere in Proverbs (3:1; 4:1; 6:20, 23; 7:2; 13:14; 28:4, 7, 9; 29:18; 31:26) and Job (22:22).

15. Lev 6:2, 7, 18; 7:1, 11; 11:46; 12:7; 13:59; 14:2, 32, 57; 15:32; Num 5:29; 6:13, 21. In all these occurrences, "*tôrāh*" is used within a genitive phrase—in its construct state "*tôrat*"—to refer to a very limited corpus of "instruction" about rules and regulations regarding a clearly defined topic: "the instruction of the burnt offering [*tôrat hā 'ōlāh*]," "the instruction of the meal offering [*tôrat hamīnḥāh*]," ". . . of the purgation offering," ". . . of the guilt offering," ". . . of the peace offering," ". . . of the forbidden and impure animals," ". . . of the postpartum mother," etc. This manner of using "*tôrāh*" to refer to a circumscribed body of instruction can be discerned elsewhere in the Pentateuch, even when it does not appear within genitive phrases; e.g., Exod 12:49; 13:9; Lev 7:7; Num 15:16, 29; 19:2, 14; 31:21; Deut 17:11.

16. Deut 1:5; 4:8, 44; 17:18–19; 27:3, 8, 26; 28:58, 61; 29:20, 28; 30:10; 31:9, 11–12, 24, 26; 32:46.

17. See Deut 31:9, 24–27, where Moses is said to write down "this book of instruction [sēfer hatôrāh hazeh]" and hand it over to the Levites, carriers of the ark of the covenant, commanding them to place the book beside the ark, where it is to remain "as a witness [lə ʿēd]" in anticipation of future national lapses. The book is to be taken out and read in public once in seven years, before a gathering of all Israel, "so that they hear, and learn, and fear YHWH your God, and observe to perform all the words of this instruction" (Deut 31:10–13; quotation at 12). Cf. Exod 24:4, where Moses is said to have written "all the words of YHWH," which thereafter is called the "book of the covenant [sēfer habərît]" (Exod 24:7). For a late dating of this passage, see Ska, "From History Writing," 160–169.

18. *Copy written by future king:* Deut 17:18–20. *Copy set up at Mt. Ebal:* Deut 27:2–8. See also Josh 8:32, where this latter inscription is called a "copy of the instruction of Moses [mišnēh tôrat mōšeh]."

19. *Not explicitly in writing:* Josh 22:5; 2 Kgs 21:8; 23:25; Mal 3:22; 1 Chr 22:12–13; 2 Chr 30:16; 33:8. For commandments communicated through Moses but not referred to as "*tôrāh*" and with no mention of any writing, see Judg 3:4; 2 Kgs 18:6, 12; Neh 1:7–8; 1 Chr 6:34; 15:15; 22:13; 2 Chr 8:13; see also Ps 99:6–7. *In a "book":* Josh 1:7–8; 8:31–35; 23:6; 2 Kgs 14:6; 2 Chr 25:4 ("in the instruction in the book of Moses [batôrāh bəsēfer mōšeh]"); 34:14. For a "book of Moses [səfar/sēfer mōšeh]" not referred to as "*tôrāh*," see Ezra 6:18; 2 Chr 35:12; see also Neh 13:1–3. "*Written*" *but not explicitly in a "book":* 1 Kgs 2:3; Dan 9:11, 13; Ezra 3:2; 2 Chr 23:18. References to a Mosaic "*tôrāh*" outside the Pentateuch should not necessarily be assumed to be dependent on anything resembling the Pentateuchal narratives; for a detailed critique of prevailing notions regarding the literary influence of the Pentateuch on these and other Hebrew Bible texts, see Choi, *Traditions at Odds* (esp. 182–237).

20. Josephus (*Ag. Ap.* 1:39) explicitly stated that "the books of Moses" number five. That authorship of the entire Pentateuch was attributed to Moses is implied, for example, by writers who attributed to Moses narratives from Genesis—despite the fact that the Pentateuch itself does not cite Moses as narrating these stories; e.g., Philo, *Creation* 8; *Names* 32; Josephus, *Ant.* 1:26–34. Additional works that at least some in antiquity may have regarded as part of a Mosaic *tôrāh* are the documents referred to by scholars as "rewritten texts" of the Pentateuch, fragmentary remains of which have been found in caves near Qumran; see White Crawford, "Reworked Pentateuch"; Brooke, "Rewritten Bible"; Zahn, *Rethinking Rewritten Scripture.* Jubilees, set within a literary context of a divine revelation to Moses at Mt. Sinai, along with the Temple Scroll, which seems to share a similar narrative framework, may also have been regarded by some as comprising part of the Mosaic *tôrāh*. For a thorough treatment of this genre of literature characterized by "Mosaic discourse," see Najman, *Seconding Sinai.*

21. *First century texts:* Philo, *Hypoth.* 7:12–13; Josephus, *Ag. Ap.* 2:175; Acts 13:14–15 (cf. 15:21); *CIIP* I.1, 9 (the "Theodotos" inscription). For details, see chapter 6. *Rabbinic texts:* e.g., *m. Yoma* 7:1; *m. Meg.* 4:1–4; *m. Soṭah* 7:7.

22. *First century texts:* e.g., Josephus, *War* 2:228–231, 291; 7:150; *Ant.* 20:113–117. See also Josephus's narration about the translation of the Pentateuch into Greek (*Ant.* 12:11–118), where "the law" appears time and again as a physical document that can be handled. *Rabbinic texts:* e.g., *m. Yoma* 7:1; *m. Beṣah* 1:5; *m. Ta'an.* 4:6; *m. Meg.* 3:1; *m. Yebam.* 16:7; *m. Soṭah* 7:7; *m. B. Meṣ.* 4:9; *m. Sanh.* 2:4.

23. The term "*tôrāh*" appears quite frequently in the Dead Sea Scrolls (see Abegg, *The Dead Sea Scrolls Concordance*, s.v. "*tôrāh*"), but the often-opaque language and the usually fragmentary condition of the texts makes it difficult to always know the precise sense of the word. Arguably, an expansive sense of the term may be found in 4QMMTᶜ (4Q398) 14–17 ii, 2–4, where the authors self-referentially use the phrase "*miqṣāt ma'aśê hatôrāh*" (some precepts of the *tôrāh*) to describe their own extensive treatments of Pentateuchal laws.

24. The largest amount of surviving text dealing with legal matters rooted in exegesis of Pentateuchal laws is found in the Temple Scroll (11Q19–20), in the Damascus Document (4Q266–273, but also in the medieval manuscripts found in the Cairo genizah), and in 4QMMT (4Q394–399). Several other compositions that discuss legal matters are preserved more fragmentarily: 4Qpap cryptA Midrash Sefer Moshe (4Q249), 4QHalakha A (4Q251), 4QHalakha B (4Q264a), 4QMiscellaneous Rules (4Q465), 4QTohorot A (4Q274), 4QTohorot Bᵃ (4Q276), 4QTohorot Bᵇ (4Q277), 4QTohorot C (4Q278), 4QPurification Liturgy (4Q284), 4QHarvesting (4Q284a), 4QRitual of Purification A (4Q414), and 4QHalakha C (4Q472). These texts have been published by several authors in the thirty-fifth volume of the *Discoveries in the Judaean Desert* series, published in 1999 under the title *Halakhic Texts*. I have not included here sectarian regulations, such as the Community Rules, which clearly govern only members of the sect and whose relationship with Pentateuchal laws is at most tenuous. To be clear, exegetical activity is in evidence not only where it is made explicit, as in literature classified as "midrash halakhah." Exegetical activity of one sort or another is undoubtably also behind works that do not present themselves as exegetical, such as the Dead Sea Scrolls cited above and the generally apodictic Mishnah and Tosefta.

25. For Josephus self-proclaiming his own expertise in interpreting Pentateuchal law, see Josephus, *Ant.* 20:263–265; *Life* 8–9. For the expert exegesis of two Jerusalem scholars (*sophistai*) at the end of Herod's reign, see Josephus, *War* 1:648–649; *Ant.* 17:149. For a charismatic pretender to expertise in interpreting the "law of Moses" in Rome, see Josephus, *Ant.* 18:81–84. For a Pharisee named Gamaliel as a "teacher of the law" (*nomodidáskalos*), respected by all the people, see Acts 5:34 (also 22:3). See also 4 Macc 5:4, 35, where a certain elderly Judean priest is said to have been one with expert "knowledge" (*epistēmē*) about the law.

26. See, e.g., 4QMMT; Josephus, *Ant.* 13:297–298; 18:15–16; Matt 15:1–20; Mark 7:1–23. See also Gal 1:14. The later rabbis also spoke of numerous disagreements between Pharisees (or "the Sages") and their Sadducean (or "Boethusian") opponents on various details of Pentateuchal and ancillary law; see, e.g., *m. Mak.* 1:6; *m. Menaḥ.* 10:3; *m. Parah* 3:3, 7; *m. Nid.* 4:2; *m. Yad.* 4:6–7. Josephus (*War* 2:162) claimed that the Pharisees, representing a "philosophical school," were generally recognized as a group whose members "are reputed to interpret the regulations with precision [*hoi met' akribeías dokoûntes exēgeîsthai tà nómima*]." For an investigation into how to best translate "*dokéō*" here (i.e., do the Pharisees *have the reputation of being* precise interpreters of the law or do they only *profess themselves to be* such), see Mason, *Flavius Josephus on the Pharisees*, 106–110. See also *War* 1:110; *Ant.* 17:41; *Life* 191. Albert Baumgarten ("The Name") has suggested that the Hebrew name for the Pharisees, "*pərušîm*," was interpreted by the Pharisees themselves as deriving from the verb "*p-r-š*" ("to specify")—i.e., to interpret with *precision*. Paul Mandel (*The Origins of* Midrash, 145–168) has recently argued that the purported expertise of the Pharisees, and indeed of all those first-century Judeans said to be expert "*exēgētai*" in the law, did not involve *interpretation* of the Pentateuch but rather instruction and exposition of an unwritten body of laws passed on from previous generations. Even if this were so, certainly any supposed unwritten corpus would have had to have been created *at some point* through some sort of exegesis of the Pentateuch.

27. The early rabbis sometimes spoke of two *tôrôt*: one "in writing" (*bīkhtāv*) and one "oral" (*bə 'al peh*); see, e.g., *Sifra, Beḥuq.* 8:12 (ed. J. H. Weiss, 112b). By "written *tôrāh*" the rabbis meant the Pentateuch, whereas by "oral *tôrāh*" they meant the dynamic interpretation of the Pentateuch. Both, however, are usually just called "*tôrāh*." A similar distinction between the Pentateuch and its oral interpretation may be behind Philo's reference to "the sacred laws and also the unwritten customs [*tōn agráphōn ethōn*]" (*Embassy* 115); but see Martens, *One God, One Law*, 87–88. Philo elsewhere (*Spec. Laws* 4:149–150) wrote of "unwritten laws" that do not carry punishments like the written laws, but here it is unclear whether he was necessarily writing about the Judean law, and if so, what exactly it was that he had in mind; see Martens, *One God, One Law*, 87–88.

28. Among the earliest appearances of the name are references to King Hezekiah "the Judean" (*Ia-ú-da-a-a*) in Akkadian texts from around the end of the eight century BCE: *Chicago Prism* II:76; *Taylor Prism* II:71–72; *Bull* 4:23, 27; *Letter to the God Ashur* 4 (English transliterations and translations collected in Mayer, "Sennacherib's Campaign").

29. See Simpson and Weiner, *The Oxford English Dictionary*, s.v. "Jew."

30. See, e.g., S. Cohen, *The Beginnings of Jewishness*, esp. 3, 69–70, 104–105; Mason, "Jews, Judaeans, Judaizing, Judaism"; D. Schwartz, "'Judaean' or 'Jew,'" "Judeans, Jews and Their Neighbors," and *Judeans and Jews*; D. Miller, "The Meaning of *Ioudaios*" and "Ethnicity"; S. Schwartz, "How Many Judaisms"; R. Bloch, "Jew

244 Notes to Pages 8–10

or Judean." For a recent critique of the premises beneath this entire debate, see Baker, *Jew*, 16–46.

31. For a detailed survey and analysis of the history of scholarship on this question, see Weitzman, *The Origin of the Jews*.

32. Thus, already in the title of John Rogerson's biography: *W.M.L. de Wette, Founder of Modern Biblical Criticism*.

33. De Wette, *Dissertatio*.

34. Ibid., 164–165 n. 5.

35. De Wette, *Lehrbuch der christlichen Dogmatik*, 1:48. English translation from Pasto, "Who Owns the Jewish Past?," 95. Pasto (ibid., 79–150; "W.M.L. de Wette") has argued compellingly that de Wette was the first scholar to have depicted the Babylonian exile as a point of complete religio-cultural rupture, and the first scholar ever to use the term "Judaism" (*Judenthum*) to mean a specifically postexilic religious development.

36. De Wette, *Lehrbuch der christlichen Dogmatik*, 1:48.

37. Aside from his observations about the literary history of the Hebrew Bible, the only ancient source de Wette cited for his novel claim was the statement of Josephus (*Ant.* 11:173), who wrote about the term "Judeans" (*Ioudaîoi*): "This name by which they have been called *from the time when they went up from Babylon*, is derived from the tribe of Judah" (emphasis mine). The tenuous connection between this statement of Josephus and the novel model posited by de Wette has been highlighted by Pasto ("Who Owns the Jewish Past?," 33–35, 104–105), who has shown that Josephus's "Judeans" are synonymous with his "Hebrews" and "Israelites," and that Josephus never intended to suggest a substantive contrast between the names as de Wette did. Pasto ("Who Owns the Jewish Past?," 79–150; "W.M.L. de Wette") has furthermore argued that de Wette's model of a radical rupture between preexilic "Hebraism" and a postexilic "Judaism" was shaped more by philosophical and political ideas current in early nineteenth-century Germany than by any specific observations of his from the ancient sources.

38. Graf, *Die geschichtlichen Bücher*. Graf's hypothesis was developed from ideas he had learned from his teacher and friend Édouard Guillaume Eugène Reuss (1804–1891), but which the latter had not published; see Ska, *Introduction*, 108.

39. Kuenen, *The Religion of Israel*, 226–307. My citations here are from the 1875 English translation of the 1869 original Dutch *De godsdienst van Israël*.

40. Kuenen, *The Religion of Israel*, 249 (italics in the original).

41. The basic outline of Wellhausen's ideas was first formulated in his article "Die composition des Hexateuchs," published in 1876 and 1877.

42. This was the second, revised edition of his 1878 *Geschichte Israels*, the first volume of an anticipated two-volume set, the second volume of which never appeared. An English translation of the 1883 German *Prolegomena* was published two years later in Edinburgh under the title *Prolegomena to the History of Israel*. The citations that follow will be from this English edition.

43. Wellhausen, *Prolegomena*, 1–13. In a slightly later work (*Israelitische und jüdische Geschichte*), Wellhausen makes another terminological distinction between "*Judentum*" and "*Judaismus*." For a discussion, see Pasto, "Who Owns the Jewish Past?," 213 n. 44.

44. Wellhausen, *Prolegomena*, 405–410.

45. Wellhausen, *Prolegomena*, 408 n. 1. It should go without saying that this sort of appeal to verisimilitude (the quality of a story *sounding* true) cannot be taken seriously as grounds to accept a story like this as historical. For a more detailed discussion, see chapter 7.

46. Meyer, *Die Entstehung des Judentums*, esp. 60–71.

47. For a review of this late nineteenth-century polemic, see Kratz, "Die Entstehung des Judentums."

48. For a history of scholarship, see Chavalas, "Assyriology and Biblical Studies."

49. For an overview of these developments, see Tov, *Textual Criticism*.

50. See Nicholson, *The Pentateuch*, 95–268; Carr, "Changes in Pentateuchal Criticism."

51. Interestingly, even scholars who argued for an early dating of "P" tended to agree with the notion that the Babylonian exile served as a bold line of demarcation when "ancient Israel" ended and "Judaism" began. Perhaps the most well-known proponent of this position was Yehezkel Kaufmann, who wrote, "The fall of Jerusalem is the great watershed of the history of the Israelite religion. The life of the people of Israel came to an end; the history of Judaism began.... Israel ceased to be a normal nation and became a religious community" (*The Religion of Israel*, 447).

52. For a recent overview of this material, see Lemaire, *Levantine Epigraphy*.

53. Wellhausen (*Israelitische und jüdische Geschichte*, 178) referred to the Elephantine community as a "fossilized remnant of unreformed Judaism [*fossile Überrest des unreformierten Judentums*]." For a recent critical examination of Wellhausen's view on this matter, and of subsequent scholarly reception of the idea, see Kratz, "Fossile Überreste."

54. I have found this to be a rather common thread running throughout much of Porten's work on the Elephantine material; see, e.g., his *Archives from Elephantine*.

55. A refreshing outlier to this trend in twentieth-century scholarship is Morton Smith's study "Jewish Religious Life in the Persian Period," where the epigraphic evidence is evaluated on its own merit without the imposition of any assumptions about the Torah being widely known and observed by Persian-era Judeans. For a more recent treatment of the evidence along similar lines, see Granerød, "Canon and Archive."

56. E. Stern, "Religion in Palestine," 253–255; *Archaeology of the Land of the Bible*, 2:478–479; "The Religious Revolution." For the debate that has arisen in recent years surrounding Stern's thesis, see below in chapter 7.

57. Sanders's exploration of "common Judaism" is concentrated in part 2 of the book,

246 Notes to Pages 14–20

which takes up more than half of the volume. While the secondary title sets the scope as "63 BCE–66 CE," most of the evidence he explores throughout the book actually dates to the first century CE (both before 66 and after).

58. Sanders ("Common Judaism Explored," 16–17) cited Morton Smith ("Palestinian Judaism"; "The Dead Sea Sect") as his inspiration for investigating the practices and beliefs of the masses. Smith himself, however, never undertook the kind of detailed investigation into this problem that Sanders did.

59. For good overviews of scholarly reception of Sanders's idea of "common Judaism" sixteen years after its initial publication, see the essays collected in two volumes published in 2008: McCready and Reinhartz, *Common Judaism*; Udoh et al., *Redefining First-Century Jewish and Christian Identities*. Sanders's discussion of the archaeological evidence, while salutary, was quite limited. For a more in-depth overview, see Magness, *Stone and Dung*. It should be noted that the term "household Judaism" coined by Andrea Berlin ("Household Judaism"; see also her "Jewish Life before the Revolt" and "Manifest Identity") refers to something rather different from Sanders's "common Judaism"; it denotes the adoption of household goods that distinguished the homes and (therefore) daily lives of Judeans from those of others. In Berlin's words: "Household Judaism developed outside legal or priestly concerns. The practice reflects a broad desire for material possessions that encoded a singular lifestyle and ethnic affiliation" ("Household Judaism," 208).

60. S. Cohen, *The Beginnings of Jewishness*, 105.

61. For a recent evaluation and critique of Cohen's emphasis on the influences of Hellenism, see Weitzman, *The Origin of the Jews*, 208–244.

62. S. Cohen, *The Beginnings of Jewishness*, 2.

63. J. Collins, *The Invention of Judaism*, esp. 60, 67, 87, 90, 184, 215 (n. 95).

64. Kratz, *Historical and Biblical Israel*, 9–57.

65. Ibid., 61–130.

66. Ibid., 200–203.

67. Ibid., 184–187, 196, 197–207 (quotation at 200).

68. Even when Josephus (*Ag. Ap.* 2:178) wished to stress how strict the Judeans were in their observance of their laws, he could at most claim that "a transgressor is a rarity." For an even more idealized (and far less believable) claim of *universal* Judean compliance to the laws of the Torah, see *Ant.* 3:223.

69. Rabbinic literature will not be consulted in the present study. As has been explained, the chronological scope of our focus is on the first century CE and earlier. The rabbinic corpus is a complex assemblage whose constituent parts as we have them began to be assembled *at the earliest* only in the late second and early third centuries CE. Although it is not uncommon to find sayings and views attributed to sages who lived in the first century CE or even in the first century BCE (only rarely are views ascribed to personalities who are thought to have lived in the second century BCE or earlier), it is usually impossible to

know the degree to which such attributions accurately reflect their purported sources. Because of this uncertainty, and because including such references would have almost invariably served only to strengthen the case which is to be made here, I decided it was best to leave this corpus of evidence out of our present investigation.

Chapter 1. Dietary Laws

1. Lev 11:1–23, 41–47; Deut 14:3–20. Note that in many cases, when the Pentateuch prohibited the consumption of certain kinds of meat, it also stated that the forbidden meat renders impurity to people and objects through contact. Although the dietary prohibitions and the purity laws share this point of juncture, the latter regulations will be treated as an essentially distinct subject in chapter 2.
2. Exod 22:30; Lev 22:8; Deut 14:21. Cf. Lev 11:39–40; 17:15–16, where these are only said to be a cause of impurity but are not explicitly forbidden as food.
3. *Blood:* Gen 9:4; Lev 3:17; 7:26–27; 17:10–14; 19:26 (but see below); Deut 12:16, 23–25; 15:23; cf. Lev 19:26. *Fat:* Lev 3:17; 7:23–25 (the fat of an "ox, lamb, and goat" is specified here).
4. Exod 21:28.
5. Lev 19:23.
6. Exod 12:14–20; 13:3–10; Deut 16:3–4. See also below, chapter 5.
7. Lev 23:14.
8. Lev 10:9; Num 6:1–4.
9. Exod 12:9.
10. Lev 7:16–18; 19:6–8.
11. Lev 7:19–21; 10:14 (in a pure "place"); 22:4–7.
12. Lev 10:14–15; 22:10–13; cf. Num 18:8–10.
13. Num 18:11–13.
14. Deut 12:17–18.
15. Gen 32:33. The rabbis later created a slew of new dietary prohibitions through interpretation of Pentateuchal passages and other legal strategies: meat cooked together with milk was forbidden, as was the flesh of animals not slaughtered according to a specific method, meat from animals that present certain pathologies, agricultural produce that had not been tithed, wine and other products obtained from (or handled by) Gentiles, and much more. Because all these dietary restrictions appear only in rabbinic literature, compiled quite some time after the first century CE, they will not be discussed here.
16. Philo, *Spec. Laws* 4:95–125.
17. Philo, *Embassy* 361–363.
18. Philo, *Flaccus* 95–96.
19. For meat offered to idols, see 1 Cor 8–10; Acts 15:20, 29; 21:25; Rev 2:14, 20. For eating in a state of impurity, or more generally eating together with Gentiles or sinners, see chapter 2.

20. Rom 14:2.

21. Rom 14:14, 20–21.

22. Similar ambiguity is found in the dangling participial phrase found in Mark 7:19b: "purifying all the food [*katharízōn pánta tà brōmata*]." Note that the comment is imbedded within a passage focused on ritual impurity, not the dietary prohibitions; see further discussion on this pericope in chapter 2. For other less-than-certain references to the dietary laws within the New Testament corpus, see Matt 23:24; Col 2:16; 1 Tim 4:3–5; Titus 1:15.

23. Acts 10:11–16. The vision is repeated in Acts 11:5–10, where Peter recounts the story to the "circumcised believers" in Jerusalem.

24. Acts 10:17–11:18.

25. Acts 15:28–29. James is said to have been the initiator of these prohibitions in Acts 15:19–20. See also Acts 21:25.

26. Thus Philo (*Spec. Laws* 4:122), who condemned the decadent Sardanapalus-like people who are said to "devise novel kinds of pleasure and prepare meat unfit for the altar by strangling and throttling the animals, and entomb in the carcass the blood which is the essence of the soul and should be allowed to run freely away."

27. Josephus, *War* 2:152; *Ant.* 1:335; 3:259–260; 6:120–121; 10:190–194 (meat is singled out); 11:346; 12:94–95; 14:215, 226–227, 261; *Ag. Ap.* 2:137, 173–174 (meat is singled out), 234–235, 281–284; *Life* 14.

28. *Animals that died on their own:* Josephus, *Ant.* 3:260. *Fats: Ant.* 3:260. *"The broad sinew": Ant.* 1:335. *Pork: Ag. Ap.* 2:137. *Unspecified animal species: Ant.* 3:259.

29. Josephus, *Ant.* 6:120–121, in a somewhat significant expansion upon the narrative in 1 Sam 14:32–34 (see further below). See also *Ant.* 3:260.

30. Josephus, *War* 2:152; *Ag. Ap.* 2:234–235. Josephus's anecdote about priests taken prisoner to Rome who sustained themselves on figs and nuts (*Life* 13–14) is likely a reference to the purity laws (see discussion in chapter 2).

31. Josephus, *Ant.* 11:346. See also *War* 7:264, where he accuses his nemesis, John of Gischala, of having had "unlawful" (*áthesmon*) food served at his table.

32. Josephus, *Ag. Ap.* 2:282.

33. Strabo, *Geogr.* 16.2:37 (*GLAJJ* 1:295, 300).

34. Josephus, *Ag. Ap.* 2:137.

35. Erotianus, *Voc. Hipp. Coll.*, F33 (*GLAJJ* 1:446).

36. Plutarch, *Quaestiones Convivales* 4.4:4–5:3 (*GLAJJ* 1:550–556). The hypothesis that the pig was revered by Judeans may have influenced the outlandish claim by Petronius (*Frag.* 37 [*GLAJJ* 1:444]) that the Judeans worship a "pig-god [*porcinum numen*]."

37. Tacitus, *Hist.* 5.4:1 (*GLAJJ* 2:18, 25).

38. Juvenal, *Sat.* 6:160; 14:98–99 (*GLAJJ* 2:99–100, 102–103).

39. Sextus Empiricus, *Hypotyposes* 3:222–223 (*GLAJJ* 2:159). The abstention of Egyptian priests from eating pork is cited also in Josephus, *Ag. Ap.* 2:141.

40. Epictetus (in Arrianus, *Dissertationes* 1.22:4) (*GLAJJ* 1:542).
41. Pliny the Elder, *Naturalis Historia* 31:95 (*GLAJJ* 1:500).
42. Carole Cope ("The Butchering Patterns"), Haskel Greenfield and Ram Bouch-nick ("Kashrut and Shechita"), and Abra Spiciarich ("Identifying the Biblical Food Prohibitions") have all published studies that sought archaeofaunal evidence for rabbinic practices such as ritual slaughter and porging of the sciatic nerve and blood vessels in archaeological contexts predating 70 CE. To succeed in such a venture, one would need to identify butchering marks on bones from sites associated with Judeans which present patterns decidedly different from marks typically found on bones from sites associated with non-Judeans—and then demonstrate that these differences are best explained by postulating the early emergence of practices otherwise known to us only from rabbinic texts dating to late antiquity, the Middle Ages, and even modern times. No study to date has accomplished this.
43. Horwitz and Studer, "Pig Production and Exploitation"; Bouchnick, *Meat Consumption*. Note that I will not indicate here where pig remains have been identified as either domestic or wild, nor where butchering marks or signs of roasting were present on the bones, since this kind of information is often unavailable.
44. *Jerusalem, eastern city dump (a):* Spiciarich, Gadot, and Sapir-Hen, "The Faunal Evidence," 109; *Jerusalem, Giv'ati Parking Lot (b):* Bar-Oz and Raban-Gerstel, "The Faunal Remains," 360; *Qumran (b):* Sade, "The Archaeozoological Finds," 457 (where it is noted: "The pig bones came from a manure heap outside of the site's eastern wall"). For all other sites, citations are provided in Bouch-nick, *Meat Consumption*, 160. Note that the assemblages from H. Burnat North, H Rimmon, Shu'afat, and Tell el-Ful are all likely to include remains from the early second century CE. Pig remains from Early Roman assemblages in a residential neighborhood on the western hill of Sepphoris are said to be "relatively scarce" (Grantham, "Faunal Remains," 873–874, fig. 34.3); I have not included these assemblages in the table, as precise NISP or percentages do not appear in the report. Also not included are sites whose identification as Judean is less than secure (such as H. 'Eleq). I have also avoided references to assemblages that are likely to include remains from periods significantly later than the first century. Also not included is a faunal assemblage from the tomb precinct on the northern slope of Herodium, as it includes loci that are associated with the rebels together with loci "from a refuse dump dated to the time when a Roman garrison took control of Herodium" (Bouchnick, "Finds of Animal Remains," 492).
45. Citations are provided in Horwitz and Studer, "Pig Production and Exploita-tion," 226 (only "northern sites" are included); Bouchnick, *Meat Consumption*, 160. Also possibly relevant is an assemblage from Qumran from loci dated to "after the Roman Conquest of 68 CE": 6 pig bones were found out of a total NISP of 77 (7.8%); see Sade, "The Archaeozoological Finds," 458.

46. Citations for all data on the fish remains are conveniently provided in Adler and Lernau, "The Pentateuchal Dietary Proscription."
47. Macrobius, *Sat.* 2.4:11 (*GLAJJ* 2:665).
48. Menahem Stern (*GLAJJ* 2:666) assumes just such an early source.
49. Josephus, *Ant.* 14:226–227. See Pucci Ben Zeev, *Jewish Rights*, 139–148.
50. Josephus, *Ant.* 14:261. See Pucci Ben Zeev, *Jewish Rights*, 217–225.
51. Diodorus Siculus, *Bibliotheca Historica* 34–35.1:2 (*GLAJJ* 1:182–183).
52. Plutarch, *Vit. Cic.* 7:6 (*GLAJJ* 1:566).
53. 1QapGen ar xi, 17; 11Q19 lii, 5–8; CD xii, 13–15.
54. In most insects, the bodily fluid analogous to the blood in vertebrates (called "hemolymph") lacks respiratory pigments such as hemoglobin which in vertebrates colors the blood red (Chapman, *The Insects*, 473). Permitted fish, as all vertebrates, have hemoglobin-carrying red blood. It seems likely, therefore, that the blood of fish would have been regarded as "blood," while permitted insects would have been regarded as essentially "bloodless." This seems to me to be the most straightforward way to understand both the fish clause and the locust clause here. For alternative explanations, which extrapolate from substantially later rabbinic discussions regarding fish and locusts, see Schiffman, "Laws Pertaining to Forbidden Foods," 67–69, and the earlier scholarship cited there.
55. 11Q19 xlviii, 5–7; 4Q251 7, 4 (the prohibition against carrion is reconstructed immediately prior to this).
56. 4Q251 7, 2. The text is fragmentary here, and conjecturally the missing words may limit the prohibition to either a late or perhaps an early stage of gestation (line 1 preserves the phrase "an ox, a sheep or a goat that have not completed"). A fragmentary passage in 4Q396 i, 3–4 and an even more fragmentary text in 4Q270 2 ii, 15 may both also refer to eating fetuses. The Temple Scroll (11Q19 lii, 5) forbids the slaughter of a sacrificial animal that is pregnant, possibly for the same reason; if the fetus is regarded as either carrion or "torn," its carcass would render the flesh of the mother impure through contact (see Lev 11:39–40; 17:15–16; 22:8). For alternative interpretations of the bans on eating fetuses and sacrificing pregnant animals, but from the perspective of later rabbinic notions regarding ritual slaughter, see Schiffman, "Laws Pertaining to Forbidden Foods," 70 (with citations to earlier scholarship).
57. 4Q158 1–2, 13. The missing text at the end of the previous line (line 12) has been reconstructed so as to turn the taboo into an explicit instruction from God to Jacob (for discussion and citations to previous scholarship, see Schiffman, "Laws Pertaining to Forbidden Foods," 73–75), but this must remain a matter of conjecture.
58. 11Q19 xlviii, 1–5.
59. CD xii, 11–13. For a discussion and citations to earlier scholarship, see Schiffman, "Laws Pertaining to Forbidden Foods," 65–67.
60. Jub. 6:12; 7:30.

61. Jub. 6:7, 10–14; 7:28–32; 21:18. It is of some interest that the Aramaic Levi Document contains no explicit blood prohibition—only an instruction to cover blood with earth before eating meat so as not to eat "upon/in the presence of the blood [*epì toũ haímatos*]" (10:9).
62. T. Ash. 2:8–10. See Lev 11:6–7; Deut 14:7–8.
63. T. Ash. 4:1–5.
64. Let. Aris. 128–171. Most scholars claim a middle to late second-century-BCE date for the work; White, Keddie, and Flexsenhar, "The Epistle of Aristeas," 34–38. See there for alternative suggested dates in the first century BCE or the beginning of the first century CE.
65. 1 Macc 1:62–63; 2 Macc 6:18–7:42 (see also 5:27); 4 Macc. 5–18 (see also 1:31–35).
66. Rappaport, *The First Book of Maccabees*, 60–61; Doran, *2 Maccabees*, 14–15. Also possibly relevant is Pseudo-Phocylides (147–148), which includes the following admonition: "Eat no meat torn from wild beasts, but to swift-footed dogs leave the remains; beasts feed on beasts." For texts that do not refer to specific Pentateuchal dietary prohibitions but only comment on Judeans keeping separate from Gentiles with regard to food (3 Macc. 3:3–7), abstaining from eating the food of Gentiles (Tob 1:10–11), or refraining from eating together with Gentiles (Jos. Asen. 7:1; Add Esth C 28; Jub. 22:16), see my comments in chapter 2. See chapter 2 also for food concerns in Judith (Jdt 10:5; 12:1–4, 9, 19); there I argue that these are to be understood as a matter of ritual purity observance.
67. 1 Sam 14:32–35.
68. Grintz, "'Do Not Eat on the Blood.'" For Josephus's interpretation informed by first-century-CE praxis, see *Ant.* 6:120–121.
69. Isa 65:3–4.
70. Isa 66:17. See also 66:3, where swine's blood is mentioned as a component of idolatrous cultic worship.
71. Ezek 44:31.
72. Ezek 4:14.
73. Dan 1:5–16.
74. The food is identified only as being of the king's "*patbag*," apparently from the Old Persian "*patibaga*" (passed into Greek as "*potíbazis*"), meaning "portion" (J. Collins, *Daniel*, 127, 139–140). For a survey of scholarly explanations for why Daniel was portrayed as refusing to eat this food, see J. Collins, *Daniel*, 141–143.
75. For a detailed discussion on the compositional history of the Daniel texts, see J. Collins, *Daniel*, 24–38.
76. Gen 32:33. The story is cited by Demetrius the Chronographer (Dem. 2:7), where a taboo against eating "the tendon of the thigh of cattle" is mentioned. For more on what the writings of Demetrius may have to teach us about what ordinary Judeans in the late third century BCE knew about and practiced, see chapter 7.
77. Gunkel, *Genesis*, xxvi.

78. *Herodium:* Bouchnick, "Finds of Animal Remains," 479; *Qumran:* Sade, "The Archaeozoological Finds," 454–456; *Nebi Samwil:* Spiciarich, "Religious and Socioeconomic Diversity," 203; *Jerusalem, Givʿati Parking Lot (Area M1):* Bar-Oz and Raban-Gerstel, "The Faunal Remains," 358; *Jerusalem, Givʿati Parking Lot (Area M2):* Spiciarich, "Religious and Socioeconomic Diversity," 147; *Jerusalem, Givʿati Parking Lot (Area M4):* Spiciarich, "Religious and Socioeconomic Diversity," 122.

79. Spiciarich, "Religious and Socioeconomic Diversity," 147 (Phase VII). For Judean assemblages dating to the "Hellenistic period" generally, and which lack pig bones, see ibid., 109, 179, 203.

80. *Ramat Raḥel:* Fulton, "The Faunal Remains," 143–144; *Givʿati Parking Lot (Area M2):* Spiciarich, "Religious and Socioeconomic Diversity," 147 (Phase VIII); *Nebi Samwil:* Spiciarich, "Religious and Socioeconomic Diversity," 203; *City of David:* Tamar and Bar-Oz, "Zooarchaeological Analysis," 499.

81. Sapir-Hen et al., "Pig Husbandry"; Sapir-Hen, "Food, Pork Consumption, and Identity"; Finkelstein, Gadot, and Sapir-Hen, "Pig Frequencies." More recently reported assemblages from Jerusalem and its environs (e.g., Spiciarich, "Religious and Socioeconomic Diversity"; Sapir-Hen, Uziel, and Chalaf, "Everything but the Oink") have not affected in any significant way the assessments of these earlier metanalyses.

82. Hesse and Wapnish, "Can Pig Remains."

83. Sapir-Hen et al., "Pig Husbandry," 12–13.

84. Hesse, "Pig Lovers," 205, 218; Sapir-Hen, "Food, Pork Consumption, and Identity," 58.

85. Hesse and Wapnish, "Can Pig Remains," 240.

86. In recent years, Avraham Faust has been a vocal supporter of the notion that an Israelite "taboo" against pig was practiced as early as the Iron Age I, writing of this period, "The Israelites (or proto-Israelites) completely avoided pork at this time, most likely building on an existing taboo to distinguish themselves from the Philistines" (Faust, "Pigs in Space," quotation at 293). Faust, like others before him, mistakenly conflates lack of pig remains with deliberate *avoidance*, and consequentially posits without adequate supporting evidence that this was the result of a "taboo." For a detailed critique of this and several of Faust's other arguments in this study, see Finkelstein, Gadot, and Sapir-Hen, "Pig Frequencies." Most recently, the idea of an early pig taboo has been adopted by Max Price in his monograph aptly titled *Evolution of a Taboo.*

87. Citations for all data on the fish remains discussed here are available in Adler and Lernau, "The Pentateuchal Dietary Proscription."

88. A significant number of catfish bones were also unearthed in Area B at Gamla (13 out of 72 total NISP). While in the original report it was assumed that this and other archaeological assemblages from Areas B/D should be associated with a supposed Judean presence at the site as early as the late second century

BCE, work by Shulamit Terem ("The Oil Lamps," 118–126) on the oil lamps and other ceramic finds from Areas B/D suggests that the town was likely settled by a non-Judean population from the second century BCE until circa 80 BCE, when according to Josephus (*War* 1:105; *Ant.* 13:394) the "fortress of Gamla" was captured by Alexander Jannaeus.

Chapter 2. Ritual Purity

1. For a cross-cultural perspective on the categories of sin and impurity in ancient Egypt, Mesopotamia, Syria-Canaan, Israel, Anatolia, Iran, Greece, and Rome, as well as in early Christianity, see D. Wright et al., "Sin, Pollution, and Purity." For a focus on ancient Judaism, see Klawans, *Impurity and Sin*. For an up-to-date annotated bibliography on these issues in the Hebrew Bible and in early Judaism, see Kazen, "Purity and Impurity." For a study on how a recent ultra-Orthodox propaganda campaign in Israel made consistent, graphic use of all three of these categories in its fight against military conscription from the Haredi community, see Simonsen, "Bacteria, Garbage, Insects and Pigs."

2. *(1)* Gen 7:2, 8; 8:20; Lev 5:2; 7:21; 11:1–28, 41–47; 20:25; 27:11, 27; Num 18:15; Deut 14:3–20. *(2)* Lev 5:2; 7:21; 11:29–38; 22:5–7. *(3)* Lev 11:39–40; 17:15–16; 22:8. *(4)* Lev 12:1–8. *(5)* Lev 13:1–46; 14:1–32, 54–57; 22:4–7; Num 5:1–4. *(6)* Lev 13:47–59; 14:54–57. *(7)* Lev 14:33–57. *(8)* Lev 15:1–15, 31–33; 22:4–7; Num 5:1–4 (see also 12:10–16). *(9)* Lev 15:16–18, 31–32; 22:4–7; Deut 23:11–12. *(10)* Lev 15:19–24, 31, 33; 18:19. *(11)* Lev 15:31, 33. *(12)* Lev 7:21; 21:1–4, 11; 22:4–7; Num 5:1–4; 6:6–12; 9:6–10; 19:11–22; 31:19–24. *(13)* Num 19:1–8. *(14)* Num 19:9–10. *(15)* Num 19:21. See also Lev 16:26–28, where the man who sends the goat into the wilderness and also the one who burns the carcasses of the bull and goat expiation offerings are not explicitly said to be impure—but both must remain outside "the camp" until they have laundered their clothes and bathed in water.

3. Arabic numerals cited here refer to verses listed in the previous note: *(a)* 4, 5, 8, 10, 11, 13, 14, 15. *(b)* 1, 2, 3, 8, 9, 10, 12. *(c)* 1, 3, 8. *(d)* 3. *(e)* 7. *(f)* 7. *(g)* 8, 10, 11. *(h)* 8. *(i)* 8. *(j)* 8, 10, 11. *(k)* 10. *(l)* 10, 11. *(m)* 12. *(n)* 12.

4. Arabic numerals cited here refer to the cause of impurity, and letters refer to the manner whereby the impurity was transferred; for Pentateuchal sources, see citations above in note 2: *(i)* 1b, 1c, 2b, 3b, 3c, 3d, 7e, 8b, 8c, 8g, 8h, 8i, 8j, 9a, 9k, 10b, 10g, 10l, 11g, 11l, 12b, 12m, 12n, 13a, 14a, 15a. *(ii)* 4a (for a male newborn), 8a, 10a, 10k, 11a, 12b, 12n. *(iii)* 4a (for a female newborn). *(iv)* 3d, 8a, 8b, 8c, 8g, 8h, 8i, 9a, 9k, 10g, 10l, 11g, 11l, 12m, 13a, 14a. *(v)* 5a, 8a, 11a. A person touched by a man with a pathological sexual discharge is said to require purification only if the latter had not washed his hand (Lev 15:11). The man with the discharge himself must bathe in "living water [*mayim ḥayim*]" (Lev 15:13). Lev 22:4–7 requires bathing and awaiting evening for anyone who touched "anything with human [corpse?] impurity [*ṭəmē᾽ nefeš*]" (12b), a creeping thing (2b), or "a person who

would render him impure with any impurity he may have"—but only if the one who was thus rendered impure wishes to partake of consecrated foods.

5. Arabic numerals cited here refer to the cause of impurity, and letters refer to the manner whereby the impurity was transferred; for Pentateuchal sources, see citations in note 2 above: *(vi)* 4a, 5a, 8a, 11a. *(vii)* 5a, 7a, 12b, 12n.

6. For Pentateuchal sources, see citations in note 2 above: 1, 3 5, 7, 8, 9, 10, 11, 12, 13, 14.

7. Lev 13:52, 55, 57.

8. Lev 15:4–5, 9, 20–21, 23–24, 26–27.

9. Lev 11:32–33, 35; 15:4, 22–23, 26–27; Num 19:14–15.

10. Num 19:18–19; 31:20–23.

11. Lev 11:32–33, 35; 15:12.

12. Lev 14:45.

13. Lev 11:34, 37–38.

14. Lev 11:36.

15. Philo, *Spec. Laws* 3:63.

16. Philo, *Spec. Laws* 1:118. Philo (and others writing in Greek, as we shall see below) followed LXX in translating the Hebrew "*ṣāraʿat*" into the Greek "*lépra*," which refers to a scaly skin disease of some sort (not the English "leprosy," also known as "Hansen's disease," which in Greek was called "*eléphas*" or "*elephantíasis*"; Milgrom, *Leviticus 1–16*, 775, 816–820). For the paradoxical character of some of the scale-disease laws, see Philo, *Unchangeable* 123–130. For more on scale disease in priests, see *Spec. Laws* 1:80.

17. Philo, *Spec. Laws* 1:119.

18. Philo, *Unchangeable* 131–135.

19. Philo, *Spec. Laws* 3:206–208.

20. Philo, *Spec. Laws* 3:205. The way Philo phrases this, it seems that full purification may be accomplished forthwith, and that the seven-day purification process is required only to permit entrance to the temple (as already noted in footnote *a* in the Colson and Whitaker edition at 3:205). For other references to exclusion of the impure from the temple, see *Unchangeable* 8–9; *Moses* 2:231; *Spec. Laws* 3:89. For purification required of those partaking of the Passover feast, see *Spec. Laws* 2:148.

21. Philo, *Spec. Laws* 1:257–272. Note that here Philo did not specify that these rituals are required only for purification from corpse impurity. For Philo's critique of those who purify their bodies through bathing but neglect to properly cleanse their minds or souls, see *Cherubim* 94–95; *Worse* 20.

22. Mark 7:1–5. The translation is based on Yarbro Collins, *Mark*, 339 (with slight emendations).

23. Lev 11: 32; 15:12; Num 31:23.

24. Lev 15:4–6, 20–24, 26. Some textual witnesses to Mark omit "and dining couches [*kai klinōn*]," probably because later transcribers had difficulty with the notion that such objects might be subject to ritual immersion; see Yarbro Collins, *Mark*, 339 n. *f.*

25. A small minority of textual witnesses here read "they sprinkle themselves [*rhantísōntai*]" instead of "they immerse themselves [*baptísōntai*]," but this is most likely a late corruption; see Yarbro Collins, *Mark*, 339, 348–349 n. 7.

26. The responses of Jesus to the Pharisees and scribes, and then to the crowds and later to his disciples, are reported in Mark 7:6–23.

27. Luke 11:37–41.

28. Luke 11:44.

29. *Handwashing:* Matt 15:1–20. *Purification of cups and dishes:* Matt 23:25–26.

30. Matt 23:27–28.

31. Mark 1:40–45 (quotation at 1:44). Parallels in Matt 8:1–4; Luke 5:12–16. The reference to Mosaic law is apparently to Lev 14:1–32.

32. Luke 17:11–19 (quotation at 17:14). For other references in the Synoptic Gospels to the "purification" of the scale-diseased, where various forms of the verb "*katharízō*" are employed, see Matt 10:8; 11:5; Luke 7:22. Although ritual purity concerns are not made explicit in the story of Jesus healing the hemorrhaging woman (Matt 9:20–22; Mark 5:25–34; Luke 8:43–48), the narrative should probably be read against the background of the Pentateuchal rules regarding the impurity that affects a woman with abnormal uterine bleeding.

33. Luke 2:22–24.

34. Acts 21:23–24, 26. See also Acts 24:18, where later on Paul recounts that on this day "they found me purified in the temple [*hēgnisménon en tǭ hierǭ*]."

35. Num 6:9–12.

36. For such a notion in later rabbinic literature, see *y. Yoma* 3:3 (40b). For the question of how Paul could have entered the temple before sunset, see my debate with Eyal Regev in Regev, "The Ritual Baths"; Adler, "The Ritual Baths near the Temple Mount"; Regev, "The Temple Mount Ritual Baths."

37. John 2:6.

38. John 3:25.

39. John 11:55.

40. John 18:28.

41. The trope of Judeans avoiding associating or eating with non-Judeans—or even with Judeans who are regarded as "sinners"—is repeated several times throughout all four Gospel accounts as well as elsewhere in New Testament writings: Matt 9:9–13; 24:48–49; Mark 2:13–17; Luke 5:27–32; 7:36–50; 15:1–2; 19:1–7; Acts 10:28–29; 11:1–18; John 4:7–9; 1 Cor 5:9–13; Gal 2:11–14. For similar notions outside the New Testament, see Diodorus Siculus, *Bibliotheca Historica* 34–35.1:2 (in Photius, *Bibliotheca*, Cod. 244) (*GLAJJ* 1:182–183); Josephus, *Ant.* 13:247; *Ag. Ap.* 2:258; Tacitus, *Hist.* 5.5:2 (*GLAJJ* 2:19, 26). While the main issue in all these cases may have been the problem of communion with "wrongdoers," avoidance of ritual impurity may also be in the background of at least some of these texts.

42. Josephus, *War* 5:226–227; *Ag. Ap.* 2:103–104; see also *Ant.* 3:261–264. For more general references to the exclusion of the impure from the temple, see *War* 1:26; 4:205; 5:194; *Ant.* 15:417–419.

43. Josephus, *Ant.* 3:269.

44. Josephus, *Ag. Ap.* 2:198. For widespread adherence to the rules of purity pertaining to the Jerusalem temple sacrifices even among non-Judeans, see *Ant.* 3:317–320.

45. Josephus, *War* 6:422–427. For the census, see also *War* 2:280–281. A strikingly similar account appears in *b. Pesaḥ.* 64b.

46. Josephus, *Ag. Ap.* 1:281.

47. Josephus, *Ant.* 18:37–38.

48. While Josephus certainly had an axe to grind with the Tiberians of his own day (see, e.g., *Life* 85–103), it seems unlikely that this is a Josephean invention from whole cloth. The story of the city's problematic foundation on graves appears to have been a well-known tradition that even found its way into legends of the later rabbis—many of whom lived in Tiberias themselves, and centuries later still found a need to provide an apology to explain how the city was no longer impure. For rabbinic legends surrounding the second-century-CE R. Simeon B. Yohai "purifying" Tiberias from its corpse impurity, see Levine, "R. Simeon B. Yohai."

49. Josephus, *War* 2:122, 149.

50. Josephus, *War* 2:129. See also *War* 2:161, where Essene women are said to be clothed and the men girdled when bathing (purification is not specified).

51. Josephus, *War* 2:138–139.

52. Josephus, *War* 2:150. For Essene purity laws being regarded as generally stricter than those of others, see also *Ant.* 18:19.

53. For the question of Gentiles as carriers of impurity, see Hayes, *Gentile Impurities.* For a compelling argument that at this time Gentiles were generally regarded as objects (although not subjects) of corpse impurity, see Noam, "Another Look."

54. Josephus, *Ant.* 18:91–95.

55. Josephus, *Life* 74. See also *War* 2:591; *Ant.* 12:120 (to be discussed in further detail below). Previous discussions on the subject (Goodman, "Kosher Olive Oil"; Rosenblum, "Kosher Olive Oil") have read Josephus's comments through the eyes of later rabbinic writings and overlooked the possibility which I am suggesting here—that Pentateuchal ritual impurity concerns were at stake.

56. Josephus, *Life* 13–14.

57. Avoidance of imported pottery is another phenomenon that may relate to ritual purity observance; see Adler, "The Archaeology of Purity," 221–280. Because the problem is quite complex, I have chosen not to delve into this issue here.

58. For a corpus of 850 pools known in 2011, see Adler, "The Archaeology of Purity," 319–343. Over 150 additional pools have been unearthed in the interim and will be published in a forthcoming updated corpus I have prepared together with Dvir Raviv.

59. The first such identification was made by Yigael Yadin in 1964 (*Masada*, 164–167). Ronny Reich was the first to research and publish extensively on the subject, in

a series of articles beginning in the 1980s, and especially in his 1990 PhD dissertation published as a monograph in 2013 (Reich, *Miqwa'ot*). For a critique of the rabbinic-centrism of Yadin and Reich, see Miller, *At the Intersection*; Miller, "New Directions." For a critique on the views of dissenters to the identification of stepped pools as "ritual immersion pools," see my discussion in Adler, "Along Ethnic Lines."

60. Adler, "The Archaeology of Purity," 42–50. The boundaries of Judean settlement in the Southern Levant during the Early Roman period are quite well known from both textual sources (especially from the writings of Josephus) and archaeological finds (such as Hebrew inscriptions and numismatic finds). Although there are a small number of sites (mostly located close to these boundaries) about which questions remain as to whether they were settled by Judeans, and several sites are either known to have been settled by a mixed population of both Judeans and non-Judeans or else are suspected of such, none of this distracts from the larger picture.

61. Josephus, *Ant.* 3:263. See also below, where the verb "immerse" is used to describe the method of purificatory bathing in earlier texts as well (e.g., Sir 34:30; Jdt 12:7; 4Q274 2 i, 4–5).

62. For the broad scope of ritual purity concerns beyond the limited spheres of the priests, the Jerusalem temple, and its cult, see Poirier, "Purity beyond the Temple"; Adler, "Between Priestly Cult."

63. I am now less inclined to my earlier suggestion ("The Ancient Synagogue") that these pools might have been associated specifically with synagogue activities.

64. Regev, "The Ritual Baths"; Adler, "The Ritual Baths near the Temple Mount"; Regev, "The Temple Mount Ritual Baths."

65. Adler, "Second Temple Period Ritual Baths."

66. Adler, "The Ritual Immersion Pools."

67. Adler, "Ritual Baths Adjacent to Tombs."

68. See surveys in Magen, *The Stone Vessel Industry*, 138–147; Deines, *Jüdische Steingefäße*, 192–246; Adler, "The Archaeology of Purity," 170–178. For the dissenters to this line of scholarship (and my critique of their positions), see Adler, "Along Ethnic Lines."

69. Adler, "The Archaeology of Purity," 182–188.

70. Lev 11:32–33; 15:12; Num 31:19–20.

71. Num 31:21–23.

72. See Adler, "The Impurity of Stone Vessels," 16 n. 42, and 22–26.

73. John 2:6.

74. See Adler, "The Archaeology of Purity," 208–210.

75. Citations are collected in the studies cited above, note 68.

76. Reed, "Stone Vessels," 390–392.

77. Adler, "Between Priestly Cult."

78. Adler and Mizzi, "A Roman-Era Chalk Quarry." In a recent study I co-wrote with researchers from the Geological Survey of Israel, we were able to show that

chalk sourced in Galilee displays a geochemical fingerprint distinct from
chalk sourced in Judea—a finding that opens up the prospect for future
large-scale provenance studies on these vessels; see Adler et al., "Geochemical
Analyses."

79. Josephus, *Ant.* 17:165–166. For a rabbinic version of this story, see *y. Yoma* 1:1;
b. Yoma 12b (and elsewhere).

80. Josephus, *War* 1:229. Ostensibly, this story presents a challenge for those scholars who deny the notion of ritual impurity affecting Gentiles at this early
stage; see Hayes, *Gentile Impurities*, 52–53.

81. Josephus, *Ant.* 12:120.

82. Skepticism of Josephus's claim here has already been voiced by Ralph Marcus
(in his "Appendix C" to the Thackeray, Marcus, and Feldman edition of *Ant.*
12) and Martin Goodman ("Kosher Olive Oil," 228–229), both of whom suggested that the order more likely dates to Antiochus III (ca. 200 BCE).

83. CD x, 10–13 (= 4Q266 8 iii, 9–10; 4Q270 6 iv, 20–21).

84. CD xii, 1–2 (= 4Q271 5 i, 17–18).

85. CD xii, 15–18 (= 4Q266 9 ii, 2–5).

86. 4Q266 6 i, 1–13; 4Q269 7, 1–13; 4Q270 2 ii, 12; 4Q272 1 i, 1–20; 1 ii, 1–2; 4Q273 4
ii, 2–11.

87. 11Q19 xlv, 7–li, 10 (= 11Q20 xii–xv, 3).

88. 11Q19 xlix, 11–21.

89. 11Q19 l, 10–19 (= 11Q20 xiv, 11–17).

90. 4Q394, 4Q395, 4Q396, 4Q397.

91. 4Q394 8 iv, 5–8 (= 4Q396 ii, 6–9). Much has been written about the parallel
between this passage and *m. Yad.* 4:7, which reports on a polemic between the
Sadducees and the Pharisees on this precise question; see, e.g., Sussmann,
"The History of the Halakha," 28–30.

92. 4Q394 3–7 i, 16–19 (= 4Q395 8–10). For the likely parallel between this passage
and *m. Parah* 3:7, which reports on a polemic involving the Sadducees on the
question of whether the priest who burns the red heifer can do so immediately after immersing prior to sunset, see e.g., Sussmann, "The History of the
Halakha," 28.

93. 4Q394 3–7 ii, 16–18 (= 4Q397 3, 3).

94. 4Q274 2 i, 4–5.

95. 1QS vi, 13–23. See above, note 51.

96. Let. Aris. 128–171.

97. Let. Aris. 106.

98. Jub. 3:8–14.

99. Jdt 10:5.

100. Jdt 12:1–3.

101. Jdt 12:7–9. Note that elsewhere where Judith is said to bathe herself in a nonritual manner (Jdt 10:3), the verb "immerse" is not used.

102. Jdt 12:19.

103. It should be noted that some scholars have interpreted Judith's actions as adherence to the laws of "kashrut" (e.g., Hayes, *Gentile Impurities*, 49, 139–140). Everything I have cited here suggests that ritual purity was at stake rather than the sort of dietary restrictions that are the focus of our previous chapter. For another likely reference to ritual impurity in Judith's own words, see Jdt 11:12–13.

104. 2 Macc 12:38. The anecdote is set between a skirmish with a Seleucid force and a return of Judas's men to the battlefield following the Sabbath to retrieve the corpses of the fallen Judean fighters. If the author of this narrative had in mind purification from corpse impurity, nothing is said of the Pentateuch's requirement for a seven-day purification process.

105. Sir 34:30. This verse has not survived in any extant Hebrew manuscripts. Note that the Syriac version in the Peshitta here reads, "One that washes from a corpse [*dəsāḥāʾ mīn mêtāʾ*]," which may suggest that the original Hebrew verb was "*r-ḥ-ṣ*" rather than "*ṭ-b-l*." Tobit is said to have washed himself (*elousámēn*) once immediately after moving a corpse and then again immediately after burying it (Tob 2:1–9), but the author of this text may have had in mind regular cleansing rather than ritual purification.

106. 3 Macc. 3:3–7; Tob 1:10–11; Jos. Asen. 7:1; Add Esth C 28; Jub. 22:16.

107. Josephus, *Ant.* 12:145–146.

108. E.g., Josh 22:17; Isa 6:5; 64:5; Jer 13:27; Ezek 14:11; 20:7, 18, 30–31, 43; 22:4–5; 23:7, 30; 24:13; 36:17, 25, 33; 37:23; 39:24; 43:7–8; Hos 5:3; 6:10; Hab 1:13; Ps 51:4, 9, 12; 106:39; Prov 15:26; 22:11; Job 4:17; 17:9.

109. For excellent recent surveys, see D. Wright et al., "Sin, Pollution, and Purity"; Kazen, "Purification." See also Milgrom, *Leviticus 1–16*, passim.

110. E.g., Isa 30:22; Ezek 7:19–20; 36:17; Lam 1:8, 17; Ezra 9:11; 2 Chr 29:5. For ritual impurity, see Ezek 18:6; 22:10.

111. See, e.g., Milgrom, *Leviticus 1–16*, 763–765, 949–953; D. Wright et al., "Sin, Pollution, and Purity"; Kazen, "Purification," 226–228. For a wider geographic and temporal scope, see Buckley and Gottlieb, *Blood Magic*.

112. E.g., 2 Kgs 23:6, 14, 16; Ezek 39:12–16; 43:27; 44:25–26; Hag 2:13; 2 Chr 34:4. For corpse impurity among other cultures, see D. Wright et al., "Sin, Pollution, and Purity"; Kazen, "Purification," 229–230.

113. 2 Kgs 5:1–27; 7:3–11; 15:5; 2 Chr 26:19–23. See also 2 Sam 3:29. For skin diseases treated as ritually impure among other cultures, see Milgrom, *Leviticus 1–16*, 818, 820–821; Kazen, "Purification," 228–229.

114. Ezek 4:14; 44:31. For carrion as ritually impure in Mesopotamia and Persia, see D. Wright et al., "Sin, Pollution, and Purity," 500, 506.

115. 1 Sam 20:26 has been commonly interpreted from the time of Josephus (*Ant.* 6:235) onward as a reference to semen impurity, but this is hardly a certain explanation. 2 Sam 3:29 refers to a pathological genital discharge in males

(together with skin disease) as a curse, but ritual impurity is not necessarily implied.

116. *Metaphorical washing or laundering:* Isa 1:16; 4:4; Jer 2:22; 4:14; Ezek 16:4, 9; 36:25; Ps 26:6; 51:4, 9; 73:13; Prov 30:12; Job 9:30. *Literal washing or laundering:* Judg 19:22; 1 Sam 25:41; 2 Sam 11:2, 8; 12:20; 19:25; 1 Kgs 22:38; Mal 3:2; Ruth 3:3. 2 Chr 4:6 speaks of priests washing in the courtyard of Solomon's temple, but while the washing may be ritual, ritual *impurity* per se does not seem to be the issue. The famous scene of Bathsheba bathing in 2 Sam 11:2 is not portrayed as a ritual purification, although some commentators have interpreted the statement following the account of the sexual encounter with David—"and she was sanctifying from her impurity [*wahi' mitqadešet miṭūm 'ātāh*]" (2 Sam 11:4)—as a retroactive explanation for the bath described two verses earlier. Even if this awkward explanation were correct, it would have to assume an impurity other than semen impurity, as the bathing precipitated the sexual liaison with David rather than the other way around. This has compelled many commentors to assume that Bathsheba bathed in order to purify herself from *menstrual* impurity, but this would hardly comport with Pentateuchal regulations where a seven-day wait is all that is necessary to remove menstrual impurity—nothing is said of bathing! For Naaman's immersion in the Jordan, see below, note 118.

117. Ezek 44:26 speaks of a seven-day waiting period *after* one has been purified from contact with a corpse! Nothing is indicated about how the purification itself is to be accomplished nor how much time this might take.

118. In 2 Kgs 5:10–14, the Aramean Naaman is "purified" (*wayiṭhār*) of his skin disease by immersing in the Jordan river seven times; nothing even close to resembling the procedures outlined in Lev 13–14 is cited. While this may be because Naaman is a non-Israelite, the fact remains that, outside the Pentateuch, the Hebrew Bible contains no allusions to the existence of any purification procedures for skin diseases or for corpse impurity resembling those found within the Pentateuch.

119. Publications on all these pools are conveniently collected in Adler, "The Imperial Cult," 409. In this article I suggest that another eight immersion pools unearthed at the acropolis of Samaria may also be associated with a palace of Herod the Great at this site.

120. Reich, *Miqwa'ot*, 84–87, 105–106.

121. Publications on all these pools are conveniently collected in Adler, "The Hellenistic Origins," 8–10. For a suggestion that historical evidence may be used to date the stepped pools found at Gezer and on the acropolis of Maresha to the period immediately following the Hasmonean conquests, see Reich, *Miqwa'ot*, 146, 150–151, 209.

122. For details, see Adler, "The Hellenistic Origins," 8–9. See also Reich, *Miqwa'ot*, 209.

123. Magen and Dadon, "Nebi Samwil," 126–128. The lack of any stepped water installations was noted in a visit I made to the site with one of its excavators, Benny Har-Even, on November 2, 2016. I thank Benny for guiding me on this visit, for discussing the issue with me, and for allowing me to mention his findings here prior to final publication of excavations at the site.

124. Adler, "The Archaeology of Purity," 51–62; Adler, "The Hellenistic Origins."

125. Avraham Faust and Hayah Katz ("The Archaeology of Purity"—not to be confused with the title of my own doctoral dissertation, submitted six years prior to the publication of this article!) have posited that a limestone basin found in an Iron Age II house excavated by these authors at Tel ʿEton was used in a purification ceremony that involved pouring water over women following their menstruation. The basin was found outside the door of a room that they identified as a space meant to house menstruating women. This identification was proffered primarily because no pottery was unearthed in this room, which they postulated was due to the regular presence of menstruating women who would have been regarded as endangering the ritual purity of the pottery. Curiously, the authors failed to explore alternative, no less plausible (although perhaps less imaginative!) explanations for why an excavated room might lack pottery, or what a stone basin might have been used for. Faust and Katz's article also rehashed a hypothesis that Faust had published previously in several other publications (e.g., Faust and Bunimovitz, "The Four-Room House," 29), according to which the four-room house plan was ideally suited for Israelite society in that it facilitated regulation of contact between pure and impure persons living in a single home. The hypothesis assumes wide-scale observance of ritual purity laws resembling the Pentateuchal rules as early as the Iron Age, an assumption that lacks an evidentiary basis. For a more detailed critique of Faust's and Katz's hypotheses, see Maeir, "On Defining Israel."

126. Geva, "Stone Artifacts," 222.

127. Geva, "Stone Artifacts from Areas J and N," 275.

128. Bar-Nathan and Gärtner, "The Stone Artifacts," 206–210.

129. Ben-Ami and Eshel, "Stone Bowl," 17.

130. See my excursus on this subject in Adler, "The Archaeology of Purity," 219–220.

131. *TAD* D7.44; Lozachmeur, *La collection Clermont-Ganneau*, no. 125. The text was previously discussed in Lozachmeur, "Un ostracon araméen d'Eléphantine"; Porten and Yardeni, "Ostracon Clermont-Ganneau 125(?)" (from which I have taken the reconstruction and translation).

132. Porten and Yardeni, "Ostracon Clermont-Ganneau 125(?)," 453–454.

133. Lemaire, "Judean Identity," 371–372. These are published in Lozachmeur, *La collection Clermont-Ganneau*, no. 97 (*ṭmʾ*), no. 137 (*lṭmʾw*), no. 107 (*bṭhr*). For a supposed use of the adjective "pure/clean" (*dəkhin*) in the so-called Passover Letter from Elephantine, see below, chapter 5.

Chapter 3. Figural Art

1. Exod 20:2–3; Deut 5:6–7.

2. Exod 20:4–6; Deut 5:8–10. For this way of accounting for the "ten command-ments," see Philo, *Decalogue* 51, 65–82, 154–156; Josephus, *Ant.* 3:91. Throughout, I have put references to the "commandments" of the Decalogue in quotation marks because the Pentateuch itself never refers to these as such (they are al-ways called "statements" [*dəvārîm*]), nor does it ever signify exactly how the "ten" should be divided up.

3. For a convenient presentation of various Jewish and Christian divisions of the Decalogue, see Kleist, "The Division of the Ten Commandments," 240. The mainstream rabbinic view (cited by Kleist only as the "Upper Cantillation" of the Masoretic tradition) is first in evidence in *Mekhilta de-Rabbi Ishmael, Baḥodesh* 8 (ed. Horovitz and Rabin, 233–234) and *b. Mak.* 24a and is taken up again in later rabbinic literary sources, in the work of the Medieval Masoretes, and in later synagogue art.

4. Deut 4:12, 15–18 (see also 4:23–25).

5. Deut 4:23–27.

6. Deut 27:15.

7. Contra Steven Fine (*Art and Judaism*, 73–81) and Eric Meyers ("Were the Has-moneans Really Aniconic?"), who both argued that the phenomenon was pred-icated on an ideology of "anti-idolism" (Fine's term) rather than on obedience to a legal interpretation within Torah law that regarded all anthropomorphic and zoomorphic depictions to be forbidden—as I argue here. Jason von Ehren-krook (*Sculpting Idolatry*) attempted to "problematize" the phenomenon but it seems to me that this attempt to bring nuance to the subject ultimately did more to obfuscate the matter at hand by emphasizing the negligible number of exceptions within the inestimably larger pattern of (especially archaeological) evidence.

8. See Mettinger, *No Graven Image?*, who traces the development in ancient Israel of a broader "de facto aniconism," an approach to deity worship that makes no use of icons and yet *tolerates* images, into a "programmatic aniconism," which makes a point to *repudiate* the use of images in the worship of its deity.

9. Philo, *Decalogue* 66.

10. Philo, *Decalogue* 67–68. But see the continuation (69–81), where Philo reverts to deriding the *worship* of images. Perhaps Philo understood the "second com-mandment" as composed of two distinct parts: (1) a proscription against *making* any image (Exod 20:4; Deut 5:8) and (2) a prohibition against *worshiping* such images (Exod 20:5; Deut 5:9). The impression seems to be that each of these is forbidden in its own right; see discussion in Tatum, "The LXX Version," 187–190. But see S. Stern, "Figurative Art," 418, and also the following note.

11. Philo, *Giants* 59. See also *Spec. Laws* 1:28–29. But cf. *Drunkenness* 109 and *Heir* 169, where (especially in the latter) the prohibition is presented as one of "mak-ing a god [*theoplasteîn*]." See also the previous note.

12. See commentary by Colson and Whitaker on Philo, *Giants* 59. Also, cf. Wis 25:4–6.

13. Josephus, *War* 2:169–174 (= *Ant.* 18:55–59); *Ant.* 18:120–122; *War* 2:184–203 (= *Ant.* 18:261–309).

14. Josephus, *Ag. Ap.* 2:73–75. Even though elsewhere (*Ant.* 3:91) Josephus paraphrased the "second commandment" of the Decalogue as proscribing the making of any "image of any living creature for adoration [*proskunein*]," this and the following examples clearly show that Josephus regarded even profane figural art as forbidden. But see S. Stern, "Figurative Art," 419, who takes *Ant.* 3:91 as Josephus's primary "halakhic" position. Cf. Tatum, "The LXX Version," 191, who understood the qualification "*proskunein*" as implying that the prohibition includes "the making and/or adoration of" images (i.e., each on its own is forbidden).

15. Josephus, *Ant.* 3:113.

16. Josephus, *Ant.* 3:126.

17. Exod 26:1, 31; 36:8, 35.

18. Josephus, *Ant.* 3:137. Similarly, in describing the cherubim in Solomon's temple, Josephus wrote, "As for the cherubim themselves, no one can say or imagine what they looked like" (*Ant.* 8:73–74).

19. Josephus, *Ant.* 8:195. But note that Josephus voiced no critique upon his first mention of the bulls and lions: *Ant.* 8:80, 140.

20. 1 Kgs 7:25, 44 (= 2 Chr 4:3–4, 15); 10:19–20 (= 2 Chr 9:18–19). See also 2 Kgs 16:17, where the evil King Ahaz is portrayed as acting sacrilegiously by removing Solomon's molten "sea" from atop the brazen oxen.

21. Josephus, *Life* 65. The nephew of Antipas, Agrippa I, also appears to have been lax in observing this prohibition; Josephus (*Ant.* 19:357) implies that he had statues depicting his own daughters set up in the Greek cities of Sebaste and Caesarea.

22. Strabo, *Geogr.* 16.2:35 (*GLAJJ* 1:294, 300). While this remark appears in a passage generally concerned with worship, the phrase "all image-carving" may suggest that even secular art is intended.

23. Tacitus, *Hist.* 5.5:4 (*GLAJJ* 2:19, 26).

24. I am not convinced that the examples cited by Lee Levine (*The Ancient Synagogue*, 111) from Berenice (Cyrenaica), Acmonia (Asia Minor), and Alexandria and Naucratis (Egypt) represent figural art, nor that the finds from Delos he cited which *do* bear figural images have any connection with Judeans known to have been living on the island. For images on the menorah depicted on the Arch of Titus, see below, note 69.

25. See Mattingly, *Roman Imperial Coinage*, vols. 1–2.

26. Meshorer, *Nabataean Coins.*

27. *TJC* nos. 67–74.

28. *TJC* nos. 75–94.

29. *TJC* nos. 95–111.

30. Josephus, *War* 1:668 (= *Ant.* 17:188–189); *War* 2:93–97 (= *Ant.* 17:317–320).
31. Meshorer, *TJC*, 90. I disagree with Eric Meyers ("Were the Hasmoneans Really Aniconic?," 24), who interpreted Philip's coins as evidence that Judeans did not commonly observe a prohibition against images. When viewed in its appropriate context, the exception of Philip actually proves the general rule.
32. *TJC* nos. 112–119. As in the previous note, Eric Meyers ("Were the Hasmoneans Really Aniconic?," 24) interpreted these early coins of Agrippa I as evidence against a commonly observed ban on images.
33. Meshorer, *TJC*, 97–98.
34. *TJC* no. 120.
35. See, e.g., Meshorer, *TJC*, 96.
36. *TJC* nos. 121–126.
37. *TJC* nos. 183–217.
38. *TJC* nos. 127–128.
39. *TJC* no. 134.
40. *TJC* nos. 129–133b, 135–182. For Paneas as the location of Agrippa II's mint, see Meshorer, *TJC*, 105–106.
41. *TJC* nos. 311–330, 340–346. Attributions to the prefects and procurators listed here are based on the dates displayed on the coins which refer to the regnal years of various emperors.
42. *TJC* nos. 331–339.
43. Meshorer, *TJC*, 167.
44. Braund, *Rome and the Friendly King*, 123–128.
45. Although focused primarily on the late first century BCE and the early first century CE, see the excellent overview of Ariel and Fontanille, *The Coins of Herod*, 30–36. Meshorer's innovative speculation that these coins were actually minted in Jerusalem from the time of Herod until 66 CE (Meshorer, *TJC*, 72–78) has been roundly rejected by scholars; see Ariel and Fontanille, *The Coins of Herod*, 38–41.
46. Ariel and Fontanille, *The Coins of Herod*, 30–36.
47. The often-made claim that the Tyrian sheqel was somehow the "official" currency of the temple is based on a misreading of a later rabbinic ruling (*m. Bek.* 8:7; *t. Ketub.* 13:3 [ed. Zuckermandel, 275]) that refers neither to the temple nor to its purported "official" currency. All we may learn from this source is that the later rabbis accurately preserved a memory that a high silver content characterized the silver coinage from the mint of Tyre (as well as from the mint of Jerusalem during the Great Revolt).
48. Contra Meyers, "Were the Hasmoneans Really Aniconic?"; von Ehrenkrook, *Sculpting Idolatry*, 27.
49. Hachlili, *Ancient Mosaic Pavements*, 5–15.
50. De Luca and Lena, "The Mosaic."
51. For the Jerusalem frescoes, see Avigad, *Discovering Jerusalem*, 103, 113–114, 149–150, 157–159.

52. Broshi, "Excavations on Mount Zion," 83–85, pl. 19.

53. Avigad, *Discovering Jerusalem*, 99–103.

54. Hachlili, *The Menorah*, 21–23. To the best of my knowledge, the only example of a relief (carved or stucco) depicting figural images which is purported to be associated with first-century-CE Judean architecture is a stucco molding found in a residential building located to the south of the Temple Mount in which lions, a gazelle, a boar, and a rabbit are depicted; see Ben-Dov, *In the Shadow of the Temple*, 150–151. We should await the final report before deciding that the stratigraphic context warrants this dating.

55. Hachlili, *Jewish Funerary Customs*, 43–54, 127–133.

56. Hachlili, *Jewish Funerary Customs*, 96–110, 152–156.

57. Shadmi, "The Ossuaries and Sarcophagus," 45 (no. 17), fig. 2.12. A fragment of a lead sarcophagus found at the Tomb of the Kings and decorated with images of a sphinx and a dolphin (Kon, *The Tombs of the Kings*, 71), while cited by Steven Fine (*Art and Judaism*, 78) as an example of late Second Temple–period Judean figural art, is almost certainly a Late Roman import from the Phoenician coast, deposited during a later reuse of the tomb by pagan residents of Aelia Capitolina.

58. Hachlili, *Jewish Funerary Customs*, 107–109, 133–152.

59. Rahmani, "Jason's Tomb," 69–75. Rahmani identified humans on the ships and also suggested that another grafitto at the site (75, fig. 8) "may possibly depict a bearded human face wearing a helmet," but I am left unconvinced by these interpretations.

60. Ornamented examples of each of these materials may be found conveniently in Avigad, *Discovering Jerusalem*, 99–103, 107–108 (stone and glass), 116–119 (glass, metal, pottery, and stone), 169–175 (stone), 179 (pottery), 199 (ceramic lamps and bone).

61. Rosenthal-Heginbottom, "The Imported Hellenistic and Early Roman Pottery," 381.

62. Rosenthal-Heginbottom, "Innovation and Stagnation," 431–432. In explaining the popularity of these lamps, Jodi Magness (*Stone and Dung*, 65) has suggested that "the motivating factor was a desire to avoid the figured images that typically decorate Roman mold-made lamps."

63. Rosenthal-Heginbottom, "Innovation and Stagnation," 432–433.

64. Rosenthal-Heginbottom, "Innovation and Stagnation," 433.

65. Sussman, "Early Jewish Iconoclasm," 46.

66. Sussman, "Early Jewish Iconoclasm," 47. For defacement of figural images on bronze utensils found in a Bar Kokhba–period deposit in the Judean Desert "Cave of the Letters," see Yadin, *Bar-Kokhba*, 100–107.

67. *Fish and animal's paw*: Avigad, *Discovering Jerusalem*, 169–170. *Human hand*: Avigad, *Discovering Jerusalem*, 193–194, 200. *Birds*: Ben-Dov, *In the Shadow of the Temple*, 160.

68. Hershkovitz, "Gemstones." See there for several parallel finds, most of which were found in archaeological contexts that are likely non-Judean.

69. Hachlili, *The Menorah*, 49–51.

70. Josephus, *War* 1:648–655 (quotation at 649); *Ant.* 17:149–164. For a recent reconsideration of the historicity of this episode, see Bourgel, "Herod's Golden Eagle." Whether or not the incident took place as described, the story itself reflects a reality at the time it was first created—apparently some time prior to its retelling by Josephus.

71. Josephus, *War* 1:650.

72. Josephus, *Ant.* 17:151.

73. Josephus, *War* 1:653.

74. Josephus, *Ant.* 17:159.

75. In several other instances where Josephus blames Herod for impiety over statuary (e.g., Herod's setting up of trophies in a Jerusalem theater in *Ant.* 15:267–291; but also *Ant.* 15:328–329; 16:157–158), it is more difficult to decide whether the transgression at stake is profane figural art or perhaps actual idolatry.

76. A rare reference to sculptured animals appears in Josephus's narrative about the Judean aristocrat Hyrcanus son of Joseph, who is said to have built a fortress in Transjordan during the reign of Seleucus IV Philopator, in the early second century BCE, upon which he had "beasts of gigantic size carved" (*Ant.* 12:230); for the archaeological remains commonly identified with this structure, see below, note 100.

77. See above, note 20.

78. 1 Kgs 6:23–29, 32, 35; 7:29, 36; 8:6–7 (= 2 Chr 3:7–14, 5:7–8).

79. *TJC* nos. 44–65.

80. *TJC* no. 66.

81. Meshorer, *TJC*, 67–69. See also Ariel and Fontanille, *The Coins of Herod*, 115–119.

82. Hachlili, *Ancient Mosaic Pavements*, 6–8.

83. Rozenberg, "The Absence of Figurative Motifs."

84. Corbo, "L'Herodion di Gebal Fureidis," 24; Rozenberg, "Figurative Paintings."

85. Netzer et al., "Herodium," 144–145. Orit Peleg-Barkat ("Herod's Western Palace," 67) has recently conjectured that fragmentary remains of a limestone lion's head sculpture, incorporated in secondary use in a Byzantine-era wall unearthed in the Jewish Quarter excavations, originally derived from Herod's palace in the western section of the city. (She cites Josephus, *War* 5:181, where water-spewing "works of bronze" [*khalkourgēmátōn*] are said to have been placed throughout the gardens of this palace.) I have not included this find in our discussion because a post-70-CE pagan context for the sculpture seems preferable; see Palistrant Shaick, "A Lion in Jerusalem."

86. Peleg-Barkat, *The Temple Mount Excavations*, 25–90.

87. Peleg-Barkat, *The Temple Mount Excavations*, 121–168.

88. Rosenthal-Heginbottom, "Innovation and Stagnation," 430.

89. Geva and Hershkovitz, "Local Pottery," 113, pl. 4.6:2–3; Rosenthal-Heginbottom, "Innovation and Stagnation," 430. Rosenthal-Heginbottom noted that an image

of a face has also been found painted on the wall of a vessel (possibly a lagynos) found in excavations along Jerusalem's eastern cardo.

90. Rosenthal-Heginbottom, "Late Hellenistic and Early Roman Lamps," 156–159, pl. 5.5.

91. *TJC* groups A–V.

92. *TJC* nos. 41–42. Another coin, *TJC* no. 43, features a wreath instead of the table.

93. *TJC* groups A–J, P–V. For a convenient summary of scholarship regarding the enigmatic phrase "*ḥever hayəhūdim*," see Meshorer, *TJC*, 31–32.

94. Donald Ariel ("A Second Seleucid Coin," 52 n. 17) counted ten types in the entire Seleucid corpus that qualify as nonfigural, but none of these replace the portrait of the king on the obverse with a dense "textual portrait" as in the Hasmonean coins.

95. For a recent survey of scholarship on these coins, see Ariel, "A Second Seleucid Coin."

96. Ariel, "A Second Seleucid Coin."

97. Josephus, *Ant.* 17:236–248.

98. See Ariel, "A Second Seleucid Coin."

99. Hachlili, *Ancient Mosaic Pavements*, 6; Rozenberg, "The Absence of Figurative Motifs," 283.

100. Lapp and Lapp, "Iraq el-Emir."

101. Josephus, *Ant.* 12:230.

102. *TJC* nos. 31–35. The identification of these coins as belonging to both Ptolemy I and Ptolemy II is in accordance with the conclusions in Gitler and Lorber, "A New Chronology for the Ptolemaic Yehud Coinage."

103. *TJC* nos. 1–26; Gitler, "The Earliest Coin." Meshorer identified another four types (*TJC* nos. 27–30) as transitional between the Persian and Macedonian eras. According to Gitler and Lorber ("A New Chronology for the Ptolemaic Yehud Coinage"), *TJC* no. 25 dates to the pre-301-BCE Macedonian era, while *TJC* nos. 29–30 are early Ptolemaic. Elsewhere ("A New Chronology for the Yehizkiyah Coins") they lowered Meshorer's Persian-period dating of *TJC* 14, 20–23, 25a, and 27 to the pre-Ptolemaic "Macedonian period."

104. For further discussion on this and some of the other previously described motifs, see chapter 7.

105. E. Stern, *Archaeology of the Land of the Bible*, 2:541; Lipschits and Vanderhooft, "Continuity and Change," 49–51.

106. See previous note.

107. Lipschits and Vanderhooft, "Continuity and Change," 51–61. For an unusual stamped handle with a depiction of an insect found in Persian levels at Jerusalem, see Ariel and Shoham, "Locally Stamped Handles," 140.

108. R. Schmitt, "Gab es einen Bildersturm"; Cornelius, "'East Meets West'"; de Hulster, *Figurines*; Balcells Gallarreta, *Household and Family Religion*, 68–72.

109. Balcells Gallarreta, *Household and Family Religion*, 72.

110. Cornelius, "'East Meets West,'" 81, 92–93.

111. E. Stern, *Archaeology of the Land of the Bible*, 2:479; "The Religious Revolution" (quotation at 204). See also his "Religion in Palestine," 253–255.

112. For a collection of recent challenges to Stern's theory, see Frevel, Pyschny, and Cornelius, *A "Religious Revolution."* For further discussion, see chapter 7.

113. Stern, *Material Culture*, 165–171, 179 (at ʿEin-Gedi); Balcells Gallarreta, *Household and Family Religion*, 64, 72, 102, 108 (at Tell en-Naṣbeh).

114. Stern, *Material Culture*, 160.

115. Ariel and Shoham, "Locally Stamped Handles," 163–165. Also discussed there are similar handles found at Bethel, Ramat Raḥel, and Beth Zur but dated to the Hellenistic period.

116. The artifact has been reported upon in the electronic media (e.g., Ruth Schuster, "Found in Jerusalem's City of David: The Egyptian God Bes," Haaretz, March 21, 2019, https://www.haaretz.com/archaeology/MAGAZINE-found-in-jerusalem-s-city-of-david-egyptian-god-bes-1.7042407). Further details have been graciously provided by one of the excavation's directors, Yiftah Shalev (personal communication, September 20, 2020).

117. Alstola, *Judeans in Babylonia*, 213–218, 267.

118. Ibid., 214–215.

119. Ibid., 141.

120. Levine, "Figural Art," 12.

121. Smith, "Goodenough's 'Jewish Symbols,'" 60.

122. Frey, "La question des images," 274; Goodenough, *Jewish Symbols*, 1:132; 4:11.

123. B. Cohen, "Art in Jewish Law," 167; Avigad, *Beth Sheʿarim*, 3:277–278. A similar position was put forward by Steven Fine (*Art and Judaism*, 73–81), who argued that an "increasingly strident" attitude of many Judeans toward Greco-Roman visual culture "may simultaneously reflect both greater integration into that culture and a desire by some to restrict connections with it through the construction of social boundaries."

124. Avigad, *Beth Sheʿarim*, 3:277–278.

125. Levine, "Figural Art," 16.

126. It bears noting that in later periods the Pentateuchal ban on images came to be interpreted leniently as forbidding only idolatrous images. By the third century CE, figural art had begun to appear almost ubiquitously in Judean material culture; for an overview, see Levine, "Figural Art," 16–23. The rabbis, too, generally chose a more lenient exegetical pathway; see S. Stern, "Figurative Art" (but note that he believed this to have been true of "the rabbis" of the first century CE as well; the massive quantity of archaeological finds to the contrary he dismissed as "folk custom" [415, 419]!). It appears that Levine and others assume that this kind of lenient approach to the otherwise widely known and observed Pentateuchal law characterized the period before the supposed Hasmonean turn to stringency.

Chapter 4. Tefillin and Mezuzot

1. The entire passage is addressed in the second-person singular.
2. Deut 11:18–20. The instructions here are in the second-person plural.
3. Exod 13:8–9; addressed in the second-person singular.
4. Exod 13:14–16; addressed in the second-person singular.
5. For a compelling argument that Exod 13:1–16 borrows from the Deuteronomy passages (and from elsewhere in the Pentateuch), see Zahn, "'Remember This Day.'"
6. Philo, *Spec. Laws* 4:137.
7. Philo, *Spec. Laws* 4:138.
8. Philo, *Spec. Laws* 4:139.
9. See discussion in the appendices to the Colson and Whitaker edition, §137. For more on the Septuagint's renderings here, see below in the section "Early Evidence."
10. Philo, *Spec. Laws* 4:142.
11. For the Hebrew " ʿal" as "before" or "over against," see, e.g., Gen 41:1, where Pharaoh is said to have dreamt that he was "standing before [not on!] the Nile [ʿōmēd ʿal hay ʾōr]" (but cf. LXX: "hestánai epì toû potamoû," where the genitive likely implies "on [the bank of] the river"). For the Greek preposition "epì" (+ accusative) as "before" or "over against," see, e.g., Luke 12:11: "they bring you before the synagogues, the rulers, and the authorities [epì tàs sunagōgàs kaì tàs arkhàs kaì tàs exousías]."
12. Matt 23:5.
13. Cohn, *Tangled Up*, 109–111.
14. Bartelink, "φυλακτήριον—Phylacterium," 25–29.
15. The hypothesis I posit here preliminarily merits further development, a task to which I plan to attend in the near future.
16. Josephus, *Ant.* 4:213.
17. References to both are included among the Judean Desert tefillin; see below.
18. See sources cited in Adler, "The Distribution," 162–163.
19. For publication information and a survey of distribution patterns of these finds among the various caves, see Adler, "The Distribution." I have excluded from my count here 4Q141, identified by the original publisher as tefillin, but different from all other slips in the assemblage in terms of its scriptural contents (Deut 32:14–20, 32–33). For an argument against identifying this text as a tefillin slip, see Nakman, "The Contents and Order," 35–37. For a critique of Nakman's position as "reductionist and highly problematic," see Cohn, *Tangled Up*, 75–77. I have also excluded from my count two slips (4Q47, 4Q148) that have recently been deciphered and identified as amulets; see Feldman and Feldman, "4Q147: An Amulet?"; "4Q148 (4QPhylactère U)."
20. The straps themselves have survived *in situ* in only three of the cases; see Harding, "The Archaeological Finds," 7, pl. 1:7; de Vaux, "Archéologie," pl. 8:5 (on the left), 6.

21. Every slip includes verses from one or more of the following blocks of text: (1) Exod 12:43–51; (2) Exod 13:1–10; (3) Exod 13:11–16; (4) Deut 5:1–18; (5) Deut 5:19–6:3; (6) Deut 6:4–9; (7) Deut 10:12–11:12; (8) Deut 11:13–21.

22. See *Mekhilta de-Rabbi Ishmael, Bō'* 17 (ed. Horovitz and Rabin, 66); *Sifre on Deuteronomy*, 35 (ed. L. Finkelstein, 63–64).

23. While in most of the known textual witnesses from the Judean Desert the orthographic form at the end of the word is given without the letter *wāw*—"*lṭ(w)ṭft*"—in a single surviving textual witness from Qumran (4Q135, 20) the word appears (in Exod 13:16) with the *wāw*—"*wlṭwṭfwt*"—an orthographic form reminiscent of the vowelized Masoretic Text "*ûlṭôṭāfōt*." This indicates that already in the late Second Temple period, at least some Judeans were reading the word in the plural as "*ṭôṭāfōt*" rather than in the singular as "*ṭôṭefet*." See Adler, "Two Types," 40, n. 24.

24. This was already assumed by the original publishers of the finds (e.g., Harding, "Archaeological Finds," 7; Milik, "Tefillin," 34–35), but probably only because of rabbinic prescriptions. For a further typological distinction between two types of four-compartment tefillin cases, which I have argued also stems from contemporary exegetical debates, see Adler, "Two Types."

25. See above, note 22.

26. For this distinction, see already Milik, "Tefillin," 36–37, 47–48, 51, 53, 56, 58. Milik consistently referred to the first type as "Pharisaic" and the second type as "Essene" (labels he claimed to use only "for convenience"). For a more in-depth discussion on these two types and their distribution among the Judean Desert caves, see Adler, "The Distribution," 166–169.

27. This type exactly prefigures the kind of tefillin called for by the Tannaitic rabbis; see *Sifre on Deuteronomy* 35:8 (ed. L. Finkelstein, 63).

28. Baillet, "Textes," 158–161.

29. Cohn, *Tangled Up*, 61.

30. Milik, "Tefillin," 80–85. I will not consider here Mur5, for which a recent attempt at decipherment has discounted its use either as a mezuzah (as its publisher Milik had assumed) or as tefillin (as Hartmut Stegemann and Jürgen Becker had subsequently suggested); see Feldman and Feldman, "Is Mur 5 a Mezuzah?"

31. Milik, "Tefillin," 36. He noted three questionable exemplars: 4Q146, 4Q148, and 4Q155.

32. For somewhat similar conclusions, see Cohn, *Tangled Up*, 60–62.

33. Let. Aris. 128–171.

34. Let. Aris. 158–159.

35. For a positive assessment, see B. Wright, "Three Jewish Ritual Practices." For a more skeptical reading, see Cohn, *Tangled Up*, 80–82.

36. White, Keddie, and Flexsenhar, "The Epistle of Aristeas," 34–38. See there for alternative suggested dates in the first century BCE or the beginning of the first century CE.

37. Wevers, *Septuaginta, Exodus*; *Septuaginta, Deuteronomium* (note here that another variant in the Deuteronomy verses reads "*asáleuta*"—in the plural).

38. See also Prov 3:1–4.

39. Milik, "Tefillin," 37. A proper paleographic analysis of the entire assemblage is planned within the framework of a current project dedicated to a comprehensive analysis and publication of the entire assemblage of tefillin and "mezuzot" from the Judean Desert; see Adler, "The Assemblage."

40. *CPJ* 4, no. 609. See also Albright, "A Biblical Fragment."

41. See citations and brief discussion in Cohn, *Tangled Up*, 67–68.

42. See, e.g., Keel, "Zeichen der Verbundenheit."

43. The two plaques are likely amulets that contain an early apotropaic formula, a version of which eventually came to be included in the Pentateuch; see recent discussion in Smoak, *The Priestly Blessing*, 67–88. As the apotropaic formula these plaques contain may well predate by decades or even centuries the compilation of Num 6:24–26, these finds cannot be taken as evidence of an already existing Pentateuch or Pentateuchal "source."

Chapter 5. Miscellaneous Practices

1. Gen 17:9–14. For Pentateuchal narratives regarding circumcision, all pre-Siniatic, see Gen 17:23–27; 21:4; 34:14–25; Exod 4:25–26. For a post-Siniatic commandment, see Lev 12:3.

2. Exod 12:48–49.

3. E.g., Josephus, *Ant.* 1:192; 12:241; Persius, *Sat.* 5:184; Petronius, *Sat.* 102:14; *Frag.* 37; Martial, *Epigr.* 7:30; Tacitus, *Hist.* 5.5:2.

4. Philo, *Migration* 92; *QG* 3:38, 47, 52.

5. E.g., Rom 2:25–29; 3:30; 4:10–16.

6. Acts 15:1; 21:21.

7. John 7:22–23.

8. Josephus, *Ant.* 20:44. See also *War* 1:34; *Life* 113.

9. For circumcision among non-Judeans around this time, see Artap. frag. 3 (in Eusebius, *Praep. ev.* 9.27:10; see *OTP* 2:899); Diodorus Siculus, *Bibliotheca Historica* 1.28:3, 1.55:5; *Geogr.* 17.2:5; Celsus, *De Medicina* 7.25:1; Philo, *Spec. Laws* 1:1–11; *QG* 3:47–48; Josephus, *Ant.* 1:214; 8:262; *Ag. Ap.* 1:168–171; 2:137–144.

10. Diodorus Siculus, *Bibliotheca Historica* 1.28:3, 1.55:5. For slightly later non-Judean authors, see Strabo, *Geogr.* 16.2:37, 4:9; 17.2:5; Horace, *Serm.* 1.9:70. Herodotus (*Hist.* 2.104:3), writing in the fifth century BCE, mentioned the practice of circumcision among the Phoenicians, "the Syrians of Palestine," the Egyptians, and other peoples. While Josephus (*Ant.* 8:262; *Ag. Ap.* 1:168–171) understood that "the Syrians of Palestine" could mean no one other than the Judeans, there appears to be little reason to accept this assessment.

11. Josephus, *Ant.* 13:257–258, 318–319 (where a report on the circumcision of the Itureans is attributed to Strabo drawing on Timagenes). The forced circumcision of

the Idumeans is also reported by an otherwise unknown Ptolemy, author of a history of Herod (in Ammonius, *De adfinium vocabulorum differentia*, no. 243). For further discussion about this episode, see chapter 7.

12. Jub. 15:25–34.

13. Theod. frag. 5 (in Eusebius, *Praep. ev.* 9.22.7; see *OTP* 2:792). For the date and identity of Theodotus, see J. Collins, "The Epic of Theodotus"; *OTP* 2:785–789.

14. 1 Macc 1:11–15. See also T. Mos. 8:1–5, which prophesizes that an evil king will *compel* a reversal of circumcision by physicians on the young, circumcised boys.

15. 1 Macc 1:57–61.

16. 1 Macc 2:46–48. See also the likely later 2 Bar. 66:5, where King Josiah is said to have been "strong in the law [Syriac: *bənīmôsā*] at that time so that he left no one uncircumcised."

17. 2 Macc 6:1–10. Cf. 4 Macc 4:24–25.

18. Dan 11:30.

19. Dan 11:30, 32.

20. J. Collins, *Daniel*, 61.

21. Honigman, *Tales of High Priests*, 237.

22. Sir 44:20 (MS B).

23. Judg 14:3; 15:18; 1 Sam 14:6; 17:26, 36; 18:20–27; 31:4 (cf. 1 Chr 10:4); 2 Sam 1:20; 3:14. For other noncircumcised peoples, see Gen 34:14–25; Ezek 32:17–32; 44:6–9. The only direct reference to Israelites undergoing the actual procedure appears in Josh 5:2–9; note that no legal rationale is given for why this mass circumcision is said to have taken place.

24. Sasson, "Circumcision." For circumcision among Idumeans at Maresha, see Kloner, "The Identity of the Idumeans," 569; I. Stern, "Ethnic Identities"; Levin, "The Religion of Idumea," 15. See also Jer 9:24–25 and above, note 10.

25. For work in general: Exod 20:9–10; 23:12; 31:14–15; 35:2; Lev 23:3; Deut 5:13–14; see also Gen 2:2–3. For plowing and reaping: Exod 34:21. For kindling fire: Exod 35:3. For gathering wood: Num 15:32–36. For leaving one's "place": Exod 16:29. For prohibitions against "work" on festivals: Exod 12:16; Lev 16:29; 23:7–8, 21; Num 28:18, 25–26; 29:1, 7, 12, 35; Deut 16:8.

26. For good overviews, see Doering, *Schabbat*, 315–383; H. Weiss, *A Day of Gladness*, 32–51.

27. Philo, *Migration* 89–93.

28. Philo, *Embassy* 158.

29. Philo, *Dreams* 2:123–132 (quotations here at 123–124).

30. Matt 12:9–14; Mark 3:1–6; Luke 6:6–11; 13:10–17; 14:1–6; John 5:1–18; 7:23; 9:1–41. For in-depth analyses of these and the following narratives, see Doering, *Schabbat*, 398–478; H. Weiss, *A Day of Gladness*, 86–110.

31. Matt 12:1–8; Mark 2:23–28; Luke 6:1–5.

32. John 5:8–12.

33. Matt 12:5–8, 11–12; Luke 13:15; 14:5; John 7:21–24.

34. Matt 28:1; Mark 15:42–16:1; Luke 23:50–56 (quotation at 56).

35. Josephus, *War* 1:60 (= *Ant.* 13:234), 146; 2:147, 392–393, 456, 517–518, 634; 4:99–100, 582; 7:52; *Ant.* 1:33; 3:91; 11:346; 12:4–7, 274–276; 13:12–13, 251, 337; 14:226, 241; 16:27, 163, 168; 18:3–320, 354; *Life* 161; *Ag. Ap.* 1:209; 2:27, 175, 282.

36. Josephus, *Ant.* 12:277–278. See Doering, *Schabbat*, 498–502; H. Weiss, *A Day of Gladness*, 73–80; Borchardt, "Sabbath Observance."

37. Josephus, *Ant.* 13:251–253; 14:226.

38. Josephus, *War* 2:147–148.

39. Josephus, *War* 4:582. It is on the basis of this remark that Aaron Demsky ("The Trumpeter's Inscription") has suggested reconstructing the fragmentary inscription found on a stone balustrade unearthed near the southeast corner of the Temple Mount: "To the place of trumpeting to se[parate between the holy (i.e., Sabbath) and the profane (i.e., weekdays)]."

40. Josephus, *Ag. Ap.* 2:282.

41. Apion, *Aegypt.* (in Josephus, *Ag. Ap.* 2:21); Seneca the Younger, *De Superst.* (in Augustine, *Civ.* 6:11); Frontinus, *Strat.* 2.1:17; Tacitus, *Hist.* 5.4:3–4. For other first-century non-Judean references to the Judean Sabbath that do not cite abstinence from work per se (fasting is sometimes cited), see Persius, *Sat.* 5:176–184; Petronius, *Frag.* 37; Martial, *Epigr.* 4:4; Plutarch, *Quaest. conv.* 4.6:2.

42. Clarysse, Remijsen, and Depauw, "Observing the Sabbath." Most of these texts appear in *CPJ* 2, nos. 160–408. For an earlier (and far more limited) treatment, see S. Stern, "The Babylonian Calendar," 169 n. 55 (where he also identified *CPJ* 2, nos. 424 and 483 as having been signed on Sabbaths). Stern noted that caution is warranted before drawing conclusions about Sabbath observance from these documents since it is essentially unknown if signing any kind of document would have been regarded by most Judeans at this time as prohibited "work," and in any event the identification of some of these papyri as "Judean" is open to debate. For the identification of *CPJ* documents as "Jewish," see *CPJ* 1, xvii–xix. It has been suggested that three unprovenanced Aramaic ostraca that report "giving" and (perhaps) "delivering" food items on the Sabbath may reflect some degree of laxity in first-century-CE Sabbath observance; see Yardeni, "New Jewish Aramaic Ostraca"; Doering, *Schabbat*, 387–397. Space limitations prevent me from engaging in a thorough treatment of the interesting questions raised by all these finds.

43. Josephus, *Ant.* 14:226, 241–242, 245, 258, 263–264; 16:163, 168.

44. Josephus, *War* 1:146; *Ant.* 14:63–64. Cf. Strabo, *Geogr.* 16.2:40 (cited in Josephus, *Ant.* 14:66–68), where Pompey is said to have taken advantage of "the day of fasting," which may simply be the way pagan writers like Strabo commonly viewed the Judean Sabbath; see *GLAJJ* 1:276–277, 307. A fragmentary papyrus from the Herakleopolite nome in Egypt, dated "year 3, Epeiph 28" (= 28 July, 49 BCE), tells of a military incident that took place one day prior, "which was the eve of a Sabbath [*hē estin prosámbaton*]" (*CPJ* 4, no. 583). The 27th of July, 49 BCE, did indeed fall on a Friday; see the editors' introduction to this papyrus in the *CPJ* edition. Another papyrus, apparently sent to the same

addressee, includes the explanation "because of the intervening Sabbath [*dià tò tèn anà méson sábbaton eînai*]" (*CPJ* 4, no. 582). In both cases, however, it remains unclear precisely how the "Sabbath" may have been relevant to the matter at hand.

45. Jub. 2:17–33 (esp. 29–30); 50:6–13. See Doering, *Schabbat*, 43–118.

46. CD x, 14–xi, 18a. Compare some of these rules with matters discussed in the Gospels; see above, notes 30–34.

47. 4Q451 1–2; 4Q264a; 4Q265 6–7, 1–5; 4Q274 2 i, 2–3; 4Q421. For in-depth investigations into Sabbath prohibitions in CD and elsewhere in the Qumran corpus, see Doering, *Schabbat*, 119–282; Noam and Qimron, "A Qumran Composition"; Hidary, "Revisiting the Sabbath Laws."

48. Aristob. frag. 5 (in Eusebius, *Praep. ev.* 13.12:12; see *OTP* 2:842).

49. 1 Macc 2:29–38. Cf. Josephus, *Ant.* 12:274–275.

50. 1 Macc 2:40–41. Cf. Josephus, *Ant.* 12:276–278.

51. 1 Macc 9:43–49. Cf. Josephus, *Ant.* 13:12–13.

52. Some scholars (e.g., Bar-Kochva, *Judas Maccabaeus*, 474–493; Holladay and Goodman, "Religious Scruples," 167–171) have argued on this basis that the story (and others like it) should not be viewed as evidence of a pre-Hasmonean practice to refrain from self-defensive fighting on Sabbath. If, however, the Sabbath prohibitions themselves were only recently adopted as authoritative—as the evidence investigated here would allow—the difficulty disappears.

53. 2 Macc 6:11. Observance of Sabbath was prohibited by Seleucid decree according to 2 Macc 6:6.

54. See 2 Macc 5:25; 8:25–28; 12:38–39; 15:1–5.

55. Josephus, *Ag. Ap.* 1:209–210. See more below, note 59.

56. Meleager, *Anth.* 5.160; For Augustan-era writers, see Horace, *Sat.* 1.9:68–72; Pompeius Trogus, *Hist. Phil.* 36 (in Justin, *Epit.* 2:14); Ovid, *Ars* 1:413–416. Pompeius Trogus, like other ancient writers, thought that the Judean Sabbath was a fast day (see above, note 44).

57. *CPJ* 1, no. 10. The term "*Sábbata*" here takes the plural, as in LXX (e.g., Exod 20:8, 10) and other Judean texts in Greek. For a discussion of this (and of the difficult-to-read verso), see commentary by Tcherikover in *CPJ*, ad loc.; Doering, *Schabbat*, 289–291.

58. Peter Altmann ("The Significance," 11) has recently voiced a similar assessment: "This provides evidence neither for a widespread practice nor for any connection to a *written nomos* functioning as law. It could just as easily concern one individual (or even group), assumedly of Judeans, basing their action on the traditional ethnic custom, though a custom that became increasingly important in the exilic and later periods." A similar problem obtains also with a reference to "*Sábbata*" in a different papyrus (*CPJ* 4, no. 605), dated on paleographic grounds to the end of the second century or the beginning of the first century BCE.

59. Josephus, *Ag. Ap.* 1:210–212.

60. Wacholder, *Eupolemus*, 272. See also Bar-Kochva, *Judas Maccabaeus*, 477–481; Holladay and Goodman, "Religious Scruples," 168; Kasher, *Against Apion*, 213–214.

61. 2 Kgs 4:23; 11:5, 7, 9; 16:18; Isa 1:13; 66:23; Ezek 44:24; 45:17; 46:1, 3–4, 12; Hos 2:13; Ps 92:1; Lam 2:6; Neh 9:14; 10:34; 1 Chr 9:32; 23:31; 2 Chr 2:3; 8:13; 23:4, 8; 31:3.

62. See, e.g., Meinhold, "Die Entstehung des Sabbats"; Robinson, *The Origin and Development*; Grund, *Die Entstehung des Sabbats*. Robinson (*The Origin and Development*, 53–57) argued that Amos 8:5, which tells of unscrupulous wheat vendors who would wait for the day of "the (new) month" and "the Sabbath" to pass before selling their grain, does not necessarily imply that it was regarded as *prohibited* to engage in commerce on the Sabbath (or on the new moon for that matter); it may only assume that many people were involved with these festivals, and as a result, these days did not function as normal times for business. The same suggestion is made by Tchavdar Hadjiev (*The Composition and Redaction*, 104–108), who also concludes that the entire passage (Amos 8:3–14) is a late redactional composition secondarily inserted into the surrounding textual unit.

63. Both Nehemiah passages are set in the Persian period. For the problem of determining their date of composition, see chapter 7, note 19.

64. Many scholars regard Jer 17:19–27 as a late, "postexilic" supplement to the book, with some even positing that the passage presupposes Neh 13:15–22 and therefore postdates it; see discussions in Veijola, "Die Propheten"; J. Wright, *Rebuilding Identity*, 229–233.

65. Ezek 20:12–13, 16, 20–21, 24; 22:8, 26; 23:38.

66. Isa 56:2, 4, 6. For the late date of Isa 56–66, see Blenkinsopp, *Isaiah 56–66*, 42–54.

67. *TAD* D7.16. Porten (*Archives from Elephantine*, 126–127) noted a clear resonance with the narratives about Sabbath commerce in Neh 13:15ff. but then proposed a highly dubious suggestion that "the threat to take Islaḥ's life unless she met the boat on the Sabbath may imply some extraordinary situation and indirectly attest the regular observance of the Sabbath." Three other ostraca cited by Porten (126–127) which refer to the Sabbath have little if anything to contribute to our investigation; for extensive analysis of all these texts, see Doering, *Schabbat*, 23–42. For a more recent study that considers additional ostraca that appeared only after Doering's monograph was written, see Granerød, *Dimensions of Yahwism*, 182–206. André Lemaire (*Levantine Epigraphy*, 55) has summarized the Elephantine evidence about the Sabbath as follows: "Ultimately we do not learn anything certain about the way of marking or celebrating the 'day of Sabbath' and we can only wonder whether it was the festival of the full moon, as it was probably during the First Temple period, or already the seventh day of the week, as specified in the Pentateuch."

68. S. Stern, "The Babylonian Calendar," 168–170. The documents are *TAD* B2.7, B3.1, B3.2, and B4.6. For a suggestion that all these documents were written

after nightfall, see Y. Bloch, "Judean Identity," 57–66. Stern noted an additional four Egyptian papyri dating to the Ptolemaic period (from 154, 152, 140, and 121 BCE) and identified by the editors of *CPJ* as Judean documents (*CPJ* 1, nos. 60, 63, 69, and 93) which were also signed on a Saturday. See also above, note 42.

69. Y. Bloch, "Judean Identity" (quotation at 55): "Both the tablets from Āl-Yāḫūdu and its vicinity and the tablets of the Murašu archive reveal no conscious effort on the part of ethnic Judeans in Babylonia to refrain from participating in transactions concluded on a Sabbath." See also Y. Bloch, "Was the Sabbath Observed," which critiques a claim posited by Oded Tammuz ("The Sabbath") that Judeans at Yāhūdu *were* observing Sabbath prohibitions.

70. Bultrighini and Stern, "The Seven-Day Week," esp. 11–17.

71. The word "*š-b-t*" found on a late seventh-century-BCE ostracon from Meṣad Ḥashavyahu (near Yavneh-Yam) should probably be vowelized and read as "my rest/stopping [*šivtī*]" rather than as "Sabbath"; see Naveh, "A Hebrew Letter," 133–134; Lindenberger, *Ancient Aramaic and Hebrew Letters*, 109–110. Even if the word were vowelized as "*šabāt*" (Lindenberger, *Ancient Aramaic and Hebrew Letters*, 112 n. g), the term may simply refer to a chronological marker; certainly nothing is implied about "work" or any other activities being prohibited at such a time.

72. It has been suggested (e.g., Porten, *Archives from Elephantine*, 127; Doering, *Schabbat*, 36–39) that prevalence of the name Shabbethai at Elephantine, along with its appearance in Ezra-Nehemiah (Ezra 10:15; Neh 8:7; 11:16), reflects the significant perception of Sabbath held by some Judeans in the Persian period. As Naomi Cohen ("The Name 'Shabtai'") has conclusively shown, however, the name was by no means a distinctly Judean one. Porten's claim that non-Judeans named Shabbethai must have been "attracted by Sabbath observance" is nothing but a case of special pleading. For a valuable recent study, see Granerød, *Dimensions of Yahwism*, 196–204.

73. Exod 12:1–13, 21–28, 43–49.

74. In contrast to Exod 12, Deut 16 provides that the Passover may be taken not only from sheep and goats (*ṣōʾn*) but also from cattle (*bāqār*), and instructs that it should be boiled (*ûvišaltā*). Briefer Pentateuchal references to the Passover sacrifice (Exod 34:25; Lev 23:5; Num 28:16) add no significant additional details.

75. Exod 12:14–20; 13:3–10; 23:15; 34:18; Lev 23:6–8; Num 28:17–18, 25; Deut 16:3–4, 8.

76. Philo, *Spec. Laws* 2:145; see also *Moses* 2:224; *QE* 1:10; *Decalogue* 159. Sarah Pearce ("Notes," 208) has suggested that "*leōs*" is used here as a literary tool to identify the contemporary Judean practitioners of the Passover with the original Israelite nation that left Egypt.

77. Philo, *Spec. Laws* 2:148. Singing of hymns as part of the Passover meal is attested also in Mark 14:26 and Matt 26:30 (see below), and a debate surrounding the precise parameters of these "hymns" is also attributed to the Houses of Hillel and Shammai in *m. Pesaḥ.* 10:6.

78. Sanders, *Judaism*, 134; Martola, "Eating the Passover Lamb"; de Lange, "The Celebration of the Passover."

79. Josephus, *War* 6:422–428. A strikingly similar account appears in *b. Pesaḥ.* 64b. Cf. also *War* 2:280–281.

80. Josephus, *War* 2:224–227 (= *Ant.* 20:105–112), 244, 280–281; 5:98–105; 6:290, 420–421.

81. Josephus, *Ant.* 3:320–321. Henry Thackeray (Thackeray, Marcus, and Feldman edition, ad loc., note *d*) notes the difficulty of identifying "flour" with "leavened" and suggests that the "flour" was brought in the form of leavened loaves; cf. Colautti, *Passover*, 123. For other references to contemporary observance of the Passover and the Festival of Unleavened Bread, see Josephus, *Ant.* 2:313, 317; 3:248–249; 18:29, 90. For a comprehensive study on Josephus's treatment of these two observances, see Colautti, *Passover*.

82. Matt 26:17–30; Mark 14:12–26; Luke 22:7–19. As opposed to the Synoptics, it seems that the setting of the meal scene in John 13–17 is *before* the Passover (see John 18:28).

83. See above, note 77. Wine is also mentioned, but this may simply have been a standard feature of *any* meal. However, cf. Jub. 49:6.

84. Matt 26:2–5; Mark 14:1–2; Luke 2:41–43; 22:1–6; John 2:13, 23; 6:4; 11:55–57; 12:1; 13:1; 18:28, 39; Acts 12:3–4; 20:6.

85. 1 Cor 5:6–8.

86. Tacitus, *Hist.* 5.4:3.

87. Josephus, *War* 2:10–13 (= *Ant.* 17:213–218).

88. Josephus, *Ant.* 14:25–29. Cf. the rabbinic version (*b. Soṭah* 49b; *b. B. Qam.* 82b; *b. Menaḥ.* 64b), where no connection to Passover is made.

89. Jub. 49:1–23; 11Q19 xvii, 6–xviii, 10; Ezek. Trag. 156–192 (see *OTP* 2:814–816); Aristob. frag 1 (in Eusebius, *Hist. Eccl.* 7.32:18; see *OTP* 2:837).

90. Jub. 49:10–12, 19. Cf. Philo, *Spec. Laws* 2:145, where the sacrifice is said to be slaughtered "from noon until the evening," and Josephus, *War* 6:423, where the time given is "from the ninth to the eleventh hour."

91. Jub. 49:16–17, 20–21; 11Q19 xvii, 8b–9a. Contra Philo, Josephus, and the Synoptic Gospel accounts; see above, notes 76–83.

92. Jub. 49:17; 11Q19 xvii, 8. The Qumran fragment is 4Q265 4, 3, where "a youth [*na'ar za'ṭûṭ*]" is excluded. Contra Philo (above, note 76), who explicitly included "old and young alike" as participants in the slaughter of the sacrifice.

93. 4Q265 3, 3; Jub. 49:17; 11Q19 xvii, 7–8. Contra Josephus (above, note 79), who excluded only menstruating women.

94. For an excellent survey of early hypotheses, see Segal, *The Hebrew Passover*, 78–113. Note that aside from the Pentateuchal references and the four narratives cited above, the Festival of Unleavened Bread is mentioned also in Ezek 45:21–25 (where the Passover is also mentioned) and in 2 Chr 8:13.

95. Michael Fishbane (*Biblical Interpretation*, 135–137) has famously argued that, in writing "and they boiled the Passover in fire [*wayəvaśəlû hapesaḥ bā'ēš*]" (2 Chr

35:13), the author of the Josiah Passover account was engaging in exegetical harmonization of Exod 12:9 (where the instruction is to roast the Passover in fire and boiling is forbidden) and Deut 16:7 (where boiling is called for). Similarly, Fishbane has argued that mention of both sheep and goats as well as cattle in 2 Chr 35:7–9 is an attempt to conflate Exod 12:5 (which allows only sheep and goats for the Passover) and Deut 16:2 (which allows also cattle). If he is correct (one might question whether "*b-š-l*" really means "boil" and not simply "cook"), this would indicate only that a well-educated author of 2 Chr 35 was aware of the *existence* of the Exodus and Deuteronomy sources (or something like them) and that he was of the opinion that both sources should be preserved. It says nothing about the "authoritative status" of these documents among the Judean masses, or that the general populace would have even know that these sources existed.

96. For citations and detailed treatment, see excursus below.

97. *TAD* A4.1 (often called "The Passover Letter").

98. *TAD* D7.6. But see Arnold, "The Passover Papyrus," 13 n. 19.

99. *TAD* D7.24. There is little reason to consider a third ostracon (*TAD* D7.8) as at all related to Passover, despite claims that the letter may allude to a Tannaitic prohibition against eating leavened products after mid-morning on the fourteenth of Nisan; see Porten, *Archives from Elephantine*, 132. Anachronistic readings of this sort within the Elephantine material are all too common; see below for more examples.

100. See above, note 97. The reading and translation below are my own and are based on recent high-resolution photographs prepared at the Staatlichen Museen zu Berlin and available online (accessed March 13, 2020): https://elephantine. smb.museum/record/ID100463/.

101. For this and additional examples where "the gods" are invoked in correspondence by Judeans at Elephantine, see chapter 7.

102. The standard reading of the final two letters on this line is " '*r*" and is often reconstructed to read "fou[rteen days]." Recently, Idan Dershowitz ("Darius II Delays the Festival of Matzot") proposed reading the second letter as a *dālet* rather than a *rêš* and reconstructed the word as "Ad[ar . . .]," suggesting that the letter is a royal instruction to intercalate the year by adding a second month of Adar.

103. The standard reading is "pure/clean" (*dəkhîn*), but these letters (or with the first letter read as a *rêš*) may simply be the ending of a longer word whose beginning has not been preserved.

104. "*wəkōl minda'am zî ḥāmîr*"; see Jastrow, *Dictionary*, s.v. "*ḥāmar*" (def. 2). Cf. Ps 75:9. I was elated to find that Morton Smith ("Jewish Religious Life," 231) had preceded me with the translation I have provided here. For the standard but entirely anachronistic translation "leaven(ed)," see below. For abstinence from wine as a mourning ritual among Elephantine Judeans, see *TAD* A4.7:20–21.

105. For an attempt to reconstruct the document as significantly wider than had previously been assumed, see Grelot, "Le papyrus pascal d'Éléphantine: nouvel examen"; "Le papyrus pascal d'Éléphantine: Essai de Restauration."

106. Thus already in the initial publication by Eduard Sachau (*Aramäische Papyrus*, 13) this letter is classified as "Sendschreiben betreffend das Passahfest." The large number of subsequent treatments does not permit adequate bibliographic citations here; for the first waves of research, see publications cited in Porten, *Archives from Elephantine*, 128–133, 311–314. For a recent questioning of this still axiomatic interpretation, see Gass, "Der Passa-Papyrus."

107. See, e.g., Arnold, "The Passover Papyrus," 7–9; Grelot, "Etudes sur le 'Papyrus Pascal,'" 361–362; Grelot, "Le papyrus pascal d'Éléphantine et le problème du Pentateuque," 255–256; Porten, *Archives from Elephantine*, 82, 313. The rabbinic prohibition is first attested in *m. Pesaḥ.* 3:1.

108. This has been the standard translation already from the initial publication by Eduard Sachau (*Aramäische Papyrus*, 13). The word is alternatively rendered as the noun "leaven" (i.e., sourdough; that which causes bread to rise) or as the adjective "leavened" (i.e., bread that has risen); see Grelot, "Etudes sur le 'Papyrus Pascal,'" 362–363. See also Beit-Arieh and Cresson, "An Edomite Ostracon," 99. For a rare critique of this otherwise almost consensual reading, see Gass, "Der Passa-Papyrus," 58 n. 18, 67.

109. Lev 16:29–31; 23:27–32; Num 29:7. Cf. Lev 25:9, where no self-affliction is mentioned.

110. Philo, *Spec. Laws* 1:186; see also 2:193–203.

111. Josephus, *War* 5:236. For other references to fasting on the Day of Atonement, see Josephus, *Ant.* 3:240; 18:94; and perhaps also *Ag. Ap.* 2:282 ("the fasts").

112. Acts 27:9.

113. See Strabo, *Geogr.* 16.2:40 (also probably cited by Josephus in *Ant.* 14:66–68); Pompeius Trogus, *Hist. Phil.* 36 (in Justin, *Epit.* 2:14); Plutarch, *Quaest. conv.* 4.6:2; Tacitus, *Hist.* 5.4:3; Suetonius, *Aug.* 76:2 (in a purported quotation from Augustus to Tiberius).

114. Josephus, *Ant.* 17:165–166. For a rabbinic version of this story, see *y. Yoma* 1:1; *b. Yoma* 12b (and elsewhere).

115. 1QpHab xi, 2–8. See also 4Q265 7 ii, 4, where a "fast" (*ṣôm*) is mentioned in connection with a conjecturally reconstructed "day [of Atonement]."

116. Cross, Freedman, and Sanders, *Scrolls from Qumrân Cave I*, 4.

117. For this and other considerations regarding the dating of this composition, see Eshel, "The Two Historical Layers."

118. CD vi, 19. For other occurrences of the term "*ta'anit*" in the Dead Sea Scrolls in possible references to the Day of Atonement, see 4Q171 ii, 10; 4Q417 3, 4; 4Q508 ii, 3; 4Q509+4Q505 16 iv, 3.

119. 11Q19 xv, 10–12; xvii, 6–10. The intervening lines prescribe the cultic rites of the day.

120. Jub. 34:18–19. The day is alluded to also in 5:17–18.

121. 11Q13 ii, 7–8.

122. The late-antique rabbis were acutely aware of this problem and provided an apologetic (although of course not historical) solution; see *b. Mo 'ed Qat.* 9a.

123. Some scholars have claimed that Neh 9:1, where the people are said to have assembled on the twenty-fourth of the seventh month "with fasting and in sackcloth, and with earth upon them," represents some sort of precursor to a Day of Atonement (see, e.g., Wellhausen, *Prolegomena*, 111), but I find this suggestion rather dubious. For other equally unconvincing apologetic explanations, see Yoo, *Ezra and the Second Wilderness*, 153–156.

124. Zech 8:19 speaks of "the fast of the fourth (month), and the fast of the fifth, and the fast of the seventh, and the fast of the tenth" (see also Zech 7:5), but these were apparently commemorations of cataclysmic historical events surrounding the Babylonian destruction of the Judean kingdom; there is little reason to associate "the fast of the seventh" with anything resembling a "Day of Atonement" (see Hoffman, "The Fasts," esp. 177–180).

125. Other instructions associated with the Festival of Sukkot (or "Ingathering") are the obligation of pilgrimage incumbent upon all males, a directive to "rejoice" during the holiday, a unique sacrificial schedule for each day of the festival, and a prohibition against work on the first day and the eighth day—a day of "assembly" (*'ăṣeret*) appended to the seven-day holiday (Exod 23:16; 34:22; Lev 23:33–36, 39; Num 29:12–38; Deut 16:13–16). Also on Sukkot, but only once every seven years, "the instruction" (*hatôrāh*) that Moses is said to have written down is to be read publicly before all of Israel upon their pilgrimage to "the place [YHWH] will choose" (Deut 31:10–13).

126. Philo, *Flaccus* 116–117. For an allegorical explanation of this law, see *Spec. Laws* 2:204–214. For the sacrifices offered on this holiday, see *Spec. Laws* 1:189–191; *Migration* 202; *Flight* 186. Philo never mentions the four species of Lev 23:40.

127. Josephus, *War* 6:301. Almost identical terminology is used when narrating an incident from the end of the second century BCE (*War* 1:73; *Ant.* 13:304)—but where it seems that Josephus is simply describing the custom of his own day. For a unique explanation for why Moses legislated this practice, see *Ant.* 3:244.

128. Josephus, *Ant.* 13:372. Josephus here is describing an incident from the time of Alexander Jannaeus in the early first century BCE, but from his language he appears to describe the widespread practice in his own day. See further below.

129. Josephus, *Ant.* 3:245. For the "Persian apple" (or "Persian fruit") as "citron," see Rubenstein, *The History of Sukkot*, 75 n. 113, 194.

130. It appears likely that Pseudo-Philo (LAB 13:7) also knew of the same four species specified by Josephus, as he listed along with the palm branch and willow also the myrtle and "*cedrum*," which Jeffrey Rubenstein (*The History of Sukkot*, 73–74) has suggested may be a mistake that befell the Latin translation from an original (but now lost) Greek, which would have read "*kítron*" (citron).

131. Rubenstein, *The History of Sukkot*, 77–78. That this is a temple-centered practice may have been understood from the end of the verse containing the four-species commandment: "and you shall rejoice *before YHWH your God* for seven days." For other Josephean references to Sukkot, see *War* 2:515; *Ant.* 4:209; 8:100, 123, 225–231; 11:75–78; 13:46, 242; 15:50.

132. *TJC*, 125–126 (nos. 211–214). The motif appears on coins from the Bar Kokhba revolt as well (*TJC*, 145–146, nos. 218, 229–233, 267–271).

133. Plutarch, *Quaest. conv.* 4.6:2. See the valuable commentary of M. Stern, *GLAJJ* 1:560–562.

134. Josephus, *Ant.* 13:372.

135. Jub. 16:20–31 (quotations at 30–31). Elsewhere (Jub. 32:4–7, 27–29), Jacob is said to offer sacrifices for seven days beginning on the fifteenth of the seventh month, and afterward for one additional (eighth) day. The numbers of animals sacrificed by both patriarchs deviates from the Pentateuchal prescriptions.

136. 11Q19 xlii, 10–17 (quotation at 13–17). See also 11Q19 xliv, 6–7.

137. Some have suggested identifying references to Sukkot rituals in other texts that may also date to this period (CD xi, 8; 4Q409 1 i, 11; 4Q502), but none of these are particularly convincing; see Rubenstein, *The History of Sukkot*, 64–68.

138. 2 Macc 10:6–7. Annual commemoration of this event is called "the Festival of Booths of the month of Kislev" in the first epistle cited at the beginning of the book (1:9), while in the second epistle (1:18) the recipients are told explicitly to celebrate it "as the Festival of Booths." For celebratory use of palm fronds, see 1 Macc 13:51.

139. A seven-day holiday in the seventh month is mentioned in 1 Kgs 8:2, 65–66 (≈2 Chr 5:3; 7:8–9) but is not called "*sūkôt*," and nothing is said of living in "booths" or of taking plant species. 1 Kgs 12:32–33 speaks of a holiday on the fifteenth of the *eighth* month—again with no mention of booths or taking plant species. Ezek 45:25 tells of sacrifices to be offered on "the festival" lasting seven days from the fifteenth of the seventh month. The name "*sūkôt*" appears only in Zech 14:16–19, Ezra 3:4, and 2 Chr 8:13, but again without any explicit reference to either of the two central rituals of Lev 23:40–43 ("*sūkôt*" as the name of a festival hardly implies the existence of a ritual involving living in booths).

140. Neh 8:14–17. No parallel has been preserved in 1 Esdras.

141. See citations in Rubenstein, *The History of Sukkot*, 37 n. 16.

142. The precise form of the menorah is prescribed in Exod 25:31–40; 37:17–24. Other directives regarding the menorah appear in Exod 26:35; 30:27; 31:8; 35:14; 39:37; 40:4, 24–25; Lev 24:4; Num 3:31; 4:9; 8:1–4.

143. Josephus, *Ant.* 3:144–146. See also *War* 5:216–217. For a description of the lamp in Onias's temple at Heliopolis contrasted with the one in Jerusalem, see *War* 7:428–429.

144. Josephus, *War* 7:148–150. Although not cited specifically, the menorah is presumably included among those "vessels of gold from the temple of the Judeans" placed in Vespasian's new temple (*War* 7:160–162).

145. Fine, "The Arch of Titus in Color."

146. Josephus, *Ant.* 8:89–90. For Philo's allegorical interpretations of the menorah, see *QE* 2:73–81; *Moses* 2:102–103; *Prelim. Studies* 6–8.

147. Hachlili, *The Menorah*, 6, 15–17; Wiegmann, Misgav, and Friedman, "A Ritual Bath." For a debunking of the fallacious notion that artistic depiction of the temple menorah was forbidden by Judean law (rabbinic or otherwise), see Adler, "Representations of the Temple Menorah."

148. *TJC*, 41–43.

149. Josephus, *Ant.* 14:72.

150. 1 Macc 1:21; 4:49–50. Reported secondarily by Josephus in *Ant.* 12:250, 318–319. Cf. 2 Macc 10:3.

151. Sir 26:17 (MS C). Or perhaps "burned" (*śāraf*)? In Greek: "*lúkhnos eklámpōn epì lukhnías hagías.*"

152. 1 Kgs 7:49; 2 Chr 4:7; Jer 52:19.

153. 1 Chr 28:15. Josephus (*Ant.* 8:90) was clearly bothered by the lack of congruity between the number of lampstands in Solomon's temple (our versions of Josephus has Solomon provide ten thousand lampstands!) and apologetically explained that only one of these was set up in the sanctuary itself to burn all day "in accordance with the commandment of Moses." For a strikingly similar rabbinic explanation, see *t. Menaḥ.* 11:10 (ed. Zuckermandel, 530).

154. 2 Chr 13:11. Gary Knoppers ("Battling against Yahweh," 519–520) has argued that the author of this passage drew on Pentateuchal (Priestly) sources. Compare references to a divine "lamp" (but not "lampstand") in 1 Sam 3:3 (*"nēr 'elōhîm"*) and Prov 20:27 (*"nēr YHWH"*).

155. Ezra 1:7–11; 5:14–15; 6:5.

156. Zech 4:1–7 (quotation at 2–5).

157. Wellhausen, *Prolegomena*, 341 (Sabbath and circumcision); Blenkinsopp, *The Pentateuch*, 218–219 (Sabbath, circumcision, and Passover).

Chapter 6. The Synagogue

1. See surveys and discussions in Runesson, *The Origins*, 67–168; Levine, *The Ancient Synagogue*, 21–44.

2. This is clearly evident, for example, in the fact that Philo used precisely the same language in describing both "*tà sunagōgia*" (*Embassy* 312) and "*proseuktḗria*" (*Moses* 2:216) as "schools . . . of temperance and justice [*didaskaleîa . . . sōphrosúnēs kaì dikaiosúnēs*]." See also *Spec. Laws* 2:62.

3. Philo, *Hypothetica* 7:11–13. For the question of whether this work is correctly attributed to Philo, see Barclay, *Against Apion*, 353–355. The description presented

here, however, is found elsewhere in Philo's writings: *Embassy* 156; *Spec. Laws* 2:62; *Moses* 2:215–216; *Good Person* 81–82; *Dreams* 2:127. For a somewhat similar description of the Sabbath assemblies of the Therapeutae, see *Contempl. Life* 30–33.

4. Philo, *Hypothetica* 7:14.

5. Philo, *Moses* 2:216. See also *Embassy* 312; *Spec. Laws* 2:62.

6. Philo, *Embassy* 311–316. He also asserted (*Flaccus* 48–50) that synagogues served as a place where Judeans would pay homage to the emperor, but there is reason to suspect that this may be little more than an apologetic claim.

7. Philo, *Spec. Laws* 2:62. Cf. *Moses* 2:216; *Flaccus* 47.

8. Philo, *Embassy* 132.

9. Philo, *Embassy* 156–157, 311–316.

10. Matt 12:9–10; Mark 1:21; 3:1–2; 6:2; Luke 4:16, 31; 6:6; 13:10.

11. Acts 6:9; 13:14, 42, 44; 17:2; 18:4. See also Acts 16:13.

12. Matt 4:23; 9:35; 13:54; Mark 1:21–22; 6:2; Luke 4:15, 31–32; 6:6; 13:10; John 6:59. In Mark 1:39 and Luke 4:44, Jesus is said to "preach" (*kērússō*) in the synagogue.

13. Luke 4:16–30.

14. Matt 12:9–14; Mark 3:1–6; Luke 6:6–11; 13:10–17.

15. Acts 15:21.

16. Acts 13:14–15.

17. Acts 13:44; 14:1; 17:1–4, 10–12, 17; 18:4–7, 26; 19:8.

18. Matt 10:17; 23:34–35; Mark 13:9; Luke 21:12; Acts 22:18–19. Cf. Acts 26:11.

19. Matt 6:1–6.

20. Matt 4:23; 9:35; 12:9–14; 13:54–58; Mark 1:21–28, 39; 3:1–6; 6:1–6; Luke 4:14–37, 44; 6:6–11; 13:10–17.

21. Acts 9:2, 20; 13:14; 14:1; 17:1, 10, 16–17; 18:4, 26; 19:8.

22. Josephus, *Ag. Ap.* 2:175 (translation follows Barclay, *Against Apion*). For a possible reliance on Philo's *Hypothetica* (cited above), see citations in Baumgarten, "The Torah," 18 n. 8; Gerber, *Ein Bild des Judentums*, 106; Barclay, *Against Apion*, 269–270, 353–361.

23. Josephus, *Ag. Ap.* 2:178 (translation follows Barclay, *Against Apion*). See also Josephus, *Ag. Ap.* 2:257, where he asserted that Plato followed Moses in mandating complete fluency in the law on the part of all the people: "He prescribed as the primary duty of the citizens a study of their laws, which they must all learn word for word by heart."

24. Josephus, *War* 2:285–292. For another narrative about conflict between Judeans and Greeks at a synagogue (*sunagōgê*) located in a non-Judean city, see *Ant.* 19:300–311.

25. Elsewhere (*Life* 276–303), Josephus tells of a "general assembly [*sunágontai pántes*]" held one Sabbath after the outbreak of the Great Revolt in "the [place of] prayer [*tèn proseukhên*]" of Tiberias, which he describes as "a huge building, capable of accommodating a large crowd." Whether any Torah reading took

place is not stated; Josephus tells only of a heated political debate that erupted, one that eventually broke off upon "the arrival of the sixth hour, at which it is our custom on the Sabbath to take our midday meal." The next day the community was reassembled in the building, but Josephus notes that the people "had no idea why they were being convened"—probably because Sunday was not a regular time for meeting in the synagogue. Again, a factional dispute broke out, and when no conclusion was reached, it was decided to reconvene in the "(place of) prayer" once again on the following day (a Monday) in order to hold a "public fast." Josephus recalls that, upon entering the building on the third day, "we were proceeding with the ordinary service and engaged in prayer [*tà nómima poioúntōn kaì pròs eukhàs trapoménōn*]" (the rest of the narrative does not concern us here). The unusual setting of this account—during the momentous days of the Great Revolt—makes it difficult to draw clear conclusions regarding what a typical assembly in Tiberias's "(place of) prayer" might have looked like. The most we may conclude is that Saturday morning was a normal time for gathering, and that aside from Sabbath assemblies the institution could host a program of prayer on a day declared to be a "public fast."

26. *CIIP* I.1, 9 (with commentary ad loc. by Jonathan J. Price).
27. The inscription also tells of several apparently ancillary architectural elements associated with the main structure of the synagogue itself: "the guest-house [*tòn xenōna*], and the rooms [*tà dōmata*], and the water installations[?] [*tà khrēstēria tōn hudátōn*] for the lodging of those who are in need of it from abroad." While the precise nature of all these architectural features remains a matter of speculation, the assertion that they were intended for the use of individuals "from abroad," together with the fact that the inscription was found in Jerusalem, suggests that these elements were specially adjoined to this particular synagogue as a service to fellow Judeans on pilgrimage to the holy city. Although it may be assumed that both the synagogue and its ancillary structures were located somewhere in the general vicinity of the inscription's find-spot in the Lower City of Jerusalem, architectural remains of these buildings have yet to be identified.
28. Reproduced in Levine, *The Ancient Synagogue*, 103. Two earlier inscriptions commissioned by the Judean community of Berenice (one from the late first century BCE and the other from 24/25 CE) mention the local "amphitheater," which many scholars have argued should be identified with the community's synagogue; see ibid., 96–102.
29. *JIGRE*, no. 126. No references to the synagogue have been found in Egyptian papyri dating to the first century CE. For a papyrus dating to 113 CE which mentions both a "*proseukhḗ*" and an "*eukheíon*," see *CPJ* 2, no. 432.
30. *CIJ* 2, no. 766. For another example of a non-Judean sponsoring the construction of a synagogue, see Luke 7:5.
31. Gibson, *The Jewish Manumission Inscriptions*.

32. First reported upon by Yadin (*Masada*, 180–191); the final report was eventually published by Ehud Netzer (*Masada*, 402–413).

33. Brief descriptions and citations to published reports for most of these buildings are conveniently provided in Hachlili, *Ancient Synagogues*, 26–28, 33–36. For Tel Rekhesh, see Aviam et al., "A 1st–2nd Century CE Assembly Room." For Khirbet Di'ab, see Har-Even, "A Second Temple Period Synagogue." In some cases (e.g., Khirbet 'A-Taw'ani and Tel Rekhesh), an early second-century-CE date is possible. The discovery of a second building identified as a synagogue at Magdala has recently been announced by Dina Avshalom-Gorni in a paper presented at the Annual Conference of the Zinman Institute of Archaeology, University of Haifa, December 2021.

34. While some scholars have identified additional synagogues elsewhere (Korazim, Capernaum, the "fountain house" at Magdala, Khirbet Burnat [North], Jericho, Shu'afat, Khirbet Qumran [Room 77], and Horvat 'Ethri), these structures lack surviving benches, and as a result their identification as synagogues has been largely rejected by scholarship; for discussions and citations to published reports, see Hachlili, *Ancient Synagogues*, 23–26, 28–30, 36–39. The dating of the earliest phase of the synagogue at Ostia and the identification of the building as a synagogue during this phase are both highly contested; see discussion and citations in Levine, *The Ancient Synagogue*, 276–277. Mary Jane Cuyler and Jaimie Gunderson recently presented a paper (at the 118th Annual Meeting of the Archaeological Institute of America, January 2017) in which they argued that the first phase of the building dates to the mid-second century CE at the very earliest, and that its identification as a synagogue during this phase remains an open question. The building unearthed at Delos will be discussed below.

35. This is how Yadin (*Masada*, 187) described his notion of a "genizah": it is "where orthodox Jews buried—since they would not destroy—documents in the holy language, Hebrew, which had gone out of use, either because they were old and tattered or because they contained mistakes." Suffice it to say that no such practice is known from such an early date. My sense is that Yadin was unduly influenced by the spectacular discovery of the Cairo Genizah a few decades prior to his excavations at Masada, in an annex to a medieval synagogue in Fustat, Cairo.

36. Philo, *Embassy* 156–157.

37. Philo, *Embassy* 311–316. Citation of this letter to the governors appears in a letter addressed to Caligula from Agrippa I.

38. Josephus, *Ant.* 16:164.

39. See Josephus, *Ant.* 16:164, and the Thackeray, Marcus, and Feldman edition, note 6.

40. Josephus, *Ant.* 16:43.

41. Josephus, *War* 7:43–45.

42. Josephus, *Ant.* 14:256–258. For a historical analysis of this document, see Pucci Ben Zeev, *Jewish Rights*, 206–216.

43. Josephus, *Ant.* 14:259–261; see Pucci Ben Zeev, *Jewish Rights*, 217–225. Cf. *Ant.* 14:235.

44. Ed P. Sanders (*Judaism*, 133–134) suggested that the Passover sacrifice was meant, while Anders Runesson (*The Origins*, 465) has gone so far as to suggest that the edict "may well refer to regular offerings, animal or non-animal," and that "the building the Jews were allowed to construct was a temple."

45. 1QS vi, 7b–8a. Immediately prior to this (1QS vi, 6–7a), the scroll instructs that in a place where ten men are gathered, someone must always be engaged in Torah study on a continuous basis. For another binary reference to "reading" and "studying" among the scrolls, see 4Q251 1, 5: "to study and to read in a book [*lidrôš wəliqrō' bəsēfer*] on [Sabba]th." For "reading" and "learning," see 4Q264a 1 i, 4–5: "a book . . . they may read [and] learn from them [*yiqrə'û (wə)lāmədû bām*]."

46. For a suggested mid-second-century-BCE date for "the first shaping" of the Community Rule, see Qimron and Charlesworth, "Rule of the Community," 2. The earliest suggested paleographic dates for 1QS and the other Community Rule manuscripts are slightly later (ibid.).

47. 3 Macc 7:20. The literary setting is the late third century BCE, but the composition itself was likely authored a considerable time after this; see *OTP* 2:510–512. See also 3 Macc 2:28, where Judeans are denied access to "their temples [*tà hierà autōn*]."

48. *JIGRE*, no. 22.

49. *JIGRE*, no. 117. The lower right-hand corner of the stele is missing. For another reference to a *proseukhē* at Crocodilopolis, see note 60 below. A recently published papyrus (*CPJ* 4, no. 619), dated on paleographic grounds to the third century BCE, mentions contributions to a "*proseu[khē]*" by a list of named individuals presumed to be Judeans.

50. *JIGRE*, no. 24. The inscription opens: "On behalf of King Ptolemy, and Queen Cleopatra the sister, and Queen Cleopatra the wife," figures commonly identified with Ptolemy VIII Physcon, Cleopatra II, and Cleopatra III, all of whom acted as co-regents for part of the time between 140 and 116 BCE. Xenephyris is located southeast of Alexandria, near Damanhur.

51. *JIGRE*, no. 25. Nitriai is identified with el-Barnûgi, southwest of Damanhur.

52. See commentary in *JIGRE*, 14, 42.

53. *JIGRE*, no. 27. The inscription opens: "On behalf of King Ptolemy and Queen Cleopatra," which may refer to one of five kings named Ptolemy (V, VI, VIII, XI, and XII) who were married to a Cleopatra; see *JIGRE*, 47. Athribis is identified with Tell Atrib, near modern Banha in the southern Nile Delta.

54. *JIGRE*, no. 28.

55. See commentary in *JIGRE*, 49–50.

56. *JIGRE*, no. 13. The inscription opens with the words "On behalf of the queen and king" and mentions a "(year) 15," which may refer to the year 37 BCE during the co-regency of Cleopatra VII and Ptolemy XV.

57. *JIGRE*, no. 125. The inscription twice refers to "the queen and king," once in Greek and once in Latin, which may therefore mean Cleopatra VII and one of her co-regents, Ptolemy XIV (47–44 BCE) or Ptolemy XV (44–30 BCE). For the identity of "King Ptolemy Euergetes" and for the possibility that this "replacement copy" dates to the late Roman period, see commentary by Horbury and Noy, *JIGRE*, 214. For additional inscriptions of questionable significance for our purposes here (especially as their dates and/or association with a Judean institution are not well established), see *JIGRE*, nos. 9, 16–18, 20, 26, 105, 127, 129.

58. *CPJ* 1, no. 129.

59. For this and the role of Nikomachus the "*neōkóros*," see Tcherikover's commentary in *CPJ* 1, 240–241.

60. *CPJ* 1, no. 134. According to Tcherikover (commentary in *CPJ*), the structure appears to be located on the outskirts of the city. For another reference to a *proseukhē* at Crocodilopolis, see note 49 above.

61. *CPJ* 1, no. 138.

62. While Yadin (*Masada*, 185–187) had suggested that the synagogue at Masada originally functioned as such already during the time of Herod, Ehud Netzer (*Masada*, 405–413) in his final report dated the conversion of the building into a synagogue to the period of the Great Revolt (66–73/74 CE). A similar reevaluation of the dating of the synagogue at Gamla (Yavor, "The Synagogue," 60–61) has established that this synagogue too was constructed only in the first century CE.

63. Onn and Weksler-Bdolah, "Khirbet Umm el-'Umdan"; Weksler-Bdolah, "Khirbat Umm el-'Umdan."

64. See bibliography cited in Trümper, "The Oldest Original Synagogue" (representing the maximalist position that the structure functioned as a synagogue throughout its lifespan) and Matassa, *Invention*, 37–77 (representing the minimalist position that the building never was a synagogue).

65. For the most detailed argument to date for the absence of organized prayer in synagogues (or anywhere else) prior to 70 CE, see Fleischer, "On the Beginnings." A detailed argument in support of prayer in the ancient synagogue has been presented in Binder, *Into the Temple Courts*, 404–415.

66. See above, note 25.

67. Matt 6:5.

68. Fleischer ("On the Beginnings," 409) suggested that diaspora synagogues adopted this name in order to provide protection from attack. Levine (*The Ancient Synagogue*, 164–165) rightly critiqued this idea, but his solution—that the name "*proseukhē*" must indicate that it functioned as a place for prayer even in the first century CE—does not comport with the evidence adduced here. My proposal would appear to solve these problems.

69. Josephus, *Ant.* 14:259–261.

70. Runesson, *The Origins*, 429–454. He may well be correct with regard to the earlier institution, but I doubt that sacrifices were being offered in first-century-CE *proseukhaí*. Contra Runesson, I do not think that Philo's two references to sacrifices and prayers in a "temple" (*hieròn*) (*Spec. Laws* 3:171; *Unchangeable* 7–9) have anything to do with Judean practices in synagogues.

Chapter 7. The Origins of Judaism Reappraised

1. For a recent history of research on the redaction history of Ezra-Nehemiah, see Yoo, *Ezra and the Second Wilderness*, 6–12.

2. Ezra 7:1–9; cf. Ezra 7:11–12, where he is described as "the priest Ezra, the scribe, a scribe of the words of the commandments [*sōfēr divrê miṣwōt*] of YHWH and his statutes [*wəḥuqāyw*] upon Israel" and as "the priest Ezra, the scribe of the law [Aramaic: *sāfar dātā'*] of the God of heaven." Here and below, I have chosen to quote from Ezra-Nehemiah without attending to the Greek 1 Esdras, as the latter is widely viewed as a second-order source that provides no significant information on the matter at hand which is not found in the Hebrew/Aramaic Ezra-Nehemiah.

3. Ezra 7:10.

4. Ezra 7:25–26. For the suggestion that the Persian word "*dātā*" originally carried the meaning of an ad hoc decree but in later Hellenistic Judean writings came to be understood as a permanent set of laws, see Kleber, "*dātu ša šarri*"; Fried, *Ezra and the Law*, 14–18, 39.

5. Ezra 9:10b–12. Note that Ezra cites the commandments commanded by "the prophets"—in the plural. The alleged quotation cited by Ezra here appears nowhere in our biblical sources, although certain parallels might be sought; see Myers, *Ezra. Nehemiah*, 79.

6. Ezra 10:3.

7. Neh 8:1.

8. Neh 8:2–8 (quotation at 7b–8). For "*p-r-š*" as "to specify," see Schiffman, *Halakhah at Qumran*, 32–41.

9. Neh 8:13–15. Cf. Lev 23:39–43. See also discussion in chapter 5, in the section on Sukkot.

10. Neh 8:16–17.

11. Neh 8:18. Cf. Lev 23:36, 39; Num 29:35.

12. Neh 9:6–23 (quotation at 13–14).

13. Neh 10:1–40 (quotation at 30).

14. For another reference to heave offerings, tithes, and first fruits brought in accordance with "the instruction" (*hatôrāh*), see Neh 12:44.

15. Neh 13:1–3. Cf. Deut 23:4–7.

16. Neh 13:15–22 (quotation at 15–16).

17. While some scholars have argued for a relatively complete version of the Pentateuch that closely resembled the Pentateuch in its more-or-less final form,

others have argued for a pre-Pentateuchal text differing in many details from the Pentateuch as we know it. For a recent survey, see Yoo, *Ezra and the Second Wilderness*, 29–31.

18. Neh 8:8. For the idea that these narratives reflect intensive exegetical endeavors, see Fishbane, *Biblical Interpretation*, 107–134. For the possibly "descriptive" rather than "prescriptive" character of the laws as they are presented in Ezra-Nehemiah, see LeFebvre, *Collections, Codes, and Torah*, 96–145; Vroom, *The Authority of Law*, 174–201. See also the detailed discussion of LeFebvre's thesis below.

19. For a Persian-period date, see Albright, "Date and Personality"; Rudolph, *Esra und Nehemía*, xxiv–xxv; Myers, *Ezra. Nehemiah*, lxviii–lxx; Bright, *A History of Israel*, 398–399; Ackroyd, *I & II Chronicles*, 25–26; Cross, "A Reconstruction," 11–12; Clines, *Ezra, Nehemiah, Esther*, 12–14; Williamson, *Ezra, Nehemiah*, xxxv–xxxvi; Pakkala, *Ezra the Scribe*, 243–255. For a Hellenistic-period date, see Torrey, *Ezra Studies*, 30, 35; Pfeiffer, *Introduction*, 811–812, 824–828; Noth, *The Chronicler's History*, 69–73; Lebram, "Die Traditionsgeschichte der Esragestalt," 126–132; Garbini, *History and Ideology*, 151–169; J. Wright, *Rebuilding Identity*, 313–340; Fried, *Ezra and the Law*, 28. Recently, Israel Finkelstein (*Hasmonean Realities*) has argued on the basis of archaeological evidence that certain texts in Ezra-Nehemiah reflect Hasmonean-era realities. The relevant texts include the story about the construction of Jerusalem's city wall in Neh 3, the lists of returnees in Ezra 2:1–67 and Neh 7:6–68, references to the adversaries of Nehemiah, and descriptions of the territorial extent of Yehud. Finkelstein's argument has little ramifications for our study, however, as even if these texts could be established as Hasmonean creations, this would still not guarantee that all the *other* texts that came to be incorporated into Ezra-Nehemiah—such as those that refer to promulgation of the Mosaic "*tôrāh*"—necessarily date to this same time as well.

20. Contra Wellhausen's startling claim regarding Neh 8 (cited above in the introduction): "The credibility of the narrative appears on the face of it" (*Prolegomena*, 408 n. 1). For a notable appraisal of all these stories as fictional, see Torrey, *Ezra Studies*. For a recent survey of scholarship on the historicity of the Ezra-Nehemiah narratives, see Yoo, *Ezra and the Second Wilderness*, 10–12. Some scholars have argued that the letter purportedly written by a King Artaxerxes and quoted in Ezra 7:12–26 is an authentic Persian document; however, even if they are correct, the letter may well be so heavily edited by later hands that its original contents are no longer identifiable; see Grabbe, *A History of the Jews*, 1:76–78; Blenkinsopp, *Ezra-Nehemiah*, 146–147; Blenkinsopp, *Judaism*, 54–57.

21. J. Collins, *The Invention of Judaism*, 60. There is little reason to assume that Nehemiah's purported efforts would have been any more successful than Ezra's.

22. We should judge in a similar vein the story in 2 Kgs 22:8–23:25 (with a parallel but somewhat different version in 2 Chr 34–35) about Josiah reading from a recently discovered "book of the covenant" (*sēfer habərit*) before all the people

and subsequently initiating a sweeping crusade to uproot and destroy anything pertaining to cultic worship of deities other than YHWH; see Davies, "Josiah and the Law Book"; Lemche, "Did a Reform like Josiah's Happen?"

23. Frei, "Zentralgewalt und Lokalautonomie im Achämenidenreich"; "Zentralgewalt und Lokalautonomie im achämenidischen Kleinasien"; "Persian Imperial Authorization."

24. Blum, *Studien zur Komposition des Pentateuch*, 345–360; Kippenberg, *Die vorderasiatischen Erlösungsreligionen*, 181–182; Kratz, *Translatio imperii*, 233–255; Steck, *Der Abschluß der Prophetie*, 13–21; Steck, "Der Kanon," 16; Albertz, *A History of Israelite Religion*, 2:466–471; Blenkinsopp, *The Pentateuch*, 239–242 (however, cf. his "Was the Pentateuch"); Crüsemann, *The Torah*, 334–351; Knauf, *Die Umwelt*, 171–175; Berquist, *Judaism in Persia's Shadow*, 138–139; Zenger, *Einleitung in das Alte Testament*, 39–42 (but see modifications in the volume's 5th ed. [2004], 129–31); Zenger, "Der Pentateuch," 5–34; Carr, *Reading the Fractures of Genesis*, 325–333; Carr, "The Rise of Torah"; Seebaß, "Pentateuch," 189–190; Watts, *Reading Law*, 137–143; Schmid, *Erzväter und Exodus*, 291 n. 658; Schmid, "Persische Reichsautorisation"; Schmid, "The Persian Imperial Authorization"; Lee, *The Authority*. See also Hagedorn, "Local Law"; Kratz, "Temple and Torah," 79–81.

25. Wiesehöfer, "'Reichsgesetz' oder 'Einzelfallgerechtigkeit'?"; Rüterswörden, "Die persische Reichsautorisation"; Otto, "Kritik der Pentateuchkomposition," 169 n. 5; Otto, "Gesetzesfortschreibung," 375 n. 14; Otto, "Die nachpriesterschriftliche Pentateuchredaktion," 66–70; Otto, *Die Tora des Mose*, 51–52 n. 174; H. Schmitt, "Die Suche," 263–267; H. Schmitt, "Das spätdeuteronomistische Geschichtswerk"; Ska, *Introduction*, 217–226; Ska, "'Persian Imperial Authorization'"; Kuhrt, "The Persian Kings"; Knoppers, "An Achaemenid Imperial Authorization"; Yoo, *Ezra and the Second Wilderness*, 13–17. See also Grabbe, "The Law of Moses."

26. Yahwistic theophoric elements generally consisted of the abbreviated forms "YH" and "YHW"; see, e.g., *TJC*, nos. 20, 22–26; Lipschits and Vanderhooft, *The Yehud Stamp Impressions*; Avigad, *Bullae and Seals*; Eshel and Misgav, "Jericho papList" (see Lemaire, *Levantine Epigraphy*, 86, who wrote that the document likely dates to around 312 BCE, but the list of names probably did not change from the end of the Persian period). I will not engage here with evidence for YHWH venerators outside Yehud who probably did not self-identify as "Judeans"; evidence for such groups is suggested by Yahwistic names found in Samaria (see, e.g., Eshel, "Israelite Names") and in Idumea (see, e.g., Naveh, "Aramaic Inscriptions"; Lemaire, "New Aramaic Ostraca," 416–417), along with a YHWH temple on Mt. Gerizim (Magen, *Mount Gerizim Excavations*) and two possible YHWH shrines in Idumea (see Knowles, *Centrality Practiced*, 44–47; Lemaire, "New Aramaic Ostraca," 416–417).

27. *TAD*, A4.7:17–19 (cf. *TAD*, A4.8:16–18).

28. See discussion and bibliography in Fried, "A Silver Coin." The coin is nearly identical to a coin bearing the legend "Jehezekiah the governor" (*yǝḥizqīyāh*

hapeḥāh), which suggests that "the priest," like "the governor," held a highly influential position within governance of the province of Yehud. But see more recently Gitler and Lorber, "A New Chronology for the Yehizkiyah Coins," where the dates of these coins are lowered to the pre-Ptolemaic "Macedonian period."

29. E. Stern, "The Religious Revolution" (quotation at 201–202). See also his "Religion in Palestine," 253–255; *Archaeology of the Land of the Bible*, 2:478–479.

30. For surveys of scholarly reception of Stern's thesis, see Frevel and Pyschny, "A 'Religious Revolution' in Yehûd?"; de Hulster, *Figurines*, 1–12.

31. Frevel, Pyschny, and Cornelius, *A "Religious Revolution."*

32. R. Schmitt, "Gab es einen Bildersturm"; Cornelius, "'East Meets West'"; de Hulster, *Figurines*; Balcells Gallarreta, *Household and Family Religion*, 68–72.

33. Cornelius, "'East Meets West,'" 82–84. There has been much discussion in the scholarly literature about whether the so-called Judean pillar figurines should be regarded as "cultic"; for a recent discussion, see Darby, *Interpreting Judean Pillar Figurines*. Christian Frevel and Katharina Pyschny ("A Religious Revolution Devours Its Children") have forwarded a similar contention regarding the absence of miniature incense burners from the material culture of Yehud, arguing that there is no reason to assume that these objects had a specifically cultic use. For numerous incense "altars" found in the Persian stratum at the Judean site of Tell en-Naṣbeh, see Balcells Gallarreta, *Household and Family Religion*, 65–68.

34. Frevel and Pyschny, "A 'Religious Revolution' in Yehûd?," 8; R. Schmitt, "Continuity and Change," 103. The small volume of such finds should also be evaluated against the backdrop of a small population living in a small geographic area. Recent estimates of the population of Yehud have been suggested at 30,000 (Lipschits, "Demographic Changes," 364), 20,000 (Carter, *The Emergence of Yehud*, 195–205), and as little as 12,000 (I. Finkelstein, *Hasmonean Realities*, 57–59). The population of Jerusalem has been estimated at either 1,500 (Lipschits, "Achamenid Imperial Policy," 32), at 1,200 (Carter, *The Emergence of Yehud*, 288), or at "a few hundred people" (I. Finkelstein, *Hasmonean Realities*, 22, 57–58). For differing evaluations regarding the precise geographical boundaries of Yehud, see Carter, *The Emergence of Yehud*, 75–113; E. Stern, *Archaeology of the Land of the Bible*, 2:428–431; Lipschits, *The Fall and Rise*, 134–184; I. Finkelstein, *Hasmonean Realities*, 51–70.

35. *TJC*, nos. 2–12.

36. E.g., Meshorer, *TJC*, 7.

37. For Athena as Anat among the Phoenicians, see Bianco and Bonnet, "Sur les traces d'Athéna." For the possibility that the Judeans of Yehud may have made this connection as well, see Smith, "Jewish Religious Life," 239.

38. *TJC*, nos. 20–26.

39. *TJC*, no. 1. For a comprehensive and judicious discussion of earlier scholarship, see Kienle, *Der Gott auf dem Flügelrad*. For a more recent discussion, see Shenkar, "

40. It should be noted here that the theophoric elements in names of Judeans that have been preserved on coins, stamp impressions, bullae, and a papyrus document dating to this period invariably relate to either YHWH or ʾĒl (the latter usually thought to be identified with YHWH by this time). I am not aware of any epigraphic material found in Judea proper that includes names of Judeans bearing clearly non-Yahwistic theophoric elements. Morton Smith ("Jewish Religious Life," 236–237) has suggested that two seals may contain Judean theophoric names that refer to Horus and one may contain a theophoric name referring to Shamash, but he notes that "all three are of uncertain provenance and two of dubious interpretation."

41. The standard edition for most of these texts today is Porten and Yardeni's *TAD*. Ostraca from the Clermont-Ganneau collection published only after the last volume of *TAD* appeared may be found in Lozachmeur, *La collection Clermont-Ganneau*.

42. In some cases, the Judean deity is referred to as "YHH of hosts [*ṣəvāʾōt*]" (Porten, *Archives from Elephantine*, 105–110). His blessing is invoked in salutations included in correspondences, by his name various oaths were sworn, and on his behalf monies were collected. In one document addressed to an Achaemenid official (*TAD*, A4.10:8), Judeans refer to YHW as "our god [ʾelāhāʾ zílān]." Another document (*TAD*, A4.7:15, 27–28) describes him as "YHW lord of the heavens [*YHW mārēʾ šəmayāʾ*]" and as "YHW god of the heavens [*YHW ʾelāh šəkhan*]." Elsewhere (*TAD*, B3.12:3; cf. B3.3:2; B3.5:2; B3.10:2; B3.11:1–2), the Judean deity is described as "the god dwelling (in) Elephantine the fortress [ʾelāhāʾ šəkhan yēv bîrtāʾ]." Judean personal names with Yahwistic elements are found frequently on ostraca and in papyrus documents (Porten, *Archives from Elephantine*, 133–150). For a survey and analysis of these names aimed at deciphering Elephantine Judeans' perceptions of YHW's powers and his role in human affairs, see Smith, "Jewish Religious Life," 227.

43. This has been duly noted in Knauf, "Elephantine und das vor-biblische Judentum"; Grabbe, "Elephantine and the Torah"; Kratz, "Temple and Torah"; Kratz, *Historical and Biblical Israel*, 137–147. Lemaire (*Levantine Epigraphy*, 87–88) has apologetically suggested that the lack of any references to Torah at Elephantine is a "strong argument in favour of the dating of the Ezra mission to 398"—i.e., after the Elephantine documents were written.

44. *TAD*, B2.8:5. Even if we were to interpret an oath of this sort as something other than explicit veneration, it is difficult to imagine how such an act could have been regarded as permissible by the Torah; see, e.g., Exod 23:13. Note that the name "Jedania" (*yədanyāʾ*) is spelled here with a final ʾaleph rather than with the hēh in the usual theophoric "yāh."

45. *TAD*, B7.2:7. For a different interpretation, see Rohrmoser, *Götter, Tempel und Kult*, 425. For critique, see Granerød, *Dimensions of Yahwism*, 250. Karel van der Toorn's recent study of Amherst Papyrus 63 ("Eshem-Bethel and

Herem-Bethel") led him to conclude that "Herembethel" should be identified as an aspect of the deity "Bethel" ("Bethel-*as*-Herem") and as certainly distinct from YHW.

46. *TAD*, B7.3:3. For various interpretations, see Porten, *Archives from Elephantine*, 154–156. For a somewhat different reconstruction, see Rohrmoser, *Götter, Tempel und Kult*, 147–148.

47. Granerød, *Dimensions of Yahwism*, 250–252.

48. *TAD*, A4.1:1. See chapter 5, in the excursus on Passover at Elephantine.

49. *TAD*, A3.7:1; cf. A4.2:1; A4.4:1, 6.

50. *TAD*, D7.21:3. For considerations of other possible readings, see Lemaire, *Levantine Epigraphy*, 52–53 n. 69. For apologetic (and ultimately unconvincing) interpretations of the above references, see Porten, *Archives from Elephantine*, 153–160.

51. *TAD*, C3.15. The date given is "year 5," which may refer to the fifth regnal year of Darius II, who began his reign in 423 BCE, or else of Amyrtaeus, a native Egyptian who led a successful insurrection against the Persians in 404 BCE. See studies cited in Porten, *Archives from Elephantine*, 162 nn. 38–39.

52. Karel van der Toorn's recent study of Amherst Papyrus 63 ("Eshem-Bethel and Herem-Bethel") led him to conclude that "Eshembethel," like "Herembethel," should be identified as an aspect of the deity "Bethel" ("Bethel-*as*-Eshem") and as certainly distinct from YHW. Anathbethel, he argues, is a distinct, female deity whose name means "Anat, the consort of Bethel" (i.e., "Anat-*of*-Bethel"). For other detailed discussions regarding the polytheistic beliefs of the Elephantine Judeans, see Rohrmoser, *Götter, Tempel und Kult*; Granerød, *Dimensions of Yahwism*. For apologetic interpretations that downplay the apparent ramifications of this document, see Porten, *Archives from Elephantine*, 163 n. 41, 164.

53. Porten, *Archives from Elephantine*, 148–149 nn. 132–133. Porten himself apologetically (and unconvincingly) conjectured that in cases where a Judean child with a Yahwistic name had a father with a non-Yahwistic theophoric name, "many of these may have been non-Jews who married Jewish women and were absorbed into the Jewish community." In cases where the father bore a Judean name but the son a non-Yahwistic theophoric name, Porten posited that the mother had been a non-Judean prior to her marriage to a Judean and had named the child after her own father.

54. Deut 12:5, 11; 14:23–25; 15:20; 16:2, 6–7, 11; 17:8–10; 18:6; 26:2; 31:11.

55. *TAD*, A4.9:3, 10; A4.7:26; A4.8:25. The temple is usually referred to in Aramaic as an "ʾagōrāʾ," the same term used to refer to the temples of native Egyptian deities in other Aramaic documents, and sometimes also as "the house of YHW" (*bêt YHW*); see discussion in Granerød, *Dimensions of Yahwism*, 104–108. Structural finds excavated at the southern end of Elephantine in 1997 by a German archaeological team led by Cornelius von Pilgrim have been identified as

remains of this temple; see von Pilgrim, "Temple des Jahu"; Rohrmoser, *Götter, Tempel und Kult*, 161–185; Granerød, *Dimensions of Yahwism*, 95–104.

56. *"kāhănayā'"*: *TAD*, A4.1:1; A4.3:1; A4.7:1. *"ləḥēn"*: *TAD*, B3.2:2; B3.3:2; B3.4:3, 25; B3.5:2, 23; B3.7:2; B3.10:2, 23, 27; B3.11:1, 9, 17; B3.12:1, 10, 33; C3.13:45, 48. *"ləḥēnāh"*: *TAD*, B3.12:2.

57. *TAD*, A4.7:21, 25, 28; A4.8:21, 24–25, 27.

58. *TAD*, A4.7 (the better-preserved earlier draft) and A4.8 (the more fragmentary later draft). This incident is apparently also described in the fragmentary A4.5. *"Bagôhi"* is the Aramaic form of the Persian name *"Bagavahya,"* rendered in Greek as *"Bagôsēs"* or *"Bagôas"*; see Josephus, *Ant.* 11:297–301.

59. *TAD*, A4.7:17–19, 22–29 (cf. *TAD*, A4.8:16–18, 21–27).

60. *TAD*, A4.9.

61. *TAD*, A4.10.

62. Several scholars have conjectured that the Judean authorities in Jerusalem looked askance at the Elephantine temple, which would explain why the Judeans of Elephantine received no answer to the earlier letter they had sent to Jerusalem's high priest Jehohanan and the other dignitaries of Yehud (see Porten, *Archives from Elephantine*, 293 n. 29). Even if this were the case (obviously one can imagine other reasons why the letter might have gone unanswered), the Elephantine Judeans appear to have been unaware of any such sensitivities on the part of the Judean officials in Jerusalem. In the memorandum recording the joint reply of the governors of Yehud and Samaria, Bagohi and Delaiah requested that in the temple to be rebuilt "meal-offering and incense" should be brought to the altar (*TAD*, A4.9:9–11), implicitly excluding animal sacrifices. This exclusion is spelled out clearly in the letter written by Jedaniah and his colleagues to a (probably) Persian official, where the Judeans pledge that if the official allows the temple to be rebuilt, they will offer only incense and meal offerings but not "sheep, ox and goat [as] burnt-offering" (*TAD*, A4.10:10–11). Again, there is little reason to think that any of this may have been triggered by a desire to conform with a Deuteronomistic call for cult centralization, which presumably would have rejected both animal and vegetable sacrifices outside Jerusalem (see, e.g., Deut 14:22–26; 26:1–11). Scholars have suggested that the offering of sheep may have been a contentious issue for priests serving in the adjacent temple dedicated to the Egyptian ram-headed god Khnum, and that the sacrifice of *any* animal might have been offensive to Persian sensibilities surrounding the profanation of fire; see citations in Porten, *Archives from Elephantine*, 293 n. 29.

63. For a similar assessment, see Kratz, *Historical and Biblical Israel*, 135–147; "Fossile Überreste." As against Wellhausen's comment (*Israelitische und jüdische Geschichte*, 178) that the community at Elephantine represented a "fossilized remnant of unreformed Judaism [*fossile Überrest des unreformierten Judentums*]," Kratz argued that this community was in fact a "living species [*lebendige*

Spezies]" far more representative of other Judean communities than Wellhausen and others would have.

64. The entire corpus consists of 250 or more texts, of which 113 were published in 2014 by Laurie Pearce and Cornelia Wunsch (*Documents of Judean Exiles*) and an additional 42 have been consulted by Tero Alstola (*Judeans in Babylonia*) in his synthetic work on the corpus published in 2020.

65. The precise location of all these sites remains unknown, although it has been suggested that they were to be found in the Nippur region, southeast of Babylon; see Pearce and Wunsch, *Documents of Judean Exiles*, 6–7; Alstola, *Judeans in Babylonia*, 104–108.

66. Most were published between 1898 and 1912, and the remainder appeared in 1985 and 1997; for full publication information, see Alstola, *Judeans in Babylonia*, 45 nn. 261–262. For an online database that presents photos, transliterated transcriptions, and translations, see Zadok et al., *Cuneiform Texts*.

67. See Alstola, *Judeans in Babylonia*, 161–163, 218, 268–272. While Elias Bickerman ("The Generation of Ezra and Nehemiah") had claimed in 1978 that naming patterns in the Murašû archive suggest that a "break with syncretism occurred in the generation of Ezra," Tero Alstola (*Judeans in Babylonia*, 269–270) has now shown that naming patterns in the newly published archive from Yāhūdu may not support Bickerman's earlier conclusions.

68. See Pearce and Wunsch, *Documents of Judean Exiles*, 13–14; Alstola, *Judeans in Babylonia*, 270.

69. See Alstola, *Judeans in Babylonia*, 141, 213–218, 267.

70. See Alstola, *Judeans in Babylonia*, 267.

71. For a funerary stele from Persian Cyprus mentioning a man named "Matan ʿaštārt" (i.e., gift of the goddess ʿAštārt) who was the son of a man bearing the Yahwistic name " ʿazaryāhû," see Heltzer, *The Province Judah*, 97–100. For doubtful epigraphic evidence of Judeans in Persian Asia Minor, see Lemaire, *Levantine Epigraphy*, 68–70.

72. Josephus, *Ag. Ap.* 1:183–204. For the most detailed treatment to date, see Bar-Kochva, *Pseudo-Hecataeus*.

73. Diodorus Siculus, *Bibliotheca Historica* 40.3 (in Photius, *Bibliotheca*, Cod. 244); English translation from Bar-Kochva, *The Image of the Jews*, 100–103.

74. Among the possible verses intended here: Lev 26:46; 27:34; Num 36:13; Deut 4:44–45; 28:69.

75. Photius, *Bibliotheca*, Cod. 244; English translation from Bar-Kochva, *The Image of the Jews*, 102–103.

76. See, e.g., Bar-Kochva, *Pseudo-Hecataeus*, 18–43; *The Image of the Jews*, 90–135; Grabbe, "Hecataeus of Abdera"; J. Collins, "Hecataeus as a Witness to Judaism."

77. See scholarship cited in the previous note. Even these scholars usually understand that the last sentence of the Diodorean excerpt ("But during the [foreign] rules that happened later . . .") is not from Hecataeus but rather was added by Diodorus himself; see, e.g., Bar-Kochva, *The Image of the Jews*, 102 n. 31.

78. For the almost universal reception of this emendation within scholarship, see Bar-Kochva, *The Image of the Jews*, 105–106 n. 43. For a recent critique of this redaction, see Kratz, "Greek Historians," 272 nn. 36–37.

79. See, e.g., Albertz, "An End to the Confusion?," 40–45; Grabbe, "The Law of Moses," 98–99.

80. Daniel Schwartz ("Diodorus Siculus 40.3") has forwarded a number of considerations for thinking that Diodorus drew from a "Pseudo-Hecataeus" that may have been the work of a Hasmonean-period Judean author, much like—if not identical with—the composition cited by Josephus and generally regarded by scholars to be a pseudepigraphic work. See also Gmirkin, *Berossus and Genesis*, 38–71; "Greek Evidence." Noting that the excerpt of Diodorus itself does not mention its source at all, and that it is only Photius who puts the ascription to Hecataeus into the mouth of Diodorus, Reinhard Kratz ("Greek Historians," 271–272) has questioned whether Diodorus had at all ever really credited Hecataeus as his source of information. See also ibid. (272–273) for critiques against source-critical and *Tendenzkritik* arguments for an authentic Hecataean attribution.

81. Katell Berthelot ("Hecataeus of Abdera," 5 n. 19) has summarized current scholarship on the matter quite succinctly: "Contemporary commentators of Diodorus' work tend to consider him less dependent on his sources than was previously thought. . . . Moreover, Diodorus used several sources, not just one, and certainly mingled them." Concerning Diodorus's use of Hecataeus's work, Berthelot cited Anne Burton (*Diodorus Siculus, Book 1*, 34), who wrote, "It is too easy to attribute to an author, the major part of whose work has been lost, passages for which an alternative source is not immediately apparent. Moreover, it cannot be ignored that certain passages may well have had their origins in authors considerably later than Hecataeus, and that Diodorus is himself responsible for others." Returning to our passage, I would just note that a reference is made to unique Judean customs surrounding burial of the dead; this reference is most readily understandable if it was first written in the mid to late first century BCE. It was only at this time that Judeans had begun to observe the unique practice of secondary burial in ossuaries; the practice certainly did not yet exist ca. 300 BCE.

82. Let. Aris. 15, 31.

83. Let. Aris. 39.

84. Let. Aris. 122.

85. Let. Aris. 128–166. The regulations mentioned in this passage are discussed above in the sections on early textual evidence in chapters 1, 2, and 4.

86. The work refers to a living Queen Arsinoe, sister of Ptolemy (Let. Aris. 41), a historical figure who is known to have reigned from the time of her marriage in the early to mid-270s BCE until her death ca. 270 BCE.

87. White, Keddie, and Flexsenhar, "The Epistle of Aristeas," 34–38.

88. Dating is based primarily on supposed citations in the works of third- and second-century-BCE authors; for a critical discussion, see Clancy, "The Date of LXX." For a third-century-BCE date argued on the basis of language, see Lee, *A Lexical Study*.

89. Mélèze-Modrzejewski ("Jewish Law"; "The Septuagint as Nomos") has argued that the translation of the Septuagint was motivated by a need for a legal code to be used for adjudication purposes in Ptolemaic Egypt. For a detailed critique of Mélèze-Modrzejewski's hypothesis, see Altmann, "The Significance," who argued that the fact of the Septuagint's translation suggests the importance of the Pentateuch in philosophical terms and that it had value in promoting group affiliation, but not that it served any practical judicial function. See also the discussion of LeFebvre's hypothesis below.

90. Blank, "The LXX Renderings."

91. Dem. frags. 1–5 (in Eusebius, *Praep. ev.* 9.19:4; 9.21:1–19; 9.29:1–3, 15–16; see *OTP* 2:848–854).

92. Josephus, *Ant.* 12:142 (translation from Bickerman, "The Seleucid Charter," 316).

93. Josephus, *Ant.* 12:145–146.

94. Josephus, *Ant.* 12:150.

95. Bickerman, "The Seleucid Charter"; "A Seleucid Proclamation."

96. Bickerman, "The Seleucid Charter," 355. For critique of Bickerman's interpretation, see Honigman, *Tales of High Priests*, 25–26, 303–306. For a rebuttal, see J. Collins, *The Invention of Judaism*, 194 n. 60.

97. See discussions and bibliographies in Grabbe, "Jewish Historiography and Scripture," 139–142; Grabbe, "Hyparchs, *Oikonomoi*, and Mafiosi," 81–84; Gera, "The Seleucid Road."

98. Williams, "The Date of Ecclesiasticus."

99. Eckhard Schnabel (*Law and Wisdom*, 40–41) listed over fifty of these terms throughout the work.

100. See, inter alia, Sir 44:1–45:26.

101. See citations in B. Wright, "Torah and Sapiential Pedagogy," nn. 3–6.

102. J. Collins, *The Invention of Judaism*, 90

103. The same may be said with regard to the few copies of Pentateuchal scrolls found at Qumran that have been dated on paleographic grounds to the Early Hellenistic period. The earliest (4Q17) has been dated by Frank Moore Cross to the mid-third century BCE, while two others (4Q15 and 5Q1) have been dated to the late third or early second centuries BCE (see references to official publications in Webster, "Chronological Index," 378–380). Another three Pentateuchal manuscripts written in paleo-Hebrew script have been dated to a similar period of time (ibid., 378). As far as all these dates are concerned, however, it is crucial to cite here the caution noted by Cross ("The Development," 135) regarding early scripts thought to predate the Hasmonean era:

"The dating of documents in the Archaic or proto-Jewish period (ca. 250–150 B.C.) is less precise, still being largely based on typological sequence." Aside from the Hebrew texts, one fragment of a Greek translation of Deuteronomy (4Q122) has been tentatively dated to the early or mid-second century BCE, but here too the publisher emphasized that the very small sample available for comparative analysis means that "the dating must be more than usually uncertain" (Parsons, "The Palaeography," 12). Note that only one Pentateuchal manuscript (4Q22) has ever been dated using radiocarbon dating, but the results were inconclusive; it was dated to either 164–144 BCE or 116 BCE–48 CE (see survey and citations in Webster, "Chronological Index," 364–367, esp. 366).

104. LeFebvre, *Collections, Codes, and Torah*.

105. J. Finkelstein, "Ammiṣaduqa's Edict," 103.

106. Malul, *The Comparative Method*, 129 (emphasis in the original).

107. Kraus, "Ein zentrales Problem"; Westbrook, "Cuneiform Law Codes"; Westbrook, "Introduction," 16–19.

108. Westbrook, "The Nature and Origins," 89.

109. Westbrook, "Introduction," 14.

110. Gagarin, *Early Greek Law*, 132–133, 144–146; *Writing Greek Law*, 145–175. Gagarin tied his argument to the work of legal philosopher H. L. A. Hart (*The Concept of Law*, 8–13, 92–107, 245–247), who posited that true "laws" are distinguished from other societal rules (such as morals or etiquette) only where there exists what he called a "rule of recognition"—a foundational criterion for determining which subset of rules is specially singled out as authoritatively binding "law." Cf. Thomas, "Written in Stone?," esp. 61.

111. Gagarin, *Early Greek Law*, 19–50; *Writing Greek Law*, 13–38.

112. Gagarin, *Early Greek Law*, 81–97; *Writing Greek Law*, 39–66. For an assessment that dates the beginning of large-scale legislation to a somewhat later period, see Hölkeskamp, "Written Law."

113. Gagarin, *Early Greek Law*, 51–80. For the problematic character of these literary accounts, see Hölkeskamp, "Written Law," 87–89.

114. Gagarin and Woodruff, "Early Greek Legal Thought," 24–25.

115. Gagarin and Woodruff, "Early Greek Legal Thought," 13, 23–24. For the Spartan notion that Lycurgus's laws derived from the Delphic oracle, see Plutarch, *Lyc.* 6:1.

116. Gagarin, *Early Greek Law*, 144.

117. Gagarin, *Writing Greek Law*, 38.

118. Gagarin, *Early Greek Law*, 144.

119. Gagarin, *Writing Greek Law*, 50.

120. Gagarin, *Writing Greek Law*, 60–63; Stroud, *The Axones and Kyrbeis*.

121. Hölkeskamp, "Written Law," 101; Gagarin, *Writing Greek Law*, 50. Cf. Thomas, "Written in Stone?," 73.

122. Gagarin, *Early Greek Law*, 133. See also Gagarin, *Writing Greek Law*, 1.

123. Gagarin, *Early Greek Law*, 146. See also Gagarin, *Writing Greek Law*, 174–175.

124. For important recent overviews and discussions, see Parker, "What Are Sacred Laws?"; Parker, "Law and Religion"; Lupu, *Greek Sacred Law*, 3–112; Carbon and Pirenne-Delforge, "Beyond Greek 'Sacred Laws.'" An extremely useful corpus titled "The Collection of Greek Ritual Norms" (CGRN) is available online at http://cgrn.ulg.ac.be/.

125. A convenient survey of these ideas and their relationship to written law is found in Martens, *One God, One Law*, 1–66. See also Hayes, *What's Divine about Divine Law?*, 54–89.

126. Smith, "Hellenization," 125–126; Gagarin, *Writing Greek Law*, 225–241 (see 232–241 for how Ptolemaic Egypt may have differed from contemporary Greece). For excellent surveys of Greek philosophers of law during both the Classical and Hellenistic periods, see the variously authored chapters 2–5 in Miller and Biondi, *A History of the Philosophy of Law*.

127. LeFebvre, *Collections, Codes, and Torah*, 146–182.

128. Wolff, "Plurality of Laws"; "Law in Ptolemaic Egypt"; *Das Recht der griechischen Papyri.*

129. Wolff, "Plurality of Laws," 215; Wolff, *Das Recht der griechischen Papyri*, 1:55; Mélèze-Modrzejewski, "Jewish Law," 81–84; Mélèze-Modrzejewski, "The Septuagint as Nomos," 190–193. An important datum for this argument is a document from the Faiyum (*CPJ* 1, no. 128, dated 218 BCE) that has been reconstructed as referring to an agreement "[in accordance with the c]ivic [law] of the [Ju]deans [*(katà tòn nómon p)olitikòn tõn (Iou)daíōn*]" (but see the alternative reconstructions in Victor Tcherikover's commentary in *CPJ*, ad loc.).

130. For a critique of LeFebvre's hypothesis, see Altmann, "The Significance." To the best of my knowledge, the earliest surviving reference to the Judeans' "ancestral law" (*tòn pátrion nómon*) in the papyri from Egypt dates to the second half of the second century BCE; see Cowey and Maresch, *Urkunden des Politeuma*, 105 (no. 9:7–8, 28–29).

131. LeFebvre, *Collections, Codes, and Torah*, 183–240.

132. Josephus (*Ag. Ap.* 2:154, 161–163, 223–224, 279) explicitly compared Moses to the Greek lawgivers and polemically argued that Moses preceded (and therefore is to be held in higher esteem than) Greek lawgivers such as Lycurgus, Solon, and Zaleucus. For further parallels between features found within the Greek legends surrounding the ancient lawgivers and the biblical narratives surrounding Moses, see Knoppers, "Moses and the Greek Lawgivers."

133. Contra Knoppers and Harvey, "The Pentateuch," who contend that indirect knowledge about the publication of local law codes in Archaic and Classical Greece, along with the "Twelve Tables" in fifth-century-BCE Rome, had some sort of influence in "the promulgation of the Pentateuch as Torah" as early as the Persian period.

134. 1 Macc 13:41–42.

135. J. Collins, *Daniel*, 61.
136. Dan 7:1–14 (quotation at 8).
137. Dan 7:16–27 (quotation at 25).
138. Dan 8:1–12 (quotation at 10–12).
139. Dan 8:13–26 (quotation at 24).
140. Dan 9:20–27 (quotation at 26–27). Instead of "and on the corner [*wə ʿal kənaf*]," some suggest reading "and in their place [*wə ʿal kanām*]," meaning that the desolating abomination will take the place of the proper "sacrifice and offering"; see J. Collins, *Daniel*, 346 n. 69 (where it is noted that the Greek and Latin read "on the temple"). The phrase "abomination that desolates" has merited much treatment among scholars; see ibid., 63, 357–358.
141. Dan 11:29–39 (quotation at 30–32).
142. 1 Macc 1:56–57.
143. 1 Macc 1:43–64.
144. See, e.g., 1 Macc 6:59.
145. 1 Macc 1:60–64.
146. 1 Macc 2:27.
147. 1 Macc 2:49, 56; 4:47; 6:53.
148. 1 Macc 2:31–41. For further discussion, see chapter 5, in the section on early evidence relating to Sabbath prohibitions.
149. 2 Macc 3:1.
150. 2 Macc 6:1.
151. E.g., 2 Macc 6:6–11, 18–20; 7:1; 11:31.
152. 2 Macc 6:10–7:42.
153. 2 Macc 7:30.
154. *Invokes defense of the law*: 2 Macc 8:21; 13:14; 15:9. "*Read aloud the holy book*": 2 Macc 8:23.
155. Rappaport, *The First Book of Maccabees*, 60–61.
156. Doran, *2 Maccabees*, 14–15.
157. Honigman, *Tales of High Priests*, 229–258 and passim.
158. J. Collins, "Temple or Taxes?"; Werman, "On Religious Persecution"; Bar-Kochva, "The Religious Persecutions."
159. Kratz, *Historical and Biblical Israel*, 178. For somewhat analogous views, see Davies, "Scenes from the Early History of Judaism," 173–182; Niehr, "Religio-Historical Aspects," 242–244.
160. Kratz, *Historical and Biblical Israel*, 185.
161. Ibid., 186.
162. Ibid.
163. J. Collins, *The Invention of Judaism*, 184–185. See also Kratz, "Temple and Torah," 103.
164. Josephus, *Ant.* 13:257–258. Cf. Josephus, *War* 1:63; *Ant.* 15:253–256.
165. Strabo, *Geogr.* 16.2:34; Ptolemy, *Historia Herodis*, in Ammonius, *De adfinium vocabulorum differentia*, no. 243 (Stern, *GLAJJ* 1:356). For archaeological evidence

indicating that the residents of Idumea observed the purity laws of the Torah by the first century CE, see Adler, "The Archaeology of Purity," 301–304.

166. Josephus, *Ant.* 13:318.

167. Strabo, *Historica hypomnemata*, in Josephus, *Ant.* 13:319.

168. See scholarship cited in S. Cohen, *The Beginnings of Jewishness*, 116 n. 21; Levin, "The Religion of Idumea," 17 n. 143.

169. For the conquest of "the nation of the Cutheans" and the destruction of their temple at Mt. Gerizim by John Hyrcanus I, see Josephus, *War* 1:62; *Ant.* 13:255. For the numismatic and archaeological evidence that dates these events to ca. 110 BCE, see Barag, "New Evidence," 7–8; Magen, *Mount Gerizim Excavations*, 98.

170. See the scholarship cited in Bourgel, "The Samaritans," 1 n. 2.

171. For accessible surveys of scholarship on this question, see Pummer, "The Samaritans and Their Pentateuch"; Anderson and Giles, *The Samaritan Pentateuch*, 7–23. Note that the question of a possible Samari(t)an contribution to the composition of the Pentateuch is a separate matter that will not detain us here, as is the question of when the distinct Samaritan revisions were later introduced into the text.

172. Bourgel, "The Destruction"; "The Samaritans."

173. As fellow venerators of YHWH, the Samaritans would have had to contend with far fewer consequences as a result of their "conversion" than would the pagan Idumeans and Itureans. This notwithstanding, the incorporation of the Samaritans into the Judean sphere was not to endure. Unlike the Idumeans, who retained their ethnic identity well into the first century CE but were eventually absorbed into their surroundings and lost to history, the Samaritans ultimately went their own way—holding on to the Pentateuch but developing their own distinct Samaritan identity apart from Judaism.

174. See S. Cohen, *The Beginnings of Jewishness*, esp. 109–197.

175. For accusations of improper practice of the Torah in the Dead Sea Scrolls, see Doering, "Law and Lawlessness," 24–27.

176. Smith, "The Dead Sea Sect," 360. See also Sussmann, "The History of the Halakha," 61–64.

177. Baumgarten, *The Flourishing of Jewish Sects*, 18–28.

178. While some scholars have argued for the advent of some form of sectarianism among Judeans as early as the Persian period, there are simply no grounds to suspect that what was at stake might have been polemics over how to understand legal matters in the Pentateuch. For early Judean sectarianism, see, e.g., Smith, "The Dead Sea Sect"; Rofé, "The Onset of Sects"; Blenkinsopp, "A Jewish Sect"; Blenkinsopp, "The Development of Jewish Sectarianism."

Bibliography

Abegg, Martin G. *The Dead Sea Scrolls Concordance*. Vols. 1–3. Leiden: Brill, 2003–2010.

Ackroyd, Peter R. *I & II Chronicles, Ezra, Nehemiah: Introduction and Commentary*. London: SCM, 1973.

Adler, Yonatan. "Along Ethnic Lines: The Case for Stepped Pools and Chalk Vessels as Markers of Jewish Purity Observance." In *Negotiating Identities: Conflict, Conversion, and Consolidation in Early Judaism and Christianity (200 BCE–600 CE)*, edited by Karin Hedner Zetterholm, Anders Runesson, Magnus Zetterholm, and Ceciia Wassén. Lanham, MD: Lexington/Fortress, forthcoming.

———. "The Ancient Synagogue and the Ritual Bath: The Archaeological Evidence and Its Relevance to an Early Rabbinic Enactment." *Cathedra* 128 (2008): 51–72 (Hebrew).

———. "The Archaeology of Purity: Archaeological Evidence for the Observance of Ritual Purity in Ereẓ-Israel from the Hasmonean Period until the End of the Talmudic Era (164 BCE–400 CE)." PhD diss., Bar-Ilan University, 2011 (Hebrew).

———. "The Assemblage of Ancient Tefillin Remains from the Judean Desert: A Preliminary Report on a New In-Progress Research Project." *Te'uda* 32–33 (2021): 855–871 (Hebrew).

———. "Between Priestly Cult and Common Culture: The Material Evidence of Ritual Purity Observance in Early Roman Jerusalem Reassessed." *JAJ* 7 (2016): 228–248.

———. "The Distribution of Tefillin Finds among the Judean Desert Caves." In *The Caves of Qumran: Proceedings of the International Conference, Lugano 2014*, edited by Marcello Fidanzio, 161–173. Leiden: Brill, 2016.

———. "The Hellenistic Origins of Jewish Ritual Immersion." *JJS* 69 (2018): 1–21.

———. "The Imperial Cult Meets Judaism: The Stepped Pools Adjacent to the Augusteum at Samaria-Sebaste." *Journal of Eastern Mediterranean Archaeology and Heritage Studies* 9 (2021): 395–414.

————. "The Impurity of Stone Vessels in 11QTᵃ and CD in Light of the Chalk Vessel Finds at Kh. Qumran." *DSD* 27 (2020): 66–96.

————. "Representations of the Temple Menorah in Ancient Jewish Art in Light of Rabbinic Halakhah and Archaeological Finds." *Recent Innovations in the Study of Jerusalem* 13 (2007): 161–172 (Hebrew).

————. "Ritual Baths Adjacent to Tombs: An Analysis of the Archaeological Evidence in Light of the Halakhic Sources." *JSJ* 40 (2009): 55–73.

————. "The Ritual Baths near the Temple Mount and Extra-Purification before Entering the Temple Courts: A Reply to Eyal Regev." *IEJ* 56 (2006): 209–215.

————. "The Ritual Immersion Pools." In *Excavations at the Site of the Jerusalem International Convention Center (Binyanē Ha-'Uma–Crowne Plaza Hotel) 2009–2010: Pottery Workshops from the Second Century BCE to the Second Century CE near Jerusalem*, vol. 1, edited by Ron Beeri and Danit Levi. Jerusalem: IAA, forthcoming.

————. "Second Temple Period Ritual Baths Adjacent to Agricultural Installations: The Archaeological Evidence in Light of the Halakhic Sources." *JJS* 59 (2008): 62–72.

————. "Two Types of Four-Compartment Tefillin Cases from the Judean Desert Caves." *DSD* 29 (2022): 27–51.

Adler, Yonatan, Avner Ayalon, Miryam Bar-Matthews, Rick Flesher, Gal Yasur, and Tami Zilberman. "Geochemical Analyses of Jewish Chalk Vessel Remains from Roman-Era Production and Settlement Sites in the Southern Levant." *Archaeometry* 63 (2021): 266–283.

Adler, Yonatan, and Omri Lernau. "The Pentateuchal Dietary Proscription against Finless and Scaleless Aquatic Species in Light of Ancient Fish Remains." *Tel Aviv* 48 (2021): 5–26.

Adler, Yonatan, and Dennis Mizzi. "A Roman-Era Chalk Quarry and Chalk-Vessel Workshop at ʿEinot Amitai in the Lower Galilee: A Preliminary Report." *IEJ* 72 (2022): 113–132.

Albertz, Rainer. "An End to the Confusion? Why the Old Testament Cannot Be a Hellenistic Book!" In *Did Moses Speak Attic? Jewish Historiography and Scripture in the Hellenistic Period*, edited by Lester L. Grabbe, 30–46. Sheffield: Sheffield Academic, 2001.

————. *A History of Israelite Religion in the Old Testament Period*. Vol. 2, *From the Exile to the Maccabees*. Translated by John Bowden. London: SCM, 1994.

Albright, William F. "A Biblical Fragment from the Maccabaean Age: The Nash Papyrus." *JBL* 56 (1937): 145–176.

————. "The Date and Personality of the Chronicler Author(s)." *JBL* 40 (1921): 104–124.

Alstola, Tero. *Judeans in Babylonia: A Study of Deportees in the Sixth and Fifth Centuries BCE*. Leiden: Brill, 2020.

Altmann, Peter. "The Significance of the Divine Torah in Ptolemaic Egypt in Documentary and Literary Sources from the Third and Second Centuries BCE." *JSJ* 52 (2021): 1–31.

Anderson, Robert T., and Terry Giles. *The Samaritan Pentateuch: An Introduction to Its Origin, History, and Significance for Biblical Studies*. Atlanta: SBL, 2012.

Ariel, Donald T. "A Second Seleucid Coin Attributed to Jerusalem." *Israel Numismatic Research* 14 (2019): 41–72.

Ariel, Donald T., and Jean-Philippe Fontanille. *The Coins of Herod: A Modern Analysis and Die Classification*. Leiden: Brill, 2012.

Ariel, Donald T., and Yair Shoham. "Locally Stamped Handles and Associated Body Fragments of the Persian and Hellenistic Periods." In *Excavations at the City of David, 1978–1985, Directed by Yigal Shiloh*, vol. 6, *Inscriptions*, 137–171. Jerusalem: IAHUJ, 2000.

Arnold, William R. "The Passover Papyrus from Elephantine." *JBL* 31 (1912): 1–33.

Aviam, Mordechai, Hisao Kuwabara, Shuichi Hasegawa, and Yitzhak Paz. "A 1st–2nd Century CE Assembly Room (Synagogue?) in a Jewish Estate at Tel Rekhesh, Lower Galilee." *Tel Aviv* 46 (2019): 128–142.

Avigad, Nahman. *Beth She'arim: Report on the Excavations during 1936–1940*. Vol. 3, *Catacombs 12–23*. New Brunswick, NJ: Rutgers University Press on behalf of the IES; IAHUJ, 1976.

———. *Bullae and Seals from a Post-Exilic Judean Archive*. Translated by R. Grafman. Jerusalem: IAHUJ, 1976.

———. *Discovering Jerusalem*. Nashville: Nelson, 1983.

Baillet, M., J. T. Milik, and R. de Vaux, eds. *Les "petites grottes" de Qumrân: Exploration de la falaise: Les grottes 2Q, 3Q, 5Q, 6Q, 7Q à 10Q: Le rouleau de cuivre*. DJD 3. Oxford: Clarendon, 1962.

Baillet, M. "Textes des grottes 2Q, 3Q, 6Q, 7Q, à 10Q." In Baillet, Milik, and de Vaux, *Les "petites grottes" de Qumrân*, 45–164.

Baker, Cynthia M. *Jew*. New Brunswick, NJ: Rutgers University Press, 2017.

Balcells Gallarreta, José E. *Household and Family Religion in Persian-Period Judah: An Archaeological Approach*. Atlanta: SBL, 2017.

Barag, Dan. "New Evidence on the Foreign Policy of John Hyrcanus I." *Israel Numismatic Journal* 12 (1992–1993): 1–12.

Barclay, John M. G., trans. *Against Apion*. Vol. 10 of *Flavius Josephus: Translation and Commentary*. Edited by Steve Mason. Leiden: Brill, 2007.

Bar-Kochva, Bezalel. *The Image of the Jews in Greek Literature*. Berkeley: University of California Press, 2010.

———. *Judas Maccabaeus: The Jewish Struggle against the Seleucids*. Cambridge: Cambridge University Press, 1989.

———. *Pseudo-Hecataeus, "On the Jews": Legitimizing the Jewish Diaspora*. Berkley: University of California Press, 1996.

————. "The Religious Persecutions of Antiochus Epiphanes as a Historical Reality." *Tarbiz* 84 (2016): 295–344.

Bar-Nathan, Rachel, and Judit Gärtner. "The Stone Artifacts from the Hasmonean and Herodian Palaces at Jericho and Cypros." In *Hasmonean and Herodian Palaces at Jericho: Final Reports of the 1973–1987 Excavations*, vol. 5, *The Finds from Jericho and Cypros*, edited by Rachel Bar-Nathan and Judit Gärtner, 205–234. Jerusalem: IES; IAHUJ, 2013.

Bar-Oz, Guy, and Noa Raban-Gerstel. "The Faunal Remains." In *Jerusalem: Excavations in the Tyropoeon Valley (Giv'ati Parking Lot)*, 1:349–380. Jerusalem: IAA, 2013.

Bartelink, G.J. M. "φυλακτήριον—Phylacterium." In *Mélanges Christine Mohrmann: Nouveau recueil, offert par ses anciens élèves*, 25–60. Utrecht: Spectrum, 1973.

Batnitzky, Leora F. *How Judaism Became a Religion: An Introduction to Modern Jewish Thought*. Princeton, NJ: Princeton University Press, 2011.

Baumgarten, Albert I. *The Flourishing of Jewish Sects in the Maccabean Era: An Interpretation*. Leiden: Brill, 1997.

————. "The Name of the Pharisees." *JBL* 102 (1983): 411–428.

————. "The Torah as a Public Document in Judaism." *Studies in Religion* 14 (1985): 17–24.

Beit-Arieh, Itzhaq, and Bruce Cresson. "An Edomite Ostracon from Ḥorvat 'Uza." *Tel Aviv* 12 (1985): 96–101.

Ben-Ami, Doron, and Esti Eshel. "Stone Bowl Bearing the Name Hyrcanus from the Givati Excavations at the City of David." *Eretz-Israel* 32 (2016): 16–20 (Hebrew).

Ben-Dov, Meir. *In the Shadow of the Temple: The Discovery of Ancient Jerusalem*. Translated by Ina Friedman. New York: Harper & Row, 1985.

Berlin, Andrea. "Household Judaism." In *Galilee in the Late Second Temple and Mishnaic Periods 100 BCE–200 CE*, vol. 1, *Life, Culture, and Society*, edited by David A. Fiensy and James R. Strange, 208–215. Minneapolis: Fortress, 2014.

————. "Jewish Life before the Revolt: The Archaeological Evidence." *JSJ* 36 (2005): 417–470.

————. "Manifest Identity: From *Ioudaios* to Jew: Household Judaism as Anti-Hellenization in the Late Hasmonean Era." In *Between Cooperation and Hostility: Multiple Identities in Ancient Judaism and the Interaction with Foreign Powers*, edited by Rainer Albertz and Jakob Wöhrle, 151–175. Göttingen: Vandenhoeck & Ruprecht, 2013.

Berquist, Jon L. *Judaism in Persia's Shadow: A Social and Historical Approach*. Minneapolis: Fortress, 1995.

Berthelot, Katell. "Hecataeus of Abdera and Jewish 'Misanthropy.'" *Bulletin du Centre de recherche français à Jérusalem* 19 (2008). https://journals.openedition.org/bcrfj/5968.

Bianco, Maria, and Corinne Bonnet. "Sur les traces d'Athéna chez les Phéniciens." *Pallas* 100 (2016): 155–179.

Bickerman, Elias J. "The Generation of Ezra and Nehemiah." *Proceedings of the American Academy for Jewish Research* 45 (1978): 1–28.

———. "The Seleucid Charter for Jerusalem." In *Studies in Jewish and Christian History*, edited by Amram Tropper, 315–356. Leiden: Brill, 2007.

———. "A Seleucid Proclamation Concerning the Temple in Jerusalem." In *Studies in Jewish and Christian History*, edited by Amram Tropper, 357–375. Leiden: Brill, 2007.

Binder, Donald D. *Into the Temple Courts: The Place of the Synagogues in the Second Temple Period.* Atlanta: SBL, 1999.

Blank, Sheldon H. "The LXX Renderings of Old Testament Terms for Law." *HUCA* 7 (1930): 259–283.

Blenkinsopp, Joseph. "The Development of Jewish Sectarianism from Nehemiah to the Hasidim." In *Judah and the Judeans in the Fourth century B.C.E.*, edited by Oded Lipschits, Gary N. Knoppers, and Rainer Albertz, 385–402. Winona Lake, IN: Eisenbrauns, 2007.

———. *Ezra-Nehemiah: A Commentary.* Philadelphia: Westminster, 1988.

———. *Isaiah 56–66: A New Translation with Introduction and Commentary.* New York: Doubleday, 2003.

———. "A Jewish Sect of the Persian Period." *CBQ* 52 (1990): 5–20.

———. *Judaism, the First Phase: The Place of Ezra and Nehemiah in the Origins of Judaism.* Grand Rapids: Eerdmans, 2009.

———. *The Pentateuch: An Introduction to the First Five Books of the Bible.* New York: Doubleday, 1992.

———. "Was the Pentateuch the Civic and Religious Constitution of the Jewish Ethnos in the Persian Period?" In Watts, *Persia and Torah*, 41–62.

Bloch, René. "Jew or Judean: The Latin Evidence." In *Torah, Temple, Land: Constructions of Judaism in Antiquity*, edited by Markus Witte, Jens Schröter, and Verena M. Lepper, 229–240. Tübingen: Mohr Siebeck, 2021.

Bloch, Yigal. "Judean Identity during the Exile: Concluding Deals on a Sabbath in Babylonia and Egypt under the Neo-Babylonian and the Achaemenid Empires." In *A Question of Identity: Social, Political, and Historical Aspects of Identity Dynamics in Jewish and Other Contexts*, edited by Dikla Rivlin-Katz, Noah Hacham, Geoffrey Herman, and Lilach Sagiv, 43–69. Berlin: de Gruyter Oldenbourg, 2019.

———. "Was the Sabbath Observed in Al-Yahudu in the Early Decades of the Babylonian Exile?" *ZAW* 132 (2020): 117–120.

Blum, Erhard. *Studien zur Komposition des Pentateuch.* Berlin: de Gruyter, 1990.

Borchardt, Francis. "Sabbath Observance, Sabbath Innovation: The Hasmoneans and Their Legacy as Interpreters of the Law." *JSJ* 46 (2015): 159–181.

Bouchnick, Ram. "Finds of Animal Remains from the Excavations on the Northern Slope of Herodium (Area A), 2006–2010." In *Herodium: Final Reports of the 1972–2010 Excavations Directed by Ehud Netzer*, edited by Roi Porat, Rachel Chachy, and Yakov Kalman, 476–503. Jerusalem: IES; IAHUJ, 2015.

———. "Meat Consumption in the Society of Judea in the Late Second Temple Period." PhD diss., University of Haifa, 2010 (Hebrew).

Bourgel, Jonathan. "The Destruction of the Samaritan Temple by John Hyrcanus: A Reconsideration." *JBL* 135 (2016): 505–523.

———. "Herod's Golden Eagle on the Temple Gate: A Reconsideration. *JJS* 72 (2021): 23–44.

———. "The Samaritans during the Hasmonean Period: The Affirmation of a Discrete Identity?" *Religions* 10 (2019): 628.

Boyarin, Daniel. *Judaism: The Genealogy of a Modern Notion.* New Brunswick, NJ: Rutgers University Press, 2019.

———. "No Ancient Judaism." In *Strength to Strength: Essays in Honor of Shaye J.D. Cohen*, edited by Michael L. Satlow. Providence: Brown Judaic Studies, 2018, 75–102.

Braund, David. *Rome and the Friendly King: The Character of the Client Kingship.* London: Croom Helm; New York: St. Martin's Press, 1984.

Bright, John. *A History of Israel.* London: SCM, 1972.

Brooke, George. "Rewritten Bible." In *Encyclopedia of the Dead Sea Scrolls*, edited by Lawrence H. Schiffman and James C. VanderKam, 777–781. New York: Oxford University Press, 2000.

Broshi, Magen. "Excavations on Mount Zion, 1971–1972: Preliminary Report." *IEJ* 26 (1976): 81–88.

Buckley, Thomas, and Alma Gottlieb, eds. *Blood Magic: The Anthropology of Menstruation.* Berkeley: University of California Press, 1988.

Bultrighini, Ilaria, and Sacha Stern. "The Seven-Day Week in the Roman Empire: Origins, Standardization, and Diffusion." In *Calendars in the Making: The Origins of Calendars from the Roman Empire to the Later Middle Ages*, 10–79. Leiden: Brill, 2021.

Burton, Anne. *Diodorus Siculus, Book 1: A Commentary.* Leiden: Brill, 1972.

Carbon, Jan-Mathieu, and Vinciane Pirenne-Delforge. "Beyond Greek 'Sacred Laws.'" *Kernos* 25 (2012): 163–182.

Carr, David M. "Changes in Pentateuchal Criticism." In *Hebrew Bible/Old Testament: The History of Its Interpretation*, vol. 3, *From Modernism to Post-modernism (The Nineteenth and Twentieth Centuries), Part 2: The Twentieth Century—From Modernism to Post-modernism*, edited by Magne Sæbø, Peter Machinist, and Jean L. Ska, 433–466. Göttingen: Vandenhoeck & Ruprecht, 2015.

———. *Reading the Fractures of Genesis: Historical and Literary Approaches.* Louisville: Westminster, 1996.

———. "The Rise of Torah." In Knoppers and Levinson, *The Pentateuch as Torah*, 39–56.

Carter, Charles E. *The Emergence of Yehud in the Persian Period: A Social and Demographic Study.* Sheffield: Sheffield Academic, 1999.

Chapman, Reginald F. *The Insects: Structure and Function.* Cambridge: Cambridge University Press, 1998.

Charlesworth, James H., ed. *The Old Testament Pseudepigrapha.* 2 vols. Garden City, NY: Doubleday, 1983–1985.

Chavalas, Mark W. "Assyriology and Biblical Studies: A Century and a Half of Tension." In *Mesopotamia and the Bible: Comparative Explorations,* edited by Mark W. Chavalas and K. Lawson Younger, 21–67. Grand Rapids: Baker Academic, 2002.

Choi, John H. *Traditions at Odds: The Reception of the Pentateuch in Biblical and Second Temple Period Literature.* New York: T&T Clark, 2010.

Clancy, Frank. "The Date of LXX." *Scandinavian Journal of the Old Testament* 16 (2002): 207–225.

Clarysse, Willy, Sofie Remijsen, and Mark Depauw. "Observing the Sabbath in the Roman Empire: A Case Study." *Scripta Classica Israelica* 29 (2010): 51–57.

Clines, David J. A. *Ezra, Nehemiah, Esther: Based on the Revised Standard Version.* Grand Rapids: Eerdmans; London: Marshall, Morgan & Scott, 1984.

Cohen, Boaz. "Art in Jewish Law." *Judaism* 3 (1954): 165–176.

Cohen, Naomi G. "The Name 'Shabtai' in the Hellenistic-Roman Period." In *These Are the Names: Studies in Jewish Onomastics,* edited by Aaron Demsky, 2:11–29. Ramat Gan: Bar-Ilan University Press, 1999.

Cohen, Shaye J. D. *The Beginnings of Jewishness: Boundaries, Varieties, Uncertainties.* Berkeley: University of California Press, 1999.

———. "Purity, Piety, and Polemic: Medieval Rabbinic Denunciations of 'Incorrect' Purification Practices." In *Women and Water: Menstruation in Jewish Life and Law,* edited by Rahel R. Wasserfall, 82–100. Hanover, NH: Brandeis University Press/University Press of New England, 1999.

Cohn, Yehudah B. *Tangled Up in Text: Tefillin and the Ancient World.* Providence: Brown Judaic Studies, 2008.

Colautti, Federico M. *Passover in the Works of Josephus.* Leiden: Brill, 2002.

Collins, Billie Jean, Bob Buller, and John F. Kutsko, eds. *The SBL Handbook of Style: For Biblical Studies and Related Disciplines.* 2nd ed. Atlanta: SBL Press, 2014.

Collins, John J. *Daniel: A Commentary on the Book of Daniel.* Minneapolis: Fortress, 1993.

———. "The Epic of Theodotus and the Hellenism of the Hasmoneans." *Harvard Theological Review* 73 (1980): 91–104.

———. "Hecataeus as a Witness to Judaism" (forthcoming).

———. *The Invention of Judaism: Torah and Jewish Identity from Deuteronomy to Paul.* Oakland: University of California Press, 2017.

———. "Temple or Taxes? What Sparked the Maccabean Revolt?" In *Revolt and Resistance in the Ancient Classical World and the Near East: In the Crucible of Empire,* edited by John J. Collins and J. G. Manning, 189–201. Leiden: Brill, 2016.

Colson, F. H., and G. H. Whitaker, eds. and trans. *Philo.* 10 vols. Cambridge, MA: Harvard University Press, 1929–1943.

Cope, Carole. "The Butchering Patterns of Gamla and Yodefat: Beginning the Search for 'Kosher' Practice." In *Behaviour behind Bones: The Zooarchaeology of*

Ritual, Religion, Status and Identity, edited by Sharyn Jones O'Day, Wim Van Neer, and Anton Ervynck, 25–33. Oxford: Oxbow, 2004.

Corbo, Virgilio C. "L'Herodion di Gebal Fureidis: Relazione preliminare della due prime campagne di scavo 1962–1963." *Liber Annuus* 13 (1963): 219–277.

Cornelius, Izak. "'East Meets West': Trends in Terracotta Figurines." In Frevel, Pyschny, and Cornelius, *A "Religious Revolution,"* 67–93.

Cotton, Hannah M., et al., eds. *Corpus Inscriptionum Iudaeae/Palaestinae: A Multilingual Corpus of the Inscriptions from Alexander to Muhammad.* 4 vols. Berlin: de Gruyter, 2010–2018.

Cowey, James M. S., and Klaus Maresch. *Urkunden des Politeuma der Juden von Herakleopolis (144/3–133/2 v. Chr.) (P. Polit. Iud.): Papyri aus den Sammlungen von Heidelberg, Köln, München und Wien.* Wiesbaden: Westdeutscher Verlag, 2001.

Cross, Frank M. "The Development of Jewish Scripts." In *The Bible and the Ancient Near East: Essays in Honor of William Foxwell Albright*, edited by G. E. Wright, 133–202. Garden City, NY: Doubleday, 1961.

———. "A Reconstruction of the Judean Restoration." *JBL* 94 (1975): 4–18.

Cross, Frank M., David N. Freedman, and James A. Sanders, eds. *Scrolls from Qumrân Cave I: The Great Isaiah Scroll, the Order of the Community, the Pesher to Habakkuk.* Jerusalem: Albright Institute of Archaeological Research, 1972.

Crüsemann, Frank. *The Torah: Theology and Social History of Old Testament Law.* Translated by W. Mahnke. Minneapolis: Fortress, 1996.

Darby, Erin. *Interpreting Judean Pillar Figurines: Gender and Empire in Judean Apotropaic Ritual.* Tübingen: Mohr Siebeck, 2014.

Dávid, Nóra, Armin Lange, Kristin De Troyer, and Shani Tzoref, eds. *The Hebrew Bible in Light of the Dead Sea Scrolls.* Göttingen: Vandenhoeck & Ruprecht, 2012.

Davies, Philip R. "Josiah and the Law Book." In *Good Kings and Bad Kings*, edited by Lester L. Grabbe, 65–77. New York: T&T Clark, 2005.

———. *On the Origins of Judaism.* London: Equinox, 2011.

———. "Scenes from the Early History of Judaism." In *The Triumph of Elohim: From Yahwisms to Judaisms*, edited by Diana V. Edelman, 145–182. Kampen: Kok Pharos, 1995.

de Hulster, Izaak J. *Figurines in Achaemenid Period Yehud: Jerusalem's History of Religion and Coroplastics in the Monotheism Debate.* Tübingen: Mohr Siebeck, 2017.

Deines, Roland. *Jüdische Steingefäße und pharisäische Frömmigkeit: Ein archäologisch historischer Beitrag zum Verständnis von Joh 2,6 und der jüdischen Reinheitshalacha zur Zeit Jesu.* Tübingen: Mohr Siebeck, 1993.

de Lange, Nicholas. "The Celebration of the Passover in Graeco-Roman Alexandria." In *Manières de penser dans l'Antiquité méditerranéenne et orientale*, edited by Christophe Batsch and Mădălina Vârtejanu-Joubert, 157–166. Leiden: Brill, 2009.

De Luca, Stefano, and Anna Lena. "The Mosaic of the Thermal Bath Complex of Magdala Reconsidered: Archaeological Context, Epigraphy and Iconography."

In *Knowledge and Wisdom: Archaeological and Historical Essays in Honour of Leah Di Segni*, edited by Giovanni C. Bottini, L. Daniel Chrupcala, and Joseph Patrich, 1–33. Milan: Edizioni Terra Santa, 2014.

Demsky, Aaron. "The Trumpeter's Inscription from the Temple Mount." *Eretz-Israel* 18 (1985): 40–42 (Hebrew).

Dershowitz, Idan. "Darius II Delays the Festival of Matzot in 418 BCE." TheTorah .com. Accessed March 13, 2020. https://www.thetorah.com/article/darius-ii-delays-the-festival-of-matzot-in-418-bce.

de Vaux, Roland. "Archéologie." In Baillet, Milik, and de Vaux, *Les "petites grottes" de Qumrân*, 3–41.

de Wette, Wilhelm Martin Leberecht. *Dissertatio critica-exegetica qua Deuteronomium a prioribus Pentateuchi libris diversum alius cuiusdam recentioris auctoris opus esse monstratur.* Jena: Leteris Etzdorfii, 1805. Reprinted in *Opuscula theologica.* Berlin: Reimer, 1830.

———. *Lehrbuch der christlichen Dogmatik, in ihrer historischen Entwickelung dargestellt.* Vol. 1, *Biblische Dogmatik Alten und Neuen Testaments. Oder kritische Darstellung der Religionslehre des Hebraismus, des Judenthums und Urchristenthums.* Berlin: Realschulbuchhandlung, 1813.

Doering, Lutz. "Jewish Law in the Dead Sea Scrolls: Some Issues for Consideration." In Dávid et al., *The Hebrew Bible in Light of the Dead Sea Scrolls*, 449–462.

———. "Law and Lawlessness in Texts from Qumran." In *Law and Lawlessness in Early Judaism and Early Christianity*, edited by David Lincicum, Ruth Sheridan, and Charles Stang, 9–28. Tübingen: Mohr Siebeck, 2019.

———. *Schabbat: Sabbathalacha und-praxis im antiken Judentum und Urchristentum.* Tübingen: Mohr Siebeck, 1999.

Doran, Robert. *2 Maccabees: A Critical Commentary.* Minneapolis: Fortress, 2012.

Eshel, Hanan. "Israelite Names from Samaria in the Persian Period." In *These Are the Names: Studies in Jewish Onomastics*, edited by Aaron Demsky, Joseph A. Reif, and Joseph Tabory, 1:17–31. Ramat Gan: Bar-Ilan University Press, 1997 (Hebrew).

———. "The Two Historical Layers of Pesher Habakkuk." In *Northern Lights on the Dead Sea Scrolls: Proceedings of the Nordic Qumran Network 2003–2006*, edited by Anders Klostergaard Petersen et al., 107–117. Leiden; Boston: Brill, 2009.

Eshel, Hanan, and Hagai Misgav. "Jericho papList of Loans ar." In *Miscellaneous Texts from the Judaean Desert*, by James Charlesworth et al. in consultation with James VanderKam and Monica Brady, 21–30. DJD 38. Oxford: Clarendon, 2000.

Faust, Avraham. "Pigs in Space (and Time): Pork Consumption and Identity Negotiations in the Late Bronze and Iron Ages of Ancient Israel." *Near Eastern Archaeology* 81 (2018): 276–299.

Faust, Avraham, and Shlomo Bunimovitz. "The Four-Room House: Embodying Israelite Society." *Near Eastern Archaeology* 66 (2003): 22–31.

Faust, Avraham, and Hayah Katz. "The Archaeology of Purity and Impurity: A Case-Study from Tel ʿEton, Israel." *Cambridge Archaeological Journal* 27 (2017): 1–27.

Feldman, Ariel, and Faina Feldman. "4Q147: An Amulet?" *DSD* 26 (2019): 1–29.

———. "4Q148 (4QPhylactère U): Another Amulet from Qumran?" *JSJ* 50 (2019): 197–222.

———. "Is Mur 5 a Mezuzah?" *Revue de Qumrân* 31 (2019): 291–298.

Fine, Steven. "The Arch of Titus in Color: Polychromy and the Spoils of Jerusalem." *City of David Studies of Ancient Jerusalem* 12 (2017): 18*–37*.

———. *Art and Judaism in the Greco-Roman World: Toward a New Jewish Archaeology.* Cambridge: Cambridge University Press, 2005.

———. "The Open Torah Ark: A Jewish Iconographic Type in Late Antique Rome and Sardis." In *Viewing Ancient Jewish Art and Archaeology: VeHinnei Rachel—Essays in Honor of Rachel Hachlili*, edited by Ann E. Killebrew and Gabriele Faßbeck, 121–134. Leiden: Brill, 2016.

Finkelstein, Israel. *Hasmonean Realities behind Ezra, Nehemiah, and Chronicles.* Atlanta: SBL, 2018.

Finkelstein, Israel, Yuval Gadot, and Lidar Sapir-Hen. "Pig Frequencies in Iron Age Sites and the Biblical Pig Taboo: Once Again." *Ugarit-Forschungen* 49 (2018): 109–116.

Finkelstein, J. J. "Ammiṣaduqa's Edict and the Babylonian 'Law Codes.'" *Journal of Cuneiform Studies* 15 (1961): 91–104.

Finkelstein, Louis, ed. *Sifre on Deuteronomy.* New York: Jewish Theological Seminary of America, 1993 (Hebrew).

Fishbane, Michael. *Biblical Interpretation in Ancient Israel.* Oxford: Clarendon, 1985.

Fleischer, Ezra. "On the Beginnings of Obligatory Jewish Prayer." *Tarbiz* 59 (1989–1990): 397–441 (Hebrew).

Fraade, Steven. "Looking for Legal Midrash at Qumran." In *Biblical Perspectives: Early Use and Interpretation of the Bible in Light of the Dead Sea Scrolls; Proceedings of the First International Symposium of the Orion Center for the Study of the Dead Sea Scrolls and Associated Literature, 12–14 May 1996*, edited by Michael E. Stone and Esther G. Chazon, 59–79. Leiden: Brill, 1998.

Frei, Peter. "Persian Imperial Authorization: A Summary." In Watts, *Persia and Torah*, 5–40.

———. "Zentralgewalt und Lokalautonomie im Achämenidenreich." In *Reichsidee und Reichsorganisation im Perserreich*, by Peter Frei and Klaus Koch, 5–131. Fribourg: Universitätsverlag; Göttingen: Vandenhoeck & Ruprecht, 1984.

———. "Zentralgewalt und Lokalautonomie im achämenidischen Kleinasien." *Transeuphratène* 3 (1990): 157–171.

Frevel, Christian, and Katharina Pyschny. "A Religious Revolution Devours Its Children: The Iconography of the Persian-Period Cuboid Incense Burners." In *Religion in the Achaemenid Persian Empire: Emerging Judaisms and Trends*, edited by Diana Edelman, Anne Fitzpatrick-McKinley, and Philippe Guillaume, 91–133. Tübingen: Mohr Siebeck, 2016.

———. "A 'Religious Revolution' in Yehûd? The Material Culture of the Persian Period as a Test Case: Introduction." In Frevel, Pyschny, and Cornelius, *A "Religious Revolution,"* 1–22.

Frevel, Christian, Katharina Pyschny, and Izak Cornelius, eds. *A "Religious Revolution" in Yehûd? The Material Culture of the Persian Period as a Test Case.* Fribourg: Academic Press; Göttingen: Vandenhoeck & Ruprecht, 2014.

Frey, Jean-Baptiste, ed. *Corpus inscriptionvm ivdaicarvm: Recueil des inscriptions juives qui vont du IIIe siècle avant Jésus-Christ au VIIe siècle de notre ère.* 2 vols. Vatican City: Pontificio istituto di archeologia cristians, 1936–1952.

———. "La question des images chez les Juifs à la lumière des récentes découvertes." *Biblica* 15 (1934): 265–300.

Fried, Lisbeth S. *Ezra and the Law in History and Tradition.* Columbia: University of South Carolina, 2014.

———. "A Silver Coin of Yoḥanan Hakkôhen." *Transeuphratène* 26 (2003): 65–85.

Fulton, Deirdre N. "The Faunal Remains." In *Ramat Raḥel VI: The Renewed Excavations by the Tel Aviv—Heidelberg Expedition (2005–2010): The Babylonian-Persian Pit,* edited by Oded Lipschits, Liora Freud, Manfred Oeming, and Yuval Gadot, 142–147. University Park, PA: Eisenbrauns, 2021.

Gagarin, Michael. *Early Greek Law.* Berkeley: University of California Press, 1986.

———. *Writing Greek Law.* Cambridge: Cambridge University Press, 2008.

Gagarin, Michael, and Paul Woodruff. "Early Greek Legal Thought." In *A History of the Philosophy of Law from the Ancient Greeks to the Scholastics,* edited by Fred D. Miller Jr. and Carrie-Ann Biondi, 7–34. 2nd ed. Dordrecht: Springer, 2015.

Garbini, Giovanni. *History and Ideology in Ancient Israel.* Translated by John Bowden. New York: Crossroad, 1988.

Gass, Erasmus. "Der Passa-Papyrus (Cowl 21)—Mythos oder Realität." *Biblische Notizen* 99 (1999): 55–68.

Gera, Dov. "The Seleucid Road towards the Religious Persecutions of the Jews." In *La mémoire des persécutions: Autour des livres des Maccabées,* edited by Marie-Françoise Baslez and Olivier Munnich, 21–57. Paris: Peeters, 2014.

Gerber, Christine. *Ein Bild des Judentums für Nichtjuden von Flavius Josephus: Untersuchungen zu seiner Schrift Contra Apionem.* Leiden: Brill, 1997.

Geva, Hillel, ed. *Jewish Quarter Excavations in the Old City of Jerusalem: Conducted by Nahman Avigad, 1969–1982.* Vol. 3, *Area E and Other Studies: Final Report.* Jerusalem: IES; IAHUJ, 2006.

———, ed. *Jewish Quarter Excavations in the Old City of Jerusalem: Conducted by Nahman Avigad, 1969–1982.* Vol. 6, *Areas J, N, Z and Other Studies: Final Report.* Jerusalem: IES; IAHUJ, 2014.

———. "Stone Artifacts." In Geva, *Jewish Quarter Excavations,* 3:218–238.

———. "Stone Artifacts from Areas J and N." In Geva, *Jewish Quarter Excavations*, 6:272–287.

Geva, Hillel, and Malka Hershkovitz. "Local Pottery of the Hellenistic and Early Roman Periods." In Geva, *Jewish Quarter Excavations*, 3:94–143.

Gibson, E. Leigh. *The Jewish Manumission Inscriptions of the Bosporus Kingdom.* Tübingen: Mohr Siebeck, 1999.

Gitler, Haim. "The Earliest Coin of Judah." *Israel Numismatic Research* 6 (2011): 21–33.

Gitler, Haim, and Catharine Lorber. "A New Chronology for the Ptolemaic Yehud Coinage." *American Journal of Numismatics* 18 (2006): 1–41.

———. "A New Chronology for the Yehizkiyah Coins." *Schweizerische numismatische Rundschau* 87 (2008): 61–82.

Gladson, Jerry A. "Jeremiah 17:19–27: A Rewriting of the Sinaitic Code?" *CBQ* 62 (2000): 33–40.

Gmirkin, Russell E. *Berossus and Genesis, Manetho and Exodus: Hellenistic Histories and the Date of the Pentateuch.* New York: T&T Clark, 2006.

———. "Greek Evidence for the Hebrew Bible." In *The Bible and Hellenism: Greek Influence on Jewish and Early Christian Literature*, edited by Thomas L. Thompson and Philippe Wajdenbaum, 56–88. Durham: Acumen, 2014.

Goodenough, Erwin R. *Jewish Symbols in the Greco-Roman Period.* 13 vols. New York: Pantheon, 1953–1968.

Goodman, Martin. "Kosher Olive Oil in Antiquity." In *A Tribute to Geza Vermes: Essays on Jewish and Christian Literature and History*, edited by Philip R. Davies and Richard T. White, 227–245. Sheffield: Sheffield Academic, 1990.

Gove, Philip B., et al., eds. *Webster's Third New International Dictionary of the English Language Unabridged.* Springfield, MA: Merriam-Webster, 1993.

Grabbe, Lester L. "Elephantine and the Torah." In *In the Shadow of Bezalel: Aramaic, Biblical, and Ancient Near Eastern Studies in Honor of Bezalel Porten*, edited by Alejandro F. Botta, 125–135. Leiden: Brill, 2013.

———. "Hecataeus of Abdera and the Jewish Law: The Question of Authenticity." In *Berührungspunkte: Studien zur Sozial-und Religionsgeschichte Israels und seiner Umwelt; Festschrift für Rainer Albertz zu seinem 65. Geburtstag*, edited by Ingo Kottsieper, Rüdiger Schmitt, and Jakob Wöhrle, 613–626. Münster: Ugarit-Verlag, 2008.

———. *A History of the Jews and Judaism in the Second Temple Period.* Vol. 1, *Yehud: A History of the Persian Province of Judah.* London: T&T Clark International, 2004.

———. "Hyparchs, *Oikonomoi*, and Mafiosi: The Governance of Judah in the Ptolemaic Period." In *Judah between East and West: The Transition from Persian to Greek Rule (ca. 400–200 BCE)*, edited by Lester L. Grabbe and Oded Lipschits, 70–90. London: T&T Clark, 2011.

———. "Jewish Historiography and Scripture in the Hellenistic Period." In *Did Moses Speak Attic? Jewish Historiography and Scripture in the Hellenistic Period*, edited by Lester L. Grabbe, 129–155. Sheffield: Sheffield Academic, 2001.

————. "The Law of Moses in the Ezra Tradition: More Virtual than Real?" In Watts, *Persia and Torah*, 91–113.

Graf, Karl Heinrich. *Die geschichtlichen Bücher des Alten Testaments: zwei historisch-kritische Untersuchungen.* Leipzig: T. O. Weigel, 1866.

Granerød, Gard. "Canon and Archive: Yahwism in Elephantine and Āl-Yāḫūdu as a Challenge to the Canonical History of Judean Religion in the Persian Period." *JBL* 138 (2019): 345–364.

————. *Dimensions of Yahwism in the Persian Period: Studies in the Religion and Society of the Judaean Community at Elephantine.* Berlin: de Gruyter, 2016.

Grantham, Billy. "Faunal Remains." In *Sepphoris III: The Architecture, Stratigraphy, and Artifacts of the Western Summit of Sepphoris*, edited by Eric M. Meyers, Carol L. Meyers, and Benjamin D. Gordon, 2:871–888. University Park, PA: Eisenbrauns, 2018.

Greenfield, Haskel J., and Ram Bouchnick. "Kashrut and Shechita—the Relationship between Dietary Practices and Ritual Slaughtering of Animals on Jewish Identity." In *Identity Crisis: Archaeological Perspectives on Social Identity: Proceedings of the 42nd (2010) Annual Chacmool Archaeology Conference, University of Calgary, Calgary, Alberta*, edited by Lindsay Amundsen-Meyer, Nicole Engel, and Sean Pickering, 1–10. Calgary: Chacmool Archaeological Association, University of Calgary, 2010.

Grelot, Pierre. "Etudes sur le 'Papyrus Pascal' d'Elephantine." *VT* 4 (1954): 349–384.

————. "Le papyrus pascal d'Éléphantine: Essai de Restauration." *VT* 17 (1967): 201–207.

————. "Le papyrus pascal d'Éléphantine et le problème du Pentateuque." *VT* 5 (1955): 250–265.

————. "Le papyrus pascal d'Éléphantine: nouvel examen." *VT* 17 (1967): 114–117.

Grintz, Jehoshua M. "'Do Not Eat on the Blood': Reconsiderations in Setting and Dating of the Priestly Code." *Annual of the Swedish Theological Institute* 8 (1972): 78–105.

Grund, Alexandra. *Die Entstehung des Sabbats: Seine Bedeutung für Israels Zeitkonzept und Erinnerungskultur.* Tübingen: Mohr Siebeck, 2011.

Gunkel, Hermann. *Genesis: übers. und erklärt von Hermann Gunkel.* Göttingen: Vandenhoeck & Ruprecht, 1901.

Hacham, Noah, and Tal Ilan, eds. *Corpus Papyrorum Judaicarum.* Vol. 4. Berlin: de Gruyter; Jerusalem: Magnes, 2020.

Hachlili, Rachel. *Ancient Mosaic Pavements: Themes, Issues, and Trends; Selected Studies.* Leiden: Brill, 2009.

————. *Ancient Synagogues—Archaeology and Art: New Discoveries and Current Research.* Leiden: Brill, 2013.

————. *Jewish Funerary Customs, Practices and Rites in the Second Temple Period.* Leiden: Brill, 2005.

————. *The Menorah: Evolving into the Most Important Jewish Symbol.* Leiden: Brill, 2018.

Hadjiev, Tchavdar S. *The Composition and Redaction of the Book of Amos*. Berlin: de Gruyter, 2009.

Hagedorn, Anselm. "Local Law in an Imperial Context: The Role of Torah in the (Imagined) Persian Past." In Knoppers and Levinson, *The Pentateuch as Torah*, 57–76.

Harding, G. L. "The Archaeological Finds: Introductory. The Discovery, the Excavation, Minor Finds." In *Qumran Cave I*, edited by D. Barthélemy and J. T. Milik, 3–7. DJD 1. Oxford: Clarendon, 1955.

Har-Even, Benny. "A Second Temple Period Synagogue at Ḥorvat Diab in Western Benjamin." *Qadmoniot* 151 (2016): 49–53 (Hebrew).

Hart, H. L. A. *The Concept of Law*. Oxford: Clarendon, 1961.

Hayes, Christine E. *Gentile Impurities and Jewish Identities: Intermarriage and Conversion from the Bible to the Talmud*. Oxford: Oxford University Press, 2002.

———. *What's Divine about Divine Law? Early Perspectives*. Princeton: Princeton University Press, 2015.

Heltzer, Michael. *The Province Judah and Jews in Persian Times: Some Connected Questions of the Persian Empire*. Tel Aviv: Archaeological Center Publication, 2008.

Hershkovitz, Malka. "Gemstones." In *Jewish Quarter Excavations in the Old City of Jerusalem*, vol. 2, *The Finds from Areas A, W, and X-2: Final Report*, edited by Hillel Geva, 296–301. Jerusalem: IES; IAHUJ, 2003.

Hesse, Brian. "Pig Lovers and Pig Haters: Patterns of Palestinian Pork Production." *Journal of Ethnobiology* 10 (1990): 195–225.

Hesse, Brian, and Paula Wapnish. "Can Pig Remains Be Used for Ethnic Diagnosis in the Ancient Near East?" In *The Archaeology of Israel: Constructing the Past, Interpreting the Present*, edited by Neil A. Silberman and David Small, 238–270. Sheffield: Sheffield Academic, 1997.

Hidary, Richard. "Revisiting the Sabbath Laws in 4Q264a and Their Contribution to Early Halakha." *DSD* 22 (2015): 68–92.

Hoenig, Sidney B. "Dorshé Ḥalaḳot in the Pesher Nahum Scrolls." *JBL* 83 (1964): 119–138.

Hoffman, Yair. "The Fasts of the Book of Zechariah and the Fashioning of National Remembrance." In Lipschits and Blenkinsopp, *Judah and the Judeans in the Neo-Babylonian Period*, 169–218.

Hölkeskamp, Karl-J. "Written Law in Archaic Greece." *Proceedings of the Cambridge Philological Society* 38 (1992): 87–117.

Holladay, A. J., and M. D. Goodman. "Religious Scruples in Ancient Warfare." *The Classical Quarterly* 36 (1986): 151–171.

Honigman, Sylvie. *Tales of High Priests and Taxes: The Books of the Maccabees and the Judean Rebellion against Antiochos IV*. Oakland: University of California Press, 2014.

Horbury, William, and David Noy. *Jewish Inscriptions of Graeco-Roman Egypt: With an Index of the Jewish Inscriptions of Egypt and Cyrenaica*. New York: Cambridge University Press, 1992.

Horovitz, H. S., and I. A. Rabin, eds. *Mekhilta de-Rabbi Ishmael*. Frankfurt: Kauff-mann, 1931 (Hebrew).

Horwitz, Liora K., and Jacqueline Studer. "Pig Production and Exploitation during the Classical Periods in the Southern Levant." In *Archaeozoology in the Near East VI: Proceedings of the Sixth International Symposium on the Archaeozoology of Southwestern Asia and Adjacent Areas*, edited by H. Buitenhuis, A. M. Choyke, L. Martin, L. Bartosiewicz, and M. Mashkour, 222–239. Groningen: ARC-Publicaties, 2005.

Jastrow, Marcus. *A Dictionary of the Targumim, the Talmud Babli and Yerushalmi, and the Midrashic Literature*. New York: Choreb, 1926.

Kasher, Aryeh. *Against Apion: A New Hebrew Translation with Introduction and Commentary*. Jerusalem: Zalman Shazar Center for Jewish History, 1996 (Hebrew).

Kaufmann, Yehezkel. *The Religion of Israel: From Its Beginnings to the Babylonian Exile*. Translated and abridged by Moshe Greenberg. Chicago: University of Chicago Press, 1960.

Kazen, Thomas. "Purification." In *The Oxford Handbook of Early Christian Ritual*, edited by Risto Uro, Juliette J. Day, Richard E. DeMaris, and Rikard Roitto, 220–244. Oxford: Oxford University Press, 2019.

————. "Purity and Impurity in Ancient Israel and Early Judaism." In *Oxford Bibliographies Online in Jewish Studies*, 2019. https://www-oxfordbibliographies-com .yale .idm .oclc .org/ view/ document/ obo -9780199840731/ obo -9780199840731–0178.xml.

Keel, Othmar. "Zeichen der Verbundenheit: Zur Vorgeschichte und Bedeutung der Forderungen von Deuteronomium 6,8f. und Par." In *Mélanges Dominique Barthélemy: Études bibliques offertes à l'occasion de son 60e anniversaire*, edited by Pierre Casetti, Othmar Keel, and Adrian Schenker, 159–240. Fribourg: Éditions Universitaires; Göttingen: Vandenhoeck & Ruprecht, 1981.

Kienle, Helmut. *Der Gott auf dem Flügelrad: Zu den ungelösten Fragen der "synkretistischen" Münze BMC Palestine S. 181, Nr. 29*. Wiesbaden: Harrassowitz, 1975.

Kippenberg, Hans G. *Die vorderasiatischen Erlösungsreligionen in ihrem Zusammenhang mit der antiken Stadtherrschaft*. Frankfurt: Suhrkamp, 1991.

Kirchner, Paul C. *Jüdisches Ceremoniel, oder, Beschreibung dererjenigen Gebräuche, welche Die Juden sowol inn-als ausser dem Tempel, bey allen und jeden Fest-Tägen, im Gebet, bey der Beschneidung, bey Hochzeiten, Auslösung der Erst-Geburt, im Sterben, bey der Begräbnüß und dergleichen, in acht zu nehmen pflegen*. Nuremberg: P. C. Monath, 1724.

Klawans, Jonathan. *Impurity and Sin in Ancient Judaism*. Oxford: Oxford University Press, 2000.

Kleber, Kristin. "*dātu ša šarri*: Gesetzgebung in Babylonien unter den Achämeniden." *ZAR* 16 (2010): 49–75.

Kleist, Aaron J. "The Division of the Ten Commandments in Anglo-Saxon England." *Neuphilologische Mitteilungen* 103 (2002): 227–240.

Kloner, Amos. "The Identity of the Idumeans Based on the Archaeological Evidence from Maresha." In Lipschits, Knoppers, and Oeming, *Judah and the Judeans in the Achaemenid Period*, 563–573.

Knauf, Ernst Axel. *Die Umwelt des Alten Testaments*. Stuttgart: Katholisches Bibelwerk, 1994.

———. "Elephantine und das vor-biblische Judentum." In *Religion und Religionskontakte im Zeitalter der Achämeniden*, edited by Reinhard G. Kratz, 179–188. Gütersloh: Gütersloher Verlaghaus, 2002.

Knoppers, Gary N. "An Achaemenid Imperial Authorization of Torah in Yehud?" In Watts, *Persia and Torah*, 115–134.

———. "'Battling against Yahweh': Israel's War against Judah in 2 Chr 13:2–20." *Revue Biblique* 100 (1993): 511–532.

———. "Moses and the Greek Lawgivers: The Triumph of the Torah in Ancient Mediterranean Perspective." In *Writing Laws in Antiquity / L'écriture du droit dans l'Antiquité*, edited by Dominique Jaillard and Christophe Nihan, 50–77. Wiesbaden: Harrassowitz, 2017.

Knoppers, Gary N., and Paul B. Harvey Jr. "The Pentateuch in Ancient Mediterranean Context: The Publication of Local Lawcodes." In Knoppers and Levinson, *The Pentateuch as Torah*, 105–141.

Knoppers, Gary N., and Bernard M. Levinson, eds. *The Pentateuch as Torah: New Models for Understanding Its Promulgation and Acceptance*. Winona Lake, IN: Eisenbrauns, 2007.

Knowles, Melody D. *Centrality Practiced: Jerusalem in the Religious Practice of Yehud and the Diaspora in the Persian Period*. Leiden: Brill, 2006.

Kon, Maximilian. *The Tombs of the Kings*. Tel Aviv: Devir, 1947 (Hebrew).

Krakowski, Eve. "Maimonides' Menstrual Reform in Egypt." *Jewish Quarterly Review* 110 (2020): 245–289.

Kratz, Reinhard G. "Die Entstehung des Judentums: zur Kontroverse zwischen E. Meyer und J. Wellhausen." *Zeitschrift für Theologie und Kirche* 95 (1998): 167–184.

———. "'Fossile Überreste des unreformierten Judentums in fernem Lande'? Das Judentum in den Archiven von Elephantine und Al-Yaḫudu." *ZAW* 132 (2020): 23–39.

———. "Greek Historians on Jews and Judaism in the 3rd Century BCE." In *Times of Transition: Judea in the Early Hellenistic Period*, edited by Sylvie Honigman Christophe Nihan, and Oded Lipschits, 263–278. University Park, PA: Eisenbrauns; Tel Aviv: The Institute of Archaeology, Tel Aviv University, 2021.

———. *Historical and Biblical Israel: The History, Tradition, and Archives of Israel and Judah*. Translated by Paul M. Kurtz. Oxford: Oxford University Press, 2015.

———. "Temple and Torah: Reflections on the Legal Status of the Pentateuch between Elephantine and Qumran." In Knoppers and Levinson, *The Pentateuch as Torah*, 77–103.

———. *Translatio imperii: Untersuchungen zu den aramäischen Danielerzählungen und ihrem theologiegeschichtlichen Umfeld*. Neukirchen-Vluyn: Neukirchener Verlag, 1991.

Kraus, Fritz R. "Ein zentrales Problem des altmesopotamischen Rechtes: Was ist der Codex Hammu-rabi?" *Genava* 8 (1960): 283–296.

Kuenen, Abraham. *The Religion of Israel to the Fall of the Jewish State*. Vol. 2. Translated by Alfred H. May. London: Williams & Norgate, 1875.

Kuhrt, Amélie. "The Persian Kings and Their Subjects: A Unique Relationship?" *Orientalistische Literaturzeitung* 96 (2001): 166–173.

Lapp, Paul W., and Nancy L. Lapp. "Iraq el-Emir." In *NEAEHL*, 646–649.

Lebram, Jürgen C. H. "Die Traditionsgeschichte der Esragestalt und die Frage nach dem historischen Esra." In *Achaemenid History*, vol. 1, *Sources, Structures and Synthesis Achaemenid History*, edited by Heleen Sancisi-Weerdenburg and Amélie Kuhrt, 103–138. Leiden: NINO, 1987.

Lee, J. A. L. *A Lexical Study of the Septuagint Version of the Pentateuch*. Chico, CA: Scholars Press, 1983.

Lee, Kyong-Jin. *The Authority and Authorization of Torah in the Persian Period*. Leuven: Peeters, 2011.

LeFebvre, Michael. *Collections, Codes, and Torah: The Re-characterization of Israel's Written Law*. New York: T&T Clark, 2006.

Lemaire, André. "Judean Identity in Elephantine: Everyday Life according to the Ostraca." In Lipschits, Knoppers, and Oeming, *Judah and the Judeans in the Achaemenid Period*, 365–373.

———. *Levantine Epigraphy and History in the Achaemenid Period (539–332 BCE)*. Oxford: Oxford University Press, 2015.

———. "New Aramaic Ostraca from Idumea and Their Historical Interpretation." In Lipschits and Oeming, *Judah and the Judeans in the Persian Period*, 413–456.

Lemche, Niels Peter. "Did a Reform like Josiah's Happen?" In *The Historian and the Bible: Essays in Honour of Lester L. Grabbe*, edited by Philip R. Davies and Diana V. Edelman, 11–19. London: T&T Clark, 2010.

Levenson, Jon D. "The Sources of Torah: Psalm 119 and the Modes of Revelation in Second Temple Judaism." In *Ancient Israelite Religion: Essays in Honor of Frank Moore Cross*, edited by Patrick D. Miller Jr., Paul D. Hanson, and S. Dean McBride, 559–574. Philadelphia: Fortress, 1987.

Levin, Yigal. "The Religion of Idumea and Its Relationship to Early Judaism." *Religions* 11 (2020): 487. https://doi.org/10.3390/rel11100487.

Levine, Lee I. *The Ancient Synagogue: The First Thousand Years*. New Haven: Yale University Press, 2005.

———. "Figural Art in Ancient Judaism." *Ars Judaica* 1 (2005): 9–26.

———. "R. Simeon B. Yohai and the Purification of Tiberias: History and Tradition." *HUCA* 49 (1978): 143–185.

Lindenberger, James M. *Ancient Aramaic and Hebrew Letters*. 2nd ed. Edited by Kent Richards. Leiden: Brill, 2003.

Lipschits, Oded. "Demographic Changes in Judah between the Seventh and the Fifth Centuries B.C.E." In Lipschits and Blenkinsopp, *Judah and the Judeans in the Neo-Babylonian Period*, 323–376.

———. *The Fall and Rise of Jerusalem: Judah under Babylonian Rule*. Winona Lake, IN: Eisenbrauns, 2005.

Lipschits, Oded, and Joseph Blenkinsopp, eds. *Judah and the Judeans in the Neo-Babylonian Period*. Winona Lake, IN: Eisenbrauns, 2003.

Lipschits, Oded, Gary N. Knoppers, and Manfred Oeming, eds. *Judah and the Judeans in the Achaemenid Period: Negotiating Identity in an International Context*. Winona Lake, IN: Eisenbrauns, 2011.

Lipschits, Oded, and Manfred Oeming, eds. *Judah and the Judeans in the Persian Period*. Winona Lake, IN: Eisenbrauns, 2006.

Lipschits, Oded, and David S. Vanderhooft. "Continuity and Change in the Persian Period Judahite Stamped Jar Administration." In Frevel, Pyschny, and Cornelius, *A "Religious Revolution,"* 43–66.

———. *The Yehud Stamp Impressions: A Corpus of Inscribed Impressions from the Persian and Hellenistic Periods in Judah*. Winona Lake, IN: Eisenbrauns, 2011.

Lozachmeur, Hélène. *La collection Clermont-Ganneau: Ostraca, épigraphes sur jarre, étiquettes de bois*. Paris: Diffusion de Boccard, 2006.

———. "Un ostracon araméen d'Eléphantine: Collection Clermont-Ganneau nº 125?" *Semitica* 39 (1989): 29–36.

Lupu, Eran. *Greek Sacred Law: A Collection of New Documents (NGSL)*. Leiden: Brill, 2005.

Maeir, Aren M. "On Defining Israel: Or, Let's Do the *Kulturkreislehre* Again!" *Hebrew Bible and Ancient Near East* 10 (2021): 106–148.

Magen, Yitzhak. *Mount Gerizim Excavations*. Vol. 2, *A Temple City*. Jerusalem: SOA; IAA, 2008.

———. *The Stone Vessel Industry in the Second Temple Period: Excavations at Ḥizma and the Jerusalem Temple Mount*. Jerusalem: IES; IAA; SOA, 2002.

Magen, Yitzhak, and Michael Dadon. "Nebi Samwil (Montjoie)." In *One Land, Many Cultures: Archaeological Studies in Honour of Stanislao Loffreda OFM*, edited by G. Claudio Bottini, Leah Di Segni, and L. Daniel Chrupcala, 123–138. Jerusalem: Franciscan Printing Press, 2003.

Magness, Jodi. *Stone and Dung, Oil and Spit: Jewish Daily Life in the Time of Jesus*. Grand Rapids: Eerdmans, 2011.

Malul, Meir. *The Comparative Method in Ancient Near Eastern and Biblical Legal Studies*. Kevelaer: Butzon & Bercker; Neukirchen-Vluyn: Neukirchener Verlag, 1990.

Mandel, Paul D. *The Origins of Midrash: From Teaching to Text*. Leiden: Brill, 2017.

Martens, John W. *One God, One Law: Philo of Alexandria on the Mosaic and Greco-Roman Law*. Leiden: Brill, 2003.

Martola, Nils. "Eating the Passover Lamb in House-Temples in Alexandria: Some Notes on Passover in Philo." In *Jewish Studies in a New Europe: Proceedings of* the *Fifth Congress of Jewish Studies in Copenhagen 1994 under the Auspices of the European Association for Jewish Studies*, edited by Ulf Haxen, Hanne Trautner-Kromann, and Karen L. Goldschmidt Salamon, 521–531. Copenhagen: C. A. Reitzel A/S International; Det Kongelige Bibliotek, 1998.

Mason, Steve. *Flavius Josephus on the Pharisees: A Composition-Critical Study.* Leiden: Brill, 1991.

———. "Jews, Judaeans, Judaizing, Judaism: Problems of Categorization in Ancient History." *JSJ* 38 (2007): 457–512.

Matassa, Lidia D. *Invention of the First-Century Synagogue.* Edited by Jason M. Silverman and J. Murray Watson. Atlanta: SBL, 2018.

Mattingly, Harold, et al., eds. *The Roman Imperial Coinage.* 9 vols. London: Spink, 1923–1981.

Mayer, Walter. "Sennacherib's Campaign of 701 BCE: The Assyrian View." In *"Like a Bird in a Cage": The Invasion of Sennacherib in 701 BCE*, edited by Lester L. Grabbe, 168–200. London: Sheffield Academic, 2003.

McCready, Wane O., and Adele Reinhartz, eds. *Common Judaism: Explorations in Second-Temple Judaism.* Minneapolis: Fortress, 2008.

Meier, John P. "Is There Halaka (the Noun) at Qumran?" *JBL* 122 (2003): 150–155.

Meinhold, Johannes. "Die Entstehung des Sabbats." *ZAW* 29 (1909): 81–112.

Mélèze-Modrzejewski, Joseph. "Jewish Law and Hellenistic Legal Practice in the Light of Greek Papyri from Egypt." In *An Introduction to the History and Sources of Jewish Law*, edited by N. S. Hecht et al., 75–99. Oxford: Clarendon, 1996.

———. "The Septuagint as Nomos: How the Torah Became a 'Civic Law' for the Jews of Egypt." In *Critical Studies in Ancient Law, Comparative Law and Legal History: Essays in Honour of Alan Watson*, edited by John W. Cairns and Olivia F. Robinson, 183–199. Oxford: Hart, 2001.

Meshorer, Yaakov. *Nabataean Coins.* Translated by I. H. Levine. Jerusalem: IAHUJ; IES, 1975.

———. *A Treasury of Jewish Coins: From the Persian Period to Bar Kokhba.* Jerusalem: Yad Ben-Zvi, 2001.

Mettinger, Tryggve N. D. *No Graven Image? Israelite Aniconism in Its Ancient Near Eastern Context.* Stockholm: Almqvist & Wiksell International, 1995.

Meyer, Eduard. *Die Entstehung des Judentums: Eine historische Untersuchung.* Halle: Niemeyer, 1896.

Meyers, Eric M. "Were the Hasmoneans Really Aniconic?" *Images* 1 (2007): 24–5.

Milgrom, Jacob. *Leviticus 1–16: A New Translation with Introduction and Commentary.* New York: Doubleday, 1991.

Milik, J. T. "Tefillin, Mezuzot et Targums (4Q128–4Q157)." In *Qumrân Grotte 4.II: I. Archéologie; II. Tefillin, Mezuzot et Targums (4Q128–4Q157)*, edited by R. de Vaux and J. T. Milik, 33–91. DJD 6. Oxford: Clarendon, 1977.

Miller, David M. "Ethnicity, Religion and the Meaning of *Ioudaios* in Ancient 'Judaism.'" *Currents in Biblical Research* 12 (2014): 216–265.

———. "The Meaning of *Ioudaios* and Its Relationship to Other Group Labels in Ancient 'Judaism.'" *Currents in Biblical Research* 9 (2010): 98–126.

Miller, Fred D., Jr., and Carrie-Ann Biondi, eds. *A History of the Philosophy of Law from the Ancient Greeks to the Scholastics*. 2nd ed. Dordrecht: Springer, 2015.

Miller, Stuart S. *At the Intersection of Texts and Material Finds: Stepped Pools, Stone Vessels, and Ritual Purity among the Jews of Roman Galilee*. Göttingen: Vandenhoeck & Ruprecht, 2015.

———. "New Directions in the Study of Ritual Purity Practices: Implications of the Sepphoris Finds." In *The Architecture, Stratigraphy, and Artifacts of the Western Summit of Sepphoris*, edited by Eric M. Meyers, Carol L. Meyers, and Benjamin D. Gordon, 445–475. University Park, PA: Eisenbrauns, 2018.

Myers, Jacob M. *Ezra. Nehemiah*. Garden City, NY: Doubleday, 1965.

Najman, Hindy. *Seconding Sinai: The Development of Mosaic Discourse in Second Temple Judaism*. Atlanta: SBL, 2009.

Nakman, David. "The Contents and Order of the Biblical Sections in the Tefillin from Qumran and Rabbinic Halakhah: Similarity, Difference, and Some Historical Conclusions." *Cathedra* 112 (2004): 19–44 (Hebrew).

Naveh, Joseph. "Aramaic Inscriptions from Arad." In *Arad Inscriptions*, edited by Yohanan Aharoni, 153–177. Jerusalem: IES, 1981.

———. "A Hebrew Letter from the Seventh Century B.C." *IEJ* 10 (1960): 129–139.

Netzer, Ehud. *Masada: The Yigael Yadin Excavations 1963–1965, Final Reports*. Vol. 3, *The Buildings: Stratigraphy and Architecture*. Jerusalem: IES; IAHUJ, 1991.

Netzer, Ehud, Roi Porat, Yakov Kalman, and Rachel Chachy. "Herodium." In *Herod the Great: The King's Final Journey*, edited by Silvia Rozenberg and David Mevorah, 126–161. Jerusalem: The Israel Museum, 2013.

Neusner, Jacob. "Preface." In *Judaisms and Their Messiahs at the Turn of the Christian Era*, edited by Jacob Neusner, William S. Green, and Ernest Frerichs, ix–xiv. Cambridge: Cambridge University Press, 1987.

Nicholson, Ernest W. *The Pentateuch in the Twentieth Century: The Legacy of Julius Wellhausen*. Oxford: Clarendon, 1998.

Niehr, Herbert. "Religio-Historical Aspects of the 'Early Post-Exilic' Period." In *The Crisis of Israelite Religion: Transformation of Religious Tradition in Exilic and Post-exilic Times*, edited by Bob Becking and Marjo C. A. Korpel, 228–244. Leiden: Brill, 1999.

Noam, Vered. "Another Look at the Rabbinic Conception of Gentiles from the Perspective of Impurity Laws." In *Judaea-Palaestina, Babylon and Rome: Jews in Antiquity*, edited by Benjamin Isaac and Yuval Shahar, 89–110. Tübingen: Mohr Siebeck, 2012.

———. "Embryonic Legal *Midrash* in the Qumran Scrolls." In Dávid et al., *The Hebrew Bible in Light of the Dead Sea Scrolls*, 237–262.

Noam, Vered, and Elisha Qimron. "A Qumran Composition of Sabbath Laws and Its Contribution to the Study of Early Halakah." *DSD* 16 (2009): 55–96.

Noth, Martin. *The Chronicler's History*. Translated by H. G. M. Williamson. Sheffield: JSOT Press, 1987.

Onn, Alexander, and Shlomit Weksler-Bdolah. "Khirbet Umm el-'Umdan." In *NEAEHL* 5:2061–2063.

Östborn, Gunnar. *Tōrā in the Old Testament: A Semantic Study*. Lund: Håkan Ohlssons Boktryckeri, 1945.

Otto, Eckart. "Gesetzesfortschreibung und Pentateuchredaktion." *ZAW* 107 (1995): 373–392.

———. "Kritik der Pentateuchkomposition." *Theologische Rundschau* 60 (1995): 163–191.

———. "Die nachpriesterschriftliche Pentateuchredaktion im Buch Exodus." In *Studies in the Book of Exodus: Redaction, Reception, Interpretation*, edited by Marc Vervenne, 61–111. Leuven: Peeters, 1996.

———. *Die Tora des Mose: Die Geschichte der literarischen Vermittlung von Recht, Religion und Politik durch die Mosegestalt*. Hamburg: Joachim Jungius Gesellschaft der Wissenschaften, 2001.

Pakkala, Juha. *Ezra the Scribe: The Development of Ezra 7–10 and Nehemiah 8*. Berlin: de Gruyter, 2004.

Palistrant Shaick, Ronit. "A Lion in Jerusalem: A Roman Sculpture of a Lion Head from the Jewish Quarter." In Geva, *Jewish Quarter Excavations*, 6:96–107.

Parker, Robert. "Law and Religion." In *The Cambridge Companion to Ancient Greek Law*, edited by Michael Gagarin and David Cohen, 61–81. Cambridge: Cambridge University Press, 2005.

———. "What Are Sacred Laws?" In *The Law and the Courts in Ancient Greece*, edited by Edward M. Harris and Lene Rubinstein, 57–70. London: Duckworth, 2004.

Parsons, P. J. "The Palaeography and Date of the Greek Manuscripts." In *Qumran Cave 4*, vol. 4, *Palaeo-Hebrew and Greek Biblical Manuscripts*, edited by Patrick W. Skehan, Eugene Ulrich, and Judith E. Sanderson, 7–13. DJD 9. Oxford: Clarendon, 1992.

Pasto, James. "Who Owns the Jewish Past? Judaism, Judaisms, and the Writing of Jewish History." PhD diss., Cornell University, 1999.

———. "W.M.L. de Wette and the Invention of Post-exilic Judaism: Political Historiography and Christian Allegory in Nineteenth-Century German Biblical Scholarship." In *Jews, Antiquity, and the Nineteenth-Century Imagination*, edited by Hayim Lapin and Dale B. Martin, 33–52. Bethesda: University Press of Maryland, 2003.

Pearce, Laurie E., and Cornelia Wunsch. *Documents of Judean Exiles and West Semites in Babylonia in the Collection of David Sofer*. Bethesda, MD: CDL Press, 2014.

Pearce, Sarah. "Notes on Philo's Use of the Terms ἔθνος and λαός." *Studia Philonica Annual* 28 (2016): 205–226.

Peleg-Barkat, Orit. "Herod's Western Palace in Jerusalem: Some New Insights." *Electrum* 26 (2019): 53–72.

———. *The Temple Mount Excavations in Jerusalem 1968–1978: Directed by Benjamin Mazar; Final Reports*. Vol. 5, *Herodian Architectural Decoration and King Herod's Royal Portico*. Jerusalem: IAHUJ, 2017.

Pfeiffer, Robert H. *Introduction to the Old Testament*. New York: Harper & Brothers, 1941.

Poirier, John C. "Purity beyond the Temple in the Second Temple Era." *JBL* 122 (2003): 247–265.

Porten, Bezalel. *Archives from Elephantine: The Life of an Ancient Jewish Military Colony*. Berkley: University of California Press, 1968.

Porten, Bezalel, and Yardeni, Ada. "Ostracon Clermont-Ganneau 125(?): A Case of Ritual Purity." *Journal of the American Oriental Society* 113 (1993): 451–456.

———, eds. and trans. *Textbook of Aramaic Documents from Ancient Egypt*. 4 vols. Jerusalem: Hebrew University, Dept. of the History of the Jewish People, 1986–1999.

Price, Max D. *Evolution of a Taboo: Pigs and People in the Ancient Near East*. New York: Oxford University Press, 2020.

Pucci Ben Zeev, Miriam. *Jewish Rights in the Roman World: The Greek and Roman Documents Quoted by Josephus Flavius*. Tübingen: Mohr Siebeck, 1998.

Pummer, Reinhard. "The Samaritans and Their Pentateuch." In Knoppers and Levinson, *The Pentateuch as Torah*, 237–269.

Qimron, Elisha, and James H. Charlesworth. "Rule of the Community." In *The Dead Sea Scrolls: Hebrew, Aramaic, and Greek Texts with English Translations*, vol. 1, *Rule of the Community and Related Documents*, edited by James H. Charlesworth, 1–51. Tübingen: Mohr Siebeck; Louisville: Westminster John Knox, 1994.

Rahmani, L. Y. "Jason's Tomb." *IEJ* 17 (1967): 61–100.

Rajak, Tessa. "Dying for the Law: The Martyr's Portrait in Jewish-Greek Literature." In *Portraits: Biographical Representation in the Greek and Latin Literature of the Roman Empire*, edited by M. J. Edwards and Simon Swain, 39–67. Oxford: Clarendon, 1997.

Rappaport, Uriel. *The First Book of Maccabees: Introduction, Hebrew Translation, and Commentary*. Jerusalem: Yad Ben-Zvi, 2004 (Hebrew).

Reed, Jonathan. "Stone Vessels and Gospel Texts: Purity and Socio-Economics in John 2." In *Zeichen aus Text und Stein, Studien auf dem Weg zu einer Archäologie des Neuen Testaments*, edited by Stefan Alkier and Jürgen Zangenberg, 381–401. Tübingen: Francke, 2003.

Regev, Eyal. "The Ritual Baths near the Temple Mount and Extra-Purification Before Entering the Temple Courts." *IEJ* 55 (2005): 194–204.

———. "The Temple Mount Ritual Baths and the Temple Cult: A Reply to Yonatan Adler." *New Studies on Jerusalem* 13 (2007): 9*–16*.

Reich, Ronny. *Miqwa'ot (Jewish Ritual Baths) in the Second Temple, Mishnaic and Talmudic Periods*. Jerusalem: Yad Ben-Zvi; IES, 2013 (Hebrew).

Robinson, Gnana. *The Origin and Development of the Old Testament Sabbath: A Comprehensive Exegetical Approach.* Frankfurt am Main: Lang, 1988.

Rofé, Alexander. "The Onset of Sects in Postexilic Judaism: Neglected Evidence from the Septuagint, Trito-Isaiah, Ben Sira, and Malachi." In *The Social World of Formative Christianity and Judaism: Essays in Tribute to Howard Clark Kee,* edited by Jacob Neusner et al., 39–49. Philadelphia: Fortress, 1988.

Rogerson, John W. *W.M.L. de Wette, Founder of Modern Biblical Criticism: An Intellectual Biography.* Sheffield: Sheffield Academic, 1992.

Rohrmoser, Angela. *Götter, Tempel und Kult der Judäo-Aramäer von Elephantine: Archäologische und schriftliche Zeugnisse aus dem perserzeitlichen Ägypten.* Münster: Ugarit-Verlag, 2014.

Rosenblum, Jordan D. "Kosher Olive Oil in Antiquity Reconsidered." *JSJ* 40 (2009): 356–365.

Rosenthal-Heginbottom, Renate. "The Imported Hellenistic and Early Roman Pottery: An Overview of the Finds from the Jewish Quarter Excavations." In Geva, *Jewish Quarter Excavations,* 6:377–413.

———. "Innovation and Stagnation in the Judean Lamp Production in the Late Second Temple Period (150 BCE–70 CE)." In *Traditions and Innovations: Tracking the Development of Pottery from the Late Classical to the Early Imperial Periods,* edited by Sarah Japp and Patricia Kögler, 429–442. Vienna: Phoibos-Verlag, 2016.

———. "Late Hellenistic and Early Roman Lamps and Fine Ware." In Geva, *Jewish Quarter Excavations,* 3:144–167.

Rozenberg, Silvia. "The Absence of Figurative Motifs in Herodian Wall Painting." In *I Temi Figurativi nella Pittura Parietale Antica (IV sec. a.C.–IV sec. d.C.): Atti del VI Convegno Internazionale sulla Pittura Parietale Antica,* edited by Daniela Scagliarini Corlàita, 283–285. Imola: University Press Bologna, 1997.

———. "Figurative Paintings in Herodium: New Discoveries." In *Antike Malerei zwischen Lokalstil und Zeitstil,* edited by Norbert Zimmermann, 371–376. Vienna: Verlag der Österreichischen Akademie der Wissenschaften, 2014.

Rubenstein, Jeffrey L. *The History of Sukkot in the Second Temple and Rabbinic Periods.* Atlanta: Scholars Press, 1995.

Rudolph, Wilhelm. *Esra und Nehemía samt 3. Esra.* Tübingen: Mohr Siebeck, 1949.

Runesson, Anders. *The Origins of the Synagogue: A Socio-Historical Study.* Stockholm: Almqvist & Wiksell, 2001.

Rüterswörden, Udo. "Die persische Reichsautorisation der Thora: Fact or Fiction?" *ZAR* 1 (1995): 47–61.

Sachau, Eduard. *Aramäische Papyrus und Ostraka aus einer jüdischen Militär-Kolonie zu Elephantine; Altorientalische Sprachdenkmäler des 5. Jahrhunderts vor Chr.* Leipzig: Hinrichs, 1911.

Sade, Moshe. "The Archaeozoological Finds." In *Back to Qumran: Final Report (1993–2004),* edited by Yitzhak Magen and Yuval Peleg, 453–459. Jerusalem: IAA and SOA, 2018.

Sanders, E. P. "Common Judaism Explored." In McCready and Reinhartz, *Common Judaism*, 11–23.

———. *Judaism: Practice and Belief, 63 BCE–66 CE*. London: SCM; Philadelphia: Trinity Press International, 1992.

Sapir-Hen, Lidar. "Food, Pork Consumption, and Identity in Ancient Israel." *Near Eastern Archaeology* 82 (2019): 52–59.

Sapir-Hen, Lidar, Guy Bar-Oz, Yuval Gadot, and Israel Finkelstein. "Pig Husbandry in Iron Age Israel and Judah New Insights Regarding the Origin of the 'Taboo.'" *Zeitschrift des Deutschen Palästina-Vereins* 129 (2013): 1–20.

Sapir-Hen, Lidar, Joe Uziel, and Ortal Chalaf. "Everything but the Oink: On the Discovery of an Articulated Pig in Iron Age Jerusalem and Its Meaning to Judahite Consumption Practices." *Near Eastern Archaeology* 84 (2021): 110–119.

Sasson, Jack M. "Circumcision in the Ancient Near East." *JBL* 85 (1966): 473–476.

Schiffman, Lawrence H. *The Halakhah at Qumran*. Leiden: Brill, 1975.

———. "Laws Pertaining to Forbidden Foods in the Dead Sea Scrolls." In *Halakhah in Light of Epigraphy*, edited by Albert I. Baumgarten, Hanan Eshel, Ranon Katzoff, and Shani Tzoref, 65–80. Göttingen: Vandenhoeck & Ruprecht, 2011.

Schmid, Konrad. *Erzväter und Exodus: Untersuchungen zur doppelten Begründung der Ursprünge Israels innerhalb der Geschichtsbücher des Alten Testaments*. Neukirchen-Vluyn: Neukirchener Verlag, 1999.

———. "The Persian Imperial Authorization as an Historical Problem and as a Biblical Construct: A Plea for Distinctions in the Current Debate." In Knoppers and Levinson, *The Pentateuch as Torah*, 22–38.

———. "Persische Reichsautorisation und Tora." *Theologische Rundschau* 71 (2006): 494–506.

Schmitt, Hans-Christoph. "Das spätdeuteronomistische Geschichtswerk Gen 1–2 Regum XXV und seine theologische Intention." In *Congress Volume Cambridge 1995*, edited by J. A. Emerton, 261–279. Leiden: Brill, 1997.

———. "Die Suche nach der Identität des Jahweglaubens im nachexilischen Israel: Bemerkungen zur theologischen Intention der Endredaktion des Pentateuch." In *Pluralismus und Identität*, edited by Joachim Mehlhausen, 259–278. Gütersloh: Gütersloher Verlagshaus, 1995.

Schmitt, Rüdiger. "Continuity and Change in Post-exilic Votive Practices." In Frevel, Pyschny, and Cornelius, *A "Religious Revolution,"* 95–109.

———. "Gab es einen Bildersturm nach dem Exil? Einige Bemerkungen zur Verwendung von Terrakottafigurinen im nachexilischen Israel." In *Yahwism after the Exile: Perspectives on Israelite Religion in the Persian Era*, edited by Rainer Albertz and Bob Becking, 186–198. Assen: Van Gorcum, 2003.

Schnabel, Eckhard J. *Law and Wisdom from Ben Sira to Paul: A Tradition Historical Enquiry into the Relation of Law, Wisdom, and Ethics*. Tübingen: Mohr Siebeck, 1985.

Schwartz, Daniel R. "Diodorus Siculus 40.3: Hecataeus or Pseudo-Hecataeus?" In *Jews and Gentiles in the Holy Land in the Days of the Second Temple, the Mishnah, and the Talmud*, edited by Menahem Mor, Aharon Oppenheimer, Jack Pastor, and Daniel R. Schwartz, 181–197. Jerusalem: Yad Ben-Zvi, 2003.

———. "'Judaean' or 'Jew': How Should We Translate *Ioudaios* in Josephus?" In *Jewish Identity in the Greco-Roman World / Jüdische Identität in der griechisch-römischen Welt*, edited by Jörg Frey, Daniel R. Schwartz, and Stephanie Gripentrog, 3–27. Leiden: Brill, 2007.

———. *Judeans and Jews: Four Faces of Dichotomy in Ancient Jewish History*. Toronto: University of Toronto Press, 2014.

———. "Judeans, Jews and Their Neighbors: Jewish Identity in the Second Temple Period." In *Between Cooperation and Hostility: Multiple Identities in Ancient Judaism and the Interaction with Foreign Powers*, edited by Rainer Albertz and Jakob Wöhrle, 13–31. Göttingen: Vandenhoeck & Ruprecht, 2013.

Schwartz, Seth. "How Many Judaisms Were There? A Critique of Neusner and Smith on Definition and Mason and Boyarin on Categorization." *JAJ* 2 (2011): 208–238.

———. *Imperialism and Jewish Society: 200 B.C.E. to 640 C.E.* Princeton: Princeton University Press, 2001.

Seebaß, Horst. "Pentateuch." *Theologische Realenzyklopädie* 26 (1996): 185–209.

Segal, J. B. *The Hebrew Passover: From the Earliest Times to A.D. 70*. London: Oxford University Press, 1963.

Shadmi, Tamar. "The Ossuaries and Sarcophagus." In *The Akeldama Tombs: Three Burial Caves in the Kidron Valley, Jerusalem*, edited by Gideon Avni and Zvi Greenhut, 41–56. Jerusalem: IAA, 1996.

Shemesh, Aharon. *Halakhah in the Making: The Development of Jewish Law from Qumran to the Rabbis*. Berkeley: University of California Press, 2009.

Shenkar, Michael. "The Coin of the 'God on the Winged Wheel.'" *Boreas* 30/31 (2007/2008): 13–23.

Simonsen, Sandra. "Bacteria, Garbage, Insects and Pigs: Conceptual Metaphors in the Ultra-Orthodox Anti-Military 'Ḥardakim' Propaganda Campaign." *Journal of Language and Politics* 19, no. 6 (2020): 938–963.

Simpson, J. A., and E. S. C. Weiner, eds. *The Oxford English Dictionary*. Oxford: Clarendon; New York: Oxford University Press, 1989.

Ska, Jean-Louis. "From History Writing to Library Building: The End of History and the Birth of the Book." In Knoppers and Levinson, *The Pentateuch as Torah*, 145–169.

———. *Introduction to Reading the Pentateuch*. Translated by Sr. Pascale Dominique. Winona Lake, IN: Eisenbrauns, 2006.

———. "'Persian Imperial Authorization': Some Questions Marks." In Watts, *Persia and Torah*, 161–182.

Smith, Morton. "The Dead Sea Sect in Relation to Ancient Judaism." *New Testament Studies* 7 (1961): 347–360.

—————. "Goodenough's 'Jewish Symbols' in Retrospect." *JBL* 86 (1967): 53–68.

—————. "Hellenization." In *Emerging Judaism: Studies on the Fourth and Third Centuries B.C.E.*, edited by Michael E. Stone and David Satran, 103–128. Minneapolis: Fortress, 1989.

—————. "Jewish Religious Life in the Persian Period." In *The Cambridge History of Judaism*, vol. 1, *Introduction: The Persian Period*, edited by W. D. Davies, and Louis Finkelstein, 219–278. Cambridge: Cambridge University Press, 1984.

—————. "Palestinian Judaism in the First Century." In *Israel: Its Role in Civilization*, edited by Moshe Davis, 67–81. New York: Seminary Israel Institute of the Jewish Theological Seminary of America, 1956.

Smoak, Jeremy D. *The Priestly Blessing in Inscription and Scripture: The Early History of Numbers 6:24–26*. New York: Oxford University Press, 2016.

Spiciarich, Abra. "Identifying the Biblical Food Prohibitions Using Zooarchaeological Methods." In *Food Taboos and Biblical Prohibitions: Reassessing Archaeological and Literary Perspectives*, edited by Peter Altmann, Anna Angelini, and Abra Spiciarich, 57–71. Tübingen: Mohr Siebeck, 2020.

—————. "Religious and Socioeconomic Diversity of Ancient Jerusalem and Its Hinterland during the 8th–2nd Centuries BCE: A View from the Faunal Remains." PhD diss., Tel-Aviv University, 2020.

Spiciarich, Abra, Yuval Gadot, and Lidar Sapir-Hen. "The Faunal Evidence from Early Roman Jerusalem: The People behind the Garbage." *Tel Aviv* 44 (2017): 98–117.

Steck, Odil Hannes. *Der Abschluß der Prophetie im Alten Testament: Ein Versuch zur Frage der Vorgeschichte des Kanons*. Neukirchen-Vluyn: Neukirchener Verlag, 1991.

—————. "Der Kanon des hebräischen Alten Testaments: Historische Materialien für eine ökumenische Perspektive." In *Verbindliches Zeugnis*, vol. 1, *Kanon, Schrift, Tradition*, edited by Wolfhart Pannenberg and Theodor Schneider, 11–33. Freiburg: Herder; Göttingen: Vandenhoeck & Ruprecht, 1992.

Stern, Ephraim. *Archaeology of the Land of the Bible*. Vol. 2, *The Assyrian, Babylonian, and Persian Periods, 732–332 BCE*. New York: Doubleday, 2001.

—————. *Material Culture of the Land of the Bible in the Persian Period, 538–332 B.C.* Warminster, UK: Aris & Phillips; Jerusalem: IES, 1982.

—————, ed. *The New Encyclopedia of Archaeological Excavations in the Holy Land.* 5 vols. Jerusalem: IES & Carta; New York: Simon & Schuster, 1993–2008.

—————. "Religion in Palestine in the Assyrian and Persian Periods." In *The Crisis of Israelite Religion: Transformation of Religious Tradition in Exilic and Post-exilic Times*, edited by Bob Becking and Marjo C. A. Korpel, 245–255. Leiden: Brill, 1999.

—————. "The Religious Revolution in Persian-Period Judah." In Lipschits and Oeming, *Judah and the Judeans in the Persian Period*, 199–205.

Stern, Ian. "Ethnic Identities and Circumcised Phalli at Hellenistic Maresha." *Strata: Bulletin of the Anglo-Israel Archaeological Society* 30 (2012): 57–87.

Stern, Menahem. *Greek and Latin Authors on Jews and Judaism.* 3 vols. Jerusalem: Israel Academy Sciences and Humanities, 1974–1984.

Stern, Sacha. "The Babylonian Calendar at Elephantine." *Zeitschrift für Papyrologie und Epigraphik* 130 (2000): 159–171.

———. "Figurative Art and Halakha in the Mishnaic-Talmudic Period." *Zion* 61 (1996): 397–419 (Hebrew).

Stroud, Ronald S. *The Axones and Kyrbeis of Drakon and Solon.* Berkeley: University of California Press, 1979.

Sussman, Varda. "Early Jewish Iconoclasm on Pottery Lamps." *IEJ* 23 (1973): 46–47.

Sussmann, Yaacov. "The History of the Halakha and the Dead Sea Scrolls: Preliminary Observations on Miqsat Ma'ase Ha-Torah (4QMMT)." *Tarbiz* 59 (1990): 11–76 (Hebrew).

Tamar, Karin, and Guy Bar-Oz. "Zooarchaeological Analysis of the Faunal Remains." In *The Summit of the City of David Excavations 2005–2008: Final Reports*, vol. 1, *Area G*, edited by Eilat Mazar, 497–510. Jerusalem: Shoham Academic Research and Publication, 2015.

Tammuz, Oded. "The Sabbath as the Seventh Day of the Week and a Day of Rest: Since When?" *ZAW* 131 (2019): 287–294.

Tatum, W. Barnes. "The LXX Version of the Second Commandment (Ex. 20,3–6=Deut 5,7–10): A Polemic against Idols, Not Images." *JSJ* 17 (1986): 177–195.

Tcherikover, Victor A., ed. *Corpus Papyrorum Judaicarum.* 3 vols. In collaboration with Alexander Fuks. Cambridge, MA: Harvard University Press, 1957–1964.

Terem, Shulamit. "The Oil Lamps from the Excavations at Gamla." MA thesis, Bar-Ilan University, 2008 (Hebrew).

Thackeray, H. St. J., Ralph Marcus, and Louis Feldman, eds. and trans. *Josephus.* 10 vols. Cambridge, MA: Harvard University Press, 1926–1965.

Thomas, Rosalind. "Written in Stone? Liberty, Equality, Orality and the Codification of Law." *Bulletin of the Institute of Classical Studies* 40 (1995): 59–74.

Torrey, Charles C. *Ezra Studies.* Chicago: University of Chicago Press, 1910.

Tov, Emanuel. *Textual Criticism of the Hebrew Bible.* 3rd ed. Minneapolis: Fortress, 2012.

Trümper, Monika. "The Oldest Original Synagogue Building in the Diaspora: The Delos Synagogue Reconsidered." *Hesperia* 73 (2004): 513–598.

Udoh, Fabian E., Susannah Heschel, Mark Chancey, and Gregory Tatum, eds. *Redefining First-Century Jewish and Christian Identities: Essays in Honor of Ed Parish Sanders.* Notre Dame, IN: University of Notre Dame Press, 2008.

Ulrich, Eugene. "Index to Passages in the 'Biblical Texts.'" In *The Texts from the Judaean Desert: Indices and an Introduction to the Discoveries in the Judaean Desert Series*, edited by Emanuel Tov, 185–201. DJD 39. Oxford: Clarendon, 2002.

van der Toorn, Karel. "Eshem-Bethel and Herem-Bethel: New Evidence from Amherst Papyrus 63." *ZAW* 128 (2016): 668–680.

Veijola, Timo. "Die Propheten und das Alter des Sabbatgebots." In *Prophet und Prophetenbuch: Festschrift für Otto Kaiser zum 65. Geburtstag*, edited by Volkmar

Fritz, Karl-Friedrich Pohlmann, and Hans-Christoph Schmitt, 246–264. Berlin: de Gruyter, 1989.

von Ehrenkrook, Jason. *Sculpting Idolatry in Flavian Rome: (An)Iconic Rhetoric in the Writings of Flavius Josephus*. Leiden: Brill, 2012.

von Pilgrim, Cornelius. "Tempel des Jahu und 'Strasse des Königs': Ein Konflikt in der Späten Perserzeit auf Elephantine." In *Egypt: Temple of the Whole World: Studies in Honour of Jan Assmann = Ägypten: Tempel der gesamten Welt*, edited by Sibylle Meyer, 303–317. Leiden: Brill, 2003.

Vroom, Jonathan. *The Authority of Law in the Hebrew Bible and Early Judaism: Tracing the Origins of Legal Obligation from Ezra to Qumran*. Leiden: Brill, 2018.

Wacholder, Ben Zion. *Eupolemus: A Study of Judaeo-Greek Literature*. Cincinnati: Hebrew Union College-Jewish Institute of Religion, 1974.

Watts, James W., ed. *Persia and Torah: The Theory of Imperial Authorization of the Pentateuch*. Atlanta: Scholars Press, 2001.

———. *Reading Law: The Rhetorical Shaping of the Pentateuch*. Sheffield: Sheffield Academic, 1999.

Webster, B. "Chronological Index of the Texts from the Judaean Desert." In *The Texts from the Judaean Desert: Indices and an Introduction to the Discoveries in the Judaean Desert Series*, edited by Emanuel Tov, 351–446. Oxford: Clarendon, 2002.

Weiss, Herold. *A Day of Gladness: The Sabbath among Jews and Christians in Antiquity*. Columbia: University of South Carolina Press, 2003.

Weiss, J. H., ed. *Sifra. Commentar zu Leviticus*. Vienna: Schlossberg, 1862 (Hebrew).

Weitzman, Steven. *The Origin of the Jews: The Quest for Roots in a Rootless Age*. Princeton: Princeton University Press, 2017.

Weksler-Bdolah, Shlomit. "Khirbat Umm el-'Umdan." *Excavations and Surveys in Israel* 126 (2014). https://www.jstor.org/stable/26604648.

Wellhausen, Julius. "Die composition des Hexateuchs." *Jahrbuch für deutsche Theologie* 21 (1876): 392–450, 531–602; 22 (1877): 407–79.

———. *Israelitische und jüdische Geschichte*. 7th ed. Berlin: Reimer, 1914.

———. *Prolegomena to the History of Israel*. Edinburgh: Black, 1885.

Werman, Cana. "On Religious Persecution: A Study in Ancient and Modern Historiography." *Zion* 81 (2016): 463–496.

Westbrook, Raymond. "Cuneiform Law Codes and the Origins of Legislation." *Zeitschrift für Assyriologie* 79 (1989): 201–222.

———. "Introduction: The Character of Ancient Near Eastern Law." In *A History of Ancient Near Eastern Law*, edited by Raymond Westbrook, 1–90. Leiden: Brill, 2003.

———. "The Nature and Origins of the Twelve Tables." *Zeitschrift der Savigny-Stiftung für Rechtsgeschichte / Romanistische Abteilung* 105 (1988): 74–121.

Wevers, John W. *Septuaginta, Exodus*. Göttingen: Vandenhoeck & Ruprecht, 1991.

———. *Septuaginta, Deuteronomium*. Göttingen: Vandenhoeck & Ruprecht, 1977.

White, L. Michael, G. Anthony Keddie, and Michael A. Flexsenhar III. "The Epistle of Aristeas: Introduction." In *Jewish Fictional Letters from Hellenistic Egypt:*

The Epistle of Aristeas and Related Literature, by L. Michael White and G. Anthony Keddie, 31–43. Atlanta: SBL, 2018.

White Crawford, Sidnie. "Reworked Pentateuch." In *Encyclopedia of the Dead Sea Scrolls*, edited by Lawrence H. Schiffman and James C. VanderKam, 775–777. New York: Oxford University Press, 2000.

Wiegmann, Alexander, Hagai Misgav, and Zaraza Friedman. "A Ritual Bath on Hebron Road, Jerusalem: Epigraphic and Iconographic Findings." *New Studies in the Archaeology of Jerusalem and Its Region* 11 (2017): 47–64.

Wiesehöfer, Josef. "'Reichsgesetz' oder 'Einzelfallgerechtigkeit'? Bemerkungen zu P. Freis These von der achaimenidischen 'Reichsautorisation.'" *ZAR* 1 (1995): 36–46.

Williams, David S. "The Date of Ecclesiasticus." *VT* 44 (1994): 563–565.

Williamson, H. G. M. *Ezra, Nehemiah*. Waco: Word Books, 1985.

Wolff, Hans Julius. "Law in Ptolemaic Egypt." In *Essays in Honor of C. Bradford Welles*, 67–77. New Haven: American Society of Papyrologists, 1966.

———. "Plurality of Laws in Ptolemaic Egypt." *Revue Internationale des droits de l'antiquité* 3 (1960): 191–223.

———. *Das Recht der griechischen Papyri Ägyptens in der Zeit der Ptolemaeer und des Prinzipats*. Vol. 1, *Bedingungen und Triebkräfte der Rechtsentwicklung*. Munich: Beck, 2002.

Wright, Benjamin G., III. "Three Jewish Ritual Practices in Aristeas §§158–160." In *Heavenly Tablets: Interpretation, Identity and Tradition in Ancient Judaism*, edited by Lynn LiDonnici and Andrea Lieber, 11–29. Leiden: Brill, 2007.

———. "Torah and Sapiential Pedagogy in the Book of Ben Sira." In *Wisdom and Torah: The Reception of "Torah" in the Wisdom Literature of the Second Temple Period*, edited by Bernd U. Schipper and D. Andrew Teeter, 157–186. Leiden: Brill, 2013.

Wright, David P., et al. "Sin, Pollution, and Purity." In *Religions of the Ancient World: A Guide*, edited by Sarah Iles Johnston, 496–513. Cambridge, MA: Belknap Press of Harvard University Press, 2004.

Wright, Jacob L. *Rebuilding Identity: The Nehemiah-Memoir and Its Earliest Readers*. Berlin: de Gruyter, 2004.

Yadin, Yigael. *Bar-Kokhba: The Rediscovery of the Legendary Hero of the Last Jewish Revolt against Imperial Rome*. London: Weidenfeld & Nicolson, 1971.

———. *Masada: Herod's Fortress and the Zealot's Last Stand*. Translated by Moshe Pearlman. New York: Random House, 1966.

———. *The Temple Scroll*. 3 vols. Jerusalem: IES; IAHUJ; The Shrine of the Book, 1977–1983.

Yarbro Collins, Adela. *Mark: A Commentary*. Edited by Harold W. Attridge. Minneapolis: Fortress, 2007.

Yardeni, Ada. "New Jewish Aramaic Ostraca." *IEJ* 40 (1990): 130–152.

Yavor, Zvi. "The Synagogue and Miqveh Complex." In *Gamla II: The Architecture;*

The Shmarya Gutmann Excavations, 1976–1989, edited by Danny Syon and Zvi Yavor, 40–61. Jerusalem: IAA, 2010.

Yoo, Philip Y. *Ezra and the Second Wilderness*. Oxford: Oxford University Press, 2017.

Zadok, Ran, Yoram Cohen, Kathleen Abraham, and Shai Gordin. *Cuneiform Texts Mentioning Israelites, Judeans, and Related Population Groups (CTIJ)*. ORACC, 2019. http://oracc.museum.upenn.edu/ctij/corpus.

Zahn, Molly M. "'Remember This Day': Grounding Law in Narrative through Redactional Composition (Exod 13:1–16)." MPhil thesis, University of Oxford, 2003.

———. *Rethinking Rewritten Scripture: Composition and Exegesis in the 4QReworked Pentateuch Manuscripts*. Leiden: Brill, 2011.

Zenger, Erich. *Einleitung in das Alte Testament*. Stuttgart: Kohlhammer, 1995.

———. "Der Pentateuch als Tora und als Kanon." In *Die Tora als Kanon für Juden und Christen*, edited by Erich Zenger, 5–34. Freiburg: Herder, 1996.

Zuckermandel, M.S., ed. *Tosefta*. Pasewalk: n.p., 1880 (Hebrew).

Acknowledgments

The efforts that have gone into the research undergirding the work presented here have been a collaborative endeavor shared with innumerable colleagues over the course of the past fifteen years. Limitations of space allow me to acknowledge here only those most directly connected to the preparation of the present book.

The introduction has benefited greatly from many marvelous conversations I shared at Yale University with Steven Fraade, John Collins, Christine Hayes, and Joel Baden, from my participation in John Collins's thought-provoking course on Ezra-Nehemiah at Yale Divinity School, and from my scintillating discussions with Reinhard Kratz at the University of Göttingen. Chapter 1 profited considerably from my friendly collaboration over the past few years with Omri Lernau and from information kindly provided by Abra Spiciarich, Ram Bouchnick, and Lidar Sapir-Hen. My work on chapter 2 is deeply indebted to my close and dear collaboration over the course of many years with the late David Amit, my long-running conversations with Stuart Miller, Ronny Reich, Thomas Kazen, Dennis Mizzi, and Rachel Bar-Nathan, and the mentorship (during my doctoral studies) of Zeev Safrai. My discussion of the coins in chapter 3 was very kindly reviewed by my friend Yoav Farhi. Chapter 4 has benefited from many friendly conversations I have shared over the years with Yehudah Cohn, from information and material kindly shared by Marcello Fidanzio, and from collaboration on paleographic matters with Gemma Hayes and with the late Ada Yardeni. My thinking about Sabbath in chapter 5 has been sharpened through conversations I have had with Ezra Zuckerman Sivan. Chapter 6 was greatly enriched from thoughtful exchanges with students in my course The Ancient Synagogue, delivered at Yale in the spring of 2020. In chapter 7, my treatment of the Persian-period archaeological data has benefited much from conversations I have had with Shai Gordin and Aharon Tavger, and my discussion on law in ancient Greece is indebted to wonderful exchanges I have shared with Joseph David and with David Small.

I have had the pleasure to discuss and work through various aspects of the book with several other dear colleagues: James Aitken, Carol Bakhos, Stéphanie Binder, Levi Cooper, Idan Dershowitz, Lutz Doering, Steven Fine, Yuval Gadot, Ingrid Hjelm, Aren Maeir, Eric Meyers, Laura Nasrallah, Anders Runesson, Lawrence Schiffman, Shlomo Shulman, Elli Stern, Guy Stiebel, Shulamit Terem, Thomas Thompson, Holger Zellentin, Karin Zetterholm, and Magnus Zetterholm.

I would also like to acknowledge the support and encouragement of my colleagues at Ariel University: Oren Ackermann, David Ben Shlomo, Adi Eliyahu, Shai Gordin, Eshbal Ratzon, Itzhaq Shai, and our rector Prof. Albert Pinhasov.

Nicole Greenspan has been of inestimable assistance in helping to get the word out about the project and enlisting public support.

Components of the research have been generously supported by two grants provided by the Israel Science Foundation (grant nos. 358/15 and 371/18).

My sincerest appreciation goes out to everyone at Yale University Press who has worked tirelessly to bring this book to print: on the scholarly side John Collins, as general editor of the Anchor Yale Bible series, and on the more technical aspects Jennifer Banks, Abbie Storch, Ann-Marie Imbornoni, and my copyeditor Ryan Davis.

And last, but certainly not least, my unending appreciation goes out to my family, whose devotion and sacrifices over the years are the true reason why this book has come to see the light of day. Without doubt, my greatest debt of gratitude is owed to Sandra, who not only has sharpened my thinking on each and every topic touched upon in this study but also—and most vitally—has ceaselessly infused me with a burning ardor to see this book through to fruition.

Index of Ancient Sources

Rabbinic Literature

Index of Names and Subjects

menorah, 164–165; on the name
"Judean," 244n37; on Passover,
146–148; on ritual purity, 58–61,
72–73; on Sabbath, 30, 38, 137–139;
on Sukkot, 158–161; on the synagogue, 174, 180–181, 187–188; on
tefillin and mezuzah, 117–118. *See
also* temple, Jerusalem
Joshua/Jeshua son of Nun, ix, 163–164,
192
Josiah, King, ix, 9, 150–151, 230, 272n16,
278n95, 289n22
Jubilees: concerned with "halakah," 15;
on circumcision, 134; on dietary
laws, 40; as Mosaic *tôrāh*, 241n20;
on Passover, 149; on ritual purity,
77; on Sabbath, 139; on Sukkot, 161
Judaism: "biblical" and "non-biblical,"
16–17; conversion to, 15, 232,
301n173; definition of, 3–5, 238n5,
238n6; etymology from Greek,
4–5, 236, 238n8, 238n9; and "Hebraism," 9–10, 244n37; history of
scholarship on origins of, 9–17;
"household," 246n59; or "Judaisms," 239n10; "Judentum" vs.
"Judaismus," 245n43
Judas Maccabaeus, 78, 162, 165, 223, 227,
259n104
Judean: earliest use of the name, 7;
as an ethno-geographic identity,
14–15, 232; or "Jew," 8; name in
different languages, 7–8; name
explained by Josephus, 244n37
Judith, 77–78, 258n101, 259n103
Judith, Book of, 77, 251n66
Juvenal, 31

kashrut. *See* dietary laws
Katz, Hayah, 261n125
Kaufmann, Yehezkel, 245n51
Ketef Hinnom, 130–131, 271n43
Khnum, 204–205, 294n62

Kings, Books of, 91, 102, 166
Kolska Horwitz, Liora, 33
Kratz, Reinhard G., 16–17, 229–230,
294n63, 296n80
Kuenen, Abraham, 10

law collections, Mesopotamian, 12,
216–221
lawgivers, 218–219, 222, 237n1, 299n132
leaven/leavened bread, prohibition: at
Elephantine, 152, 154–155, 278n99,
278n104, 279n108; Josephus on,
147–148, 277n81; Paul on, 148; Pentateuchal sources, 26, 146
LeFebvre, Michael, 209, 216–217,
221–222
Lemaire, André, 85, 275n67, 290n26,
292n43
leprosy. *See* skin pathology impurity
Letter of Aristeas: date of composition, 128, 211–212, 251n64, 270n36;
on dietary laws, 40; Judean law in,
211–212, 215; on ritual purity, 77; on
tefillin and mezuzah, 127–128
Levine, Lee I., 111–112, 263n24, 268n126
Leviticus, 10, 25
Lipit-Ishtar, code of, 217
Lipschits, Oded, 109
Luke-Acts: on circumcision, 133; on
the Day of Atonement, 156; on
dietary laws, 28–29; on Passover,
147–148; on ritual purity, 54–57, 63;
on Sabbath, 137; on the synagogue,
172–175
Lycurgus, 298n115, 299n132

Maccabees, First: on the Antiochene
persecutions, 223–228, 230; on
circumcision, 134; date of composition, 40, 227; on dietary laws, 40;
on the menorah, 165; on Sabbath,
140–141
Maccabees, Fourth, 4, 40, 239n9